ABUSE IN THE FAMILY: AN INTRODUCTION

ALAN KEMP

Pierce College
Tacoma, Washington

Brooks/Cole Publishing Company

I(T)P® An International Thomson Publishing Company

Pacific Grove • Albany • Belmont • Bonn • Boston • Cincinnati • Detroit • Johannesburg • London
Madrid • Melbourne • Mexico City • New York • Paris • Singapore • Tokyo • Toronto • Washington

Sponsoring Editor: *Lisa Gebo*
Marketing Team: *Jean Thompson, Romy Taormina, Deanne Brown*
Marketing Representative: *Amelia Keeney*
Editorial Assistants: *Lisa Blanton, Susan Carlson*
Production Coordinator: *Karen Ralling*
Production Service: *Ex Libris/Julie Kranhold*

Manuscript Editor: *Jennifer McClain*
Permissions Editor: *Cathleen C. Morrison*
Interior Design: *Nancy Benedict*
Cover Design: *Sharon L. Kinghan*
Photo Researcher: *Julie Kranhold*
Typesetting: *Fog Press*
Cover Printing: *Malloy Lithographing, Inc.*
Printing and Binding: *Malloy Lithographing, Inc.*

Photo Credits: Page 3: *Cary Wolinsky/Stock, Boston/PNI;* Page 40: *Michael W. Thomas/Stock South/PNI;* Page 71: *David Young-Wolff/PhotoEdit/PNI;* Page 133: *Rob Crandall/Stock, Boston/PNI;* Page 157: *John Troha/Black Star/PNI;* Page 202: *Bob Daemmrich/Stock, Boston/PNI;* Page 236: *Mark Richards/PhotoEdit/PNI;* Page 295: *Ed Eckstein/Phototake/PNI.*

For more information, contact:

BROOKS/COLE PUBLISHING COMPANY
511 Forest Lodge Road
Pacific Grove, CA 93950
USA

International Thomson Publishing Europe
Berkshire House 168-173
High Holborn
London WC1V 7AA
England

Thomas Nelson Australia
102 Dodds Street
South Melbourne, 3205
Victoria, Australia

Nelson Canada
1120 Birchmount Road
Scarborough, Ontario
Canada M1K 5G4

International Thomson Editores
Seneca 53
Col. Polanco
11560 México, D.F., México

International Thomson Publishing GmbH
Königswinterer Strasse 418
53227 Bonn
Germany

International Thomson Publishing Asia
221 Henderson Road
#05-10 Henderson Building
Singapore 0315

International Thomson Publishing Japan
Hirakawacho Kyowa Building, 3F
2-2-1 Hirakawacho
Chiyoda-ku, Tokyo 102
Japan

Printed in the United States of America

10 9 8 7 6 5 4 3 2 1

Library of Congress Cataloging-in-Publication Data

Kemp, Alan R.
    Abuse in the family / Alan Kemp.
      p. cm.
    Includes index.
    ISBN 0-534-34198-5
    1. Family social work. 2. Family violence. 3. Problem families.
    I. Title
    HV697.K46   1998
    362.82′ 92—dc21

                                       97-15009
                                        CIP

This text is dedicated to anyone who has ever suffered abuse at the hands of someone in their family . . . and to each of you who wants to help. I would like to add a special dedication in memory of Judi Clark, a bright spirit, whose life ended before she could complete her training.

Alan Kemp, MSW (University of Washington), is professor of Social Services/Mental Health and the director of the Social Service/Mental Health Program at Pierce College. He is a certified clinical social worker, marriage and family therapist, and mental health counselor who has had extensive experience with abuse recovery and in treating abuse in the family, especially child maltreatment and domestic violence. He is a Diplomate in Clinical Social Work (DCSW) with nearly 20 years of experience, including 5 years under contract with the United States Air Force.

CONTENTS

CHAPTER 1
Survey of the Family Abuse Landscape   1

    Family Abuse as a Matter of Public Concern   2

    Family Abuse as a Focus of Professional Attention   2

    Defining Abuses   5
        Considering Basic Human Needs   6
        Fuzzy Lines Between Types of Abuse   8
        Continuums of Abuse   8
        A Continuum in Child Sex Abuse Cases   10
        Family Abuse Spillover   10

    Using Social Science Methods to Study Abuse in the Family   11
        Social Science and Scientific Method   11
        Correlational Studies   12
        Descriptive and Inferential Statistics   13
        Some Key Research Issues   13
        Official Reports and Survey Data   14
        Confusion and Misuse of Research Data   14
        The Need for a Conceptual Framework   15

    Systems or Ecological Approaches   15
        A Systems-Oriented Model: General Systems Theory   16

A Pioneering Ecological Model   18
The Ecological Framework Adopted in This Text   19
A Big Picture Look at Family Maltreatment: The Macro Level   19
Family and Small Group Influences: The Meso Level   23
Individualistic Explanations: The Micro Level   28

Relationships Between Forms of Abuse   30

Chapter Summary   31
Legal and Ethical Concerns: Critical Thinking Questions   32
Suggested Activities   33
Review Guide   33
Suggested Reading   35
Chapter Glossary   35

CHAPTER 2
Child Physical Abuse   39

Social and Historical Context   41

Defining the Problem   43
Intent and Result   43
Considering Culture when Defining Abuse   44
Child Abuse Prevention and Treatment Act of 1974   44
Toward a Working Definition   45
Continuum of Abuse   46

Overview of Major Types of Injuries   47

Psychological Impacts   49
General Psychological Impact of All Types of Child Abuse   50
Psychological Impact Specific to Child Physical Abuse   50
The Developmental Factor   51

Intergenerational Transmission: The Violence-Begets-Violence Theory   52

A Systems or Ecological Approach to Understanding Risk
and Resiliency Factors   56
Risk Factors   56
A Blending of Factors   61

Resiliency or Protective Factors   62

A Special Category of Child Physical Abuse: Munchausen
Syndrome by Proxy   63

Chapter Summary 63
 Legal and Ethical Concerns: Critical Thinking Questions 65
 Suggested Activities 66
 Review Guide 66
 Suggested Reading 68
 Chapter Glossary 68

CHAPTER 3
Child Psychological Maltreatment
and Child Neglect 70

Child Psychological Maltreatment 71

What Is Psychological Maltreatment? 72
 Controversies 73
 Definitions 74

What Do We Need to Know About Psychological Maltreatment? 77
 Basic Human Needs and Psychological Maltreatment 77
 Human Development and Psychological Maltreatment 78
 Research on the Impact of Psychological Maltreatment 81
 Explanations of Causes and Risk Factors 85
 Resiliency: Protective Factors 90

Child Neglect 92
 Neglect of Neglect 92
 The Serious Nature of Child Neglect 93
 Some Possible Causes for the Inattention to the Problem 93
 Social Costs of Neglecting Neglect 94
 Definitions and Categories of Neglect 95
 Failure to Thrive Syndrome (FTT): A Special Category 96
 Explanations of Causes and Risk Factors 97
 Resiliency: Protective Factors 100

Chapter Summary 101
 Legal and Ethical Concerns: Critical Thinking Questions 102
 Suggested Activities 103
 Review Guide 103
 Suggested Reading 105
 Chapter Glossary 106

CHAPTER 4
Child Sexual Abuse 109

The Problem 110
Professional and Societal Neglect of the Issue 111
Rediscovering Child Sexual Abuse 112
How Big Is the Problem 113

The Victims 118
Basic Information about Victimization 118
Impact of Child Sexual Abuse On Victims 121
Indicators of Abuse 124

Models of Victimology and Emerging Trends 125
The Medical Model 125
Psychiatric Diagnosis 126
Diagnostic Labeling and Child Sexual Abuse 129
The Four-Factor Traumagenic Model 130
Abuse-Related Accommodation: An Emerging Model 132
Current State of the Art in Victimology 135

Chapter Summary 136
Legal and Ethical Concerns: Critical Thinking Questions 136
Suggested Activities 137
Review Guide 138
Suggested Reading 138
Chapter Glossary 139

CHAPTER 5
Child Maltreatment:
Investigation, the Courts, and Intervention 143

Reporting Suspected Child Maltreatment 144

Child Protective Services Investigation and Interviewing Procedures 145
Validated Interviewing Procedures 146
The Issue of Multiple Interviews 148
Videotaping Interviews 148
The Use of Anatomically Detailed Dolls 149
Classic Work on Investigatory Interviewing 150

Risk Assessment   151

Initial Intervention by CPS   152

Juvenile Civil Court Action—Dependency Proceedings   153

Social Service Intervention   156

Child Abuse and Criminal Proceedings   157
Coordinated Response and Law Enforcement Investigation   158
Prosecution of Criminal Cases   159
Testimony in Criminal Cases   160
Sentencing   165

False Memory/Repressed Memory Controversy   165

Problems, Issues, and Trends in Intervention   168
Traditional Interventions   168
State-Funded Care: Problems and Issues   168
The Family Preservation/Child Protection Controversy   169
An Overview of Intervention Approaches   172

Chapter Summary   178
Legal and Ethical Concerns: Critical Thinking Questions   179
Suggested Activities   180
Review Guide   181
Suggested Reading   183
Chapter Glossary   184

CHAPTER 6
Sexual Offenders   188

Types of Offenders   190

Psychiatric Diagnosis and Sexual Offenders   192

Profile Models   193
The Fixated-Regressed Profile Model   193
The Situational-Preferential Profile Model   195

The Four-Factor Offender Model   196

The Addiction Model   198

A Special Class of Offenders: Children and Adolescents   200

Concluding Comments About Sexual Offenders   203

Intervention and Treatment   203
   Federal Initiatives   203
   State Initiatives   204
   Local Initiatives   205
   Overview of Sex Offender Treatment   205
   Does Sex Offender Treatment Work?   206
   Comprehensive Treatment Approaches   208

Chapter Summary   212
   Legal and Ethical Concerns: Critical Thinking Questions   213
   Suggested Activities   214
   Review Guide   214
   Suggested Reading   216
   Chapter Glossary   216

CHAPTER 7
Domestic Violence   221

A Brief Look at the Historical Context   222

What Is Domestic Violence? A Working Definition   225

How Common Is Domestic Violence? Incidence and Prevalence   229

The Controversy About the Rate of Male and Female
Domestic Violence   232

What Is the Impact of Battering on Its Victims?   235
   Children Who Witness Abuse   238
   Toward a More Client-Friendly Approach to Understanding Victims   238

The Cycle of Violence   240

Why Do Women Stay?   242

Explanations and Risk Factors   243
   The Macro Level—Broad Cultural and Social Factors   244
   The Meso Level—Family and Relationship Factors   245
   The Micro Level—Individual and Personality Factors   246

Classifying Perpetrators   248

Intervention   252
   Services for Victims   252
   Intervention with Perpetrators   256
   Perpetrator Treatment Issues   260

Chapter Summary   262
   Legal and Ethical Concerns: Critical Thinking Questions   263
   Suggested Activities   264

Review Guide   264
Suggested Reading   266
Chapter Glossary   267

CHAPTER 8
Elder Maltreatment   270

Historical Context   271

What Is Elder Maltreatment?   273

How Big Is the Problem?   274

What Are the Indicators of Maltreatment?   277
Behavioral Indicators of Elder Abuse   277
Indicators of Suspected Physical Abuse   278
Physical Indicators of Neglect   278
Indicators of Financial or Material Exploitation   279

What is The Impact of Elder Maltreatment?   280

Explanations and Risk Factors   282
The Macro Level—Broad Cultural and Societal Factors   282
The Meso Level—Family and Relationship Factors   283
The Micro Level—Individual and Personality Factors   287
Concluding Words on Explanations and Risk Factors   290

Efforts to Deal with Elder Maltreatment   291
Federal Initiatives   291
State and Local Efforts   293
Intervention with Domestic Maltreatment   293
When Maltreatment Is Defined as Domestic Violence   296
Involuntary Services—Conservatorship
and Involuntary Commitment   298
Intervention with Institutional Maltreatment   298

Chapter Summary   300
Legal and Ethical Concerns: Critical Thinking Questions   301
Suggested Activities   302
Review Guide   303
Suggested Reading   305
Chapter Glossary   305

References   308
Index   327

PREFACE

Why Do We Need an Introductory Text on Abuse in the Family?

I don't think we can deny that family abuse, in one form or another, is now a major social concern. Over the last 35 years or so, both the public and members of the professional community have become increasingly interested in this issue. Attorney General Janet Reno asserts that it may be the leading contributor to most of today's social problems.

In addition to being a human service educator, I am also a clinician. My clinical experience has convinced me that understanding family maltreatment is vital to being competent at dealing with some of the most important real-life concerns of clients.

When I was in school preparing for my career in human services, I didn't get formal training on handling abuse issues. I got most of my training after I left school and when I was already in practice, usually through workshops, self-directed study, and professional supervision. Learning to handle abuse cases in the field is something like reading the repair manual after your car has broken down. Because this is how many clinicians learn, I've become convinced that we ought to start teaching prospective human service providers about family abuse issues before they start to practice.

When I began my college teaching career, one of the first courses I taught was a course dealing with family maltreatment. It made perfect sense to offer such a course, yet I soon learned that formal courses on the subject were something of a new thing. I also discovered that finding a textbook wasn't so easy. While there were a number of scholarly books dealing with one or more aspects of family maltreatment, I couldn't find anything that really seemed geared for the classroom.

Who Is This Text For?

This book is written for students in a variety of disciplines, who need a comprehensive introduction to the subject of family maltreatment. I hope it will meet the need for a readable, yet instructive, text on the subject. It is intended to serve as an introduction, not as an exhaustive examination of all aspects of the field. There are a number of other professional and technical volumes that deal extensively with such specialized areas as intervention and treatment (many of these are included in the Suggested Reading sections located at the end of each chapter).

Since the course I regularly teach on the subject has no prerequisites, I don't assume that the reader already has a background in the social sciences, and I certainly don't assume the student has already been out in the field, though many have. I hope the text will appeal to a broad audience, especially those who want to become human service workers, social workers, teachers, counselors, therapists, psychologists, or nurses, though I also hope it will be a useful introduction to anyone who wants to know more about the subject. It is written in a style that might be appropriate for use in community college, university, and beginning-level graduate courses.

Philosophy and Structure

Each major topic area will be looked at from an *ecological* or *systems* perspective. This means that we aren't interested in just single explanations but, rather, interacting explanations from a variety of levels: social and cultural, family, and individual. When this happens, a number of important questions seem to get raised, reminding us that the kind of issues we're dealing with are complex. What social and cultural influences are at play? How do family relationships influence maltreatment? What personality and individual factors are at work?

The family abuse domain is not a unified field of study, but is divided into a number of semiautonomous specialty areas: child physical abuse, child neglect, child emotional or psychological maltreatment, child sexual abuse, sexual offenders, domestic violence, and elder abuse. There seems to have been a tendency for professionals and researchers to focus their attention on one or more very specialized areas. Sometimes even within a particular specialty, such as child physical abuse, they might concentrate on just a small part of the issue. As a consequence, researchers and professionals sometimes carry out their work independently, unaware of what others are doing. By bringing each of the maltreatment topic areas together in one text, I hope to give students a more unified view.

The text is divided into eight chapters. The first chapter serves as a survey of the family abuse landscape. It includes an overview of the various forms of maltreatment but also introduces the systemic or ecological perspective adopted throughout the rest of the text. In this vein, the reader is oriented to the *macro-meso-micro* format, with which we explore the interacting levels of explanation. We will be examining broad social and cultural influences, relationship factors, and individual characteristics in our effort to understand what happens in family maltreatment. This survey chapter also introduces the reader to some basic discussion about the social sciences, the scientific method, and how to interpret what we read when it comes to family maltreatment. Chapters 2 through 4 deal with child physical abuse, child psychological maltreatment and neglect, and child sexual abuse. Chapter 5 discusses intervention in child abuse cases, including investigation, risk assessment, court involvement, treatment, and other forms of intervention. In Chapter 6 we discuss sex offenders and also touch on society's attempts to deal with them. In Chapter 7 we cover the problem of domestic violence, and in our discussion we look at its definitions, possible causes (including society's attitudes about women), and some new (and, I think, exciting) research about batterers. We discuss steps that are being taken to help victims and things we can do to deal with perpetrators. In the final chapter, Chapter 8, we explore the often neglected issue of elder maltreatment. Here again, we explore its reasons, including society's attitudes about the elderly, and we look at what is being done to help solve the problem.

Studies and research are cited, and wherever possible we try to use that research as we test and explore various concepts and theories. Whenever appropriate, I also include clinical experiences, case examples, media reports, and other supplemental information to add relevance and enhance interest. These are usually highlighted in a box and placed near relevant text or discussion. Figures, charts, tables, and other aids to assist in understanding the data are also included whenever appropriate.

The reader will find that each chapter is structurally similar. Once you become familiar with the organization of one chapter, you'll find considerable consistency in each of the others. Each chapter contains a chapter summary at its conclusion. Since critical thinking has become an increasingly important concern, at the end of each chapter you will find a section titled "Legal and Ethical Concerns: Critical Thinking Questions." Much like the questioning of Socrates in ancient times, these questions are designed to encourage students to critically examine issues that raise significant moral and ethical questions. You will also find a review guide, suggested activities, and a few suggested readings at the conclusion of each chapter. Key terms and concepts are highlighted in bold type throughout the text. While descriptions and definitions accompany the terms and concepts in the discussion, you will also find a glossary at the end of each chapter.

A Few Personal Comments to Students

Before turning to how to use this text, it may be appropriate to make a few comments of a more personal nature. Those of us working in human services do not do our work in a vacuum. We live in families too, and some of us may have been exposed to family abuse in one form or another. The kind of material presented here has a way of "kicking up" personal issues related to maltreatment that may have occurred in your own life. One of the reviewers of this text really brought this issue home. She commented that over half of all students taking her courses are in various stages of dealing with maltreatment that they themselves have experienced in their own family spheres. I have found this to be true among students in my courses as well. If reading this material brings up issues for you, I will tell you that it may be better to grapple with this now, rather than bumping into it later, when you're already in the field. Working with abuse issues can be emotionally challenging for anyone, so be prepared to do some personal introspection and experience a certain amount of discomfort. If you get into major distress, seek professional assistance outside the classroom. Should you find yourself becoming particularly troubled by the material presented in this text, I strongly encourage you to consult a professional therapist. You may also want to notify your professor, and perhaps even consider taking the course at another time, if you suspect the distress you experience is unmanageable.

In addition to monitoring any reactions you may have relating to prior maltreatment, I also hope you will look at the feelings and attitudes you have about each of the topics and themes. I want to challenge you to examine whatever feelings may surface, and use them as a way to learn more about your own attitudes and beliefs. Why do you think or feel as you do? How well do your old beliefs fit with the new information you are being exposed to? What are the implications of this new information? Does it change your preexisting attitudes? If so, why? If not, why not?

How to Use This Text

I think it's always good to initially skim through the book and stop to take a close look at material that interests you. You may also want to skim the chapters before sitting down to read and study them. After completing a chapter, you may want to go back and give a second look at some of the topic areas. The chapter summaries may help you organize your thinking into a more coherent whole. As mentioned earlier, each chapter contains a series of legal and ethical questions which are designed to spark discussion and critical thinking. The review guide is designed to help you as you study and try to master the material. Initially, I suggest that you may want to use it to assess how much of the material you've learned. While terms are defined within the context of the discussion, you might want to use the glossary at the back of each chapter for quick reference. Since a text such as this cannot possibly deal with every issue related to family maltreatment, a number of other suggested readings are included at the end of each chapter. A number of these readings are considered classics, while others represent cutting-edge works in the field. Reading material and discussing it is one thing, but when it comes to really getting a grasp of the issues, sometimes the best way to do this is by doing something active and getting involved. As a way of providing you with some direction in this regard, I've included a number of suggested activities at the back of each chapter. While you probably don't have time to do them all, you may find that doing at least some of them will make the written material more meaningful.

A Few Concluding Comments

One of the things I always like to tell my students is this: Any system of education is also a system of ignorance. Let me explain. Any time an educator prepares a lecture or writes a paper or chapter, we tell the student or reader what we think is important. There are many other things that might be important that we don't include. The danger of this is that important insights and ideas can be overlooked. While this text tries to be as comprehensive as space allows, there is much that isn't included. I encourage you to be a critical consumer of the concepts, positions, and information presented. By all means, go to the original sources and explore any issue that sparks your interest.

Finally, let me say that, regardless of whether or not you decide to purchase or adopt this text, I want to thank you for taking the time to consider it. If you have comments or questions, I'd be happy to hear from you.

Acknowledgments

When I began to think about writing this acknowledgment, I came to realize just how many people I need to thank. Each in his or her own way has not only helped make this a better text but me a better person, and for this I am truly grateful.

First of all I need to say a special thank-you to my friend and colleague Dennis Morton. As a sociologist, not only has Dennis given me a broader perspective about human relationships, but he has taught me how important it is for a social scientist to have a big heart. He's done this by modeling it. Dennis has read drafts of the manuscript in various stages of development and has been there to bounce some of the big-picture ideas back and forth with me. I hate to confess this, but sometimes I even woke him up, forgetting that, unlike myself, teaching in the afternoon and evening, he has to get up very early every day to teach his first course. Dennis not only helped with his insights and encouragement, but when I was considering taking an extra year to write the text, he gave me the good counsel to finish it sooner rather than later. I'm glad this book is here now, and I can truly thank Dennis for the encouragement and support that helped make it happen.

I also want to say a special thank-you to my friend and colleague Pam Slyter, who served as another sounding board. When I needed a "writing break" or someone to talk to about one or another part of the manuscript, she was always willing to talk. She has always been clear and honest in the feedback she provides, something I really admire in her. My friends Arthur and Susan Tirotta were there when the book was just an idea. Not only have they given me their love and support along the way, but they've also read various drafts, providing important input. My friends Willis and Laurie McNabb have been a constant source of encouragement and support. My friend Elizabeth Warren is another person who's been there from the beginning—encouraging, listening, and supporting in intangible but critical ways. My friends John and Lynn Civitello helped me even before I began working on this project, as they knew and supported me when I worked on some extremely challenging cases. It was this experience that gave me the seasoning I needed to become a more mature abuse-trauma therapist. In this regard I can't say enough about my many past and present clients who, through their lives, have demonstrated how to survive brilliantly and courageously despite incredible challenges.

I have many other friends, family members, colleagues, and students who have also helped me in important ways, and I'm sure they don't understand how, so I'll tell them. First of all, they were tolerant when I was caught up with the writing. When I got stretched too thin and even got a little cranky (okay, a lot cranky), they put up with me. They were understanding when I couldn't make it to one function or another because of my writing schedule. My students are always a source of inspiration, and at least two classes became guinea pigs when I "field-tested" various drafts of the manuscript. I want to thank my former division chair, Sam Samuelson, as well as my current division chair, Karen Colleran, each of whom has encouraged me at various times. The people in my own department also deserve some special thanks, especially my assistant, Clemintene Benjamin, who is a very special person and who gives of herself so freely. The other faculty members in the Social Service/Mental Health program at Pierce College, Dinah Martin and Larry Ruiz, helped by reading portions of the manuscript at various stages and offering feedback guided by their own experience and wisdom. Dinah helped with the discussion about innovations in child welfare. Larry assisted with his perspective about domestic violence intervention as well as Native American culture. Economist and statistician Tom Phelps assisted with the discussion about correlation. Marty Lobdell offered important perspectives on the false memory/repressed memory debate. Teaching at a community college like Pierce can be a wonderful experience. There is a wealth of diversity and talent in such places. I also owe Pierce a debt of gratitude for giving me a chance at the greatest opportunity in the world: community college teaching.

If I completed this book and didn't thank a special class of people—librarians—I wouldn't feel right. In a way they're almost like a staff that someone else has to pay. I want to especially thank Barb Perkins, librarian at Pierce College, who tracked down copies of the many books and journal articles I needed. When I was late returning things (which was often) she was persistent in her efforts to get them back, but always did so in a good-humored way. I asked a lot from Barb and I really appreciate how helpful she was. I am also indebted to the library at Pacific Lutheran University, which made its electronic databases available to me. Sharon Brewer and all the staff of the library at Western State Hospital in historic Ft. Steilacoom, Washington, also deserve special kudos. They were always most welcoming. They provide a little-known service in an out-of-the-way gold mine of a library.

I have many other friends and colleagues, each of whom has taught me something important. One lesson I appreciate most of all is the value of diversity. My colleague Dale McGinnis, who has now stepped over into the other world, was an especially good teacher in this regard. I don't think I would have the appreciation for culture that I now have had it not been for

Dale's understanding, humor, wit, and genius for teaching. By sitting at his feet, I learned what it means to be a "real teacher." I also want to thank April West-Baker, director of our Title III Native American Program, who encouraged me to include discussion about culture when it came to the subject of child physical maltreatment. Anthropologist Lynn Stagg helped me with a better understanding of the material about Iroquois culture, which I included in the survey chapter. I also want to thank Michelle Andreas, Mike Avey, and Dr. Boatamo Mosupyoe for being my colleagues and for sharing their insights about human behavior and multiculturalism.

Many community professionals have also contributed in various ways. Some gave of their time in telephone interviews, some reviewed draft material, and some put me in touch with additional contacts. These professionals include Gary Benton, former Executive Director, New Hope Child and Family Service; Rick Crozier, Program Manager, Elder Services, Good Samaritan Mental Health Center; Dr. Art Gordon, Director, Sex Offender Treatment Program, Twin Rivers Correctional Center; Karen D. Hausrath, Regional Long-Term Care Ombudsman; Jina Pickford, Washington Adult Protective Services; Debra Lambourn, formerly of the YWCA Women's Support Shelter; Bill Notorfrancisco, formerly of Family Counseling Service; Ray Raschko, Director of Elder Services, Spokane Community Mental Health Center; Mary Lee Doran, social worker for the Washington Department of Social and Health Services; and, Tom Rolff, Secretary, Department of Corrections, State of Washington. My friend and colleague Nancy Watson lent her wisdom and experience on the subject of elder maltreatment. There are many others, but space is too limited to mention them all by name.

I also want to thank Lisa Gebo, my editor at Brooks/Cole Publishing Company. Lisa became more like a partner than a mere editor. Right now, I can hear her saying something like, "I don't deserve the credit." She does deserve the credit. Her spirit and enthusiasm for this project have meant a lot, and I can't say enough about what a nice experience it was to have this kind of partnership. The rest of the staff at Brooks/Cole has been great, too. Just to mention a few, I want to thank Amelia Keeney, the Brooks/Cole representative in my area; Lisa Gebo's assistants, Lisa Blanton and Susan Carlson; and Cat Collins, my permissions editor. They've all been a big help, as have the staff at Ex Libris for shepherding the project through production; Nancy Benedict for the crisp, open design, and Jennifer McClain for her thorough editing of the manuscript.

I am also grateful for the comments and suggestions of the reviewers: Janice Adams, Indiana Wesleyan University; Mary Cail, Private Practice; Robin Russel, University of Nebraska at Omaha; Pam Slyter, Lake Washington Individual Progress Center; Cindy Stevenson-McClure, Walla Walla Community College; and Stephanie Vaughn, New Mexico State University.

Finally, dear reader, I want to thank you. Were it not for you, this book would not exist. I hope you find it a useful tool.

Alan Kemp
Pierce College
Tacoma, Washington

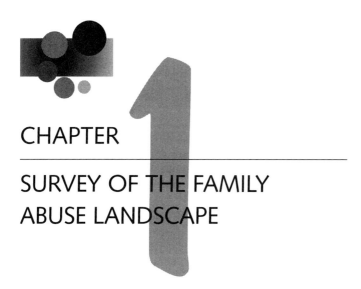

CHAPTER

SURVEY OF THE FAMILY ABUSE LANDSCAPE

Family Abuse as a Matter of Public Concern

Family Abuse as a Focus of Professional Attention

Defining Abuses

Using Social Science Methods to Study Family Abuse

Systems or Ecological Approaches

Relationships Between Forms of Abuse

The purpose of this text is to serve as a starting point for students and human service professionals who want to understand more about abuse in the family. There are good reasons to do so. Public attention to the problems of abuse in the family has intensified. The helping professions are increasingly aware that understanding abuse in the family is crucial to professional practice. All the major mental health disciplines—psychiatry, social work, psychology, psychiatric nursing, marriage and family therapy, mental health counseling, and human services—are taking the issues to heart. Educators and professional school personnel are being required to get specialized training in family abuse as part of their credentialing requirements. Family abuse is surfacing more often as the focus of in-service training programs and workshops. Larger numbers of colleges and universities throughout the country are offering courses in family maltreatment both in major academic departments and in continuing education programs. Human service and education programs often call for completion of family abuse coursework as part of their graduation requirements. Aside from the professional attention the subject has been getting, it is, plain and simple, an important subject because it affects so many people.

The material in this text is sensitive, and many of you who are reading it are likely to have been impacted by this subject in one form or another. Consequently, you will be wise to monitor your own reactions, pay attention to your feelings, and use your personal support network. Even if you haven't been affected directly, you may still find it necessary to work with your own feelings and attitudes, since issues of abuse go to the heart.

FAMILY ABUSE AS A MATTER OF PUBLIC CONCERN

When I use the term "abuse in the family," I include child physical maltreatment, psychological maltreatment, child neglect, child sexual abuse, domestic violence, and elder maltreatment. The terms "family maltreatment," "family abuse," "family violence," and so on, have all been used more or less synonymously. United States Attorney General Janet Reno says family violence is the leading contributor to most of today's social problems. The attorney general's statement is extraordinary if factual. It does have a ring of truth, since it is in families that we learn our basic values as well as how to behave within the family unit.

Family maltreatment has also caught the public's attention. One has only to look at some of the recent celebrated media cases to see this. Those of Susan Smith, O. J. Simpson, John Wayne Bobbit, and the Menendez brothers are examples (see Box 1–1). This media attention can be for good or for ill: for good when it awakens us to problems that exist in our midst; for ill when the shock leads to knee-jerk reactions that, in the end, don't contribute to either a better understanding of the issues or to finding long-range solutions.

FAMILY ABUSE AS A FOCUS OF PROFESSIONAL ATTENTION

Professional involvement in the area of family abuse can be thought of as a reflection or extension of community needs and demands. The public has essentially said that it is concerned about the problem and wants something done about it. It is only appropriate for the human service field to respond since it is the "mission" of the field to try to help human beings solve their problems and get their needs met.

To find the involvement of the human service field in these issues, you don't have to go any further than the person credited with launching the whole business of psychotherapy, Sigmund Freud. Based on reports of his patients, Freud first attributed early trauma, often in the form of sexual

We all deserve a happy childhood. Unfortunately, many children don't have one because of abuse in their families.

abuse, as the cause of a psychiatric disorder he named *hysterical neurosis*. If we have a difficult time dealing with family maltreatment issues today, it was no easier in the late 1800s and early 1900s when Freud was doing his pioneering work. In Victorian Viennese society, sex was a difficult subject, and Freud's patients were making allegations of sexual abuse by parents and other caretakers, most of whom were respected members of their society. Indications are that, when Freud asserted that the recollections of his patients represented real events, his ideas were rejected by his colleagues. Recent explorations about the development of Freud's ideas suggest that it was only when he modified his ideas to say that these disclosures were really tied in to guilt-ridden fantasies, and not real events, that Freud gained professional acceptance. The modification involved changing the assertion from that of patients claiming to have experienced real sexual abuse to one of theorizing that the patients, when children, had secret sexual fantasies involving their opposite sex parent. Some scholars (Masson, 1984) now suggest that this marked the beginning of a long period of professional neglect of child sexual abuse, lasting from the beginning of the 20th century to the early 1980s. We will discuss this in more detail in Chapter 4.

Since the time of Freud's first writings, two world wars have come and gone, and we live in a society where it used to be thought that parents had a right to treat their children almost any way they wanted, in the name of discipline. It wasn't until 1962, when a pediatrician by the name of C. Henry Kempe and his colleagues wrote a startling article, which appeared in the *Journal of the American Medical Association*. The article described what they called *battered child syndrome* (Kempe, et al., 1962). Building on reports from other physicians as well as on their own experience, Kempe and his associates

---

BOX 1-1   High-Profile Family Abuse Cases

O. J. Simpson was a legendary sports hero and media celebrity. He was charged in the murder of his former wife. Media reports before and during the trial spotlighted a troubled relationship that included allegations of previous domestic violence perpetrated by O. J. Simpson. The image of alleged abuser is in contrast to the prior media image of a charming, charismatic star.

John Wayne Bobbit had his penis severed, while he slept, by his wife Loreena, who claimed to have been abused in their relationship and raped by him. She was acquitted of the assault on the basis of having a mental disorder caused by abuse in the marriage.

Lyle and Erik Menendez were tried for the murder of their father and mother. The brothers claimed to have been physically and sexually abused by their father for years. While they said their mother did not abuse them, they claimed she knew of the abuse, and did not intervene. In explaining why they killed her in addition to their father, the Menendez brothers claimed they did so because she was so miserable and unhappy.

The McMartin day care case broke in 1984. Virginia McMartin and six employees, including family members, were accused of molesting children in their Manhattan Beach, California, day care center over a period of ten years. Therapists came into the controversy when they were accused of asking leading questions of the children, which critics charged tainted the children's testimony.

---

described in lucid detail a very scary phenomenon—one that involved repeated attacks on very young children, often resulting in numerous broken bones, each in a different stage of repair. The article by Kempe et al. (1962) is rightly credited with jolting the professional community in the 1960s into an awareness of the problem of physical child abuse and neglect.

The early 1970s marked the beginning of public and professional concern about the problem of domestic violence, or spousal abuse. It was in 1972 that the term "spouse abuse" appeared for the first time in the social science indexes (Gondolf, 1985) and battered women's shelters began to appear. In 1975 the National Organization for Women launched an effort to study the problem of battering (Gelles, 1993a); some sources say that our more enlightened contemporary awareness of family abuse began in earnest as a result of the women's movement, when women began speaking out about abuses they had suffered (see Gelles, 1980). It was also in the 1970s when the media picked up on the issue. A book and TV movie, *The Burning Bed,* appeared and stirred public sentiment (McNulty, 1980). According to one source, very little professional literature existed on the subject of domestic violence until the early seventies (Gondolf, 1985). This same source suggests that the scant professional literature found prior to that time tended to characterize the victims as provokers of their own abuse, something now called "blaming the victim." It is still pointed out that victims are often questioned about why they stay in abusive relationships—the implication being that they are somehow to blame for their own misfortune. One pioneering researcher in the area, Dr. Lenore Walker, wrote a groundbreaking book in the late seventies, applying Seligman's theory of learned helplessness to explain that severely battered women are often caught up in a cycle of violence over which they have no control (Walker, 1979). In addition to Dr. Walker's book, other works appeared in the mid-to-late seventies that are now regarded as landmarks in the field (Gondolf, 1985). The 1970s may also note the beginning of public and professional attention to the issue of elder abuse, brought about at the instigation of advocates for the elderly (Gelles, 1993a), though interest in this area has been neglected until recently (see Chapter 8).

According to one source, child sexual abuse became a semiautonomous specialty in the late seventies (Finkelhor, 1992), and by the mid-eighties it caught on as a public and professional issue. Some suggest that 1984 marked the beginning of intense public attention to the area of child sexual abuse, with the breaking of the McMartin day care case (Haugaard & Repucci, 1988) and several other cases involving multiple allegations of abuse by child care providers. Public interest in this topic intensified in the wake of publicity surrounding these cases (Haugaard & Repucci, 1988) and persists to this day. Since public intervention and research dollars are limited, a certain amount of competition exists between specialty areas; and if there is a disadvantage to all the attention about child sexual abuse, it would have to be that it takes the focus away from other areas that need help. Finkelhor (1992) suggests that, with publicity centering around child sexual abuse, funding and research has shifted away from child physical abuse in favor of sexual abuse. Finkelhor (1992) also observes that both physical abuse (see Chapter 2) and sexual abuse (see Chapter 4) pale in comparison to neglect cases (see Chapter 3), which represent the largest part of many child protective service caseloads but have been relatively overlooked. Psychological or emotional maltreatment is now regarded by many leaders in the field as a sort of master form of maltreatment (see Chapter 3), but it has received relatively less public attention.

DEFINING ABUSES

So far we've started discussion about most of the major types of family abuse: child physical abuse, child sexual abuse, child psychological maltreatment, child neglect, domestic violence, and elder maltreatment. Though most of us have a pretty clear idea about what these various forms of abuse are, we've yet to define our terms.

Any form of abuse can be loosely defined as misuse or mistreatment. An **assault** can be defined as a threat or any single abusive act, psychological or physical. Any *pattern* of physical, sexual, or emotional assaults can constitute **abuse**, whereas the failure to attend to the basic human needs of a person for whom one has responsibility constitutes **neglect**. **Physical abuse** represents a physical assault or pattern of behavior that attacks the victim's physical integrity. While there is controversy over where to draw the line between acceptable parental punishment and abuse, any act of punishment that results in injury is generally defined as abuse. Any physical assault that represents part of a pattern of harmful behavior, or is sufficiently severe, can also be considered physical abuse. **Emotional or psychological maltreatment** is a pattern of emotional or psychological attacks or the neglect of genuine psychological or emotional needs. **Sexual abuse** can be thought of as the inappropriate use of another, which includes sexual contact for the purpose of sexual gratification, domination, or both. Sexual abuse by its very nature includes an assault on a positive sense of self, including sexuality. It sometimes threatens the physical integrity and safety of the victim.

Not only is abuse usually defined according to its type but it is also classified according to the the status of the victim (child, spouse, or elder) and the relationship between victim and offender. **Domestic violence**, for instance, is a pattern of abusive behavior in which one person establishes power and control over another person with whom the abuser has or has had a personal relationship. Sexual contact with children by an adult or significantly older person is **child sexual abuse**, even if the victim participates, because children lack an understanding of the long-range consequences of their involvement and therefore can't consent. Because children are known to engage in sexual exploration with each other, a five-year age difference is generally used to differentiate abuse and exploration (Finkelhor, 1986b). Child sexual abuse can be either **incest** (if it is perpetrated by a close relative) or non-incestuous abuse (if it is perpetrated by someone other than a close relative). It is interesting that, while cultures vary in what they consider to be incestuous (for instance, what the relationship between the parties is), all cultures have the **incest taboo**; that is, all cultures define certain kinds of intimate sexual contact between family members as incest.

In the past in our own society, when people thought of sexual abuse, they usually thought of unnatural acts of non-incestuous abuse as perpetrated by sexual deviants with a sexual preference for children. These individuals are professionally classified as **pedophiles**, but most people have now come to a disturbing realization: While predatory pedophiles exist, most child sexual abuse is perpetrated by family members or close personal friends, some of whom may be pedophiles.

Considering Basic Human Needs

The matrix sketched in Table 1-1 suggests that we can differentiate between abuse and neglect on the basis of whether the person is physically, sexually, or psychologically maltreated or whether their basic needs are neglected. This assumes that basic human needs are critically important. The work of a

---

TABLE 1-1   Family Maltreatment Matrix

| | **ABUSE/NEGLECT CAN BE PHYSICAL OR NONPHYSICAL** | | | |
	Physical Assaults	**Sexual Assaults**	**Emotional Assaults**	**Failure to Attend to Basic Needs**
CHILD	Punishment assault or physical abuse	Child sexual abuse	Psychological assault or child psychological abuse	Child neglect
SPOUSE/ DOMESTIC PARTNER	Domestic violence	Spousal rape	Psychological assault or abuse	
ELDER	Elder physical abuse	Rape or elder sexual abuse	Elder psychological assault or abuse	Elder neglect

---

founding father of humanistic psychology, Abraham Maslow, suggests that each of us comes into the world with certain basic human needs. These needs exist at different levels from most basic to those of a more esoteric nature (Maslow, 1954). They include essential physical necessities such as food and water, a certain degree of safety and security, love and belonging, and self-esteem, as well as self-actualization or psychic/spiritual completion or wholeness. According to Maslow's scheme, we do not work to achieve fulfillment at higher levels unless lower-level needs are at least somewhat satisfactorily achieved. In the area of abuse, the significance of this model is that victims of abuse cannot be expected to be whole if the achievement of their needs is interrupted by abuse or neglect.

These ideas can assist us to think about ways abuse and neglect can impact the ability of their victims to experience life in a positive, creative, and fulfilling way. Maslow's simple but classic hierarchy of needs can also help us to establish such nonphysical human needs as affection, belonging, and self-esteem as essential to human existence. Studies have shown that nontangible "needs" such as love and self-esteem are essential to normal growth and development. To give an example, after the second world war one researcher did a remarkable study on European orphans (Spitz, 1945). While the children were physically well cared for, they were deprived of emotional and psychological nurturance. As a consequence, they suffered from a set of lethargic and depressive symptoms, which the researcher labeled *hospitalism*. Other observations about children reared in out-of-home placements raise similar concerns about long-term care of children in institutions.

Support for the idea that intangibles are essential to normal development can be found in a classic series of studies conducted with rhesus monkeys (Harlow & Zimmerman, 1959; Harlow & Harlow, 1966). A control group of monkeys, raised in a cage with a cloth-covered wire "mother" figure, was compared with another group that was given an identical "mother," except this one was not wrapped with cloth. When the two groups of monkeys matured, the monkeys raised with the wire mother were considerably more aggressive, antisocial, and less well adjusted than those raised with the cloth mother.

Human needs, including the need for physical safety, may be especially important to the understanding of various forms of family maltreatment. This, as well as the role of human development, will be covered more extensively when we address the problem of psychological maltreatment (see Chapter 3).

Fuzzy Lines Between Types of Abuse

When dealing with abuse in the family, there aren't always clear lines between the types of the abuse; it's common for more than one type to occur simultaneously. Psychological or emotional abuse, for instance, comes into play when any of the other forms of abuse are present. Some experts in the field believe that psychological maltreatment is the form of abuse that underlies all other types of maltreatment (see Chapter 3). We can use what happens in domestic violence as one example. As our definition states, domestic violence can be seen as a pattern of behavior in which a person is abusive as a way to establish power and control over a person with whom he has or has had a close personal relationship. In contrast to popular belief, the actual battering may be a relatively infrequent activity. It doesn't have to be used continually in order for the abuser to maintain power and control. The implied threat it causes is often powerful enough. At other times, the abuser uses various forms of manipulative, coercive, and otherwise psychologically abusive behavior as effective additional tools to establish and maintain dominance. The physical, emotional, and sexual forms of domestic violence can thus all be thought of as expressions of a more central process—that of establishing domination and control.

Continuums of Abuse

Models called **continuums of abuse** are representations of abusive behaviors arranged on a line from least to most severe. They are often employed in the domestic violence field to help educate victims and professionals about abusive patterns. Three common continuums are physical abuse continuum, sexual abuse continuum, and psychological abuse continuum.

PHYSICAL	EMOTIONAL OR PSYCHOLOGICAL	SEXUAL
Pinching	Ignoring	Treating as sex object
Squeezing	Demeaning	Minimizing sexual needs
Pushing	Withholding affection	Criticizing sexuality
Shaking	Minimizing feelings	Obsessive jealousy
Cornering	Ridiculing	Unwanted touching
Restraining	Yelling	Sexual name calling
Throwing things	Isolating	Demanding sex
Breaking bones	Insulting	Forcing to strip
Internal injuries	Accusing	Promiscuity
Denying medical care	Humiliating	Forcing to observe sex
Using weapons	Destroying valued things	Forcing unwanted acts
Disabling	Questioning sanity	Forced sex after beatings
Disfiguring	Threatening to injure pets	Use of weapons to force sex
Maiming	Threatening to abandon	Injuring during sex
Murdering	Threatening violence	

FIGURE 1–1 Continuums of Abuse in Domestic Violence

These seem so simple and obvious that one can miss their significance. As a clinician I've found that abusers are often so practiced at rationalizing their behavior that they develop a distorted view of what they are doing. Most batterers will justify and explain away their behavior as being anything *but* abuse. The continuums, which contain very practical and concrete examples, serve as a way to do a "reality check." If the suspected perpetrator is engaging in a range of specific behaviors depicted on the continuums, the abuse pattern materializes easily enough, if the human service professional is willing to ask questions about the behaviors on the continuum and if the perpetrator is willing to disclose. Sometimes the victims, if they feel safe enough to speak, can give you a better description. The range of physically, sexually, and emotionally abusive behaviors, which serve to establish and maintain domination and control, can be graphically depicted as shown in Figure 1-1.

Continuums such as these have been commonly used in domestic violence education. They are not intended to be precise but to graphically show the kinds of behaviors commonly associated with various types of abuse. Some of these may also apply to cases of child emotional and physical abuse when the motivation revolves around dominance and control.

FIGURE 1–2
A Continuum
of Grooming
Behavior in
Child Sexual
Abuse

Nonsexual game playing
Games involving touching
Innocent kissing
Mouth-to-mouth kissing
Exposing or undressing
Observing while toileting
Touching when undressed
Fondling private parts
Has child touch private parts
Penetration with objects
Sexual penetration
Taking sexual photos
Threatening to injure
Injuring during sex

A Continuum in Child Sex Abuse Cases

Though some noted child abuse experts (Sgroi, 1982; Groth & Burgess, 1977, as cited in Sgroi, 1982) argue that sexual abuse is an "acting out" of power and control needs, there also seem to be qualitatively significant differences in how these needs are expressed in child sexual abuse and other types family violence cases. These differences center on motivation. In child sexual abuse cases, the purpose of the gradation of behaviors seems to focus on gradually enticing the child into more intimate sexual activity, a process called **grooming**. In the case of the sexually abusive behaviors acted out in other types of family violence cases, the behaviors seem to be an expression of a sense of entitlement and part of a more general pattern of subjugation and control. Behaviors that could be more useful on a child sexual abuse continuum would include some very different examples from those in the domestic violence sexual abuse continuum, such as the range of behaviors that child sexual abusers engage in as part of grooming their victims. The grooming behavior involves the offender beginning his preparation of a child victim with relatively innocent forms of interaction and gradually increasing the level of activity until he gets the child to go along with intimate sexual activity (see Figure 1-2).

Family Abuse Spillover

Family violence on one family member impacts other family members. Others in the family very often witness it or become aware of it later. In the case of spouse abuse, for example, even if the children are not actually present in the room where it occurs, they are usually well aware of what's going on. Sometimes in these situations children try to intervene and end up being hurt themselves. Even when children stay clear and are not victims of the physical abuse, simply being aware of one parent abusing the other is distressing. It is probably sufficiently traumatic to constitute emotional or psychological abuse in its own right, and there are jurisdictions where exposing a child to spousal abuse is defined as a form of child abuse.

USING SOCIAL SCIENCE METHODS TO STUDY FAMILY ABUSE

Social Science and the Scientific Method

Since this text is designed for students entering the helping fields, and since there have been so many theories, models, and statistics bandied about, it seems essential for anyone studying this topic to be able to put it in the context of the social sciences. Science is the process of systematically testing ideas in order to differentiate between belief and certainty. Science is usually divided into the natural sciences (or "hard" sciences) like chemistry and physics and the social sciences (or "soft" sciences).

The social sciences hope to uncover and explain human behavior. As in the natural sciences, **scientific method** is the generally accepted process, though there is also a movement toward the acceptance of qualitative research, which we will briefly review later in this section. Scientific method essentially involves identifying a question or problem to be solved, developing some tentative ideas or guesses about what causes it (the **hypothesis**), and then testing the hypothesis to see if it is true or not. This is done by **operationalizing** the key concepts to be tested in the hypothesis, following accepted methods in doing **hypothesis testing**, and then describing and explaining the results. When social scientists believe the results apply to what we're trying to study, we say they are **valid**. When different researchers apply the same research methods and get the same results, we say the results are **reliable**. The scientific method implies that the universe, including human behavior, operates according to predictable rules that can be identified and observed. The social scientist is looking for **causation**; in other words, the cause-and-effect relationships presumed to be in operation. In order to do this, they want to exclude **extraneous** or **intervening variables** as much as possible, so they can be confident that whatever conclusions they arrive at are solid. This is important if future research is to build on the results.

Based on the challenges in carrying out systematic research on family abuse, it's not hard to see why the study of the various forms of abuse seems so segmented. Not only do the investigators have different interests but they

FIGURE 1–3
Correlation
Continuum

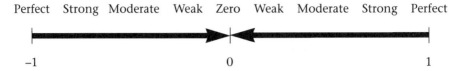

Perfect   Strong   Moderate   Weak   Zero   Weak   Moderate   Strong   Perfect

−1   0   1

must try to reduce the scope of study to manageable proportions so that the search for causative explanations can go forward.

In the area of family abuse, numerous social scientists have studied an array of suspected factors. One of the most consistent findings is that single-cause explanations do not seem to work and that the interaction of multiple interrelated factors seems to be a better way of explaining the causes of abuse. **Causative** explanations (that is, explanations that try to establish cause-and-effect relationships) are often hard to come by; the types of study that can help us arrive at causative explanations are **controlled studies** or **experimental studies**.

An important cautionary note is appropriate here. Researchers strive to be very careful about the kind of **generalizations**, or assumptions, they make about how the world really works, even when doing controlled or experimental studies. Only when the data seems valid and reliable, and the samples being studied seem to represent the population as a whole, should researchers conducting experimental studies be willing to go out on the limb and make claims about causes.

Correlational Studies

When causative explanations can't be found, social scientists generally look for the existence of factors that seem to be related to each other in *any* way. When we can establish that two factors or variables are related, but can't establish cause and effect, we call this kind of information **correlational data**. But correlation does not equal causation. If one variable increases when the other variable increases, they are said to be positively correlated. An example of a positive correlation might be if the unemployment rate goes up along with reports of domestic violence and child abuse. If one variable increases when the other variable decreases, they are said to be negatively correlated. An example of this might be when treatment services are provided to victims of abuse and their symptoms of disturbance decline.

We can measure correlation mathematically, and when we do so it is typically called r. The value of correlation is reported on a continuous scale, or continuum, from −1 to +1, as illustrated in Figure 1-3.

Correlational data is less compelling than causative data. Where cause-and-effect relationships can be established the factors associated with abuse can be called **predictors**; where the relationships are correlational, they are called **markers**.

Descriptive and Inferential Statistics

When information simply defines or describes some observation, it is called **descriptive data**. Statistics that merely describe incidence but don't establish a relationship between variables are called **descriptive statistics**. Descriptive statistics are like snapshots with numbers. They describe a phenomenon at a certain place and time and have less explanatory power than even correlational data. With **inferential statistics** we make generalizations, or inferences, about the whole population on the basis of studying a sample. Inferential statistics are used in formal, controlled research. If done properly they can tell us if it is likely that we could have obtained the results we did merely by chance.

Some Key Research Issues

As we discussed earlier, abuse in the family has only recently reemerged as a focus of professional attention. While we have been accumulating a large body of information, we still have a very long way to go in the understanding of family abuse. Studying something as personal and sensitive as abuse poses special challenges. Much of the knowledge we have been able to gather is either descriptive or correlational, with some exceptions. The two most common sources of information are **clinical samples**, from victims or offenders who have already been identified; and **population samples**, drawn from the general population. There are difficulties associated with each.

One of the chief problems is that abuse, by its very nature, is something generally carried out in secret. We can probably safely assume it is the rare perpetrator who will want to disclose his or her abusive behavior. As for victims, they often are unable to identify their mistreatment as abuse, or they may either fear the consequences of disclosing or feel unsafe about doing so. Since asking people about prior abuse may be safer, this is the approach that is often taken. Research such as this tends to be done by sampling the general population.

When we draw population samples by asking adults about their childhood experiences, we call these **retrospective studies**. While it may be safer to disclose childhood abuse from the distance of adulthood, retrospective studies have another problem—the reliability, or lack thereof, of memory. In addition to the general problems associated with reliability of memory, memory is at the heart of a major controversy in the field of family maltreatment, the false memory/repressed memory debate. Those on the "false memory" side of the debate assert that so-called repressed memories are often artifacts of subtle suggestion on the part of therapists or victim advocates. Those on the "repressed memory" side of the debate assert that memories that surface later in life are real. They counter arguments from the other side with the contention that abuse is so traumatic that memories are repressed until triggered later in life. We will discuss the false memory/ repressed memory debate at greater length in Chapter 5.

In contrast to population samples, clinical samples are not representative of the population as a whole since they are drawn from groups of people who are receiving counseling or mental health services. As a result, we need to be careful about the kinds of generalizations we make from them. Certain questions arise: Because a large number of people in clinical samples have been maltreated, can we assume that maltreatment causes the psychological or behavior problems? Do people in clinical samples report abuse partly as a way to explain their current problems, when other factors could be at play? While the results of research done with clinical samples can be interesting and informative about these specific populations, it is hard to generalize about the whole population or to answer questions such as those posed here.

Official Reports and Survey Data

The kinds of statistics the layperson is most likely to come in contact with are those from official reports or large surveys. In order to understand how to best use information from these sources, we can think of family maltreatment as being like an iceberg. The part we can see would be like the tip of the iceberg, while much of it remains unseen and submerged. The official reports of abuse would be like the tip of the iceberg, leaving much information beneath the surface. While research that uses the scientific method attempts to explain maltreatment, official reports tell us how much abuse is reported; large surveys try to inform us about abuse that has occurred but has not necessarily been reported.

One of the leading figures in the study of family violence, Richard Gelles (1992), suggests there are three main sources of data on family violence: official reports, the *FBI Official Crime Statistics* (data on fatalities), and self-report surveys. Official report information is universal for all 50 states for child abuse and neglect but nonexistent for domestic violence. The FBI *Official Crime Statistics* can help us track fatalities but are not helpful in other areas of family maltreatment. There are two well-known-self-report surveys: the **National Crime Victims Survey** and the **National Family Violence Surveys.** The National Crime Victim Survey can tell us about various acts of abuse based on a representative sampling of 60,000 households across the country, prepared by the Bureau of the Census for the Department of Justice. The National Family Violence Surveys are really two surveys, conducted by a group of researchers headed by Murray Straus, that used large representative samples taken ten years apart. Because of the national requirement to report suspected and substantiated child abuse, we have very good official information about reported child abuse through *Reports from the States to the National Center on Child Abuse and Neglect* (see NCCAN, 1996).

Confusion and Misuse of Research Data

So far we've outlined three different types of research information: experimental, correlational, and descriptive data. Sometimes even professionals can get confused about what each kind of information can tell us, especially when the issue is as emotionally charged (and sometimes polarized) as this field can be. One team of family maltreatment researchers undertook a critical examination of the explosion of research published on the subject and expressed some significant reservations about the value of much of it (Hotaling & Sugarman, 1986). Most of the studies they surveyed performed only correlational comparisons yet attempted to make assertions about causality. Another criticism of some of the early research is that it was done without using comparison groups. Hotaling and Sugarman (1986) point out that we should be extremely careful about accepting conclusions based on correlational data, especially so when these studies do not use comparison groups. (For more detailed discussion of how Hotaling and Sugarman [1986] apply social science methods to the literature on domestic violence, see Chapter 7). If we need to be careful about the conclusions we draw from correlational data, we need to be all the more careful with the kinds of conclusions we arrive at on the basis of descriptive information.

The Need for a Conceptual Framework

While the subject of family maltreatment is fascinating, it is also complex and at times confusing. Some researchers attempt to explain abuse on the basis of the characteristics of individual perpetrators, while others attempt to explain maltreatment on the basis of social or economic factors, and still others look at family dynamics. Some of the research attempts use controlled data, others make use of correlations, while still others try to ferret out answers from large-scale survey data. Since the issues are so complex, a conceptual framework may help us in our exploration of abuse in the family. In order to understand maltreatment we'll need to look at the available research, but we'll use a conceptual model to help us organize our examination. I have decided to adopt an *ecological* or *systems* model for this purpose. Before describing the simplified model adopted in this text, we'll briefly discuss ecological and systems approaches and then look at a well-known ecological model that was adopted earlier. After we sketch out the model we'll be using throughout this text, we'll take a brief look at some of the relevant research data and see how it fits.

SYSTEMS OR ECOLOGICAL APPROACHES

There seems to be a tension in the family abuse field. On the one hand are real attempts to understand and study specific abusive phenomena, such as child sexual abuse or spouse abuse, and on the other hand seems to be a growing recognition of the need for a more integrated approach to understanding family abuse. While some researchers continue to be interested in narrow fields of study, a growing number of investigators have become interested in the various interrelationships and in understanding family maltreatment in a more unified way. In their efforts to understand family maltreatment, some have proposed what they call **ecological models**, while others offer what they term **systems approaches** (for discussions see Milner & Crouch, 1993; Edleson & Tolman, 1992; Blau et al., 1993; Gondolf, 1993). Systems and ecological approaches emphasize that the complex interrelationships between individuals, families, communities, and the society at large all play a role in family abuse. These approaches stress that human behavior takes place within a social environment or ecology: family, neighborhood, school, community, society, and so on.

The terms "ecological" and "systems" are sometimes used almost interchangeably; however, "systems" is often used as a description for the dominant theoretical orientation in the field of marriage and family therapy. I should probably briefly mention that, when simultaneously discussing the area of domestic violence and the field of marriage and family therapy, there is some conflict related to key philosophical positions. I will limit discussion here since these issues will be dealt with in greater depth later in this text, but following is the crux of the conflict.

At the risk of oversimplifying, the family systems approach assumes that problems arise as the result of how the family system is organized or functions. The assumption is that there is dysfunction in significant relationships and that the best approach to therapy is to work on the relationship. In the domestic violence field, on the other hand, the dominant view suggests that domestic violence occurs because of an imbalance of power. From this point of view, it is not appropriate to assume we are dealing with equals since one member of the dyad has more power than the other. Therefore the prevailing view is that we should not work with couples together because we may endanger victims if we require them to interact with their abusing partners about potentially sensitive areas. (Anecdotally, advocates and therapists report that victims are often battered or endangered as the result of something they've said during a therapy session.)

We want to distinguish between the study of family maltreatment and the methods we employ when we try to intervene. The systems or ecological approach I'm introducing here does not necessarily mean that we want to put victims and perpetrators together in therapy; however, it does attempt to provide a framework in which to study and explore abuse in the family. With this in mind, let's turn now to a discussion of the systemic or ecological way of thinking.

A Systems-Oriented Model:
General Systems Theory

Systems theory has its roots in efforts to extend the principles long valued in the natural sciences to the social sciences. Ludwig von Bertalanffy (1934, 1968), a pioneer "systems thinker," is credited with originating a broad theoretical framework called **general systems theory**. Bertalanffy also advocated for moving beyond examining simple, linear, cause-and-effect relationships to looking at the more complex interrelationships that exist in dynamic, living systems. He was himself a biologist and suggested that many of the principles of biology could be extended to all living systems, including human beings, and even to human social systems.

One of the most interesting concepts associated with systems theory is the notion that the whole is greater than the sum of the parts. Systems theorists have coined the term **emergent characteristics** to apply to the unique characteristics that result from the interaction of people in certain special relationships. When people marry, the marriage, with all its new obligations and possibilities, is an example of how the whole (in this case, the marriage) is more than just the combined lives of two individuals. It has great social meaning, as do families, extended families, communities, and society as a whole. Systems theorists are interested in exploring the social realities that result when individuals, families, groups, and whole societies act and interact.

According to systems theory, all systems are goal directed; that is they strive to accomplish specific goals. Human beings and human social systems are no exception. Individual human beings strive to fulfill all their basic needs, but in order to accomplish many of them, especially when young, they need the support and help of other people. Families are systems, viewed in this model, and are essential to providing for the needs of the young and the old. The family is the one social institution where members should be able to fulfill their need for love, belonging, acceptance, and self esteem, and, ultimately, where they can get the support and encouragement they need to seek higher meaning and truth. Communities and societies, by extension, serve similar functions on a grander scale. States and nations provide for economy, the internal security of citizens, and defense against outside aggression. In addition to trying to accomplish the fulfillment of basic goals, systems theory also proposes that we strive to maintain **homeostasis**, or stability, within a certain range of functioning. If there is too little or too much of something, the system's feedback mechanism will give an alert so that the system can take appropriate steps to return to its desired balance.

Systems theory offers an explanation both for why systems change and why they stay the same. They change when they get feedback information that says they either need less of something they have or more of something they do not. According to the model, systems resist change if that change is perceived as a threat to stability or homeostasis. We can use this part of the model to help us understand and explore both the pain of living with family abuse and the resistance to change.

That systems strive to accomplish basic life goals is an integral part of systems theory. The goal-directedness of systems is sometimes referred to as **cybernetics**. Using an archer's target rings for a model, we can imagine that we aim our arrow and attempt to hit the bull's-eye in the center of the target. Becoming a good archer requires skill and experience, so we learn to modify what we do. If we hit too far up we lower our aim; if we hit too far to the right we go left on our next shot, and so on. The cybernetic, or goal-directed nature of systems can help us understand the role of goals and the use of **feedback** in trying to accomplish them. Much behavior, even incomprehensible behavior, is motivated by goals of one kind or another. When the feedback is ignored, the system is described as relatively *closed*. When communication is good, boundaries appropriate, and structural integrity in place, the system is said to be relatively *open*.

According to the model, all systems have boundaries that separate systems from their environments and from each other. In order for a system to have internal integrity, its boundaries must also keep harmful elements out and allow for the inclusion of those things that are needed for the system to accomplish its goals and maintain itself. When boundaries perform the function of allowing in what is needed and keeping out what is harmful, they are called **selectively permeable boundaries**.

In systems theory, living systems have a complex organization that includes many **subsystems**. Human beings, for instance, have a number of biological subsystems, including nervous, respiratory, digestive, and so on. Each subsystem has its own functions and plays its role in the maintenance and survival of the primary system. Within a human being we could also posit physical and psychological subsystems, each working in conjunction with the other. Not only do living systems have subsystems but they are also themselves parts (or subsystems) of other larger systems. On the social level, each of us exists within groups of other human beings that form families, friendship groups, classes, neighborhoods, communities, and societies. It is here, in discussing different levels of interaction, that we can apply ideas drawn from a systems or ecological perspective to help us organize our exploration of family abuse.

A Pioneering Ecological Model

One of the best-known ecological models for describing family abuse is the one adopted by Belsky (1980), based upon the earlier work of Bronfenbrenner (1977; 1979) and Tinbergen (1951) and organized into a multilevel system. Belsky's system (1980) has four levels of factors believed to be involved with family abuse: **ontogenic** level, **microsystem** level, **exosystem** level, and **macrosystem** level. In Belsky's framework (1980), the individual factors of the abuser make up the ontogenic level. The microsystems level is Belsky's term for those factors in the child's immediate environment, such as home, the parents' work, school, friends, and so on. The exosystem consists of relationships that *indirectly* affect people. Examples might include community efforts to change laws or the launching of a child abuse prevention campaign. Belsky characterizes the *macrosystem* as being all-encompassing, taking in all the other levels and including broad and sweeping factors such as culture, attitudes, norms, values, sex roles, and the like. We can also think of the macrosystem level as dealing with the interracial society in which we live.

The Ecological Framework
Adopted in This Text

Belsky's framework may be a bit more complex than is necessary here. In keeping with the principle of **parsimony**, or the idea that we should prefer the simpler models that explain as much or more, I'd like to propose a three-level system to organize the discussion in this text: **micro**, **meso**, and **macro** meaning small, middle, and large. We can use the term *micro level* to apply to everything at the individual level. This includes all explanations about individual behavior, personality, individual motivation, and psychopathology. Family systems would be at the *meso level*. Explanations about how family systems functioning contributes to or protects families from abuse is at this level. The term *macro level* is reserved for explanations and phenomena that occur at the level of communities and the society. The exploration of the contribution of the culture is at this level, and can include norms, economics, and political organization. We will be looking at individual perpetrator factors, including personality and psychopathology, at the micro level; functional and dysfunctional family systems at the meso level; and factors in our culture and society that contribute to family abuse at the macro level.

Now that we have looked at a couple of ecologically oriented models and have sketched out the framework we'll be using in this text, let's apply this framework to the broad field of family maltreatment. We begin by exploring it at the macro, or "big picture," level.

A Big Picture Look at Family
Maltreatment: The Macro Level

There are two measures of family maltreatment that can give us an estimate of the big picture, or macro level: **incidence** estimates and **prevalence** estimates. Incidence estimates refer to the number of people who are abused during a given year. Prevalence estimates tell how many people living within a particular society have been abused. In addition to discussing some proposed explanations for abuse, we will briefly survey some of the most frequently used statistics in this section. The purpose is to start "framing in" the field. Since we will be discussing incidence and prevalence estimates in greater detail for each of the major topic areas, we will only briefly discuss a few of those here.

Some basic statistics on the
incidence of family maltreatment

With issues as emotionally charged as abuse, people want to know how big a problem we have. In order to look for the answer, we turn to statistics, though most of us also appreciate that statistics can be misleading if improperly used. An often heard condemnation about statistics goes something like this: "There are liars, damn liars, and statistics." Another concern people sometimes have with statistics is that they seem so complex, technical, and analytical that we can get bogged down in them and lose sight of what we really hope to understand. We need to examine statistics, however, if we want to have any hope of determining the scope and size of the family abuse problem. As discussed earlier, statistics can be descriptive, correlational, or inferential. When trying to describe incidence and prevalence of abuse we turn to descriptive statistics, which do as the name implies: give us a snapshot of the landscape based upon our sample, or the part of the picture we choose to look at.

The incidence of various forms of abuse is somewhat hard to compare. While nationwide mandatory reporting of child abuse has been in effect since the late 1960s, no such nationwide system for reporting spouse or elder abuse exists. Even with mandatory reporting of child abuse, what gets reported varies depending upon the specific legal definitions for abuse that are in effect in each jurisdiction.

The National Center on Child Abuse and Neglect reports that 2.6 million children were reported as abused in 1990 and 2.9 million in 1994 (NCCAN, 1996). Of these complaints, about 40% were "substantiated" or "indicated," suggesting that in 1994 we can estimate that the incidence of child maltreatment was about one million. Of these, approximately 14% were determined to be sexual abuse, 5% emotional maltreatment, 25% physical abuse, and 53% neglect (NCCAN, 1996).

One incidence estimate of spousal maltreatment is drawn from the National Crime Victim Survey (U. S. Department of Justice, 1992). Based on a sample of 60,000 homes, we can arrive at an estimate of approximately 1,400,000 crimes committed by a spouse or an ex-spouse. There is some debate about whether this number represents only physical maltreatment, but most experts agree that the incidence of spousal maltreatment is in this range (see Chapter 7).

Based on an incidence rate of 32 per 1000 (Pillemer & Finkelhor, 1988), we can estimate that between 700,000 and 1,000,000 elderly people experience maltreatment each year. As with child abuse and domestic violence, there are a number of different types of elder maltreatment that this figure takes in, including physical, sexual, and psychological maltreatment as well as financial exploitation, neglect, and even "self-neglect" (see Chapter 8).

Family maltreatment deaths

Estimates of fatalities caused by child maltreatment each year range from approximately 1,100 to 1,383 (NCPCA, 1992; NCCAN, 1988; Gelles & Straus, 1988). Estimates of spousal fatalities are very similar in number. The official FBI crime statistics cited by Landes, Siegel, and Foster (1993) indicate that slightly more than 1,300 women were killed by their husbands or boyfriends in 1991.

Sometimes numbers don't seem very significant until we connect real-life people to them. The realities associated with family maltreatment

---

BOX 1-2   The Death of Eli Creekmore

Eli Creekmore was three years old when he was killed by his father, Daren Creekmore. When she was 17, Eli's mother became pregnant with Eli, left high school, and later married her boyfriend, Daren. Three weeks after Eli was born, Daren went to prison for assaulting two men. Eli and his mother moved to the town of Everett, Washington, where her family lived. Shortly after Eli's second birthday, Daren was released and moved back with his wife and Eli.

Child Protective Services became involved when Daren abused the boy, and Eli was briefly placed in foster care. Eli was returned home and the family was given intensive in-home family counseling. While counseling was underway, the family seemed to be doing well. After counseling stopped, however, Eli's grandmother and a number of others began expressing increasing concern about Eli's safety. Prior to his death, another serious incident occurred that required Eli to be seen at the emergency room. The physician suspected a fracture at the base of his skull and wrote a statement to the police expressing his opinion that Eli was at great risk.

One evening shortly thereafter, Eli became fussy at the dinner table when his father sat down. Daren sent Eli to his room, but the little boy continued to cry. Daren went into the room, kicked the little boy in the abdomen, and ruptured his intestines. Despite Eli's becoming ill and vomiting, Daren refused to allow his wife to take Eli to the hospital. Eli Creekmore died from his injuries that night.

Based on *The Unquiet Death of Eli Creekmore* (video), by D. Davis (Producer-Director), KCTS Channel 9, Seattle, 1987.

---

become especially clear in the most extreme cases, those that result in death or serious injury. Recently, the case of Susan Smith riveted the public's attention. After claiming her children were kidnapped and her car hijacked, Susan Smith tearfully pleaded on national TV for nine days for the release of her little boys. As a result of the extensive media coverage, she received an outpouring of public support and sympathy until she admitted to having killed them.

Another tragic death is that of Eli Creekmore, a three-year-old boy who, despite having been involved in the Child Protective Services (CPS) system, was killed by his father. One of the most compelling aspects of this case is how Eli was subjected to his father's abusive control despite pleas for CPS to help, especially from his grandmother. It is a case that was highlighted in a PBS documentary titled *The Unquiet Death of Eli Creekmore* (Davis, 1987). (See Box 1–2.)

A brief look at the role of culture

Dramatic and moving cases like that of Eli Creekmore tend to stir people and, once aroused, a common reaction is to want to understand why abuse happens and why it is allowed to happen. Social scientists believe that, at the macro level, there are broad cultural and societal factors that contribute to an environment that fosters, if not causes, family abuse. Anthropologists say that culture is something that is passed down from one generation to another. Beyond the physical artifacts left behind by a society, culture includes all the beliefs, values, rules, and patterns of behavior that are part of a people's adaptation to their world.

In our own society, North America in the closing days of the 20th century, we can say we live in a violent culture. References to public fear about violence are regular fare in newspapers, on TV, and on radio talk shows. If Janet Reno's claim is true that family violence is at the root, then family abuse is a momentous problem.

In order to determine the degree to which culture plays a role in influencing violence in families, we need to be able to compare cultures. Gelles and Cornell (1990) cite the work of an anthropologist (Levinson, 1981) who compared violent family behavior across a number of Western and non-Western cultures. His data suggest significant differences in the amount and types of family abuse from culture to culture. For example, both wife beating and the physical punishment of children are common among the Serbs and rare among certain other cultural groups, including Iroquois, Ona, Thai, and Andaman Islanders. The question that lingers is, "Why?" Without rigorous scientific testing, the answer is only suggestive and speculative; however, we might find clues by taking a closer look at one of the cultures identified as having low rates of wife beating.

The historic tradition of the Iroquois people provides a fascinating example (Tooker, 1978). The Iroquois was not one tribe but a confederacy of five tribes, or nations. They referred to themselves as the "Long House with Five Fires" and to colonial America as the "Long House with Thirteen Fires." Women in Iroquois society were highly valued. While they did not hold high office in the tribe, they had other sources of power. Each tribe was subdivided into clans, and each clan had its own "clan mother," who was the only person who could appoint male members of the clan to the ruling council of the Iroquois League. These appointed chiefs were known as Sachems or federation chiefs. Not only did the clan mothers appoint the Sachems but they could recall them if the clan mother felt they had proved unworthy. The Iroquois were matrilineal; that is, titles and other valued things were passed down through the female lineage. If a female in Iroquois society was murdered, the offending party would lose his own life and have to give twenty strings of wampum to the surviving family, clan, or tribe. The price was only ten strings of wampum for the murder of a man.

In the western European tradition, we have a long history in which women and children were not valued. In Roman times, women and children could be beaten, sold, or even killed. The history of western European society is replete with many examples of how the abuse of women and children was encouraged or tolerated until the present day. A prominent Adlerian family therapist and educator, Dr. Oscar Christianson, suggests that the hierarchical, male-dominated family system that has developed out of the European tradition creates the cultural climate in which children and women can be abused. Where power is shared more democratically, he suggests, abuse ceases to be a destructive force on the family. This view is certainly consistent with feminist theorists who have been saying for a long time that **patriarchy** is the key factor in the abuse of women. It is also consistent in the child maltreatment field, where we often find that some abusive parents seem to feel that their children are property and that they have a right to treat them as they wish. When I was working on a child maltreatment case between a son and his father, the father was a little startled when I suggested he think of his son as a *person* and asked him if he would treat other people the way he did his son. He responded that he hadn't really thought of his son as a person and that he would not behave toward others the way he had behaved toward his son. In the area of sexual abuse (see Chapters 4 and 6), many professionals feel that perpetrators may be influenced by the media and pornography. One TV newsmagazine reported on a group of male college students who candidly expressed the view, on camera, that their sexual attitudes about women were heavily influenced by their experiences as youth with soft porn and masturbation.

Social and economic conditions

In a discussion about the causes of family violence, Richard Gelles and Claire Cornell (1990) comment that all the available data is fairly consistent in pointing to a strong association between economic factors and family maltreatment. While Gelles and Cornell (1990) affirm that this relationship seems well established, they also point out another well-known truth: while poor families may be *more likely* to have maltreatment, abuse in the family is a problem that spans all income levels. Kaufman and Zigler (1989) echo these observations about the association between economic conditions and family maltreatment, citing economic depression, unemployment, single parenthood, poverty, and lack of social supports as all contributing to child physical maltreatment. In their review of research in the area of domestic violence, Hotaling and Sugarman (1986) identify low occupational status, low income, and low educational achievement as being risk factors associated with domestic violence. Over the years, a great deal of discussion has centered on the perceived relationship between child neglect and poverty; there is also the argument that, when we prosecute parents for neglect, we are often really prosecuting them because they are poor. See Box 1-3 for a touching story that was highlighted in a 1987 Academy Award winning documentary.

Family and Small Group Influences: The Meso Level

The culture of a society, by definition, encompasses all the attitudes and beliefs of the society. We've just looked at how these attitudes and beliefs contribute to a social environment in which aggressive and destructive

---

BOX 1-3   The Story of One Family's Tragedy

In a 1987 Academy Award–winning documentary, *Down and Out in America,* producer/narrator Lee Grant tells the story of a number of homeless people across the country. One particularly poignant story revolves around a young couple and their five children.

The story takes place in New York City at a hotel for homeless people called the Martinique. The couple in this story are living at the Martinique because they lost their apartment, his carpentry tools, and virtually everything they owned in a fire. Because he lost his tools, tools that he acquired one at a time over many years, and because of rules about how much they could earn and still receive assistance, he also lost his ability to support the family.

In addition to living in demoralizing conditions, one of the things this couple experienced was being subjected to the threat of investigation for child neglect. They explained that, because they were living at the hotel, they came under the eye of the social services department and were scrutinized in ways they never were when they had their own home.

Based on *Down and Out in America* (video), by L. Grant (Producer-Director), 1987.

---

behavior occurs between family members. If the culture of a society serves as the total social environment and blueprint for human behavior within it, then we can think of the family as the primary agency or institution through which children learn. Families act as the social institutions that succor and nurture children as well as teach them what to believe and how to behave.

Beginning in the 1950s, Bandura and Walters (1963) became interested in how aggression is learned. They developed a theory, now called **social learning theory**, to explain it. In some now-classic controlled experiments, they were able to demonstrate that children can and do learn to behave aggressively by watching and imitating others. Parents are and should be the primary models for their children, but it may also be an unfortunate reality that some of what is modeled is abusive and aggressive.

A number of writers have explored the common wisdom that children who are abused become abusers. This is sometimes referred to as **intergenerational transmission** (Gelles & Cornell, 1990), a topic that deserves sensitivity and compassion. Were we to become untrusting and suspicious of another simply because they themselves were abused as children, we could in a sense be victimizing them again by our unfair and prejudicial attitude. We need to remind ourselves that most victims don't become abusers, though it is true that a disproportionately high number of abusers were abused as children. (For a detailed discussion, see Chapter 2.)

Many advocates working to stop domestic violence suggest that spouse abusers learn to control women in childhood. They suggest that these abusers often see women as threatening and come to believe that they need to use intimidation and violence in order to subdue and control them. Available statistics seem to support this view, and at least one researcher suggests that we stop asking *if* abuse is passed down through the family and start asking *under what circumstances* it happens. Alison Landes and her colleagues review the work of Pamela Smith, who did extensive research with the families of women in a battered women's shelter. Smith's research suggests that about 53% of the sample of batterers had themselves witnessed battering by their parents and a slightly smaller proportion had been abused themselves as children (Smith, 1984, cited in Landes et al., 1991), indicating that witnessing spousal violence may have an even stronger influence than the experience of being abused. Kaufman and Zigler (1987, 1989) estimate that approximately 30% of people who abuse their children experienced such abuse in their own youth. This figure may sound small until we compare it to the 2 to 4% of the general population who we estimate engage in this kind of behavior (Gelles & Cornell, 1990).

Another way of looking at intergenerational transmission is through family roles. As sociologists suggest, it may well be true that we learn various **roles** through experience and observation. As children we learn what is expected of us, and we also observe others around us who fill various roles. So not only do we learn our roles (child, student, playmate, and so on) but through observation we also learn how "mommies," "daddies," and others behave in different situations. Whether we like our role models or not, these are all we have and what we **internalize** as we grow up. When we ourselves become parents and we don't have other internalized models, we may be inclined to behave in ways that match what we've experienced. As adults, this may be especially likely to happen in times of stress; for instance, when we're having discipline problems with children or when our partners don't do what we want.

Family systems theorists believe that families have a life of their own, one that involves patterns of behavior, communication, structure, and involvement with the world outside the family.

A family systems model— The work of Virginia Satir

One very popular figure in the family therapy movement was Virginia Satir, who is regarded as a gifted family therapist with a knack for explaining very complex clinical concepts in clear, easy-to-understand language. Satir advocated that behavior is learned in families and that it can be unlearned. In one of her last pieces of work (Satir, 1988), she describes four changeable characteristics of families which distinguish families that are working from those that are troubled: the family's rules, its communication patterns, the degrees to which the self-esteem of each member is respected, and its connections to the bigger community through friendship networks, work, church, neighborhood, and so on. In Satir's scheme, dysfunctional families have rigid rules, unclear and dishonest communication patterns, low self-esteem among members, and weak ties to the rest of the community. As we'll see later, weak social ties are consistently cited as a characteristic of abusive families, as are rigid, autocratic family power systems.

The work of Virginia Satir provides an intuitively satisfying and practical way to make "thumbnail" representations of "functional" and "dysfunctional" family systems. I find this simple, clear model helpful to many families I work with as well as to students in my classes. It should not, however, be regarded as the final word on family systems or as scientifically valid without more testing and empirical validation of these ideas.

In trying to decide how well Satir's ideas work, one thing we can do is look at the available research and see how it matches up. Consistent with Satir's model, isolation (or not being very well connected to the world outside the family) is commonly cited as a descriptive characteristic of families in which family abuse occurs (Gelles & Cornell, 1990; Smith, 1975; Landes et al., 1991; Milner, 1986, cited in Milner & Crouch, 1993). In families in which child abuse occurs, it seems that there is less support, less positive communication, and more hostile communication (for discussion of research see Milner & Crouch, 1993). In terms of family power systems, Straus, Gelles, and Steinmetz (1980) found significantly less spousal abuse among couples where decisions are arrived at democratically and where neither the wife nor the husband dominates the decision-making process. Depression and a low sense of self-worth are among the most highly correlated factors associated with child abuse (for discussion see Milner & Crouch, 1993). While self-esteem appears to be an individual marker, it is also important to consider it relevant to understanding the context, or relationship, the person is in. After all, how we get self-esteem often comes as the result of acceptance from others.

It might be noted that Satir was associated with Don Jackson and the famed **Palo Alto group**, headed by anthropologist turned family systems theorist, Gregory Bateson. Bateson is regarded as the founding father of family systems theory. The son of a noted biologist, he was fascinated by general systems theory, and many think he integrated significant general systems theory concepts into his own work. In addition to what has come to be called the **experiential school** of family therapy, which is associated with Virginia Satir, at least two family therapy branches have roots in the pioneering work of Bateson and his associates, notably **structural family therapy** and **strategic family therapy**.

The concept of addictive family systems

One popular approach to applying systems ideas is in the area of addictions. Some renowned addictions practitioners suggest that not only do families strive to adapt to their environments but that family members each find unique ways of adapting to troubled family systems (see Black, 1981;

Wegscheider, 1981). These adaptations, or coping systems, take the form of particular family roles. For example, one member might adapt by taking on the role of "hero," assuming leadership or caretaking functions; another might help the family by becoming a "mascot," or person who makes it possible for family members to feel good; another might become isolated, or the "lost child"; and yet another might react with anger and act out the family's hostility. Originally, these ideas were popularized as a way to describe adaptations to families who have a central family figure with an alcohol or drug addiction problem. More recently, these concepts have been applied to many other kinds of family systems that seem driven by similarly acting compulsive behaviors—for example, rage, obsessive sexuality, workaholism, and the like (see Bradshaw, 1988). While these concepts do provide an easy-to-understand, and intuitively interesting, model for explaining why people respond the way they do to troubled family systems, we do not have good, controlled research that can tell us how well it works in the real world.

A family addictions perspective—
The work of Patrick Carnes

Patrick Carnes, a psychologist who proposes an **addiction theory** to explain sexual abuse, has reviewed research relating to the family systems of offenders (for discussion see Carnes, 1989). This research used the Family Adaptability and Cohesion Evaluation Scales (FACES II) to measure two dimensions of family functioning—adaptability and cohesion—in the families of offenders and non-offenders. In this model, balanced family systems are seen as the ideal, extreme families as unfavorable, and mid-range families somewhere in between. As Carnes himself suggests, the results of this research need to be interpreted cautiously. They do indicate that family systems functioning contributes to sexual offending behavior by some of its members. Offenders were more likely to come from extreme family systems than non-offenders. A smaller percentage of offenders came from mid-range family systems and fewer yet from balanced family systems. What the research also suggests is that, while family systems issues are important, they do not account for all sexual abuse. Other factors are also at play.

A few concluding words about
family systems approaches

Family systems approaches do not hold all the answers, however, and one serious criticism of applying a family systems approach to family violence is that there is a danger of **victim blaming**, or unfairly viewing victims as participants in the abuse. Another more sobering caution is that we put victims at risk when we attempt family counseling. Family therapy can be extremely stressful, especially for an abuser who stands to lose control over his victim. We should ask ourselves, "What happens to the victim when they get home after a stressful family counseling session?" Many experienced clinicians tell us that victims are further victimized when they get home. Some seasoned therapists assert that even attempting to do conjoint family counseling, in which the perpetrator and victim are in the same room, is by its very nature unethical because of the danger to the victim.

Individualistic Explanations: The Micro Level

If, as our research seems to show, some individuals can refrain from behaving abusively despite having observed or experienced abuse in childhood, this suggests that individual differences play an important role in determining adult behavior. Our culture itself emphasizes the importance of the individual, and individual responsibility for behavior. Because abusive behavior appears so aberrant, it's common sense to try to ferret out the suspected deep-seated individual psychopathology. Many of those who are interested in family abuse are in fact clinicians who want to learn more about assessing and treating the problem. Being that they are clinicians and practitioners, it shouldn't surprise us if they tend to focus on emotional or psychological reasons to explain the abuse.

In terms of approaches to studying family abuse, there is probably no single approach that has been more widely used than studying the perpetrators themselves. Since many perpetrators have multiple victims and have hurt so many over the course of their deviant careers, this may not be an altogether bad thing. One popular approach to understanding perpetrators is to develop profiles. This has been an especially widespread practice in the field of sexual abuse (Groth et al., 1982), but certainly not unknown in the areas of domestic violence (Gondolf, 1988; Dutton, 1988) and child abuse (Gelles & Cornell, 1990). Later in this text, when exploring specific patterns of abuse, we'll study some of the profile models in more detail.

What we now seem to be discovering is that these profiles tend to generalize too much and aren't very accurate. With regard to male batterers, for instance, one prominent investigator, Edward Gondolf, says that, despite preliminary studies that sketch the profile of a batterer as having an "inexpressive, impulse-driven, traditional, and rigid personality with low self esteem and frequent drug and alcohol problems," there is no conclusive "batterer" profile that exists (Gondolf, 1993). In another passage, Gondolf makes a remarkable comment: "The vast majority of batterers aren't distinguishable from the normal 'good guy'—in fact, many of them may be 'good guys' on all other counts."

Based on a sample of convicted and incarcerated sexual offenders, Groth, Hobson, and Gary (1982) proposed a typology, or system, of categorizing offenders. This model proposes some general characteristics of offenders, but differentiates between two major types—fixated and regressed. In this framework, regressed offenders are often similar to what we think of as incest offenders, who abuse their older female children. The fixated offender refers to the *pedophile,* or person who is virtually exclusively attracted to children for sexual gratification. The work of Groth et al. represents a pioneering effort to understand sexual offenders, people who most would just as soon write off. A number of researchers and clinicians, however, have become disillusioned with the model because it does not seem to accurately describe the range of sexual offenders who actually exist. Conte (1993) comments: "To date, no empirical evidence exists for the accuracy of the [Groth et al.] typology to classify adult sexual offenders."

Many social scientists are coming to the conclusion that theories that propose only single causes for something as complicated as child sexual abuse are inadequate. David Finkelhor and Sharon Araji reviewed the available body of literature. Based on the kinds of questions asked in each of the studies they reviewed, they developed a four-factor model to explain why child sexual abusers develop as they do (Finkelhor & Araji, 1986). In the chapter on child sexual abuse we'll be taking a closer look at this model, but we'll summarize briefly for now. The four factors Araji and Finkelhor (1986) found in the literature are emotional congruence, sexual arousal, blockage to normal sexual outlets, and disinhibition. Emotional congruence refers to the emotional comfort molesters feel when intimate with children. The explanations for why the sexual offender feels comfortable with children include emotional immaturity and fear of intimacy with an equal. Sexual arousal refers to the heightened arousal of the offender to children. Blockage, as the name implies, refers to blocks to getting sexual needs met in culturally appropriate ways. Disinhibition refers to the breakdown of normal inhibitions to sexually inappropriate behavior with children. This model, if for no other reason than it opens up the topic to broader exploration, seems to be a significant advancement over previous approaches to studying child sexual abuse. Rather than focusing on a single factor, it looks at the interaction between a number of suspected factors.

In the area of child physical abuse, many studies have been conducted that try to isolate individual perpetrator characteristics to determine the causes of the abusive behavior (for discussion see Milner & Crouch, 1993; Gelles & Cornell, 1990). However, the emphasis on developing profiles, so evident in domestic violence perpetrator and sexual offender study, has not been as prominent in the child physical abuse arena. Milner and Crouch review a number of studies that do nevertheless look at individual perpetrator characteristics (1993). These characteristics range from unrealistic expectations of the child, to the tendency to blame outside influences for circumstances, to depression. Just based on incidence, women are more often implicated in child maltreatment than men. The experience of stress and the practice of substance abuse are often associated with physical abuse. Some studies seem to show that physical abusers have more negative sensitivity, or irritability, to children—their interaction with their children is less positive and more hostile. Abusive parents are also reported to be more socially isolated and have fewer social supports. In addition, they seem to use physical punishment more often (and reasoning less often) to get their children to behave.

RELATIONSHIPS BETWEEN FORMS OF ABUSE

Many people, professionals included, intuitively feel that there are important relationships between *forms* of abuse but have been hard pressed to describe and prove exactly what they are. As we've already discussed, the family abuse field has been specialized and segmented, with people within one specialty area perhaps not even being aware of the work of colleagues engaged in the study of another aspect of family violence. Without a high degree of awareness and communication between people working on various facets of the family maltreatment problem, it seems difficult to draw too many conclusions. What can we confidently say we really know about the relationships between the various forms of abuse? Embarrassingly, the best answer is probably something like, "Some, but not enough."

The data we do have about the relationships between forms of abuse are probably at best correlational and at worst sketchy, inconsistent, or speculative. As we review the literature reflected throughout this text, a few themes seem to emerge. One is that some family maltreatment (for instance, in child physical abuse and domestic violence) seems to involve the exertion of domination and control by a powerful family member over a weaker member. Another theme, especially in child sexual abuse and aspects of domestic violence, seems to involve the aberrant use of another in a sexual way. Yet a third theme, especially in elder maltreatment, involves the exploitation of a dependent family member. Informally comparing risk factors between various forms of abuse, we also find some common elements. These include economic problems, high levels of stress, substance abuse, social isolation and low levels of social support, verbal aggression, youth, high levels of relationship conflict, number of children, and having witnessed family violence as a child.

Where power and control seem to be the driving issues, it probably shouldn't surprise us that there seems to be a correlation between spousal violence and child abuse. We have already talked about the correlation between having witnessed spousal abuse as a child and perpetrating abuse as an adult. As we mentioned earlier, one study of battered women showed that a very large number of their abusers had seen abuse as children (53%); but we did not yet emphasize that nearly as many (46%) were victims of child abuse (for discussion see Landes et al., 1991). We don't have clear numbers that tell us how many had both seen spousal violence and been physically abused.

Straus and Smith (1990) analyzed the results of the 1985 National Family Violence Survey. They note that parents who have conflict with each other are also more likely to be abusive with their children, and parents who are verbally abusive to their children are also more likely to physically abuse them. Children are three times more likely to be hit in families where one parent is also violent toward another. In addition, children who witness aggression at home by parents tend in turn to be assaultive to siblings.

In addition to the other factors, substance abuse is often associated with family maltreatment. According to information reviewed by Straus and Gelles (1990), we can estimate that the correlation between substance abuse and spousal battering ranges from .36 to .52. Other estimates are as high as 70%. Heather Hayes and James Emshoff (1993) reviewed the literature and discuss the **comorbidity**, or co-occurrence, of substance abuse problems and family violence. Their review suggests that several published studies link over half of child abuse and neglect cases to substance abuse in the family. Among families in treatment for their substance abuse problems, they note that as many as 60% may have experienced domestic violence. Their review also cites figures that suggest that as many as two-thirds of children raised in alcoholic homes may have either been physically abused or have observed domestic violence.

CHAPTER SUMMARY

In this introductory chapter we concentrated on trying to gain an overview of the family abuse landscape. Public awareness and professional concern often go hand in hand. We traced the reawakening to the problem from Freud's time to the present. In the past 35 years child physical abuse, domestic violence, child sexual abuse, and elder abuse have each in turn captured public attention. We highlighted several high-profile cases, such as those of O. J. Simpson, Susan Smith, and John Wayne Bobbit. In order to get a better handle on the scientific study of family abuse, we surveyed how social scientists study and explain human behavior. We differentiated between descriptive, correlational, and causative data and discussed the kinds of generalizations we can make based on each type of evidence. We used a model of basic human needs as a way to give the topic a context: the assault on or neglect of one of these basic needs. We defined forms of family maltreatment in that context, looking at both abuse and neglect, and brought into our definition the status of the victim; that is, the child, spouse, or elder.

Because the subject of family abuse is so complex, we outlined a systems approach in order to give us an organizational framework. We discussed how to use a simple micro-meso-macro model in which to study the complex dynamics at various levels of explanation. Within that framework we looked at broad cultural issues, family systems, and individual factors.

In order to get a feel for the research done on family abuse, we reviewed selected statistics on the incidence and prevalence of various forms of family violence. While relatively low when compared to the overall incidence and prevalence estimates, we noted that cases in which death results can be very dramatic. When looking at the role of social and economic factors, we briefly discussed that while the risk of maltreatment is higher among the disadvantaged, poor families are sometimes misidentified as neglectful.

Official reports and prevalence estimates can give us a framework for how big the problem is. Case examples, such as that of Eli Creekmore, who is profiled in this chapter, can tell us about the impact in extreme incidents. Neither, however, helps us understand why it happens. In an effort to understand why abuse occurs, we looked at some theories and ideas about the role that social, family, and individual factors might play.

We had a brief opportunity to compare cultures and explore why abuse might occur less often in some than in others. We built on the earlier work of anthropologist David Levinson (as cited in Gelles & Cornell, 1990) and explored in some depth the question about why abuse might be more widespread in some societies than in others. In this regard we not only looked at the western European tradition but explored a culture where battering is traditionally less common, that of the Iroquois.

We also reviewed some of the ideas of family therapist Virginia Satir and discussed how family-related factors might help us distinguish between troubled and healthier families within our own society. In order to round out our discussion, we also briefly reviewed some of the literature about factors associated with individual perpetrators. We noted that, while we may want to believe that perpetrators fit a certain profile, the evidence seems to suggest that there are no definitive profiles for the various categories of perpetrators.

Finally, in the closing part of the chapter, we briefly surveyed some relatively uncharted territory, the suspected relationships between the various forms of abuse in the family.

LEGAL AND ETHICAL CONCERNS: CRITICAL THINKING QUESTIONS

1. Cases such as that of O. J. Simpson, the Menendez brothers, and the McMartin preschool case attract a lot of public attention. Publicity surrounding such cases makes the public more aware of a problem, but public sentiment can also inflame and distort. How can we balance the need for awareness and the risk of distortion due to media coverage and emotionality?

2. Social scientists identify at least three types of information about human behavior: descriptive, correlational, and inferential. Why is being conscientious in doing research important?

3. In the family abuse arena, basic human needs seem to be important, yet they are sometimes forgotten by social scientists in their quest for scientific understanding about human behavior. How do we balance the need for objective accuracy in scientific knowledge and the need to be sensitive to the subjective experience of the individual?

4. We identified three levels of explanation for abuse in the family: micro, meso, and macro. Some aspects of the problem are so compelling that it can be easy to define them too narrowly. How can we avoid focusing too much on any one factor so that we get a more rounded understanding of family violence?

5. People from around the world have very divergent world views and cultures. We know that differences exist in the use of violence within the family from culture to culture. How do we balance our own view that family violence is bad with a respect for cultural difference?

6. The field of family violence requires professionals to make hard choices. No one likes outside intervention, yet children and domestic partners are killed every year. How do we balance the right to freedom from interference in domestic affairs with protection of potential victims?

7. The research seems to suggest that socioeconomic conditions and poverty, or simply the stresses related to them, increase the risk of abuse in the family. How do we reconcile removing public economic support for people living on the margins with a commitment to reducing family violence?

SUGGESTED ACTIVITIES

1. Make a list of any feelings you might have become aware of as a result of the material we have covered in this chapter. Select one item and write a brief description about it.

2. Watch TV for an evening and make a list of references to women, children, or the elderly that negate their value. Discuss the degree to which you feel society either values or devalues members of these groups.

3. Describe your family and discuss the dynamics, explaining how they work. To what degree are your current relationships like those of family members who came before you?

4. Discuss any of your personality characteristics that influence your relationships.

5. Describe any experiences you have had in which you tried to establish dominance or control over another. How did that experience influence you and the other person?

REVIEW GUIDE

1. Discuss the development of public concern in family abuse issues.

2. Identify some of the recent high-profile cases that have sparked public interest in family abuse (for example, O. J. Simpson, Menendez brothers, and so forth). Discuss some of the basic elements in each of these cases.

3. Outline the emergence of concern about family abuse in the professional community.
- Include the place of Freud and his ideas in the history of professional attitudes about sexual abuse.
- Be able to identify the influence of the work of Kempe and his colleagues in the areas of physical abuse.
- Discuss events and influences in the 1970s with respect to domestic violence and other forms of abuse.

- Be familiar with the information about the reemergence of sexual abuse as an area of study.

4.   List all major terms and concepts associated with the scientific method as used in the social sciences (these are printed in **bold** in the text and included in the glossary at the end of the chapter). Briefly define and explain each. Be sure to include the differences between descriptive, correlational, and inferential statistics. Discuss hypothesis testing and the kinds of generalization that can and can't be made, based on the type of data we are working with (for example, what can we assert based on correlational data compared to causative data?). Know the difference between predictors and markers.

5.   Discuss how basic human needs can help us understand abuse. Be familiar with Maslow's hierarchy model. Discuss how we can define various forms of maltreatment according to whether we address any of these areas or neglect them.

6.   Be able to define each of the various forms of family abuse— child sexual abuse, child physical abuse, child neglect, elder abuse, and domestic violence.

7.   Be familiar with each of the abuse continuums; their limitations as well as ways in which they can be helpful to those working in the family abuse field. Be familiar with each of the behaviors on the continuums, and see if there are some others you might want to add.

8.   Discuss the fuzzy lines between the various types of abuse.

9.   Summarize what is meant by ecological or systems theory approaches. What are the major concepts in general systems theory? Describe each of the four levels of "ecology" outlined in Belsky's model. Define parsimony. Describe the three-level systems model introduced in this text. Define macro, meso, and micro levels of explanation. Discuss how a systems approach can be used as an organizational model. Be able to define all systems terms outlined in the text. Describe the examples and social science applications of systems theory principles.

10.   Discuss what is meant by incidence and prevalence levels. Be generally familiar with the significant statistics related to family abuse. Describe each of the major types of official reports and surveys (for example, the National Family Violence Surveys). Discuss the statistics associated with fatalities caused by family violence. Be generally familiar with the Eli Creekmore case.

11.   Discuss social (macro) level factors that seem to be associated with family abuse.

12.   Describe family systems, or interrelationship (meso) level explanations for family abuse.

13.   Discuss individual (micro) level factors associated with family abuse.

14.   Review what we know about the relationships between forms of abuse.

SUGGESTED READING

Bradshaw, J. (1988). *Bradshaw on the family*. Deerfield Beach, FL: Health Communications.
A popular book that summarizes the impact of dysfunctional family systems on individuals. Includes discussion of cultural influences and child-rearing practices.

Briere, J. (1992). *Child abuse trauma*. Newbury Park, CA: Sage Publications.
A scholarly but enormously engaging book about child abuse trauma. Attempts to look at how to work with all forms of child abuse trauma, with a particularly understanding and humane attitude toward victims.

Edleson, J. L., and Tolman, R. M. (1992). *Intervention for men who batter: An ecological approach*. Newbury Park, CA: Sage Publications.
An innovative approach to understanding and intervening with batterers, which incorporates an ecological approach.

Masson, J. M. (1984). *Assault on truth: Freud's suppression of the seduction theory*. New York: Addison-Wesley.
Controversial book about the transformation of Freud's original ideas about child abuse trauma.

Satir, V. (1988). *The new peoplemaking*. Mountain View, CA: Science and Behavior Books.
A popular and caring book about human beings in families. Written by one of the most popular and influential family therapy practitioners and teachers.

Wegscheider, S. (1981). *Another chance*. Palo Alto, CA: Science and Behavior Books.
This is a well-written, popular book about the impact of alcoholism on families and how members of the family assume specific roles in their attempt to cope and adapt.

CHAPTER GLOSSARY

Abuse
A pattern of emotionally, physically, or sexually assaultive behavior that is harmful to a human being, committed by a person with greater power or authority.

Addiction theory
A theory that attributes the causes of personal and social problems (such as abuse in the family) to a variety of compulsive behaviors, such as substance abuse, gambling, or obsessive sexual proclivities.

Assault
Individual episodes, or acts of commission, of emotionally, physically, or sexually harmful behavior that is not necessarily part of a general pattern that would constitute abuse.

Bateson, Gregory
Anthropologist, regarded by many as the father of the systems-oriented family therapy movement.

Causative data
Data or information drawn from research that establishes cause-and-effect relationships between two or more variables.

Clinical samples
Samples drawn from populations of people (including victims and perpetrators of abuse) who have already been identified as having significant psychological, emotional, or social problems.

Comorbidity
The simultaneous occurrence of two illnesses or pathologies in the same person.

Continuums of abuse
A range of specific abusive behaviors that are graphically arranged, from least to most harmful, along a line or continuum.

Correlational data   Information or data that establishes a relationship between two or more variables.

Descriptive data   Information or data that merely describes or defines but cannot establish any particular relationship between variables.

Descriptive statistics   Statistics that merely describe incidence or prevalence but make no correlations or cause-and-effect inferences. Commonly encountered in our day-to-day lives.

Domestic violence   A form of maltreatment perpetrated by a person with whom the victim has or had a close personal relationship. Usually used as a synonym for spousal, or partner, abuse.

Dynamics   The forces that act within a system.

Ecological models   Models that try to understand phenomena within the context of interacting social environments.

Emergent characteristics   Characteristics that arise out of the particular relationships between elements of a system. The common expression "the whole is greater than the sum of the parts" is often applied to this concept. An example of an emergent characteristic is a marriage—a unique relationship is created as the result of interaction between the two people who are part of it.

Emotional or psychological abuse   Abuse that causes, or can cause, harm to the sense of self, self-esteem, or psychological or emotional well-being.

Experiential school   A school of family therapy associated with Virginia Satir, which emphasizes the way people experience their social worlds.

Extraneous or intervening variables   Variables a researcher does not control but that could influence the outcome of research.

General systems theory   A theory first advocated by biologist Ludwig von Bertalannfy which asserts that scientific principles which operate in biology can be applied to the social sciences.

Generalize   To apply the results of research more broadly to a larger sample or to the whole population.

Homeostasis   A state of equilibrium or balance.

Hypothesis   A statement that asserts a testable relationship between two or more variables.

Hypothesis testing   The process by which social scientists test a hypothesis through empirical research. While 100% certainty cannot be determined, based on laws of probability it can be determined how likely it is that the results achieved could have been obtained solely by chance.

Inferential statistics   Statistics with which we can make inferences about cause-and-effect relationships, or about a larger sample or entire population, based upon a smaller sample. The process by which we generalize about a population based on studying a sample.

Intergenerational transmission   The process by which abusive behavior is believed to be passed down from one generation to another.

Macro level   Literally means "large"; in a systems-organizational sense, used to refer to large units, especially at the cultural and societal level.

Markers   Factors associated with a phenomenon but that are unable to predict its occurrence.

Maslow's hierarchy   A model developed by Abraham Maslow that attempts to describe the prioritization of basic human needs.

Meso level	Literally means "middle"; in a systems-organizational sense, used to refer to medium-sized units, especially at the level of families or small groups.
Micro level	Literally means "small"; in a systems-organizational sense, used to refer to small units, especially at the level of single individuals.
National Crime Victim Survey	A survey about crimes, conducted by the Bureau of the Census for the Department of Justice with a representative sample of 60,000 households in the United States.
National Family Violence Surveys	Two surveys, using large representative samples, conducted in 1975 and 1985 to determine the incidence and prevalence of family violence. Contains much data used to help us study family maltreatment.
Neglect	Acts of omission by which the basic human needs of a dependent person are not provided.
Official crime statistics	Statistics reported by the Federal Bureau of Investigation. In the family abuse field, the most important of these statistics are those that deal with fatalities.
Operationalize	To take an abstract concept and put it into concrete form, so that it can be observed and studied. Take, for example, the concept of empathy. Psychologists and counselors use active listening skills, such as paraphrasing, to demonstrate deep understanding of another's perspective, thereby operationalizing the concept of empathy.
Palo Alto group	A group of researchers and clinicians associated with Gregory Bateson and Don Jackson, who did pioneering work in the area of family systems. The name derives from Palo Alto, CA, where the group tested their theories.
Parsimony	A principle employed in social science where simpler theories that explain more are preferred over more complex explanations.
Patriarchy	Dominance or rule by men in a group or society.
Physical abuse	Abuse involving harm to the body.
Population samples	Samples drawn from the population at large.
Predictors	Factors associated with a phenomenon that can accurately predict its occurrence.
Reliability	The extent to which research comes up with the same result from one study to another and from one time to another.
Retrospective studies	Studies that rely upon the reflections or memories of adults about their childhood experiences.
Roles	The function of an individual in a group, for example, "parent," "son," "teacher," "policeman," "minister."
Satir, Virginia	An associate of Don Jackson of the Palo Alto Group who was a pioneering family therapist and charismatic teacher and advocate of a family systems approach to helping people.
Selectively permeable boundaries	Boundaries in a system that establish identity and allow for exchange of information or substances but that keep out harmful material.
Sexual abuse	Abuse that involves the sexual use or exploitation of another person or the use of force.
Social learning theory	A theory popularized by Bandura and Walters that explains important human behavior as being learned by observation, imitation, and vicarious reinforcement.

Strategic family therapy	A school of family therapy that can trace its roots back to some of the pioneering work done by the Palo Alto Group. Interested in disrupting dysfunctional patterns and helping to establish healthier patterns.
Structural family therapy	A school of family therapy that can trace its roots back to some of the pioneering work done by the Palo Alto Group. Interested in family structure. Associated with the Philadelphia Child Guidance Clinic.
Subsystems	Systems that are part of larger systems.
Systems approaches	Approaches that describe the relationships between people and behavior by the use of systems contexts.
Validity	The extent to which research actually measures what it says it does.
Variance	One of several measurements of dispersion, or how spread out the data is. In social science, the various factors that influence variance are studied in an attempt to understand the causes of human behavior.
Victim blaming	Attributing responsibility to victims for the bad things that happen to them.

CHAPTER

CHILD PHYSICAL ABUSE

Social and Historical Context

Defining the Problem

Overview of Major Types of Injuries

Psychological Impacts

Intergenerational Transmission: The Violence-
Begets-Violence Theory

A Systems or Ecological Approach to
Understanding Risk and Resiliency Factors

A Special Category of Child Physical Abuse:
Munchausen Syndrome by Proxy

In some respects we seem to be at an awkward place in our history in terms of studying child abuse. On one hand many people seem to feel that the state and federal governments unduly interfere with the rights of parents to freely exercise control over their own children. Some suggest that, because of government involvement in regulating how parents discipline their children, the legitimate authority of parents and traditional family values have been undermined. Greater emphasis on children's rights in recent decades has become an issue of concern for some.

Understanding
the risk factors
associated
with child
physical abuse
might help us
prevent it.

On the flip side of the coin, however, we know from the most current reports that there are approximately a million substantiated cases in which children are abused each year (NCCAN, 1995a). The unfortunate fact seems to be that the overwhelming majority of those who physically abuse children, or endanger them through neglect, are the parents. Parents and other caretakers are the same people who we and the children should be able to trust. But recent figures available from the National Center on Child Abuse and Neglect (1995a) suggest that about 77% of cases of child abuse are perpetrated by parents. Foster parents, child care providers, and other caretakers make up an additional 2%. Furthermore, the proportion of actual physical abuse perpetrated by parents is likely to be somewhat higher because the total number of substantiated cases of child abuse includes sexual abuse cases, in which fewer parents and more family friends, neighbors, and other relatives are the perpetrators (see Chapter 4). So we can probably estimate that more than 77% of the perpetrators of child physical abuse are parents.

Other statistics provided by the National Center on Child Abuse and Neglect (1995a; 1995b) indicate that about 24% of cases of child abuse involve physical abuse. While the issue of child sexual abuse may have taken center stage in recent years, child physical abuse is a vital issue. It accounts for a substantial number of deaths, not to mention permanent disability, disfigurement, and the long-range psychological problems it causes.

SOCIAL AND HISTORICAL CONTEXT

Some of the most heart-wrenching cases of physical abuse involve our youngest and most vulnerable children. You might recall from the introductory chapter the story about the death of little Eli Creekmore. Eli was three years old when he died from the internal injuries caused by his father's abuse. He was one of the estimated 1,200 to 1,400 children who suffer the same fate each year (Landes et al., 1993; NCCAN, 1995a, 1995b). According to one study, the risk of fatal child abuse is 5.9 times higher for children under the age of three than for older children (Jason and Andereck, 1983). In another study, it was found that more than 50% of victims of severe abuse were under three years of age (Rosenthal, 1988).

If we use today's definitions of child physical abuse, we could probably say that it has a long and tolerated history. In the western European tradition, we can trace the mistreatment of children back to Roman times and before. Children have been sacrificed, tortured, beaten, and disfigured (Burgess & Garbarino, 1983; Zigler & Hall, 1989). In their brief review of the literature, Zigler and Hall (1989) comment that it was not uncommon to sacrifice infant children in order to dedicate public buildings and bridges. They also suggest that the Roman doctrine of **patria potestas** gave fathers almost absolute power over their children. From the Middle Ages until the dawn of the industrial revolution, children continued to be an underprotected class. By the beginning of the industrial age, child labor abuses were common enough to eventually result in child labor legislation in the United States and elsewhere.

In addition to the child labor abuses during the latter part of the 19th century and early 20th century, children do not seem to have been well protected even in their own homes. It wasn't until the latter half of the 19th century that the issue of child abuse finally began to get some serious attention in this country. In 1874 a social worker in New York City discovered the abuse of Mary Ellen Wilson. Not only was Mary Ellen beaten, she was also confined with chains and deprived of food by her adoptive parents (Gelles, 1993a; Zigler & Hall, 1989). Henry Berg, the founder of the Society for the Prevention of Cruelty to Animals, is credited with pushing the case and ensuring that it finally got to court (Gelles, 1993a; Zigler & Hall, 1989). It apparently attracted considerable press coverage, and at its conclusion Mary Ellen's adoptive mother was sent to jail and Mary Ellen was placed in an orphanage (Zigler & Hall, 1989). By 1875 the Society for the Prevention of Cruelty to Children was formed (Zigler & Hall, 1989). (It's an interesting footnote that this happened *after* the Society for the Prevention of Cruelty to Animals was established.)

While it took the case of Mary Ellen for the public to pay attention to the problem, child welfare workers and the courts had been active on behalf of abused and neglected children for some time. It wasn't until the 1960s, however, that the issue began to become one of general social concern. As mentioned in Chapter 1, C. Henry Kempe and his colleagues wrote an article on the subject in the *Journal of the American Medical Association* (Kempe et al.,1962), which is generally regarded as the spark that fired public and professional interest in the area of child abuse. It was in this article that Dr. Kempe and colleagues coined the term **battered child syndrome.**

Kempe and his colleagues described the battered child syndrome as a condition in young children caused by serious, chronic abuse and a frequent cause of permanent injury or even death among children (Kempe et al., 1962). Prior to the article's publication, other physicians had begun to question whether or not there was a relationship between the serious injury of some children and abuse by their parents (Dubowitz & Newberger, 1989; Gelles, 1993a; Zigler & Hall, 1989), and advances in radiological technology made it possible to visually identify repeated injuries to bones. Kempe and his colleagues took these early speculations a step further, suggesting the existence of the battered child syndrome and outlining some general criteria for identifying and diagnosing child battering. Among the most dramatic and telling of the signs and symptoms they described are multiple fractures of bones in varying degrees of healing (Kempe et al., 1962). They allude to fractures and lesions of the long bones, common in severe physical abuse cases because the child's limbs make such convenient "handles" for man-handling. They suggest that if physicians find in the X rays multiple breaks in varying degrees of healing that they can conclude with a reasonable degree of certainty the presence of severe child abuse. Other highly suspicious indicators associated with severe physical abuse include subdural hematomas (blood clots with or without skull fractures), multiple soft-tissue injuries, poor skin hygiene, and marked malnutrition (Kempe et al., 1962).

In the same classic article, Kempe and his colleagues suggest that in true cases of battered child syndrome the abuse tends to be chronic and repeated. While the tragedy of Eli Creekmore occurred much later in the history of child abuse, Eli's case certainly brings this reality home. Eli had been examined in the emergency room just days before his ultimate death. The emergency room doctor reported that Eli had two "black eyes." In an interview for a PBS documentary, this physician described the black eyes as "raccoon eyes," identical discolorations around both eyes often caused by skull fractures. Because of the complicated structure of the cranium, some skull fractures are hard to detect on X rays, even though they can cause cranial bleeding. When this happens, the blood collects around the eyes, causing the raccoon-eye appearance. As a result of this observation, the emergency room physician called the police and made a strong recommendation that Eli not be returned home. Unfortunately, his plea was not heeded and Eli died as a consequence of yet another episode of abuse.

Sometimes it takes cases like that of Eli Creekmore, in addition to a commitment on the part of the professional community, to make a difference. According to many it was the work of Kempe and his colleagues, and the increasing attention they brought to the problem, that stimulated an awakening. Kempe sensitized many physicians to the problem, the news media began to cover tragic cases, and policy makers began to listen. As a result of efforts by Kempe and the U. S. Children's Bureau, a model reporting law was published in 1963, and by 1968 all 50 states had enacted laws requiring the reporting of suspected abuse (Landes et al., 1993). Initially, this legislation required only physicians to report serious physical and non-accidental injuries, but it has now been expanded to include most professionals who serve children (Landes et al., 1993). Another significant advancement often associated with the work of Kempe and his associates was the establishment of the National Center for Child Abuse and Neglect, which itself has come to play an important part in setting the stage for greater public interest in the problem (Giovannoni, 1989).

DEFINING THE PROBLEM

In addition to describing extremely catastrophic child physical abuse, the battered child syndrome as a concept became a catalyst that created heightened public and professional awareness of the problem. What began as the "battered child syndrome" ultimately broadened and became transformed into the more global concept of "child abuse." While there now seems to be a movement toward understanding the various forms of abuse in a more unified way, this is a fairly recent trend. Many professionals in the field have had an interest in one or more specialized areas; working somewhat independently of each other, they have followed their interests and inclinations. Perhaps because of this, the field has become divided into a number of specialized areas: child physical abuse, neglect, child sexual abuse, incest, and emotional or psychological abuse (Finklehor, 1992).

Intent and Result

There is no single definition of child physical abuse that is acceptable to all. For instance, up until now we have alluded to physical abuse as being a willful act on the part of parents or caretakers. While this seems true enough, this definition can also be debated. Returning to the case of Eli Creekmore as an example, we can ask, "Did his father intend to kill him?" The answer is probably no, though Eli's father should have been aware that his abusive behavior could have had this result. He probably did intend to inflict pain, perhaps in order to gain compliance, perhaps in response to some perceived misbehavior, or perhaps merely as a way to feel powerful and in control.

If we don't use intent as the key feature in our definition, how about the result? This too has problems. David Gil, a well-known professional in the field, is credited with giving us the following example (Landes et al., 1993). A parent has two children whom he disciplines at the same time, one with each hand. He pushes both children to the floor. One child lands on concrete and suffers scrapes and bruises, the other lands on the carpet and suffers no observable injuries. Gil's question, then, is this: "Is the parent only a one-handed abuser, because only one child was injured?" Of course the answer is no.

In a case as dramatic and extreme as Eli's, the consequences, or result, of the act proves this to be abuse. But what about other cases where the injuries aren't so obvious? Is it only abuse if there is death or some long-term physical consequence to the child? Finally, what about accidents that result in serious injury yet truly were unintentional and are not the by-products of abusive use of power by the parents? What about spanking? Is it abuse? Is it abuse when bruises or injury result? These are all vital questions, yet none of them have easy answers.

Considering Culture when Defining Abuse

What about cultural differences? Should we impose our values and biases on people with different cultural backgrounds? Is it fair? Cultural beliefs and practices vary considerably around the world. In principle most fair-minded people would probably agree that we should take culture into account, yet some practices are so diametrically at odds with the prevailing societal standards that they cannot be accepted. For example, clitorectomies (the practice of surgically removing the clitoris of female children) are accepted or even required as part of membership in some other cultures. On the other hand, cultural practices can also get members of certain cultural groups into trouble in our society, even though the practices are probably not abusive. Consider the example of the Pha family, as described in Box 2-1.

Child Abuse Prevention and Treatment Act of 1974

As you can see, the definition of child physical abuse, which sounds like a straightforward issue, is far from it. Definitions vary according to the purpose of the definition and who is doing the defining, and there are many legal implications. The **Child Abuse Prevention and Treatment Act of 1974** requires that all states have **mandatory reporting laws** and programs

---

BOX 2-1   The Pha Family

Mrs. Pha has five children, ranging in age from 4 to 14. She originally came from Cambodia with her husband. After fleeing Cambodia, Mr. and Mrs. Pha spent a considerable amount of time in refugee camps in Thailand. They have now divorced. Mrs. Pha has a limited income but has an extended family and other members of the Cambodian community she can turn to for help.

One of the Pha children had been out of school for several days. When the child returned to school her teacher noticed severe bruising around her neck. As is required by law in that state, the teacher notified Child Protective Services (CPS). When the child was examined at the local emergency room, the physician also found a number of circular-shaped bruises on the child's back.

This particular community has a well-run Asian refugee counseling program, and one of the Cambodian counselors was consulted on the case. What the CPS worker learned is that in many Southeast Asian cultures certain home remedies are used to try to combat illness. The little girl had been ill. Her mother, following old healing practices, had pinched the skin around the neck as a way to fight her daughter's sore throat. The circular bruises on the little girl's back were caused by placing hot cups on the child's back. Again, this was done in an attempt to help the child recover from her illness.

Because deliberate acts that result in bruising are often considered indicators of abuse in that state, this case could have gone to court had the worker not taken the effort to explore the cultural issues.

---

that address the problem of child abuse. The definitions adopted by the states are not uniform, though they are often similar. The act itself defines child abuse as

> *the physical or mental injury, sexual abuse, or exploitation, negligent treatment or maltreatment of a child under the age of eighteen, or except in the case of sexual abuse, the age specified by the child protection law of the State by a person (including any employee of a residential facility or any staff person providing out of home care) who is responsible for the child's welfare under circumstances which indicate that the child's health or welfare is harmed or threatened thereby.* (Child Abuse Prevention and Treatment Act of 1974, as cited in Landes et al., 1993)

Toward a Working Definition

So here we are. Because we know that parents who clearly abuse do not necessarily intend for their abuses to end in injury, we know that injury alone is probably not an adequate criterion for defining abuse. Visible, remaining marks or bruises are also not adequate in themselves since in some cultures bruises are deliberately inflicted in an attempt to actually provide care. How, then, do we define abuse? With the understanding that no definition is going to fit all circumstances, perhaps we can start with a working definition and agree that it is not—and should not be—cast in stone. Here is one we might use:

> *Child physical abuse is the injury, risk of injury, or fear of injury to a child caused by the actions of the child's caretaker, who disregards the welfare and safety of the child in the exercise of adult authority or whim. When defining abuse all efforts should be made to take the culture of the individuals into account, though we recognize that simply because a culture permits or endorses a given behavior does not necessarily imply that our society should accept it as desirable. Respect for human life and care about human beings should be the principles that assist us in making determinations about appropriate and inappropriate child-rearing practices.*

Approaching the definition from another angle, we can consider abuse not only from the standpoint of severity but also from the perspective of frequency. How often does the caregiver use physical means with the child? Some states distinguish between acceptable parental discipline and abuse by the marks that are left behind. In such jurisdictions, welts that last a certain length of time, or visible bruising, are the indicators used by CPS workers to define abuse. At the extreme end of the spectrum, we don't seem to have much trouble thinking of maltreatment that can result in permanent disfigurement, disability, or death as abuse.

Continuum of Abuse

As we've already mentioned, not all aggressive physical contact initiated by an adult on a child is abuse. While there is evidence to suggest that any form of hitting children is harmful (Straus, 1994) most of us accept a certain amount of physical parental discipline. Most people seem to agree that simple spanking is not abuse, though many question its appropriateness. At a certain point socially acceptable spanking can and does turn into physical abuse. A line is crossed, though the exact location of the line is often very hard to determine. How much physical discipline is acceptable? One way to try to answer this question would be to graphically display examples of physical contact, from mild to severe. We could put simple spanking on the behind at one end of the continuum. At the other end of the continuum, we would put **severe physical abuse**, including acts perilous enough to cause significant injury or death.

OVERVIEW OF MAJOR
TYPES OF INJURIES

As mentioned earlier, very young children, especially those under three years of age, are at extremely high risk of suffering the most severe consequences of physical abuse. This may be for a number of reasons. For one, they require much time and attention of the caretaker, and this can be a burdensome and frustrating task for some. For another, children this young are especially vulnerable to physical attack. Their young bodies are not developed, and they can be quite fragile.

As evidenced by the fact that head injuries are the most common type of fatal injury in children (Monteleone & Brodeur, 1994b), children's heads are extremely vulnerable. Whereas the heads of adults make up approximately 2% of our body weight, for small children the head is up to 10% of body weight (Case, 1994). Nerve cells do not yet have the myelin coating found in adult brains (Case, 1994; Monteleone & Brodeur, 1994b), and neck muscles are not yet developed (Case, 1994). A common type of injury suffered by young children is called the **shaken infant syndrome.** While shaking a child doesn't sound like a potentially lethal activity, serious damage can result (Case 1994; Monteleone & Brodeur, 1994b). Severe shaking, or worse, hitting against something, can cause tearing of the blood vessels and nerves. Subdural hemorrhaging is especially common in abuse cases (Case, 1994). It can also result in the brain hitting the walls of the cranium. Signs and symptoms associated with shaken infant syndrome can include retinal hemorrhages, bleeding (including subdural hematoma), concussion, bruising, soft-tissue swelling, skull fractures, altered consciousness, irritability, coma, convulsions or seizures, respiratory problems, and death (Monteleone & Brodeur, 1994b). Even when obvious injury is not immediately apparent, damage to the brain can cause problems, such as retardation, that might not be found until later.

According to one source, the second most common type of injuries implicated in the deaths of children are **visceral injuries** (Barry & Weber, 1994), or injuries to the smooth muscles or organs. **Thoracoabdominal trauma,** or injuries to the chest and abdomen, can be caused by kicks and blows to the abdomen and chest areas. The liver is especially vulnerable because of its forward location. Barry and Weber (1994) point out that the duodenum is also quite vulnerable. They further indicate that a number of injuries to the gastrointestinal tract can lead to serious problems. The spleen, pancreas, and kidneys are located further back, and according to Barry and Weber (1994), are less often the sites of injuries. They note that such events as auto accidents can also cause some of these problems. In comparing the two, however, Barry and Weber (1994) indicate that there is a much higher fatality rate in abuse than in accidental injury. The death rate for accidental visceral injuries ranges from 4.5 to 12.5% compared to 12 to 60% in abuse cases (Barry & Weber, 1994). The reasons they suggest are interesting and in keeping with common sense. When abuse is involved, parents tend to avoid or delay seeking medical attention. They also give less information to help the physician isolate the problem so it can be treated.

The next category of injuries is actually where we started when we discussed the pioneering efforts of physicians in the area of identifying child physical abuse—injuries to the bones. As you probably recall, one of the hallmark indicators of child physical abuse identified by Kempe and his colleagues (1962) is the presence of multiple breaks that are in various stages of healing. In their pioneering article, Kempe and associates comment that the long bones are especially implicated in abuse because they make handy things to grab. Multiple breaks in varying degrees of healing are still a hallmark in making a child physical abuse diagnosis (Launius, Silberstein, Luisiri, & Graviss, 1994). However, technology has advanced since X rays were our primary tool. Now we have other "radiological" tools as well. These include **computed tomography** and **magnetic resonance imaging**, which can reveal images of cross sections of tissue portions of the body. While bone fractures aren't the leading causes of death in abuse cases, they often seem to co-occur in severe child abuse cases (Case, 1994; Barry & Weber, 1994).

Some estimates suggest that the percentage of child abuse cases that involve burns may be as high as 28% (Scalzo, 1994). In his review of the research, Scalzo comments that the estimates of the percentage of burns caused by abuse range from 4 to 10% of all children hospitalized for burns. Burns typically injure the skin and can have life-threatening consequences. Not only can children be immediately threatened by the trauma of the burns themselves but, even after the initial trauma, the child's health and safety continues to be threatened. Because of the extensive damage that burns can cause, a number of vital systems are threatened and infection continues to pose significant risks. Burns have several sources, including scalding, flame, grease, flash, contact, electrical, and chemical (Scalzo, 1994).

According to Scalzo (1994), the most common types of burns associated with child abuse are scalding (hot water) and contact (direct contact with a hot object like an iron or stove). Scalding burns occur more often in the bathroom than in the kitchen and are often associated with hot tap water. Because children's skin is thinner than that of adults, serious burns can occur far more rapidly (Scalzo, 1994).

In evaluating burns, Scalzo (1994) suggests a few characteristics of burns caused by abuse that tend to differ from accidental burning. Burns caused by systematic abuse often leave very clear damage patterns. One common pattern is termed **stocking and mitten burns**, referring to the characteristic pattern caused when hands or feet are deliberately put in hot water leaving burns that look like stockings or mittens. Similarly, when a child is held in the bathtub, sometimes there will be two nonburned circular areas where the child's bottom has rested on the cooler surface of the tub. Irons, curling irons, and stove heating coils all have characteristic shapes, which when used in abuse leave identifiable patterns. Accidental burns, on the other hand, are more likely to appear irregular.

Injuries to the eye are another common type of injury associated with child abuse. **Retinal hemorrhaging**, previously mentioned in association with shaken infant syndrome, is especially common. Cruz and Giangiacomo (1994) review literature that suggests that between 5 and 23% of physically abused children suffer from retinal hemorrhages. While the research is not conclusive, it seems that there is at least some likelihood a relationship between shaken infant syndrome and retinal hemorrhaging (Cruz & Giangiacomo, 1994). It is believed that the bleeding in the retina of the eye is caused by increased fluid pressure from severe shaking or trauma. Other problems associated with the eyes and vision include dislocation and movement of the lens and damage to the cornea, the iris, and the optic nerve (Cruz & Giangiacomo, 1994).

Skin injuries, while perhaps not as lethal in themselves as other types of injuries, are the kinds of injuries that are often the most visible and hence the most likely to alert others that the child may be a victim of abuse. Objects used to injure children leave characteristic "signature" marks (Monteleone & Brodeur, 1994b). For example, a doubled-over extension cord might leave impressions from the loop at the end. Injuries caused from hitting with objects, such as extension cords, belts, sticks, or "switches," injure the skin as does burning. Rope burns, caused by tying children or even attempting to strangle them, are another type of injury that leaves a distinct bruise. This last example points out that, even though skin injuries aren't in themselves life threatening, they might tip us off to the possibility that other more lethal injuries may coexist with them.

It probably isn't possible or necessarily even desirable to catalog the many ways that adults have found to injure children. Even if I were to try, I'm sure we would pick up the paper or turn on the TV to hear of a new one. The reason I've included some of the major categories of child abuse injuries in this chapter is to try to provide you, the reader, with a broader understanding of the kinds of abuse that are perpetrated against children. While the types of injuries described above represent the most common types of severe injuries caused by child physical abuse, there are also other less common ones, including suffocation and poisoning.

PSYCHOLOGICAL IMPACTS

In addition to the serious physical injuries that child physical abuse can cause, the impact of abuse can influence the very way the child sees the world. A number of psychological and emotional problems can result from any form of abuse. In the chapter on child sexual abuse we discuss many of these in detail, so we will only briefly review them here. An interesting side note is in order at this point, however. While some of the negative effects of child sexual abuse do seem to be related to the sensitive nature of sexuality, cultural attitudes, and the vulnerability of young children, it also seems that one of the most important factors that influence the severity of the impact, even in sexual abuse cases, is the amount of force or violence used (Elwell & Ephros, 1987; Finklehor, 1979; Fromuth, 1986; Russell, 1984). While some of the effects of abuse are associated with abuse generally, there may be unique aspects of child physical abuse. After a brief review of the suspected effects of general child abuse, we will survey research specifically targeted to child physical abuse.

General Psychological Impact of All Types of Child Abuse

Briere and his associates (Briere, 1992; Briere & Runtz, 1993) have developed a very clean system for describing the variety of psychological effects likely to be caused by child abuse. As outlined by Briere (1992), the immediate effects of child abuse are likely to include posttraumatic responses, distortions in thinking, thinking of self as deserving of the abuse and "bad," altered emotionality, dissociation, and a damaged sense of self. Longer lasting impacts of abuse identified by Briere (Briere, 1992; Briere & Runtz, 1993) include disturbed relationships, development of avoidance strategies (withdrawal, suicidal thoughts or attempts, substance abuse, eating disorders, self-mutilation, compulsive sexual behavior, and borderline personality disorder—a disorder associated with concrete, black-and-white thinking, rage, manipulativeness, disturbed interpersonal relationships, identity disturbance, disturbed emotions, and issues of abandonment (American Psychiatric Association, 1994).

Psychological Impact Specific to Child Physical Abuse

While sometimes found with other forms of abuse, child physical abuse has its own unique characteristics. While some pioneers in the field of sexual abuse thought that sexual abuse was more an issue of power than sex, the connection between violence and abuse is not as clear as it is with child physical abuse. Because of this, it seems that the effects of child physical abuse are likely to reflect the element of violence.

David Kolko (1992), from the School of Medicine at the University of Pittsburgh, completed a review of recent research about the short- and- long-term consequences specific to child physical abuse. He comments that the family home can be a dangerous place for some children to live. His review describes an array of problems and adjustments that look very similar to those described by Briere and his associates (Briere, 1992; Briere & Runtz, 1993). These include posttraumatic memories and behavior, personality changes related to grief and rage, trauma-specific fears, denial, repression, dissociation, and even forming an identification with the abuser.

Kolko (1992) discusses several specific problem areas that physically abused children seem to be affected by, including medical or physical problems, psychiatric disturbances, attachment and self-esteem problems, thinking and developmental problems, school difficulties, behavioral problems, social and adjustment behaviors, problems associated with emotions, and family influences and interactions. His review (1992) suggests that abused children seem to have a greater need to find relationships outside the home (Lynch & Cicchetti, 1991), more impaired self-esteem and a tendency to see themselves in a more negative light (Allen & Tarnowski, 1989; Kinard, 1982; Oates et al., 1985). Abused children with anxiety problems may be more likely to be diagnosed with attention deficit hyperactivity disorder and those with aggression diagnosed with conduct disorders (Kolko, 1992). According to Kolko, some research indicates that the thinking and reasoning abilities of abused children can be impaired, including verbal ability, memory, and general thinking ability (Friedrich et al., 1983). Other research has found problems in the reading levels and perceptual motor skills of physically abused children (Oates et al., 1984; Tarter et al., 1984). Kolko's review also suggests that abused children have problems adjusting to school and display poor school performance (Salzinger et al., 1984; Wolfe & Mosk, 1983); behavioral problems, such as with aggression and resistance, are more likely with physically abused children as well. There may also be a higher rate of alcohol and drug abuse among abused children (Gelles & Straus, 1990). In addition, they may be less able to play or interact with peers and have more difficulty making friends (Gelles & Straus, 1990). Some of the research reviewed by Kolko suggests that physically abused children may have more problems with feelings of hopelessness and depression (Allen & Tarnowski, 1989; Kazdin et al., 1985). Finally, abused children get only limited positive interaction with their parents but considerable hostile, or negative, contact with them (Kavanagh et al., 1988; Oldershaw et al., 1986).

The Developmental Factor

At this point it may be appropriate to consider one of the reasons why child abuse can be so devastating to its victims. Children, by virtue of their lack of experience and dependence on adults, are particularly vulnerable to injury, both physically and psychologically. Most developmental psychologists seem to agree that children mature developmentally in stages. They are mastering new tasks at each stage, and the degree to which they are able to do so may be either hindered or helped by influences in their physical and social environment. Some suggest that, when trying to determine the impact of abuse, it may be wise, or indeed essential, that we consider the individual child—the developmental milestone the child has reached—in addition to the severity, frequency, and nature of abuse the child is subjected to (Milner & Crouch, 1993).

One of the best-known and most time-honored models for thinking about the social development of children is that of Erik Erikson (1968). He describes a series of developmental milestones, or crises, a child must pass through in order to successfully develop socially. We can speculate that a very young child, who is struggling to develop basic trust, may be more severely affected by physical abuse than an older child, who is striving to establish autonomy and independence for example. Or, children who experience repeated assaults and violations may have more difficulty learning to respect the integrity and rights of others since they have not experienced this kind of respect.

INTERGENERATIONAL TRANSMISSION: THE VIOLENCE-BEGETS-VIOLENCE THEORY

Child physical abuse, especially its most serious forms, seems senseless. It is difficult for most people to fathom how such a thing could occur. Regardless of whether it's hard for us to understand or not, the sad reality is that it does happen. When we learn about individual cases, the natural reaction for most of us is to get angry about it. If we're able to get past the anger, we may also want to understand why it happens. As with family abuse in general, the answer is not so easy.

One explanation we often hear has to do with the abuse being passed down from generation to generation. At an intuitive level this seems to make sense. Who among us has not picked up an undesirable characteristic from a parent? Our common sense seems to tell us that we often learn by example, even if the example is one we don't admire. This explanation has been around since at least the early 1960s (Curtis, 1963; Kempe et al., 1962). Widom (1989) comments in her review that one of the most commonly held beliefs in both popular and scholarly literature is that adults who were abused as children are more likely to abuse their own children. She cites a number of works that seem to suggest this (Cicchetti & Aber, 1980; Herzberger, 1983; Kadushin, 1974; Jayaratne, 1977; Stark, 1985). Kaufman and Zigler (1987; 1989), in their own review of the literature, comment that a history of abuse is commonly reported in studies about parents who mistreat their children.

Social scientists have put forward an explanation for the causes of abuse much like the commonsense explanation we just introduced. The social science explanation is often referred to as the **intergenerational transmission theory**. By way of review from Chapter 1, we can say this theory bases its explanation of abusive behavior on **social learning theory**, which asserts that people, especially children, learn behavior by observing others (Bandura, 1973; Bandura & Walters, 1963). If the person being observed is rewarded, we are more likely to imitate their behavior; if the person is punished, we are less likely to do so. Social learning theorists refer to these two processes as **vicarious reinforcement** and **vicarious punishment.**

Widom (1989) reviews the available literature with just this purpose in mind: to assess whether the intergenerational transmission theory can truly explain child physical abuse. She takes a close look at six hypotheses, or research questions, that are implied by the broader intergenerational transmission theory. These are:

- Does abuse breed abuse?
- Can abuse histories explain the behavior of certain violent and homicidal offenders?

- Does being abused cause delinquency in its victims?
- Does abuse cause aggressive behavior in infants and young children?
- What is the relationship between abuse, social withdrawal, and self-abusive behavior?
- What is the impact on children who witness domestic violence and does viewing violence on television contribute to aggressive behavior?

The first of these questions seems to be the one closest to our own: Can the intergenerational transmission theory explain child physical abuse? In her attempt to answer this question, Widom (1989) analyzes the contemporary research on the subject. She prefaces this review with cautions about the many problems with the current research designs being used and notes that much of the research is based on self-reports and retrospective recollections about past abuse. She comments that studies that are prospective, or attempt to predict and study abuse that might occur in the future, are regarded as superior to the retrospective research because they help test our beliefs in the real world of experience.

Widom found that the rate of intergenerational transmission reported in the various studies she reviewed ranged from 7 to 70%. This means, at the low end, that 7% of parents who were victimized as children in turn victimized their children and, at the high end, 70% did. As with so much social science research in the area of family maltreatment, these results varied depending upon definitions and research methods used. (Please refer to Widom [1989] for a complete discussion.) We should note, however, that the study that yielded the 70% transmission rate (Egeland & Jacobvits, 1984, cited in Widom, 1989, and in Kaufman & Zigler, 1989) counted regular spanking as abusive, even though the spanking did not injure or leave bruises. In most states, and according to most accepted definitions of abuse, this does not really constitute abuse. As Widom comments, if we subtract this category, the 70% transmission rate reported in this study drops considerably.

Widom (1989) does not believe the available research is sufficiently conclusive to establish a clear cause-and-effect relationship between being abused as a child and becoming an abusive parent. She echoes the concerns of others (Kaufman & Zigler, 1987; 1989) about unconditionally accepting the intergenerational transmission theory. While she also acknowledges that being abused is a factor in becoming abusive, she concludes that a clear, one-to-one relationship does not exist. If there is at least some relationship, however, between victimization and becoming abusive, the next logical question seems to be, "How much?" Widom defers to others on this question.

Kaufman and Zigler (1987; 1989) do attempt to estimate the extent to which violence is transmitted across generations. They introduce two important concepts in their discussion of the intergenerational transmission theory: **sensitivity** and **specificity**. *Sensitivity* refers to the ability of a theory to correctly identify those who will abuse. *Specificity* refers to the ability of the theory to correctly discriminate and identify only those who will abuse. We hope that whatever theory we adopt will be sensitive enough to correctly predict all who will abuse, but will also be specific enough so that only those who abuse are identified.

In their analysis of the problem, Kaufman and Zigler (1987; 1989) examined the available research (Altemeier et al., 1984; Conger et al., 1979; Egeland & Jacobvitz, 1984; Gaines et al., 1978; Herrenkohl et al., 1983; Hunter & Kilstrom, 1979; Quinton et al., 1984; Smith & Hanson, 1975; Spinetta, 1978; Steele & Pollock, 1968; Straus, 1979). Most of this research, they concluded, is retrospective in nature or is based on self-report. As you probably recall, retrospective studies attempt to understand what has already occurred and are often based upon perceptions about the past and memory. Most experts agree this is a major limitation, since retrospective studies and self-reports are often unreliable and inaccurate. It is difficult to objectively substantiate abuse that may have occurred years before. Prospective studies, which try to predict (especially those that have control groups), are more difficult to do but are clearly superior in their explanatory power.

While Kaufman and Zigler (1989) comment that a history of abuse is more common among parents who mistreat their children, they caution against the unconditional acceptance of the intergenerational transmission theory. In one prospective study they reviewed (Hunter & Kilstrom, 1979), a sample of 282 parents of newborns in a regional intensive care nursery was selected. The researchers took histories from the parents, which included information about their own abuse or neglect as children. Forty-nine of the parents reported having experienced abuse or neglect as children. The researchers later checked the state's child abuse central registry for confirmed abuse during the infants' first year of life. The state children's protective service found ten children in the sample had been abused during the first year. Nine out of the ten abusing parents were among those who had previously reported a history of being abused or neglected as children.

Before interpreting this to mean that abuse victims become abusers, we should remember that only 18% of the adults abused as children were implicated in abuse and 40 of the 49 previously victimized parents did not have any such confirmed complaints of abuse against their own children. This is over 80% of previously victimized parents. Kaufman and Zigler concede, however, that 18% may be too low for a number of reasons. For one, the Hunter and Kilstrom study (1979) only looked at the first year, and as time goes on, additional members of the sample might also become abusive. Based on a nationally representative sample, Straus (1979) also found an 18% intergenerational transmission rate, though this study did not include children younger than three. The problem with this study is that children under age three are precisely those most at risk for the most serious forms of abuse.

Based on their analysis of a number of factors in their review of the research, Kaufman and Zigler (1987; 1989) estimate that the rate of intergenerational transmission is approximately 30%, plus or minus 5%. If correct, this means that, as adults, an estimated 30% of victims of child abuse can be expected to become abusive to their own children. It also means that about 70% can be expected not to.

Using the concepts of sensitivity and specificity, we can say that the theory is sensitive enough to correctly predict that victims will become abusive 30% of the time. We also have to say it is not very specific since it incorrectly identifies the other 70% as potential abusers. As you can see, while the intergenerational transmission theory seems to hold promise of telling us something about a relationship between being victimized and the risk of becoming an abusive adult, it leaves a lot of other questions unanswered. Kaufman and Zigler (1987; 1989) lament that there are serious deficits in both sensitivity and selectivity. What we can say is that there is an increased risk. Gelles and Cornell (1990) comment that, even comparing substantially lower estimates of intergenerational transmission, the 30% rate is still in stark contrast to the prevalence of abusive behavior in the general population, which they estimate to be between 2 and 4%.

All right. We can now be reasonably sure that a person who experiences abuse as a child has at least some increased risk of becoming abusive, but we also know that the vast majority of victimized children don't become abusive. We have an estimate of the number of abused children who become abusive as adults; what we don't yet have is good information about the other side of the coin: the number of abusive parents who were themselves abused.

While we often assume that most, or perhaps even all, child physical abusers were themselves victims, we really have no basis for accepting this as true until it is tested. We want to be able to expect research that studies abusers to tell us. The answer to this question might lead to answers for other questions as well. For instance, if all abusers were victims, it might tell us that an abuse history is a necessary, though perhaps insufficient, requirement to becoming an abuser. If only a small number of abusers were victimized, then we might conclude that other factors contribute to becoming abusive.

Unfortunately, as is true in other aspects of the family abuse field, the answers are not so easy. Widom (1989) notes in her review that Smith and Hanson (1975) found that 30% of both fathers and mothers of battered children had childhoods described as harsh or rejecting. Based on a sample of over 500 heads of households recruited from various programs, Herrenkohl, Herrenkohl, and Toedter (1983) found that about 56%, slightly more than half, of abusive parents themselves reported a history of "harsh discipline." In the prospective study done by Hunter and Kilstrom (1979), nine out of ten, or 90%, of the abusive parents themselves had a history of being abused or neglected in childhood.

I would like nothing more than to have a straightforward, reliable, and valid answer to our question. The results of the available studies are so varied, however, that I think we need to be highly cautious about how much we read into them. The best we can probably conclude is that some, not yet clearly defined, relationship exists between a history of family abuse and becoming abusive. Indications that a substantial number of abusive parents come from loving homes without any apparent history of child maltreatment should probably give us pause for thought (see Kaufman & Zigler, 1989; Widom, 1989).

Since we know that intergenerational transmission is a factor in child physical abuse, at least some of the time, what we probably want to know is not *if* intergenerational transmission occurs but rather *under what conditions* it occurs. Kaufman and Zigler (1989) call the conditions and factors that influence intergenerational transmission **mediating variables.** They point out in their review a number of such variables, some of which place individuals at greater risk of becoming abusive while others seem to insulate individuals from abusive behavior. They call these **risk factors** and **compensatory factors** respectively. Compensatory factors are now commonly referred to as resiliency, protective, or buffering factors.

A SYSTEMS OR ECOLOGICAL APPROACH TO UNDERSTANDING RISK AND RESILIENCY FACTORS

In the introductory chapter to this text, I briefly summarized the very well known model developed by Belsky (1980) and introduced a simpler three-level systems model for examining family violence. This three-level system includes the individual (micro) level, small group or family (meso) level, and societal or community (macro) level of explanations. Kaufman and Zigler (1989) organize their mediating variables into a similar though somewhat different framework. Here we will adapt our basic three-level system to organize the risk and compensatory factors summarized by Kaufman and Zigler (1989).

Human service professionals tend to come at the issue of family abuse from a number of different angles, depending upon their interests, beliefs, and professional orientation. Many clinicians might look to individual explanations such as offender pathology, others might approach the issue from a family systems perspective, while others, like sociologists or anthropologists, might focus more on the broader social or cultural factors. Many professionals who attempt to study or intervene with family abuse are more and more interested in multifactor or multilevel explanations (Belsky, 1980; Kolko et al., 1993; Milner & Chilamkurti, 1991; Milner & Robertson, 1990). It seems that many of those who are most involved in studying the problem are looking at the interactions between factors from a variety of "levels of explanation" (see Box 2-2).

Risk Factors

All risk factors increase the risk of an individual becoming an abuser. Those identified by Kaufman and Zigler (1989) that correlate with our social or macro level include a cultural climate that supports corporal punishment, a view of children as possessions, economic depression, unemployment, single parenthood, poverty, and insufficient social supports. Those risk factors

BOX 2-2   Research on Risk Factors

Perhaps one of the most active groups of social scientists studying in the area of child physical abuse is Joel Milner and his associates at the Family Violence Research Program at Northern Illinois University.

Milner and colleague Chinni Chilamkurti recently reviewed a number of studies that attempt to explain child physical abuse from several different "levels of explanation" (Milner & Chilamkurti, 1991).

They highlight a number of specific variables that seem to be involved in child physical abuse. Among the more intriguing of these are self-esteem, "locus of control," perceptions of children by their abusive parents, parental expectations of children, alcohol abuse, social isolation, and the quality of the parent-child interactions.

The best available research seems to suggest that parents with low self-esteem, who feel they are at the mercy of outside circumstances, who view their children negatively, who have unrealistic expectations of their children, who are isolated, and who have negative versus positive interactions with their children, seem to be at greater risk of becoming abusive. There is also at least a moderate connection between alcohol use and abuse.

The authors express the belief that, if we are to be effective in handling the problem, we need to take a "multimodal approach," tackling a number of different factors from different directions.

that seem to fit within our individual or micro level include a history of abuse, low self-esteem, low IQ, poor peer relations as a child, and poor interpersonal skills. Those that correspond to a small group or family (meso) level include marital discord, behavior problems of children, and stress associated with caring for premature or unhealthy children.

Broad cultural and demographic factors

Of all the social factors we associate with child abuse, poverty and the general social and economic status of the family are just about at the top of the list. A number of people looking into the problem have commented that high poverty rates, unemployment, and poor living conditions are often associated with child physical abuse (Milner & Crouch, 1993; NCCAN, 1988; Straus & Smith, 1990). While poverty in and of itself may not cause child abuse, it may well be that the stress associated with trying to meet the needs of daily living and coping with the frustrations inherent in family living outstretches the coping abilities of many parents in these circumstances.

While many of us might not consider gender a critical social influence at first blush, it seems to be important. Gender, especially historically accepted and socially supported male dominance, plays an important role.

In the western European tradition, as is true in other cultural traditions as well, men have during times in history had the legally sanctioned right to discipline or even kill their children and wives. Can we really say that this tradition is not a part of present-day cultural beliefs and attitudes? In modern-day society role expectations that go with being a man or woman seem highly relevant. We might even assume that because of male machismo and a cultural tradition in which "dad" is the disciplinarian, he might be more implicated in child abuse. This seems true some of the time. While the most often cited literature suggests that slightly more than half of all reported child physical abusers are women (Gelles, 1980; Gil, 1970), some more recent research suggests that there may not be a gender difference (Wauchope & Straus, 1990, as cited in Milner & Chilamkurti, 1991). If it is true, however, that women are more often implicated in child physical abuse, we want to know why. We may want to consider that women have more day-to-day contact with children, are sometimes isolated, and have more opportunity to inflict abuse. If, as it seems, women are implicated about half the time, that also means men are implicated the other half. We should note that, when men physically abuse children, the abuse tends to be more severe, resulting in more of the serious injuries (Hegar et al., 1994).

In addition to looking at gender as a factor in and of itself, the relative amount of influence or power wielded by men and women in any given culture may also be an important factor. *Patriarchy* is a term that denotes a cultural pattern in which males have greater influence and power in a society. While not specifically looked at in relation to child physical abuse, patriarchal influence has been associated with spousal abuse (Dobash & Dobash, 1979). Since there is sometimes greater risk of child physical abuse when spousal violence occurs in a family, it certainly seems to be worthwhile to look at.

As discussed in an earlier section, race and ethnicity may be something that we want to be very sensitive about. In this day and age when we are struggling to understand and heal from racial divisions and conflict, it's easy enough to shy away from talking about any possible relationship between race or ethnicity and abuse. A number of social scientists have noted that people of color seem to be overrepresented in families where abuse occurs (Gelles & Cornell, 1990; Gil, 1970, as cited in Zigler & Hall, 1989; Hampton, 1987, 1991; Pecora et al., 1992). Others comment that there are no clear differences in abuse rates among people from ethnically diverse backgrounds.

Many mention that what often goes with being a member of an ethnic minority in this country includes disenfranchisement, poverty, and other socioeconomic challenges, which are the real factors that influence family violence. If family violence is higher among oppressed groups, such as African Americans, Native Americans, and people of Hispanic origin, even if we took the other socioeconomic factors into account, it would seem to raise important questions; for instance, "What is the social and family impact of historical class violence by one group against another?" Shortly, when we talk about trying to apply social science research, we will at least open discussion on this question.

Family and relationship factors

While not organizing their material quite this way, Milner and Chilamkurti (1991) identify at least three factors we can think of as social or relationship factors: social isolation, parent-child interactions, and parental discipline strategies. Their review seems to confirm that abusive families tend to withdraw from social involvement, are more isolated, don't have good support networks, and are not very involved with outside community activities. In terms of the quality of the parent-child relationships in these families, the parents tend to be more hostile with their children and less nurturing. Milner and Chilamkurti's review also seems to show that abusive parents tend to use more corporal punishment than other parents. Based on independent research David Kolko and his associates (Kolko et al., 1993) describe abusive families as experiencing more recent stress, less cohesion or closeness, less expressiveness, and less encouragement for involvement in family activities.

Generally, when we think of child physical abuse, we think of child victims and parent perpetrators. There are two related, and relatively neglected, areas that have only recently begun to get recognition. These are adolescent abuse and sibling abuse. In Box 2-3 we will briefly highlight a few of the issues associated with these areas.

Individual factors

In addition to the moderately increased risk of abuse associated with a history of having been abused as a child, Milner and Chilamkurti (1991) review a number of other risk factors reported in the research. Individual perpetrator characteristics they identify as being connected with child physical abuse include self-esteem and ego strength, "locus of control," perceptions about the child's behavior, the parent's expectations about the child's behavior, and alcohol or drug abuse. In addition, it seems when there is a child in the family who is fussier or has other problems, there is increased risk of physical abuse.

Their review included Milner's own 1988 study in which he confirmed a relationship between self-esteem and abuse. Locus of control is a concept that refers to the degree to which individuals feel able to control circumstances and outcomes in their own life. Those parents who are seen as being at risk of becoming abusive seem to have a "high external locus of control," or a feeling that their lives are controlled by things external to themselves. Other research reviewed by Milner and Chilamkurti seems to confirm the commonsense perception that abusive parents tend to see their children in a more negative light and appear to have less reasonable and flexible expectations about their children's' behavior. Another factor often associated with abuse is the degree to which the parent has psychological problems. As we might expect, some research also establishes a connection between mental illness and child abuse (Kolko et al., 1993).

Another common perception about abusers is that they are often alcoholic or substance abusers. While there is limited support for this idea, it

---

BOX 2-3   Adolescent and Sibling Abuse

Although the subject of child abuse has become an important topic in the social sciences, adolescent abuse and sibling abuse continue to be relatively neglected issues. While there are approximately 6,000 journal citations dealing with child abuse in the American Psychological Association's *PsychLit* database for the period covering 1991 to 1996, there are only 8 journal citations on the topic of adolescent abuse and 13 on sibling abuse.

Adolescent abuse. Adolescent abuse refers to the abuse of young people in their adolescent years. Gelles and Cornell (1990) assert that, while little attention has been given to the topic, it may be the most common form of family violence. The most recent data available from the National Center on Child Abuse and Neglect (1996) suggest that 21% of all reports of child maltreatment relate to adolescents aged 13 to 18. James Garbarino (1989), one of the few social scientists to take an interest in the issue, suggests a number of dynamics that may contribute to the problem. For one, adolescents have a bad image. For another, adolescence is a time when young people assert their independence and challenge the authority of adults. Garbarino (1989) reports that where adolescent maltreatment does exist a stepparent is often present. Garbarino also reports that two types of family systems are prevalent when adolescent maltreatment is present. One type of family may be very rigid and unable to adapt to the changing characteristics of their children as they begin to mature. The other seems to be chaotic and unable to enforce checks on adolescent behavior in a reasonable way.

Sibling abuse. Gelles and Cornell (1990) suggest that violence between siblings is a matter of significant concern. As indicated earlier, they point out that it is a pervasive problem. They suggest that society and parents not only tolerate violence between siblings but, especially in the case of boys, may even encourage it. Sibling violence may have a primal relationship with other forms of family violence in that it is a way of controlling the behavior of others by means of the use of physical force. By permitting and encouraging this form of family violence, we may also be reinforcing the use of violence in other family contexts. On the reverse side, Gelles and Cornell (1990) point out that, when nonviolent techniques are available, it may be less likely that violent behavior is used.

---

seems that the jury is not in on this point. Milner and Chilamkurti (1991) comment that research on any possible connection between child physical abuse and substance abuse is limited. While some have suggested such a relationship (Bradford & McCleon, 1984; Fein, 1979; Hayes & Emshoff, 1993), there may not be enough evidence to establish a clear-cut relationship between substance abuse and child physical abuse (Black & Mayer, 1980; Leonard & Jacob, 1988). Milner and Chilamkurti (1991) tell us that much more good research is needed before we can know what the relationship is between substance abuse and child abuse and how strong the relationship is.

A Blending of Factors

One person whose work has attracted attention, perhaps more in the popular market than in the professional community, is Dr. Alice Miller (1990). While herself a psychiatrist, perhaps someone we would expect to be very focused on the individual, I think she blends her analysis of the development of the individual's psychology with the family and society in an intriguing way. When discussing the psychological development of Adolf Hitler, Dr. Miller's analysis suggests that the beginnings of his anti-social policies can be traced to his childhood in which he was victimized by abusive child-rearing practices. She suggests that societies, including our own, sometimes have very harmful ideas about how to treat children and get them to behave the way we want them to. She uses the term **poisonous pedagogy** to describe the kinds of child-rearing techniques and attitudes that minimize the importance of the child's identity for the sake of conforming to the desires of the parents or society. Miller also points out that there is speculation that Hitler may have had Jewish ancestry and that he projected his self-hatred onto millions of innocent Jews. While we may not have conclusive empirical research to support her views, I think she raises some very interesting questions—questions certainly worthy of a closer look.

As mentioned previously, race and ethnicity are among the variables social scientists have looked at in their attempt to study family violence. There are many references in the literature to a higher prevalence of child abuse among groups who have historically suffered from oppression, such as African Americans and Native Americans (Gelles & Cornell, 1990; Hampton, 1987, 1991; Pecora, Whittaker, & Maluccio, 1992). Speculations about the reasons for the higher rates include some very plausible explanations. For instance, it could be that the researchers expect to find greater numbers of members of racial and ethnic groups among the ranks of abusive parents and therefore tend to find them. As some suggest, it may also be that members of minority groups tend to be reported more often. While both these explanations are plausible, and perhaps really do help to explain the numbers, it may also be that the prevalence rate is somewhat higher among members of disenfranchised racial and ethnic groups. As mentioned in an earlier discussion about risk factors, being a member of a disempowered group often also means having to contend with other economic and social stresses.

If the results some researchers have gotten from their studies are not mere artifacts of identification or prejudice, and do measure higher rates of family violence, then it seems important to try to understand why (Hampton, 1987, 1991). We might ask the following questions: "Why shouldn't we expect slavery and other forms of domination, along with the violence that was often used to enforce it, to have an impact on those who suffered under it?" If intergenerational transmission applies at all, and we have said it is at least one factor, then we might be wise to also consider the impact of societal violence, sometimes called **oppression**, on its victims and succeeding generations. In addition to the violent subjugation of Africans and African Americans, aboriginal Americans (often called "Indians" or

Native Americans) have also been subjugated to the domination of a larger culture that has at times been brutal and violent. Our society established an entire system of boarding schools for Native Americans and imposed an educational system on Native children. The abuse experienced by many at these schools is just now being explored in the literature (Caribou Tribal Council, 1991; Furniss, 1992; Knockwood, 1992).

Within our systems model, we are probably wise to think of the phenomenon of child physical abuse as having a life that takes form within a complex social and psychological world, a world in which all the factors— at the micro, meso, and macro levels— interact in a complex and dynamic way. In science, including the social sciences, we seem inclined to try to break the problem down into its discrete components and to attempt to control and isolate as many outside variables as possible, so as to be able to study the question at hand. This is all very well and good, yet a problem as complex as this doesn't always lend itself to an organizing model that tries to control and limit the variables involved. Approaches that take into account as many of the variables as possible, and that encourage a creative and dynamic way of looking for patterns and clues, may ultimately help us to more fully grasp the complexity of the problem, yet they are much more difficult to validate scientifically. Be this as it may, it might take us to a place where we can take a more fair and honest look at our society, the way our families work, and the individuals who perpetrate violence against our youngest citizens.

Resiliency or Protective Factors

On the positive side, we know that a relatively small proportion of abused children are abusive when they themselves become parents. Comparing the number of victims of abuse who do not become abusive later in life with those who do gives us cause for optimism. Despite sometimes horrendous conditions, many children are apparently very resilient.

A number of authors have suggested that there may be protective or compensatory factors that prevent abused children from developing an abusive pattern later in life. Those factors identified by Kaufman and Zigler (1989) that seem to operate at the individual or micro level include an awareness and understanding of past abuse, a history of positive relationships with at least one parent, special talents, high IQ, physical attractiveness, positive school experiences and peer relationships as a child, getting therapy as a child, and good interpersonal relationships. Factors identified by Kaufman and Zigler (1989) that seem to fit into our family system, small group, or meso levels include a supportive spouse, financial stability, healthy children, good social supports, and moderate levels of stress in adult life. Factors they identify that correspond to our macro or broad social/societal level include a cultural environment that promotes a sense of shared responsibility for caring for children, a culture opposed to violence, and economic prosperity.

A SPECIAL CATEGORY OF CHILD PHYSICAL ABUSE: MUNCHAUSEN SYNDROME BY PROXY

Munchausen Syndrome by Proxy as a term is a mouthful, and it is in a category of its own. It is the name given to a syndrome that involves a most unusual process, whereby a parent deliberately fakes or intentionally inflicts injuries on a child. In the preceding discussion about child physical abuse we dealt with the definitions, manifestations, impacts, and explanations, but we did so outside of consideration of Munchausen Syndrome by Proxy. We've saved discussion of this syndrome until now because the dynamics involved in it seem very different from the general child physical abuse patterns. With the more common forms of child physical abuse, we seem to be dealing with a problem of parental hostility or frustration often associated with issues of control, stress, and violence. We briefly look at this special category in Box 2-4.

CHAPTER SUMMARY

We began the chapter with a general discussion of the issue of child physical abuse. We acknowledged that this can be a controversial issue since many feel that the rights of parents to punish their own children has been subverted by excessive zeal on the part of child advocates. We briefly reviewed the history of the issue in this country. We noted that child physical abuse is hard to define and exists along a continuum that, to a certain extent, varies according to the age and the culture in which we live. At the extreme we noted that child physical abuse can be a tragedy, and we revisited a case we introduced in Chapter 1, that of Eli Creekmore, to bring home some of the important issues associated with serious child physical abuse. In order to familiarize the reader with the kinds of serious physical abuses, we surveyed some of the most common types of physical injury. We discussed the concept of the battered child syndrome. In addition to our discussion of physical injuries, we also took time to talk about psychological impacts. Some psychological impacts seem to go with most types of abuse, while others seem to apply specifically to child physical abuse.

We devoted some discussion to explanations for child physical abuse, giving special attention to the intergenerational transmission theory. We noted that only 30% of victims seem to become abusers, whereas 70% do not. We spent some time exploring why some victims might become abusive and why others don't. We discussed both risk factors and compensatory factors. We also briefly reviewed the ecological model of Belsky, and looked at risk factors for abuse within the simple three-level model that was introduced in

---

BOX 2-4   Munchausen Syndrome by Proxy

In Munchausen Syndrome by Proxy, a parent (usually the mother) either fakes symptoms of a physical illness in her child or else actually does things to produce these symptoms (Kahan & Yorker, 1991, cited in Karlin, 1995; Johnson, 1996; Monteleone, 1994), using the child to get attention or sympathy from members of the medical community. The term has an interesting history. Karl Friedrich Hieronymus Freihess von Munchausen was an 18th century figure who gained fame and notoriety for tall tales about outrageous adventures (Karlin, 1995). He was first written about in a children's book that appeared in the 1930s and was the subject of a 1980s movie on the same theme. Nina Karlin (1995) suggests that Richard Asher (1951) first used the term *Munchausen Syndrome* to describe patients who fabricated illnesses in order to get attention. Meadow (1977, as cited in Karlin, 1995) seems to be the first to have applied the full term, *Munchausen Syndrome by Proxy,* to mothers who fabricated symptoms in their children.

Since the syndrome involves the seeking of medical attention for a child, physicians and human service professionals working in medical settings are the most likely to have the first contacts with perpetrators. Monteleone (1994) describes two basic types: simulated and produced. In the first the mother fakes symptoms for her child and may contaminate lab specimens in order to do so. In the second category, unfortunately, the mother is likely to take steps to injure or make the child ill. Also bear in mind that some perpetrators will go to extremes in order to fake the illnesses.

Another way of categorizing different types of the syndrome divides these parents into the categories of help seekers, active inducers, and doctor addicts (Libow and Schreier, 1986, as cited in Karlin, 1995). Karlin (1995) suggests that the category of "help seekers" may be trying to convey a problem with anxiety, exhaustion, depression, or even their inability to parent their own child. Active inducers are somewhat like Monteleone's "produced" category. Doctor addicts are those who are obsessed with obtaining medical treatment for nonexistent illnesses in their children.

Munchausen Syndrome by Proxy often has a pattern that involves chronic and recurrent physical problems that do not respond to treatment (Johnson, 1996; Monteleone, 1994). When the child is hospitalized, the abusing parent might dutifully stay with the child and perhaps sabotage medical treatment (Johnson, 1996; Monteleone, 1994). The parent may be sufficiently knowledgeable to be effective at this. Monteleone (1994) suggests that the perpetrator often has a nursing background or has been employed in medical settings.

Chapter 1. We looked at some ways of applying social science thinking to the problem before moving on to our final section.

Finally, we spent a small amount of space discussing an unusual form of child physical abuse called Munchausen Syndrome by Proxy. This form of physical maltreatment seems to differ in terms of quality and motivation from the other forms of physical abuse explored in this chapter.

LEGAL AND ETHICAL CONCERNS:
CRITICAL THINKING QUESTIONS

1.   Many people today are torn over the issue of child physical abuse. On one hand they would be upset over children being truly abused. On the other hand many people feel that the issue has been carried too far and that parents have lost the right to discipline their own children. How can we reconcile these contrasting concerns?

2.   Often it's the very dramatic case, such as that of Eli Creekmore in the modern era or of Mary Ellen in days gone by, that brings our attention to the issue of child physical abuse. These are among the most extreme of cases and ought to be condemned. In other cases, where physical force is used inappropriately but not so severely, we are not so quick to condemn. Where do we draw the line when it comes to defining abuse? How do we justify calling one thing abuse and the other punishment?

3.   Sometimes, unless you have experience with another culture, it is easy to overlook the significance of the beliefs, norms, values, and behaviors that are part of culture. Our modern-day North American culture is deeply rooted in the traditions of western Europe, which include a history of misusing, abusing, and maiming children. How should we look at this particular cultural heritage? In what ways should we take culture into account when dealing with issues such as child physical abuse?

4.   Sometimes parents punish their children and injuries result, but the parents do not intend to cause injury. On the other hand sometimes parents behave very violently, yet for one reason or another the child escapes injury. Which would you define as abuse? Why? As a society how should we define abuse?

5.   We live in a multicultural society. In Box 2-1 we discussed the importance of taking culture into account when defining abuse. In this example we looked at the healing practice of "cupping" that is used in some cultures, yet which leaves marks. Other cultural practices are more dramatic; for instance, in many parts of the world female children have parts of the female anatomy surgically removed. This runs contrary to the prevailing culture in this society. Under what circumstances should cultural practices different from that of the predominant culture be tolerated, and under what circumstances should they be treated as abuse? Why?

6.   The Child Abuse Prevention and Treatment Act requires all states to enact and enforce the mandatory reporting of abuse. Some might feel that little will happen as the result of a report and perhaps the child will get even worse treatment as a result. Is it ever ethical not to report suspected abuse? Why or why not?

7.   The shaken infant syndrome sometimes results in severe medical problems or even death, yet the parent who engages in the shaking may not even realize how serious it is. How should we proceed in such cases? Why?

8.   Sometimes we do not learn of prior physical abuse until the victims become adults. What is the best way to proceed in cases where we learn of prior physical abuse?

9. The intergenerational transmission theory suggests that abusive patterns of behavior may be learned and passed on from one generation to the next. Recent research suggests that this only happens some of the time (approximately 30%). Should we be more cautious in what we imply with our theories and research, or is it justified to slant our research so as to make the public more concerned about the problem?

10. Some recent research tells us that certain risk factors are associated with child physical abuse. These risk factors in themselves do not prove that children are being abused or that they will be. How do we balance our concern for children in high-risk families with the family's right to privacy?

11. We are now becoming more sensitive to abuses perpetrated against entire cultural groups, such as African Americans and Native Americans. Violence inflicted against them and disruption to their natural cultures may have contributed to significant problems among people in these groups. What responsibility, if any, do you feel we as a society have for correcting these injustices? Please discuss your rationale.

SUGGESTED ACTIVITIES

1. About 1,200 to 1,400 children or more die each year from child physical abuse or neglect. Locate the statistics about child abuse deaths in your community. Your local social service agency or health department may be a good source of information. Through the local newspaper, select one case and research it. Develop a report to share in class or turn in to your instructor.

2. Many severe cases of child abuse end up being seen at community hospitals. Contact the social service department at a local hospital and see what they say about the kind of cases they see.

3. Each state and each community has a children's protective service component. Contact them and find out how they prioritize the reports of abuse they get.

4. Most jurisdictions have risk assessment procedures. Find out from your local children's protective service how they determine risk. Do they use a particular risk assessment instrument, or do they operate from general guidelines or state-established criteria?

REVIEW GUIDE

1. Be familiar with the debate over the balance between parents' rights to discipline their children and the state's interest in protecting children. How many substantiated cases of abuse are there each year? What are the percentages of this total who are physically abused and neglected children? Who is the usual perpetrator of these abuses?

2. Be familiar with the history of child physical abuse in western European history. Know the concept of patria potestas. Be familiar with such

practices as indenturing children, beating them, child labor abuses, and so forth. Be familiar with the cases of Mary Ellen and Eli Creekmore.

3.   Be fully familiar with the concept of the battered child syndrome, and how publicity about this syndrome ignited public interest in the issue of child abuse. Who wrote the article that became the springboard for the notoriety of the problem? What happened as a consequence?

4.   Be fully familiar with definitions of child maltreatment, especially child physical abuse. Be able to distinguish between intent and result as they relate to child abuse. What cultural considerations should we take into account when developing definitions? How does the Child Abuse Prevention and Treatment Act of 1974 define child abuse? What is the working definition developed for the purpose of discussion in this chapter?

5.   Be able to cite examples that could be placed at various points on a child physical abuse continuum.

6.   Be familiar with the various types of child physical abuse injuries surveyed in this chapter. Describe how we can differentiate between these and accidental injuries, if we can. What technological instruments or procedures are used to make the assessment? What percentage of various types of injuries are the result of abuse, if this is known?

7.   Be familiar with any psychological impacts that may result from child physical abuse. What psychological impacts are generally associated with child abuse in general compared to that for child physical abuse?

8.   Be fully prepared to discuss theories about why child physical abuse happens, with attention to the intergenerational transmission theory. What theoretical framework is this theory based on? Explain. Does the available literature tell us that persons abused as children are at greater risk of becoming abusive? Define the terms selectivity and sensitivity. Based on the work of Kaufman and Zigler, in a sample of all adults abused as children, what percentage actually become abusive? How many don't? Since we know there is increased risk of people abused as children becoming abusive, the question isn't *if* abusive behavior is transmitted intergenerationally. What then is the question?

9.   Discuss risk factors and resiliencies (compensatory factors). Which factors seem to indicate more risk? Box 2-2 summarizes the findings of Milner and Chilamkurti (1991). What are the results of this research? Be familiar with risk factors at the micro, meso, and macro levels. Which factors seem to reduce the risk of intergenerational transmission?

10.   Be fully familiar with the practical applications of social science thinking to child physical abuse. Be familiar with the work of Dr. Alice Miller, including her concept of poisonous pedagogy. What are the implications of intergenerational transmission if applied to African American and Native American populations.

11.   Be able to discuss Munchausen Syndrome by Proxy. Define it. Discuss the family dynamics believed to be involved. Describe the pattern.

SUGGESTED READING

James, B. (1994). *Handbook for treatment of attachment-trauma problems in children*. New York: Lexington Books.

Becoming a classic. A highly understandable and readable book that applies attachment theory. Discusses both healthy bonding and attachment as well as the development of what she calls trauma bonds.

Miller, A. (1990). *For your own good*. New York: The Noonday Press.

An intriguing book by German-born psychiatrist, Dr. Alice Miller. In this book Dr. Miller suggests that western European child-rearing philosophy and practice may foster violence and personal unhappiness. Included in this book is an analysis of Adolf Hitler's psychological development with application to the practices of his regime. She suggests that the seeds of Hitler's anti-Semitism may have been rooted in the secret Jewish identity of a paternal grandfather.

Monteleone, J. A., & Brodeur, A. E. (1994). *Child maltreatment: A clinical guide and reference*. St. Louis, MO: G. W. Medical Publishing.

Monteleone, J. A. (1994). *Child maltreatment: A comprehensive photographic reference identifying potential child abuse*. St. Louis, MO: G. W. Medical Publishing.

A two-volume boxed set. The clinical guide and reference contains highly readable, yet scholarly, discussions on virtually every aspect of child abuse. Intended to assist physicians, but useful to others as well. The photographic reference contains very graphic photographs depicting the effects of abuse. Highly useful to help identify and distinguish between deliberate abuse and accidental injury.

Straus, M. A. (1994). *Beating the devil out of them: Corporal punishment in American families*. New York: Lexington Book.

A very readable and passionate book by one of the pioneers in the field of family abuse. Dr. Straus discusses the potentially destructive influence of an accepted, yet insidious, parenting practice: hitting our children, sometimes called "spanking."

CHAPTER GLOSSARY

Battered child syndrome   A syndrome, or clustering of signs and symptoms, proposed by family abuse pioneer C. Henry Kempe to describe characteristics of children who have been severely physically abused.

Child Abuse Prevention and Treatment Act of 1974   An act passed by the Congress of the United States and signed into law. Among other things it defines child abuse, mandates that certain professionals such as physicians be required to report suspected abuse, and requires states to develop requirements for mandatory reporting.

Computed tomography   Commonly known as CT or CAT scan, this is a cross-sectional radiographic technique. Images produced are essentially thinly sliced two-dimensional X rays (ionizing radiation) of the body part being analyzed.

Intergenerational transmission theory   A theory proposed which states that victims of abuse will themselves perpetrate similar acts as adults.

Locus of control	Can be either internal or external. Persons with an internal locus of control are thought to believe they have more choices and control over what happens to them in their lives. Persons with an external locus of control are thought to attribute their circumstances to external events and circumstances.
Magnetic resonance imaging	An imaging technique that uses magnetic pulses capable of producing high-quality, cross-sectional representations of the human body from any angle or perspective, without the use of radiation.
Mandatory reporting	Refers to the requirement that suspected abuse be reported to the appropriate child protective agency.
Munchausen Syndrome by Proxy	A pattern in which a parent inflicts harm on a child in order to get the attention of others, including the doctors and nurses.
Oppression	The condition when one more powerful group exercises domination and control over another.
Patria potestas	A Latin term that refers to the nearly absolute power of the father.
Poisonous pedagogy	A term coined by German psychiatrist Alice Miller, which refers to a set of parenting principles in which children are required to sacrifice their own sense of self in order to comply with the demands of their parents for obedience.
Retinal hemorrhaging	Bleeding and damage to the retina of an infant caused by pressure exerted when shaken.
Sensitivity	A term used by Kaufman and Zigler (1989) that refers to the ability of a theory to correctly identify those who will abuse.
Severe physical abuse	Child abuse serious enough to cause significant injury, disfigurement, death, or the risk of these occurring.
Shaken infant syndrome	A clustering of signs and symptoms, including subdural hematomas and retinal hemorrhaging, that can result in death or permanent brain injury.
Social learning theory model	A theory in psychology suggesting that learning is acquired by observing others; vicarious reinforcement or punishment is experienced depending on whether the being observed is rewarded or punished.
Specificity	A term used by Kaufman and Zigler (1989) that refers to the ability of the theory to correctly discriminate and identify only those who will abuse.
Stocking and mitten burns	Burn marks that have the appearance of stockings or mittens, caused by deliberate immersing of the hands or feet in hot water.
Thoracoabdominal trauma	Trauma or injuries inflicted in the chest and abdomen region.
Vicarious punishment	Reduction in the probability that the observer of behavior will repeat an observed behavior of another because the model being observed was administered an undesirable consequence.
Vicarious reinforcement	Increase in the probability that the observer of behavior will repeat an observed behavior of another because the model being observed was administered a desirable consequence.
Visceral injuries	Injuries to the smooth muscle organs of the body, such as the liver, pancreas, kidneys, and so forth.

CHILD PSYCHOLOGICAL MALTREATMENT AND CHILD NEGLECT

Child Psychological Maltreatment

What Is Psychological Maltreatment?

What Do We Need to Know about Psychological Maltreatment?

Child Neglect

In this chapter we'll be dealing with two of the most important, but sometimes overlooked, issues in the family maltreatment field: child psychological maltreatment and child neglect. Professionals in the field now seem to be taking these issues more seriously, however. Psychological abuse is getting more attention, perhaps because leaders in the field are suggesting that it may be the core issue in all other forms of abuse. Child neglect is still the ignored issue, yet it is the most commonly substantiated form of child maltreatment.

Discouraged
children
who have
suffered from
psychological
maltreatment
deserve to
be helped.

CHILD PSYCHOLOGICAL MALTREATMENT

In this part of the chapter, we'll be dealing with one of the most elusive, but important, types of child maltreatment: **psychological maltreatment.** It is elusive, perhaps, because the concept itself seems vague and broad, and because professionals themselves have had a hard time trying to find adequate definitions. Psychological maltreatment is critically important as an issue. How we think, feel, and believe is at the very core of who we are as human beings. Professionals today suggest that this form of abuse can distort the most fundamental beliefs and feelings we have about ourselves as people and how we relate to the world. Not only this, but a number of professionals in the field are now saying that it is the psychological aspect of maltreatment that is responsible for the most devastating effects of all forms of child abuse (Claussen & Crittenden, 1991; Garbarino et al., 1986; Hart, Brassard, & Karlson, 1996; Hart, Germain & Brassard, 1987; Navarre, 1987).

WHAT IS PSYCHOLOGICAL MALTREATMENT?

It is sometimes easier to talk about emotional abuse through an example than to try to describe what it is in words. Most of us have enough life experience to have an opinion about what kind of behavior is abusive. In Box 3-1 you will find a brief example of child psychological maltreatment. I've titled it "Michael Can't Win."

In the case of Michael and his family, we can see that there are a number of problems. The behavior of Michael's mother is interlaced with several family issues, including her resentment over her own mother rejecting her and favoring Michael. And while we can't prove that Michael's poor school performance is the result of his family relationships, it certainly seems like a plausible explanation. In the counseling sessions, Michael seems to be in a no-win situation—no matter what he does, he is likely to be criticized for it. This happens all too often in psychological maltreatment cases. Even when we think we have a very clear example of psychological maltreatment, such as in Michael's case, there are many subtleties and ambiguities. Since all of us want to be loved, rejection from the people who are supposed to care for us can be devastating. Unless you see the victims crying or despondent after an episode, it's hard to get a true sense of the pain. Often the perpetrators hide the maltreatment from public view, and all too often victims in such cases are isolated. To compound the problem, when victims begin to suspect and protest, these already vulnerable people may be told that they're the ones who are distorting what's going on. "If you think like that, maybe there really is something wrong with you," a perpetrator might say; "maybe you really do need to see a counselor."

We will discuss the various types of psychological maltreatment later in this chapter. We still need, however, to try to explain just what we mean when we use the term *psychological maltreatment.* (In keeping with trends in the field, we will be using this term, though a number of professionals in the field have variously referred to it as emotional abuse, psychological abuse, psychological neglect, or emotional neglect. For a discussion of this, see Hart, Germain, and Brassard [1987].) While it is well accepted that abusers use psychological methods to control their domestic partners, we will limit discussion in this chapter to the psychological maltreatment of children. In Chapter 7, we will discuss psychological maltreatment in the context of adult domestic relationships.

BOX 3-1   Michael Can't Win

In order to protect confidentiality, the following case example has been significantly changed in order to protect the identities of Michael and his family.

Michael is a 13-year-old boy who lives with his mother, stepfather, and three half brothers. Michael's mother, Sylvia, was born in Australia and she had Michael when she was young and unmarried. Her own mother had mistreated her as a child. When Sylvia got pregnant with Michael, her mother berated her for getting pregnant without being married. While she helped support Sylvia and Michael, she never let Sylvia live it down. In contrast to her behavior toward Sylvia, Sylvia's mother was very nurturing of Michael.

Sylvia eventually met an American sailor and married. They had three children of their own. Michael and Sylvia's relationship was always tense, and Sylvia would often find things about Michael she didn't like that she would always tell him about. She rarely noticed positive things. When Michael began to have trouble in school, the family was referred to counseling. The counselor took note of the family history but also noticed that if Michael said something his mother did not like, she would berate him for it in session. When he became quiet in session, she would criticize him for not trying. Michael couldn't win, and he stopped trying. His stepfather supported Sylvia, and both would discuss all Michael's shortcomings in front of the other three children.

Controversies

Before going any further, it may be wise to pause for a moment to discuss a current public controversy. Many people seem to feel that we have gone too far with the whole issue of child abuse, feeling that by paying so much attention to the issue we've promoted a heightened sensitivity that fosters hysteria and exaggerated allegations. To those who feel this way, I think I can say that extending our focus to psychological abuse might seem as if we're really taking the issue to the extreme. My own position is that the maltreatment of children is a critically important issue. I agree, however, that when our concerns about the welfare of children are exploited, it harms the ultimate goal: protecting kids so they can grow up to be healthy, happy, and productive human beings. By *maltreatment* I am not referring to isolated incidents in which a child's feelings are hurt or in which his or her emotional needs go temporarily unmet. After all, who among us has not neglected the feelings of another or said something that has caused distress? Rather, what we're talking about are *patterns* of psychologically abusive or neglectful behavior that occur in a child's life that can have a destructive and perhaps permanent impact. Lest anyone accuse us of using the term irresponsibly, I ask that you take note that this concern is shared within the professional community as well. Hart, Brassard, and Karlson (1996) review the professional opinion on the subject commenting that, "The term *psychological maltreatment* and the research and coercive intervention directed toward it should be reserved for the most salient, extreme, and severe forms of psychologically damaging or limiting care and interactions." (p. 75)

For the purposes of this chapter, we will be using psychological maltreatment as a general term to refer to both **psychological abuse** and **psychological neglect,** both of which can be thought of as types of psychological maltreatment. Later in the chapter, we'll come across these concepts again when we look at a model to help us understand psychological abuse. We are also assuming that the abusive or neglectful person is an adult who has a responsibility to care for the child. By putting forth this description of psychological maltreatment, I do not mean to offer it as a formal definition. As you will soon see, defining psychological maltreatment is not such an easy thing, and professionals themselves haven't yet reached consensus.

Definitions

In order to be able to talk in a meaningful way about almost any phenomenon in the field of human services, we need to have some agreement about what it is we're dealing with; this is where definitions come into play. With a topic as broad and nebulous as psychological maltreatment, defining the issue seems especially important.

While it may be extremely important to define psychological maltreatment, it isn't so easy to do. Serious work on this task didn't begin until the mid-to-late 1980s when two groups of investigators (Garbarino et al., 1986; Hart et al., 1987) took an interest in this issue. Hart and his colleagues (1987) did two things in the process of developing their definition. First, they looked at federal law (The Child Abuse, Prevention, and Treatment Act of 1974—P.L. 93–247) as well as the proceedings of the International Conference on the Psychological Abuse of Children, convened in 1983, to tackle this issue. The federal law includes the term "mental injury," which seems to serve as a starting point.

The definitions in use today generally include the idea that there is usually a *pattern of behavior* (though sometimes single incidents are sufficiently severe) that includes both acts of commission and omission, judged by community and professional standards to be psychologically damaging. The impact of the abuse can be to the child's thoughts, feelings, or behavior (see Hart et al., 1996).

Building on this concept of mental injury, Hart and his colleagues (1987) flesh it out by including a number of examples, or categories of psychological maltreatment, agreed upon by the professionals attending the international conference. Since then the list of categories of psychological maltreatment has been modified and expanded some, though key parts of the definition remain in use today (Briere, 1992; Garbarino et al., 1986; Hart et al., 1996).

TABLE 3-1   Categories of Child Psychological Maltreatment

- Rejecting (spurning*)
- Terrorizing
- Corrupting
- Denying essential stimulation, emotional responsiveness, or availability
- Unreliable and inconsistent parenting

- Mental health, medical, or educational neglect
- Degrading/devaluing (spurning*)
- Isolating
- Exploiting

*Hart et al., 1996, refer to both rejecting and degrading as spurning.
Adapted from Briere, 1992; Garbarino et al., 1986; Hart et al., 1987, 1996.

As depicted in Table 3-1, the list of categories of psychological maltreatment in use today includes: rejecting; degrading/devaluing; terrorizing; isolating; corrupting; exploiting; denying essential stimulation; unreliable and inconsistent parenting; and the neglect of mental health, medical, or educational needs (Briere, 1992; Hart et al., 1996). With **rejection** the child is pushed away and made to feel unacceptable and unworthy. When a child is **degraded or devalued**, he or she is criticized, stigmatized, humiliated, and made to feel inferior. Hart et al. (1996) refer to both rejecting and degrading as "spurning." When a child is **terrorized** he or she is verbally assaulted and threatened. **Isolation** deprives the child of social contacts. **Corrupting** takes place when the child is mis-socialized, or is encouraged to participate in inappropriate activities, such as the use of drugs, gambling, or promiscuous sexual activity. **Exploiting** a child occurs when the child is used to meet the needs or desires of the caretaker. **Denying essential stimulation** deprives a child of loving and sensitive caregiving. The terms *unreliable* and *inconsistent* parenting are generally used to define a process whereby contradictory demands or expectations are made of the child; as a consequence, these children live in an emotionally unstable world.

What our current-day broad definitions and category lists do not do is provide clear and distinct definitions that can be used in social science research or in the courts. Having such definitions is essential for research and legal work.

Creating an operational definition for research purposes essentially involves taking an abstract concept (in this case, psychological maltreatment) and defining it in terms of operations or behaviors we can observe. One research team (McGee & Wolfe, 1991) has proposed an operational definition that gives sole consideration to psychological acts that have clear, and observable, psychological consequences. An example of a clear psychological act might be something like telling a child that he or she is "stupid." A psychological consequence might be feelings of depression or lowered evaluation of self. One problem with operational definitions that only look at psychological consequences is that they are often hard to measure. When we can measure consequences, we usually need to ask ourselves how we can be sure they are caused by the psychologically abusive behavior.

Some definitions are very focused (McGee and Wolfe, 1991), and these definitions are sometimes criticized as being too narrow or confining (Barnett, et al., 1991; Belsky, 1991; Hart & Brassard, 1991; Giovanonni, 1991). They don't adequately cover things that some of us feel should be considered when defining psychological maltreatment. Another criticism of operational definitions is that many are too broad and include factors that really shouldn't be classified as psychological maltreatment.

Psychological maltreatment is often thought of as a form of maltreatment that is part of all other forms. While this seems true enough, it can and does occur by itself in families (Claussen & Crittenden, 1991). For the purpose of trying to isolate and study psychological maltreatment, it makes sense to look for it in its "cleanest" form whenever possible. From a legal standpoint, on the other hand, psychological maltreatment is so often an intangible activity (which is more difficult to establish) that it may be more practical to litigate other, more "concrete" types of abuse if they are also present. As McGee and Wolfe (1991) point out, it is very important to keep in mind the purpose of our definition. Are we using it to help us prosecute perpetrators and protect kids? Are we using it to help us do research and better understand the problem? Sometimes these two purposes are at odds with each other, as suggested by McGee and Wolfe (1991), and it may be well to have definitions for each purpose.

We should note that the definitions we've discussed so far don't give us a lot of specificity about what differentiates psychological maltreatment from behavior that occurs as part of the normal ups and downs in family life. This is another potential problem. In a classic article, which is still among the most often cited articles on the subject, Dorothy Dean (1979) gives us a very simple approach that might help us do a better job with this. Dean defines three primary concepts: **emotional abuse**, **emotional assault**, and **emotional neglect.** An intriguing thing about Dean's work is that her definition of emotional abuse includes both emotional assault and emotional neglect. Within Dean's framework, emotional assault is an attack—an act of commission—perpetrated on the child. Emotional neglect is any act of omission, or inattention, to the child's psychological needs.

As Dean (1979) describes it, acts of emotional assault or emotional neglect would not necessarily be defined as abuse (psychological maltreatment in our terminology) unless they were serious enough, happened often enough, or were chronic enough to justify court intervention. This is also consistent with the other definitions of psychological maltreatment that emphasize (unlike other types of abuse, where even single incidents might be sufficient to classify a behavior as abusive) that a *pattern* of behavior is generally required in order to define it as abusive. According to Dean, in true cases of emotional abuse, the consequence of being subjected to emotional abuse is that it becomes the dominant characteristic in the child's life. As a result, those who are psychologically maltreated don't become competent adults, capable of developing to their full potential. Dean (1979) goes on to say that the reason this should concern us is because of the personal and social consequences, which could include behavior and character disorders, increased risk of developing severe mental illness, and becoming severely handicapped in being able to relate to others in a positive way. With a few qualifications, I think Dean still offers one of the cleanest and most practical frameworks for defining psychological maltreatment.

With regard to definitions that can be used in the courts, Dorothy Dean (1979), who was a supervisor at San Diego County prosecutor's offices, discusses three types of psychological abuse cases that have been successfully prosecuted in her county: (1) single acts sufficiently severe to establish abuse, (2) differential treatment of one child over others, and (3) reductions in a child's functioning that can be linked to abusive treatment.

WHAT DO WE NEED TO KNOW ABOUT PSYCHOLOGICAL MALTREATMENT?

Psychological maltreatment may be the most complex of the abuses to study. With physical abuse and child sexual abuse, the acts of maltreatment may be more readily identifiable because the perpetrator breaks fairly clear-cut social rules. In the case of psychological maltreatment, however, we are dealing with intangibles. It's hard to observe things that happen in the mind, and hard to observe psychological maltreatment, which is so often subtle and done in the relative privacy of the home. The abuse usually takes place over a period of time and is hard to identify without being privy to the innermost workings of the family.

Basic Human Needs and Psychological Maltreatment

In Chapter 1, we discussed the role that basic human needs seem to play in trying to understand abuse and neglect. As we discussed, there is a body of very good and classic research which establishes that such psychological intangibles as love, belonging, and self-esteem are not merely nice to have but are actually needs (Gardner, 1972; Harlow & Harlow, 1966; Harlow & Zimmerman, 1959; Spitz, 1945, 1946).

Since we now know that psychological needs are vital to human development, our next question seems to be: "How can we most productively think about these needs if we want to understand psychological maltreatment?" As suggested in the first chapter, the model developed by pioneering humanistic psychologist Abraham Maslow (1954, 1968, 1970) might provide a way. Hart and his colleagues (1987) comment that, while the efficacy of Maslow's model is still subject to debate, it has enough support, including clinical opinion, to justify using it to assist us with understanding abuse and neglect issues. What it gives us is the notion that intangibles such as love, belonging, affection, self-esteem, and so forth, are essential to human functioning. It also suggests that it is difficult for us to develop as truly human if we do not accomplish the more basic tasks.

To paraphrase Hart and his colleagues (1987), psychological maltreatment involves the denial of a person's psychological needs or interferes with the person's effort to satisfy psychological needs to the point that the person becomes seriously maladapted. This seems to be a pretty viable approach to the subject. We might, however, extend it just a bit. Children probably aren't sufficiently aware of their own self-esteem needs to be motivated to consciously take steps toward enhancement. Whereas adults in therapy might do things to improve their self-esteem, children probably won't. They are dependent upon others for this. While psychologists haven't even achieved consensus about exactly what self-esteem is, it is generally believed that self-esteem develops as a result of the approval of others (Zimbardo, 1979) and of our own growing ability to reflect positively on our attributes, abilities, and potentials. In cases where adults make repeated assaults on a child's positive sense of self (for instance, through berating or belittling), it is more than merely blocking or frustrating the child's attempts to meet his or her needs. It is an insidious attack on the child's developing psyche—insidious because the child may be unaware of what's happening until later in life, if ever. Such maltreatment carries with it the potential for lifelong consequences, both to the child and to all others with whom he or she will interact.

Human Development and Psychological Maltreatment

In addition to the importance of considering basic human needs when trying to understand psychological maltreatment, it also seems important to consider human development. Educators, mental health professionals, and many parents are becoming increasingly sensitive to the importance of child development. We've all heard someone say that a particular child is going through this or that "stage." Developmental psychologists tell us there is good reason to believe that there might actually be something to this. Childrens' ability to think and behave is not something that happens overnight but, rather, something a child learns in stages over a period of years. These stages are important for some very good reasons. For one, we can expect the effects of psychological assault and neglect, or nurturance and support, to vary depending upon the child's maturity, or level of development. For another, we as adults vary in our levels of development, and those who have many unmet psychological needs of their own may have more difficulty understanding and nurturing a child. Finally, parents who do not have a good understanding about the normal developmental milestones may have unrealistic expectations of a child and might then be more critical of the child than a more knowledgeable parent.

Developmental psychologists tell us that as human beings mature they master certain "developmental tasks" at different times, or at different stages, in their development. Each new task generally builds on tasks previously learned. The tasks themselves can be quite varied in their character. Tasks that involve the ability to perform certain kinds of thinking activities are referred to as cognitive, and the child's level of functioning in this domain is commonly referred to as **cognitive development.** Jean Piaget is the psychologist credited with much of the groundbreaking work in this area. The ability to relate socially with others is referred to as **social development.** Erik Erikson is the psychologist whose model is considered the classic for understanding social development. **Moral development** is the term used to describe the level of functioning when it comes to forming values and making moral decisions about behavior. Lawrence Kohlberg is the psychologist credited with groundbreaking work in this domain.

Garbarino and his colleagues (1986), in their now classic work on the topic, suggested that we look at four developmental stages when trying to assess the interaction between the child's developmental level and the category of psychological maltreatment; namely, infancy, early childhood, school age, and adolescence. They represented these four basic developmental periods and five types of psychological maltreatment on a basic grid.

Consider the interaction between the developmental period and the type of psychological maltreatment. Take, for example, the intersection between the early childhood developmental period and the degrading/devaluing category of psychological maltreatment. Ask yourself what kind of impact degrading statements such as, "You're stupid!" "Who could love someone as bad as you?" or "You're nothing but a little baby" could have on the child's beliefs, social behavior, and moral behavior during this time period.

Since we've had a chance to picture the kinds of interaction between developmental period and type of psychological maltreatment, it may be instructive to look at some of the kinds of developmental tasks Piaget and Erikson suggested that the child should be mastering during these time periods. See Table 3-2.

As Table 3-2 suggests, children during infancy, early childhood, school years, and adolescence strive to accomplish certain cognitive and social tasks. Those suggested by Piaget and Erikson are, respectively, the best known about cognitive and social development. As shown in Table 3-2, Piaget suggests that in infancy children are essentially egocentric but are curious, begin to learn to anticipate events, manipulate objects, and imitate. Piaget's model depicts

TABLE 3-2   Developmental Tasks and Approximate Developmental Periods

	INFANCY	EARLY CHILDHOOD	SCHOOL AGE	ADOLESCENCE
PIAGET'S COGNITIVE DEVELOP-MENT	• "Sensorimotor" stage • Curiosity • Anticipates • Manipulates objects • Imitates	• "Preoperational" and "concrete operations" stages • Perception and behavior more exploratory • Starts problem solving • Discovers that objects exist independently • Beginning imagination and speech • Centration (focusing)	• "Concrete operations" stage • Able to focus on more that one thing • Knows objects continue to exist even when can't see • Thinking can be more flexible	• "Formal operations" stage • Can imagine alternative explanations • Able to use symbols and abstract thought • Can understand metaphor
ERIKSON'S SOCIAL DEVELOP-MENT	• Develops "Basic trust vs. mistrust"	• "Autonomy vs. shame and doubt" • Muscular control • Toilet training • Sense of self-control • "Initiative vs. guilt" • High energy • Success vs. failure • Does things for the joy of it	• "Industry vs. inferiority" • Build on trust, autonomy, and initiative • Starts cooperating • Learns to complete tasks	• "Identity vs. role confusion" is major task • Identity formation • Starts thinking of a career • Sexual maturity • Physical maturity

Descriptions based on *Child Development,* Second Edition , by S. R. Ambron; Holt, Rinehart and Winston, 1977.

cognitive development as occurring in stages; Erikson proposes that social development occurs as the child moves from one developmental turning point, or crisis, to another. As Table 3-2 depicts, the turning point in infancy is establishing either trust or mistrust in the world. The implications about what happens when the child is psychologically maltreated at this stage seem fairly obvious. If both Piaget and Erikson are substantially correct, we would expect these psychologically maltreated children to anticipate abuse, perhaps learn to imitate it, and develop a nontrusting and self-protective attitude toward the world. We could develop similar projections for maltreatment that occurs at each of the other developmental periods. These projections can be displayed in summary form, as shown in Table 3-3.

If the consequences projected in Table 3-3 are even close to being true, they paint a pretty scary picture of the potentially destructive impact of psychological maltreatment. Especially for someone who may have experienced such abuse, what are the implications? For instance, does this mean that these developmental tasks can never be accomplished if the developmental period in question has already come and gone? Whereas we used to think in terms of **critical periods**, windows of time when it was considered crucial to satisfactorily complete a task or forever be impaired, we now think more in terms of **sensitive periods**, or windows during which it is optimal to accomplish developmental tasks. This view offers a bit more hope to the affected person since it implies that, while it is optimal to accomplish certain developmental tasks during the sensitive time, it is still possible to complete this work later on. This is also consistent with a **strengths-based perspective**, which calls our attention to the internal strengths and resilience that human beings seem to possess and which is increasingly getting attention within the human service and public policy fields.

As outlined by Garbarino et al. (1986), concepts about human development seem to hold out some promise of helping us develop a better framework for studying and understanding psychological maltreatment. Taking this a step further, there are some specific implications suggested by the classic work of pioneers in the field of developmental psychology, such as Piaget and Erikson. If psychological maltreatment can indeed impede cognitive and social development, then we should expect specific deficits, or problems, in kids who have been so mistreated. Some of the possible ramifications suggested by their work and depicted in Table 3-3 are fairly profound. How do the suggested possible impacts stack up against actual research on the impact of child psychological maltreatment? We will try to answer that question in the following section.

Research on the Impact of Psychological Maltreatment

While the available research in an area as abstract and ambiguous as psychological maltreatment is bound to be diverse, and might even appear a bit fuzzy, it does seem to be consistent with the impacts projected in the model depicted in Table 3-3. Before reviewing some of that research, however, a few cautionary comments are probably in order. The projected impacts tend to be worded in a fairly general way, allowing lots of room for interpretation.

TABLE 3-3   Suspected Impacts of Psychological Maltreatment at Specified Developmental Periods

	INFANCY	EARLY CHILDHOOD	SCHOOL AGE	ADOLESCENCE
SUSPECTED IMPACTS OF PSYCHOLOGICAL MALTREATMENT USING PIAGET'S COGNITIVE DEVELOPMENT MODEL	• Less curiosity • Anticipates bad experiences	• Retardation of exploratory behavior • Delayed problem solving • Altered intellectual development • Problems with concentration (focusing)	• Difficulty focusing on more than one thing • Problems learning • Difficulty looking at things from more that one point of view	• Difficulty with alternative explanations • Use of symbols and abstract thought impaired
SUSPECTED IMPACTS OF PSYCHOLOGICAL MALTREATMENT USING ERIKSON'S SOCIAL DEVELOPMENT MODEL	• Develops a sense of mistrust	• Experiences shame and doubt • Problems with toilet training • Impaired sense of self-control • Experience of guilt • Anxious energy • Sense of failure • Does not experience joy in doing things	• Sense of inferiority • Difficulty with trust, autonomy, and initiative • Hard time cooperating and making friends • Difficulty completing tasks	• Confused sense of role • Impaired identity formation • Fearful and uncertain about career • Sexual immaturity

Descriptions based on *Child Development,* Second Edition, by S. R. Ambron; Holt, Rinehart and Winston, 1977.

Developmental theory specifies developmental tasks and the sequence in which they are typically mastered, not the causes for their failure to be accomplished. Besides psychological maltreatment, there are other possible reasons why a child may have problems with one or more of the tasks. While we can suspect that certain of the developmental problems experienced by psychologically maltreated children can be attributed to the maltreatment, we can't presume that developmental problems are always caused by psychological maltreatment.

Comparing projected outcomes about
social development with the research

Hart and his colleagues (1987) surveyed the available literature and were
able to identify a virtual litany of negative consequences and characteristics
associated with psychologically maltreated children. Some of this data is
correlational and some is based on controlled research. They were interested, just as we are, in understanding the impact of psychological maltreatment. As an alternative to using psychiatric diagnostic categories, Hart
et al. (1987) chose to use the five categories of behavioral disabilities outlined in federal regulations that govern services to handicapped children
(P.L. 94–142). They did not specifically attempt to relate these impacts to the
particular developmental tasks written about in the work of Piaget, Erikson,
and others, but we will try to do so here. Earlier in the chapter we discussed
the four developmental periods outlined by Garbarino et al. (1986) in their
developmental grid: infancy, early childhood, school years, and adolescence. We will continue to use these terms as approximations of the developmental stages and periods outlined by Piaget and Erikson.

During the earliest developmental period, infancy, we would expect psychologically maltreated children to develop problems with trust. The
research cited by Hart et al. (1987) suggests that this may be the case
(Densen-Gerber, 1979).

The kinds of impacts we might expect at the early childhood period in
psychologically maltreated children would include problems with shame
and doubt, toilet training, impaired sense of self-control, guilt, sense of failure, and having difficulty finding joy in doing things. The literature
reviewed by Hart et al. (1987) suggests that the following kinds of problems
seem to be associated with children who have been psychologically maltreated: problems with soiling and wetting, or encopresis and enuresis
(Hyman, 1985; McCarthy, 1979; Pemberton & Benady, 1973); inability to
become independent (Egeland, et al., 1983; Rohner & Rohner, 1980); and
reduced emotional responsiveness (Fischoff, et al., 1979; McCarthy, 1979;
Shengold, 1979). Recent research indicates a strong relationship between
shame and a history of emotional abuse (Hoglund & Nicholas, 1995).

Problems associated with the school years in our rough model would
predict social problems with a sense of inferiority; difficulty stabilizing trust,
autonomy, and initiative; difficulty making friends and learning to cooperate; and problems with completing tasks. The research surveyed by Hart et
al. (1987) suggests the following: low self-esteem or a negative self (Krugman
& Krugman, 1984; Rohner & Rohner, 1980), problems with achievement
and ability (Dean, 1979; Moore, 1974; Pastor, 1981; Waters, et al., 1979), and
social withdrawal (Hyman, 1985; Krugman & Krugman, 1984; Main &
Goldwyn, 1984; Moore, 1974). Work done by Briere and Runtz (1990) to differentiate between the effects of the various forms of abuse suggests there is
a strong relationship between psychological abuse and low self-esteem.

Our adaptation of the developmental framework would project that
psychologically maltreated adolescents might have problems establishing

intimacy. There seems to be a lot of agreement in the literature about the high risk in psychologically maltreated people for problems with intimacy and relationships as a result (Dean, 1979; Garbarino et al., 1986; Hart et al., 1987; Ney, 1987; Rohner & Rohner, 1980). Intuitively, this makes a lot of sense since the ability to become intimate seems to involve the ability to trust another person and become vulnerable. In their cross-cultural research, Ronald and Evelyn Rohner (1980) have found that psychologically maltreated children often become either excessively dependent, because of their unmet needs or, if the maltreatment is sufficiently severe, develop **defensive independence**. This defensive independence can be thought of as a sort of learned self-protective behavior.

The Minnesota Mother-Child Interaction Project

Controlled studies where children are observed over time is a rare plum in the social sciences. When we do have one, it is to be treasured. Such is the case with the Minnesota Mother-Child Interaction Project. Byron Egeland and his associates (see Egeland & Erickson, 1987) began working with a sample of 267 high-risk children in the early 1980s and were able to follow them for a number of years. The families these children came from had the same risk factors, which included low income, age, lack of social supports, chaotic living conditions, and high stress.

The mothers were selected for inclusion in the study when pregnant. Each was on public assistance and receiving care in the clinic. The base rate of reported abuse of 1 to 2% among them was considerably higher than for the state generally. The project staff had had fairly intense contact with the participating families over a period of years. Based upon evaluation from the staff, the original sample was divided into four maltreatment groups: physically abusive, hostile/verbally abusive, neglectful, and psychologically unavailable. The physically abusive parents used methods that ranged from frequent and intense spanking to bruising, cutting, or burning the children. The hostile/verbally abusive mothers were those who constantly criticized and were harsh with their children. The negligent mothers were irresponsible or incompetent in their parenting. Those mothers in the psychologically unavailable group seemed unresponsive, detached, and uninvolved with their children. While they did not neglect their children's physical needs, they did not interact with them in a way as to respond to their emotional needs.

Using a developmental model, Egeland and Erickson (1987) assessed the children on mastery of expected developmental tasks, including their ability to establish a sense of trust, security, and autonomy, among others. To assess for self-control and self-esteem, they observed each child both with the mother and without her and evaluated self-esteem, persistence, enthusiasm, and frustration tolerance. As the children approached school years, they assessed for positive peer interactions, acceptance of direction, confidence, and assertiveness in classroom activities.

Children in each of the four abuse groups were compared with a comparison group from the time they were three months old. The results reported by Egeland and Erickson (1987) support the kind of results we would expect, based on a developmental perspective, as well as one that is more surprising. All maltreated children, regardless of which of the four categories they were in, functioned much more poorly than those children who were not maltreated. The surprising result is that children who had the psychologically unavailable parent did the worst of all. This flies in the face of intuition, since psychological unavailability, or psychological neglect, seems overtly less destructive than more deliberate forms. If it is the most destructive, it also seems to be the one that is hardest to identify and, as a consequence, perhaps the one we will be able to do the least about.

Explanations of Causes and Risk Factors

As we've already alluded, psychological maltreatment has been closely associated with other forms of child maltreatment. It has been especially linked with child physical abuse. Until Claussen and Crittenden (1991) were able to show that psychological abuse can and does occur independently from other forms of maltreatment, professionals in the field were not convinced that it is truly a discrete form of abuse. Because psychological maltreatment co-occurs so often with other forms of abuse, its suspected causes have also been associated with these other forms. While it's easier to do scientific, empirical research with simple cause-and-effect relationships, this is often difficult to do in the abuse field. Multiple variables appear to be in operation. We turn next to a review of an approach to organizing and thinking about family maltreatment, which may help us with the level of complexity we are faced with.

In Chapter 1, we briefly discussed systemic or ecological approaches to understanding family abuse. Systemic or ecological models propose that causes of social phenomena are complex and interrelated. Perhaps the two most comprehensive efforts to study the problem of psychological maltreatment, those of Garbarino, Grettmann, and Seeley (1986) and Brassard, Germain, and Hart (1987), are systemic or ecological in their orientation. This systemic or ecological approach is considered by some to be the most thorough approach to understanding the problem (Fortin & Chamberland, 1995).

One aspect of the work of Garbarino et al. (1986) may be of some help to us at this juncture. Much like the three-level model (macro, meso, micro) proposed in this text, Garbarino et al. (1986) sketch a model that includes the **environmental context** (macro level in our terminology), **family context** (meso level), and **parental and child characteristics and behaviors** (which, using our terminology, we can place at the micro level). Reproduced in Figure 3-1 is a representation of a diagram used by Garbarino et al. (1986) to explain their particular ecological approach.

As you can see, the environmental context (macro level) encompasses all the other levels of the system, or "psychological ecosystem." Within it is

FIGURE 3-1
An Ecological
Model for
Understanding
Psychological
Maltreatment
Adapted from *The
Psychologically
Battered Child*,
by J. Garbarino,
E. Guttmann, and
J. W. Seeley, p. 48.
Copyright © 1986
Jossey-Bass Inc.,
Publishers. Adapted
with permission.

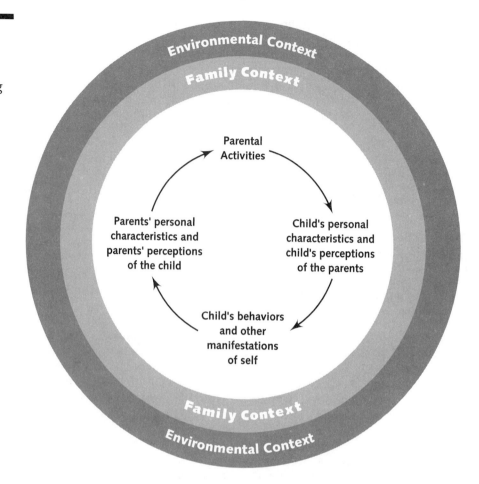

Environmental Context

Family Context

Parental
Activities

Parents' personal
characteristics and
parents' perceptions
of the child

Child's personal
characteristics and
child's perceptions
of the parents

Child's behaviors
and other
manifestations
of self

Family Context

Environmental Context

the family context (meso level), and within the family are the individual members: the adults and children (micro level). Both the parents and the children bring their own personal characteristics and perceptions into the family, and they interact and relate to one another. This is a very nice, clean way to depict the key variables we believe come into play, and it may help us understand the relationship between various levels of the larger system.

The macro level—
Broad social and cultural influences

Conditions in the social environment that have been implicated as factors contributing to maltreatment include low societal attitudes about the value of children, endorsement of hostility and verbal aggression through the media, and societal acceptance of the use of intimidation and manipulation to control. Stress associated with economic conditions, unstable work conditions, and unemployment are often suggested as contributing influences

(Claussen & Crittenden, 1991; and McCurdy, 1992, as cited in Fortin & Chamberland, 1995). The work of Rohner and Rohner (1980), while done some time ago, is particularly relevant since they took a look at psychological maltreatment from an anthropological, cross-cultural point of view. They noted that psychological maltreatment does exist in specific cultures and that in those cultures in which it occurs, it has predictable, and destructive, impacts on the psychological well-being of its victims.

We can think of culture as encompassing all the beliefs, values, attitudes, traditions, behavior, and technology of a given group of people, in a particular place and at a given time. Our own culture has been shaped by many influences, and to some degree it may be accurate to say we are multicultural; that is, an amalgam of many different cultures. A very dominant influence on present-day society has been that of the western European societies. As briefly discussed in Chapter 2, Dr. Alice Miller, a German psychiatrist, has made some telling observations about how we raise our children (Miller, 1990). She believes that the way we, as a culture, get our kids to do what we want them to do and be what we want them to become is not only psychologically devastating to them but in the long run is injurious to our society.

According to Miller (1990), a characteristic of western society is a pattern of child rearing in which we coerce children to become what we want while requiring them to deny their own true feelings, opinions, and will. Dr. Miller suggests that, in the process, children are taught to hold their true selves in contempt, resulting in a tendency to condemn one's true self and the true self in others as well. In Dr. Miller's framework, we are in a sense walking around with secret negative identities about ourselves, which we have also secretly learned to hate. This is a traumatic and disturbing experience, and one that is suppressed. According to Dr. Miller's model, if a negative identity can be found in someone whom we are allowed to devalue, we can project the hate we secretly feel for our true identity onto that other person or group, thereby making them our scapegoat. In Nazi Germany it was the Jew. In North America it has been one of many traditionally devalued groups: African Americans, Native Americans, Japanese Americans, gay and lesbian people, the chronically mentally ill, the disabled, and others.

An important consideration when looking at the social and cultural influences on psychological maltreatment is that of cultural bias and prejudice (Jones & Jones, 1987; Reschly & Graham-Glay, 1987). We noted in our discussion about the definitions of psychological maltreatment that there are nine different examples or expressions of psychological maltreatment, which include rejecting, degrading, isolating, and exploiting. If we accept the idea that there is such a thing as psychological maltreatment, and that it can have disastrous repercussions, we probably also need to carefully consider the role of prejudice and discrimination. Just as psychological abuse within a family goes to the heart of a person's identity and sense of integrity, discriminatory attitudes and behavior can be thought of as a contributory factor. Members of undervalued groups may be at increased risk for the kind of damage to the self we've been discussing in relation to psychological maltreatment. What impact does this have on their child-rearing practices and their attitudes toward their own children? We should also consider that, for many individuals, this might be combined with other risk factors such as economic stress.

There are a number of other broad social influences that are suspected of playing a role in psychological maltreatment in families. The literature reviewed by Garbarino et al. (1986) suggests (and other sources seem to confirm) that psychologically abusive families may be more isolated than other families and may lack social supports. Garbarino et al. (1986) review the work of Polansky and Gaudin (1983), who conducted research that suggests that not only do troubled families self-isolate but also are isolated by members of their neighborhoods and communities who distance themselves from them. The Garbarino review further comments that unemployment, crime, poor housing, and the lack of services are characteristics of the human social environment in which many families live. In addition, it suggests that, as a result of stressful living conditions, many families become stressed and may be so overwhelmed as to be unable to use whatever coping skills they may have had. In their review of the literature about psychological maltreatment, Fortin and Chamberland (1995) comment on the work of Vising, Straus, Gelles, and Harrop (1991), who suggest that parents seem to get mixed messages from the society about how they should talk with their kids. On the one hand, they are discouraged from being verbally abusive; on the other, harsh verbal communication is commonly accepted as being a necessary part of controlling children.

The meso level—Family and relationship influences

In the middle ground between societal influences and the behavior of individuals is family structure and functioning. The family power structure, the presence of one or both parents in the household, and the relationship between the two parents are all important considerations. The kind of communication that is permitted in the family, the rules, the degree to which self-esteem is valued, and the degree of connectedness to the neighborhood and community are the factors believed central by noted family therapist Virginia Satir (1988).

The micro level—Individual factors

In trying to answer the question, "Why would anyone behave that way toward their own child?" One of the most common and common sense answers is that the parent was a victim of the same thing as a child. We know in the area of child physical abuse that parents who were battered as children are more at risk than the general population to become abusive themselves, but we also know that less than a third actually do so (Kaufman & Zigler, 1987, 1989; Widom, 1989). With increasing publicity and public sensitivity to the issue of child abuse, we do not know how many parents restrain themselves from physically abusing their children and instead resort to verbal abuse. There is some opinion that the rate of intergenerational transmission for psychological maltreatment may be considerably higher than it is for physical abuse (Ney, 1989, cited in Fortin and Chamberland, 1995).

Earlier in this chapter, we discussed how important it is to have an appreciation of basic human needs and human development when trying to understand the impact of maltreatment. Because we are talking about individuals when we speak of development and human needs, the micro level of explanation may be the most logical category in which to put them. In the diagrammatic representation of Garbarino's ecological approach (Figure 3-1), children and parents as individuals are located in the central area. Included here are all the behaviors, personal characteristics, and perceptions they bring. Garbarino et al. (1986) also include all the back-and-forth interactions that go on between the parent and child at this level. My own view is slightly different in that I like to think of the interaction between parent and child as one of the dynamics that constitute family functioning, something I normally think of as being part of the family system.

Parent characteristics

The personal characteristics of parents, along with their own experiences and perceptions, clearly, however, belong at the micro level. Parents as adults are going through a developmental process as they move through the life cycle. Learning how to behave as a parent is part of it. Many of us have parents or other adults who served as good models. Others have not. Those who have good models probably have an easier time with parenting, while those who do not might have to muddle along and perhaps learn to parent as an adult. Part of this learning process may involve understanding child development. Garbarino et al. (1986), Belsky (1980), and Herrenkohl and Herrenkohl (1981) suggest that parents often have a poor understanding of child development and, perhaps because of their own childhood experiences, have unrealistically high expectations of the child's performance. When the child doesn't measure up, there is the risk that frustration and maltreatment could ensue.

Frustration not only results because of a mismatch between high expectations and what is reasonable but also because of the deficits a parent might have. A parent's inclination to maltreat a child may be shaped not only by what they have learned about parenting, and their developmental blind spots, but also by deficits in meeting their own basic human needs. Let's face it—parenting can be extremely demanding, and parents who have many unresolved emotional needs may have a hard time being able to give of themselves to a child. Virginia Satir (1988) has given us a very nice analogy to describe this. We can think of our needs as being like a pot. When the pot is full we have lots to share, but when it's empty, we not only have nothing to give but may demand something from others. When the only other person around happens to be a child, we have a problem. Hickox and Furnell (1989) compared characteristics of psychologically maltreating parents to a community sample. They were able to isolate nine factors, which, the results of their research suggest, are significantly different in the two groups. Without going into lots of detail about the particulars of this research, the maltreating parents had the following characteristics:

- Anxiety about the child's health during pregnancy
- Anxiety, pain, or shock during delivery
- Negative perception of self, or else another has negative perception of them
- Different treatment from other children in their family of origin
- Criminal activity in family
- Marital discord
- Lack of confidence
- Lack of use of community resources
- Substance abuse

Child characteristics

In their review of the literature, Fortin and Chamberland (1995) note that there is literature establishing a link between physical abuse and certain organic, or biological, child characteristics (premature babies, underweight babies, and children of mentally handicapped parents). We should probably remember, however, our earlier discussion, where we noted that psychological maltreatment commonly co-occurs with physical abuse. While Fortin and Chamberland (1995) suggest that there doesn't appear to be clear-cut research establishing such a relationship in identified cases of psychological maltreatment, this is an area that is probably deserving of additional attention. A noted British psychiatrist, Michael Rutter, and his colleagues have been interested in risk and protective factors for a number of years. In some of his earlier work on the subject, he makes a comment that seems particularly relevant to our discussion of psychological maltreatment (Rutter, 1979 p. 57):

> The way all of us respond to another person is determined to a considerable extent by what the other person is like. . . . When parents are depressed or irritable they do not take it out on all their children to the same extent: often, one is more or less scapegoated. The target child tends to be the temperamentally difficult one.

Resiliency: Protective Factors

When trying to understand a problem as perplexing as child psychological maltreatment, it's easy and understandable to look to all the things that have gone wrong in order to explain it. I once met a person who is regarded as a pioneer in the field of developmental psychopathology, Norman Garmezy. (Developmental psychopathology is a field of study that tries to explain how mental and emotional problems develop in people.) Dr.

Garmezy told a wonderful story about his life when he was growing up, including some of the things his mother would tell him when she got upset or frustrated with him. Since Dr. Garmezy is a renowned figure, we might not conclude that he was psychologically maltreated, and in fact he would probably say that he clearly was not. He made a very important point, however. Had he grown up, developed a drug or alcohol problem, and become a hostile person who was psychologically abusive toward his own family, people might be inclined to conclude exactly this.

The error of looking back to the past for what has gone wrong today is sometimes called **retrospective analysis.** There are probably many things that have happened to each of us in our lives that, were we to look back, we could say that this one, that one, or some combination has "caused" some problem in our lives. In our society we have a tendency to look for things to blame problems on. As we've seen in connection with psychological maltreatment, there are any number of influences, at different levels of our social system, that seem to increase its risk. What we've not yet done is look at things on the other side of the scales: things that reduce the risk of a problem with child psychological maltreatment or that protect kids from damage.

There has been a movement within social sciences—small, but growing—that emphasizes the role of **resiliency** and adaptability in insulating kids from the damage of destructive social environments. The term refers to the ability of human beings to adapt and bounce back despite adversity. In the mid-1970s, the work of Norman Garmezy and some of his colleagues was getting a fair amount of public attention. He coined the term *invulnerable children,* and it took off. He was interested in looking at the kids who had to deal with really tough circumstances yet who, for some reason, were able to come out of it apparently unaffected (Garmezy, 1976; Garmezy, et al., 1979). At the present time, the strengths-based perspective and the interest in resiliency seem alive and growing.

In a fairly recent review of the literature, Fortin and Chamberland (1995) suggest that, at the micro level, the following factors are protective for parents: having children who are easily educated; good self-esteem; low aggression, impulsivity, and defensiveness; good problem-solving skills; and good social skills. Based upon their review, parental skills and abilities that seem to reduce the risk of psychological maltreatment include having an understanding of child development, a willingness and ability to support their children emotionally and intellectually, being firm with discipline but using nonpunitive measures, and a willingness to use community resources when needed. Fortin and Chamberland's review also notes that having a personal and professional support network available also reduces the risk.

One of the most consistently mentioned protective factors for children is having at least one supportive adult in their life. Michael Rutter (1979), in some of his classic studies, notes that some schools provide the kind of supportive social environment that can prevent a child who might otherwise develop serious problems from doing so.

CHILD NEGLECT

While neglect may not seem as dramatic and troubling as some other forms of child maltreatment, statistics provided by the National Center on Child Abuse and Neglect (1995a; 1995b) indicate that 49% of all substantiated cases of child maltreatment involve neglect. This is more than twice that of the next most common form of child maltreatment, child physical abuse, which constitutes only 24% of substantiated cases. While other forms of maltreatment such as child sexual abuse and child physical abuse may have gotten more press, the consequences of neglect are no less compelling. For example, nearly as many child fatalities are caused by neglect as by physical abuse.

The problem of child neglect is qualitatively different from other forms of family abuse. It is passive rather than active, representing acts of omission rather than commission. In contrast to child physical abuse and domestic violence, where the perpetrator assaults the victim, in child neglect there is a failure to care. Since it is easier to identify bad things that we can see than to notice what is missing, it may be easier for neglect to be overlooked. Many times, Child Protective Services only becomes aware of a neglect problem when someone who cares about a particular child—a teacher, neighbor, or relative—becomes concerned enough to make a report.

In this section we'll be looking at reasons why the problem of neglect has received so little attention in comparison to other forms of child maltreatment. We will also discuss the seriousness of the problem, attempt to define it, survey types of neglect, look at risk factors. We will then look at a few things we might do to help solve the problem.

Neglect of Neglect

As a student of family abuse, you might at first blush think that child neglect is unimportant in comparison to family violence. After all, the news media frequently covers very sensational cases involving overt acts of family violence but rarely pays much attention to cases of child neglect. Occasionally, cases of neglect get media attention, such as those about a newborn baby abandoned in some dumpster, but these stories are rare in comparison to those about extreme physical abuse.

Inattention to the issue of neglect isn't isolated to the popular media. Unfortunately, family abuse professionals also seem to be guilty. The topic of neglect is itself referred to as the neglected child welfare issue (Berliner, 1994; Dubowitz, 1994; Wolock & Horowitz, 1984). In 1984 Isabel Wolock and Bernard Horowitz coined the expression "neglect of neglect." They commented, for instance, that despite the fact that the word *neglect* is frequently used in combination with abuse, (for instance, "child abuse and neglect") it is often just given lip service. At a major child abuse and neglect conference, for instance, they note that only 3% of the papers presented really focused on neglect as a separate, and important, issue. It seems that the situation hasn't changed much since then. Ten years after Wolock and Horowitz wrote their classic article on the subject, Dubowitz (1994) lamented that we still haven't awakened to see just how big a problem we have on our hands.

The Serious Nature of Child Neglect

While we may be guilty of neglecting neglect, the topic is not unimportant. Despite appearances, professional inattention, and the general lack of public concern about the issue, child neglect may be one of the most vital issues facing us today. Why? For one thing, our best estimates tell us that neglect is by far the most common form of child maltreatment. By all accounts, the number of neglect cases constitutes about half of all substantiated cases of child maltreatment, ranging from 49 to 52% (for instance, see Cantwell, 1980; DePanfilis, 1996; NCCAN, 1994, 1995b; Wiese & Daro, 1995, cited in DePanfilis, 1996). Compare this to 24% for child physical abuse and 14% for child sexual abuse (NCCAN, 1995b).

In his review of the literature, Dubowitz (1994) points out that the results of neglect can be as bad or worse than those associated with other forms of maltreatment (Rivera & Widom, 1992, cited in Dubowitz, 1994). In terms of "drama," while cases of neglect often lack the flash of severe cases of physical abuse like that of Eli Creekmore, we also know that about half of all children who die because of child maltreatment are victims of neglect (McCurdy & Daro, 1994, as cited in Dubowitz, 1994). How can this be? According to Dubowitz (1994), many of the child neglect fatalities that occur each year involve inadequately supervised children dying in house fires. Improperly supervised children also die from drowning and getting into poisons, medicines, and other dangerous substances. Some children with significant medical problems are endangered when their caregivers do not adequately attend to their needs. Not only do children really die as a consequence of neglect but they suffer other serious consequences as well. Among these are nonorganic "failure to thrive"; deficits in growth and development, in the ability to think and reason, and in the ability to relate to others; and increases in antisocial behavior (Dubowitz, 1994). Some suggest that the consequences of child neglect are equal to or more damaging than other forms of child maltreatment (Egeland, 1988, and Egeland & Sroufe, 1981, as cited in DePanfilis, 1996).

Some Possible Reasons for the Inattention to the Problem

Howard Dubowitz (1994) and others (Cantwell, 1980) suggest that among the reasons why we fail to pay much attention to neglect is that it isn't as dramatic or sensational as other, more compelling types of child maltreatment. Another possible reason for our neglect of the issue is that it hits closer to home. In this day and age when two incomes seem necessary for economic success, both partners in relationships get engrossed with the world of work and, in the process, sometimes fail to pay as much attention to other aspects of their lives, including children. This sometimes means that people feel guilty that they too may be neglecting their children.

Dubowitz (1994) suggests yet another reason: we feel so utterly unable to deal with neglect that we've given up. We often associate poverty with neglect, and it does seem that poverty is a risk factor for neglect. Unfortunately, poverty itself seems to be insurmountable. It has also been an issue long embroiled in politics. In the 1960s former President Johnson attempted to wage a "war on poverty." This effort was short lived, and some claim Johnson's war on poverty failed, pointing out that despite the outlay of large numbers of dollars poverty was not ended. Those on the other side of the debate, however, point to some impressive successes, such as that of the Head Start program. Head Start, a program designed to assist disadvantaged children, provides an enriched preschool program, nutritious food, and social supports. It is still looked upon as a boon to countless numbers of disadvantaged children. The fact that it has survived all succeeding administrations attests to its staying power.

Regardless of your view of the Johnson administration efforts, the changing political tides are a social reality. As a society we've had mounting concerns about the economy, including such issues as the national debt and the trade imbalance. Compounded by the perceived ineffectiveness of government programs and public concern about the high cost of government, we don't seem inclined to undertake ambitious investments in antipoverty programs. The current push, then, seems to be in the direction of less government intervention, not more. With this tide, it also seems that fewer government resources may be available to deal with child neglect.

Social Costs of Neglecting Neglect

While as a society we seem quite able to vent frustration and express concern about the social problems of the day, we also seem unaware, unconcerned, or apathetic to an issue that seems tangled up with them—that of child neglect. Who can deny that teen moms, perhaps among the least prepared for motherhood, are getting pregnant, having children, and often ending up in court because of their inability to care for them?

The problem does not seem to be getting better, and since governmental resources appear to be diminishing, neglect of neglect does not seem likely to improve anytime soon. Is there a social cost? Undoubtedly. We've already established that child neglect has consequences as serious for its victims as those associated with child physical abuse. We have not yet, however, discussed the long-term social consequences. It's a difficult issue, and perhaps one that is cyclical. Let's take a look at it. The rates of teenage pregnancy, promiscuity, and substance abuse are matters of public concern. Many youthful mothers end up on welfare. Because of adverse social conditions, they are also at higher risk for neglecting their children. When it becomes clear that the children have been harmed or are at risk, Child Protective Services intervenes and a slow and costly process begins. This happens regardless of our other social or political priorities since, by this time, we have an emergency. The system tends to become reactive. We lack the public will to pay adequate attention to the problem, but are not so callous that once we have an emergency we fail to take action. In other words, by the choices we make up front, we also determine what we must do later.

The child protective system, the courts, treatment, and foster care are all expensive. This is so regardless of whether we decide to try to help the mother or remove the child. By the time a family comes to the attention of the child protective service, the mother is likely to need intensive intervention and support. On the other hand, if we simply focus on the child and remove the child from the situation, we cause other problems that are also likely to be costly. Specialized foster care or residential treatment is often more financially costly than the support we provide young mothers on welfare. From a financial and logistical standpoint, finding foster parents able and willing to provide the kind of help these children need is difficult at best. When we do find them, we need to support them, not only with enough money to raise these children adequately but also with other specialized resources, including medical care, counseling or mental health treatment, child welfare supervision, and so on.

In terms of damage to the child, attachment theorists tell us that disrupting the mother-child bond interferes with the child's ability to develop socially (James, 1994). These children, too, are expected to be at higher risk for social and behavioral problems, including early pregnancy. As with our previous discussions about the intergenerational transmission theory, I do not mean to imply that this happens in every case. It does seem, however, that there are increased risks for these and other social consequences. We can also expect increased costs, both in terms of dollars and in terms of the impact on the society at large.

Definitions and Categories of Neglect

As mentioned in the introduction to this section, child neglect, rather than being an overt act, is a failure to provide care. DePanfilis (1996) comments in her review that, while there isn't consensus in the professional community about the exact nature of child neglect, there is general agreement about what it is. Based on her review of the literature, she suggests at least three basic components to a definition of child neglect: (1) the maltreatment refers to acts of omission rather than commission, (2) it is perpetrated by parents or other caregivers, and (3) it results in harm or risk of harm. Consistent with the basic family abuse matrix introduced in Chapter 1, she also notes that Howard Dubowitz and his colleagues suggest that a child is neglected when his or her basic needs are not met, whatever the reasons (Dubowitz, et al., 1993, cited in DePanfilis, 1996).

The categories of neglect vary. Pecora, Whittaker, and Maluccio (1992) review a list of 14 categories of neglect developed by Zuravin (1989). Munkel (1994) has a similar listing of types of neglect but organizes them somewhat differently. He divides forms of neglect into four basic types and then includes various specific forms of neglect within each category. The four categories in Munkel's model are as follows: (1) the kind associated with the physical environment, (2) that which is related to **hazards in the physical environment,** (3) that which is related to **inadequate care standards,** and (4) that which is related to the child's **development.** Within each category of neglect, the laundry list of specific types is fairly self-explanatory. The types of problems Munkel (1994) includes within the physical environment category include inadequate shelter, inadequate sleeping arrangements, unsanitary conditions, structural hazards, and housekeeping problems. The environmental hazards category includes fire hazards, accessibility of substances, and excessive hot water temperature. Within the field of inadequate care standards Munkel includes nutrition, clothing, personal hygiene, health care, and supervision. Finally, Munkel identifies two types under the heading of developmental neglect: education and emotional growth.

Failure to Thrive Syndrome (FTT): A Special Category

Failure to thrive syndrome, or FTT, is really a shorthand expression for the more complete title: nonorganic failure to thrive syndrome. "Failure to thrive" refers to the phenomenon in some infants (usually under two years of age but as old as three) in which they fail to develop. To call it "nonorganic" simply means that the failure to develop is not caused by some physical factor in the child's biology but rather is due to a failure to provide adequately for the infant (Kempe, Cutler, & Dean, 1980). In order to arrive at a diagnosis of nonorganic failure to thrive, the health professional needs to be able to rule out other possible biological or organic causes (Pecora, et al., 1992).

This deficit in development is not an arbitrary determination and signifies much more than a child simply being slow to achieve normal developmental milestones. As noted by Pecora and colleagues (1992), in nonorganic failure to thrive (FTT), there is no standard set of signs and symptoms that when present, constitute the disorder; however, there are a few generally accepted indicators. Those noted by Pecora et al. (1992) and others (Kempe, et al., 1980) include (1) weight or height below the third percentile, (2) weight less than about 80 or 85% of the ideal weight for the child's age, (3) failure to maintain previous weight, (4) failure to maintain growth for a specified period of time (two months for infants less than five months old, three months for infants five or more months old), and (5) delayed psychomotor development. In addition to these, another physical indicator associated with FTT is small head circumference. Munkel (1994) adds that children with FTT are often emaciated, have potbellies, poor muscle tone, episodes of diarrhea, tension, and discomfort, and cold, pale, and mottled skin. Pecora et al. (1992) also note some significant behavioral indicators, including hypervigilence or unusually high levels of watchfulness, a lack of smiling, resistance to being cuddled, and a froglike posture when on their backs, much like that of newborns. Additionally, Munkel (1994) notes that many FTT-affected infants seem insensitive to pain, inflict injuries on themselves, have sleep problems, and sometimes eat inappropriate things from the garbage or pet bowls.

Shortly, we will be talking about the risk factors associated with child neglect; however, since we've been treating FTT as a special category, we'll take just a moment to briefly skim over some of the risk factors specifically associated with it.

Ruth Kempe and her colleagues (1980) suggest that the primary care provider is often a young, immature mother who lacks child care experience and education. They also suggest that some mothers who are mentally retarded or who have low intelligence may have difficulty making decisions about the care of their children. The most recent literature reviews seem to implicate disturbed patterns of parent and infant interaction (for discussion see Munkel, 1994; Pecora et al., 1992). Some mothers with significant difficulties may find it hard to bond with a child, especially if the child is troublesome or temperamental. Pecora et al. (1992) also comment that the parent in such cases may also be experiencing depression, in addition to having unrealistic expectations about what the infant should be able to do.

With the exception of social isolation and lack of social support, one factor that does not appear to have been extensively examined is the family's place within the greater social niche. In other words, what kind of social and environmental stressors are impinging upon the family's ability to function?

The long-term effects of FTT appear to be significant. It seems that children who were failure-to-thrive infants may be at higher risk for developmental delays, personality problems, abuse, and even death (Moore, 1982, cited in Pecora et al., 1992). Kempe et al. (1980) echo this conclusion in their own review, commenting on earlier research suggesting that a number of children who had been previously hospitalized as FTT infants were later found to be seriously, or fatally, abused (Koel, 1969) or starved (Adelson, 1963).

The traditional approach to treating FTT has been a combination of medical and social service interventions. The common wisdom seems to be that thorough assessment sometimes requires hospitalization in order to establish that the infant is able to gain weight when not in the home environment. Hospitalization is also often regarded as necessary for the safety and well-being of the child when it is believed that the child may otherwise be at imminent risk. When FTT can be established and appears to be an ongoing risk, the child may be placed in longer-term foster care as a protective measure. Mental health treatment or counseling has also been a traditional part of intervention efforts. Consistent with observations about child neglect in general, innovations in treatment may now be turning to providing increased social support to parents in FTT cases (see DePanfilis, 1996; Pecora et al., 1992). It seems that increased social support may not only help the distressed parent but also provide increased opportunity for monitoring.

Explanations of Causes and Risk Factors

Most child abuse professionals seem to agree that child neglect is determined by many different forces at work in the individual, family, community, and society (DePanfilis, 1996). One way of looking at these forces is to think of them in terms of risk factors. As with the previous section on child psychological maltreatment, we will focus on three primary levels of explanation: individual factors (micro level), family factors (meso level), and socio-cultural issues (macro level).

Poverty seems to be a significant socio-cultural (macro level) issue. We believe that poverty increases the risk of child neglect, though this does not mean that all families living in poverty are neglectful of their children's needs. Social isolation can be thought of as a lack of connectedness to others within one's community. It is often a factor that, perhaps more than any other, has been identified as a significant risk associated with child neglect (Gaudin & Polansky, 1986; Polansky, et al., 1981; Polansky & Gaudin, 1983). In some respects the jury is still out on what this means, however. On one hand, it is possible that social isolation itself increases the risk of neglect since an isolated family has fewer resources for dealing with its problems. On the flip side, some research clearly suggests that people across races and classes will distance themselves from those who are thought to be neglectful of their children (Gaudin & Polansky, 1986; Polansky & Gaudin, 1983). These apparently disparate propositions present us with a paradox, since those most in need of increased social support may well be the very people most likely to be shunned by those in their communities.

Another important factor to consider is that of the neighborhood. Some suggest that, with so much of the attention having been given to parent characteristics and parent-child interaction, the neighborhood was really neglected as a risk factor for a long time until Garbarino and his colleagues (Garbarino & Crouter, 1978; Garbarino &: Kostelny, 1992; Garbarino & Sherman, 1980) called attention to it (Korbin, Coulton, & Furin, 1995). We can think of neighborhoods as that immediate part of the social environment in which individual and family dramas are played out, where the rubber meets the road, so to speak. One wonders how they could not be important. You don't have to be the proverbial rocket scientist to realize that living in neighborhoods where people are scared is not likely to foster closeness, inclusion, and social connectedness. If we accept Maslow's model (1954) about basic human needs, it makes sense that it would be hard to work on building relationships or striving for a more healthy sense of self as long as safety and security is a central issue.

Since intimacy is so central to human existence, family and relationship issues also seem important. Being single or being in a conflict-ridden relationship seems to put the parent at greater risk. Not only is the single parent often without the emotional support of a caring partner but the support and energy necessary for providing adequate care may be lacking as well. On a more practical level, the single parent may also lack having another to immediately rely upon for assistance with day-to-day caretaking functions. Being isolated from one's own family also seems likely to increase risk since there may often be fewer supports in such homes.

In terms of other individual status considerations, it seems that age, educational attainment, and the number of children are also important factors. Susan Zuravin and Frederick DiBlasio (1992) have conducted some interesting research with teen mothers, which suggests that mothers who are youngest at first pregnancy and who have completed the least amount of education are at increased risk of being neglectful. These authors also attempted to explore the role of self-esteem and sense of personal control but could not establish any increased risk factors, despite previously developed theory (Belsky, 1984) that hypothesized a connection. At an individual level, we might expect that a personal history of abuse or neglect would be expected to increase the risk that such a person would become neglectful as a parent. Pecora et al. (1992) also note that many neglectful parents had themselves been placed in foster or residential care as children. Recent findings by Zuravin and DiBlasio (1992), however, did not establish any connection between physical abuse or neglect and later becoming a neglectful parent. They did find a connection, however, between having been sexually abused and becoming a neglectful parent.

In terms of individual personality characteristics, depression is commonly cited in connection with both neglect and abuse and can be expected to increase the risk of neglect since among its features are apathy and lack of energy in the afflicted person. When trying to explain depression, we sometimes resort to the **anger turned inward hypothesis.** This hypothesis says in essence that, when a person becomes angry or frustrated and has no way to constructively direct it, the person can do nothing but hold onto it, allowing it to be turned against the self. It incapacitates the individual, decreasing the likelihood that future attempts at coping will be constructive. In a pioneering work on neglect by Polansky and his associates (1981), they suggest that there seem to be five types of neglectful parents. In addition to the depressed category, which many professionals have commented on, they include the apathetic-futile, the impulse-ridden, the retarded, and the psychotic or "borderline." We might wish to group the psychotic-borderline type into a category called the chronically mentally ill.

Polansky expresses a particular interest in the apathetic-futile category because so many of the neglecting parents who were referred to him in Appalachia seemed to fit into this group. He expanded the category into what he has come to call the **apathy-futility syndrome** (Polansky et al., 1981). Similar to depression, the apathy-futility syndrome is a kind of adaptation that, in the long run, isn't really adaptive at all. It includes eight components, as follows: (1) a pervasive conviction that nothing is worth doing, (2) emotional numbness (sometimes mistaken for depression), (3) interpersonal relationships that can be characterized as desperate and "clingy," (4) lack of competence in many areas of living (partially caused by fear of trying and failing), (5) passive aggression or reluctant and hostile compliance, (6) negativism or noncommitment to positive stands, (7) verbal inaccessibility to others, and (8) an uncanny ability in making others feel the same sense of futility.

We should not leave the topic of risk factors in neglect without first addressing the issue of alcohol and drug use. Whether we should treat the consumption of alcohol and drugs during pregnancy as abuse or neglect is a good question. Clearly, the issue of drug- and alcohol-affected babies is a social concern. We have known for some time now that the use of even small amounts of alcohol during pregnancy places the unborn child at increased risk. **Fetal alcohol syndrome** is a disorder caused by the use of alcohol by the mother during pregnancy, in which deformity, retardation, and a number of other physical anomalies are present. A less severe condition known as **fetal alcohol effect** includes less pronounced symptoms, which, among many others, include irritability or fussiness. The fussiness of the baby can in itself increase the risk of bonding problems between the parent and child and thus contribute to a neglect problem. While the connection between alcohol and drug use and neglect is not well researched or established, we do seem to be fairly clear that continued use of alcohol or other drugs after abuse or neglect problems get attention significantly reduces the likelihood of successful intervention.

Resiliency: Protective Factors

Just as risk of neglect seems to be determined by many different forces, it is probably also true that influences that protect a child from neglect are numerous. In an earlier section, we discussed several compensatory factors associated with child physical abuse, as identified by Kaufman and Zigler (1989). These were discussed in the context of understanding why so many physically abused children did not grow up to be abusers. As you might recall, the factors at the individual (micro) level include a history of a positive relationship with at least one significant person, high intelligence, positive school experiences, and good peer relations. Relationship (meso level) factors include having a supportive spouse, financial stability, healthy children, good social supports, and moderate amounts of stress in adult life. Broad social/societal (macro level) influences included a cultural environment that promotes a sense of shared responsibility for caring for children, a culture opposed to violence, and economic prosperity. Anthropology teaches us that kinship systems vary around the world, and in some cultures all adults from the generation of one's biological parents are considered to be one's "mothers" and "fathers." In such cultures it seems that the adults share more responsibility and have more concern for the welfare of their children.

While we have devoted fewer efforts to the issue of neglect, including its risk and protective factors, we should probably expect these factors to be somewhat similar to those for child physical abuse. Social and cultural attitudes that place a high value on children, and the responsibility of all adults toward them, and neighborhoods in which people are connected to others and where residents watch out for each other and the children and individuals and families can feel supported, seem to promote greater social health and less risk. Michael Rutter, in some of his early research on protective factors (1979), suggests that some schools create a sense of belonging and serve to promote the overall well-being of their students. Recent work in the area of neglect does revolve around social support (see DePanfilis, 1996). Professional work in the field is now seeing social support for and the connectedness of the mother in her social environment as being important protective factors. Despite the existence of a number of problems and risk factors,

DePanfilis (1996) suggests that "strong, positive social networks can serve as compensatory factors that act to decrease the risk of maltreatment" (p. 41).

At an individual level, there may also be some factors that decrease the risk of neglect. A good state of mental health, high intellectual functioning, having a sense of purpose and hope, a history of good childhood experiences, a positive relationship with at least one important person, and good social relations seem to reduce the risk of problems with abuse and neglect. Zuravin and DiBlasio (1992) were interested in looking at a variety of risk factors. Based on their research of 11 factors, it seems that mothers who had their children later rather than earlier and those who completed the most number of years in school were less at risk of being neglectful.

CHAPTER SUMMARY

In this chapter we covered two of the most perplexing problems facing us in the field of child maltreatment: psychological maltreatment and neglect.

First we explored the area of child psychological maltreatment, an increasingly important area. Leaders in the field suggest that it is perhaps the core issue in all types of child maltreatment. It is also the psychological trauma that is believed responsible for the impact of child abuse generally. We built on the work of Hart et al., 1987, who integrated the definition of child abuse contained in the federal Child Abuse Prevention and Treatment Act, and the definition proposed by an international conference on the subject.

In the context of trying to understand psychological maltreatment, we looked at the role of two important dimensions: basic human needs and human development. We explored why these two conceptual dimensions of the human condition may be so important to the issue of psychological maltreatment. Based on developmental theory, we projected expected impact. We explored the research about psychological maltreatment, initially paying special attention to research that bears on the projected impacts based upon our use of developmental theory.

Before looking at systemic or ecological approaches to understanding psychological maltreatment, we took a look at the literature on one long-term research project concerned with the study of child abuse and neglect: the Minnesota Mother-Child Interaction Project. We took special note of the results of this project, which suggests that all forms of maltreatment impair human development but that indifference to the psychological needs of the child is the most devastating of all.

We then discussed the place of systemic or ecological models in the understanding of child psychological maltreatment. We noted that those models regarded by some leaders in the field as being the most comprehensive are systemic or ecological in nature. Systemic or ecological models attempt to describe phenomena as a whole system, with interaction between various smaller parts of the system. Rather than looking at one level or another, systemic or ecological approaches attempt to explain psychological maltreatment by describing the interaction between forces operating at all levels of the system: societal, family, and individual. Still exploring the problem from a systemic/ecological point of view, we took a brief look at resiliency, a term used to describe human adaptability in the face of difficult circumstances, and to explain why some people survive and even do well despite the odds.

In the second half of the chapter, we introduced the topic of child neglect and discussed how it is qualitatively different from the more dramatic forms of child maltreatment. A chief characteristic is that it represents acts of omission rather than commission. We also discussed the "neglect of neglect," noting that, while child neglect is clearly the most common form of child maltreatment, it gets short shrift when it comes to both professional and public attention. In relation to this lack of attention, we reviewed the serious nature of child neglect and the social costs of ignoring this issue.

We defined child neglect and reviewed a system for categorizing a number of subtypes. We also surveyed a very specialized form of child neglect called failure to thrive syndrome (FTT), which is believed to spring from disturbed family and parent-child interactions.

We discussed a number of risk factors associated with the general problem of child neglect and examined those at the societal, family, and individual levels. Finally, we reviewed some of what we know about protective factors, or those factors that are likely to insulate and protect the child from some of the most adverse consequences of neglect.

LEGAL AND ETHICAL CONCERNS: CRITICAL THINKING QUESTIONS

1. Parents are thought to have certain rights when it comes to the discipline of their children, and sometimes this includes harsh words. At what point do the interests of the state to protect children from psychological maltreatment over-ride the rights of parents to be parents?

2. Many children have problems in school. Sometimes it is because the student has a learning or behavior problem. Students are sometimes spoken to in a negative way, disciplined, or otherwise have problems. When do the tactics the school uses to get compliance from the child constitute psychological maltreatment? Ever?

3. The friends or family of a child may become concerned about a parent psychologically maltreating a youth. Is it always better to report the abuse, even if the action might result in the parent totally rejecting the child?

4. Poverty is a significant risk factor associated with child neglect. Does the fact that this problem seems so overwhelming justify not taking steps to try to alleviate it? Why?

5. We have limited resources. We know that we might be able to prevent abuse and neglect if we invest our money in reducing risk factors and enhancing resiliencies. Under what circumstances, if ever, is it appropriate

to try this, even if it means that identified existing cases don't get the attention they need?

_____

SUGGESTED ACTIVITIES

1. Contact a librarian or federal government documents office and locate a copy of the Child Abuse Prevention and Treatment Act (P.L. 93-247). Review it in full. Prepare a report and include any issues you think go unaddressed in the law.

2. Some of the most experienced professionals in the field have been perplexed attempting to develop operational definitions of psychological maltreatment. (An operational definition is one in which the abstract idea is translated into observable operations or steps.) As an exercise, try to develop your own operational definitions of psychological maltreatment. What are the problems with doing this? What are the problems with your definition?

3. Psychologically maltreated children often develop emotional and behavior problems. When this happens, it is all too easy to point the finger at the child and fail to find out what is going on with that child. How can we deal with this problem? Write a report or paper addressing this question and talk about how we might correct the problem. What might therapists do? Teachers? Probation officers? Friends of the family? Relatives?

4. Child maltreatment laws vary from state to state, and not all contain language that specifically defines child psychological maltreatment. Research the laws in your state and determine how it defines psychological maltreatment, if at all.

5. Contact the social service department at a local hospital and find out what kinds of neglect cases they handle. What sort of physical problems do the children have? What steps do they take to work with the families and help them provide better for their children?

6. Courts have to make sensitive decisions about how to intervene in cases of child physical abuse and neglect. Contact your local court administrator or judge and find out how this is done in your community.

7. Select at least one book on child physical abuse or neglect. Read it, and evaluate it critically and honestly. Be sure to support your views, and be able to discuss the relevant literature.

_____

REVIEW GUIDE

1. Be able to discuss why psychological maltreatment is an important field of study.

2. Based on the discussion in the opening pages of the text, what do we mean when we say psychological maltreatment? The way we are using the term, can it be a single episode? Are we using it in the context of adult relationships? What other terms have been used to describe essentially the same thing?

3. What are the different basic types of psychological maltreatment?

4. Be familiar with how Dean (1979) defines emotional abuse, emotional assault, and emotional neglect. What are the differences between each of the three? Also, be familiar with the three types of psychological abuse cases that have been successfully prosecuted in San Diego County.

5. Be fully familiar with the rationale for making the model of basic human needs a central part of our study of psychological maltreatment. Be familiar with the research cited, which supports the concept that emotional and psychological needs are every bit as important as physical needs. What kinds of psychological needs were identified?

6. Be able to discuss what the developmental approach is. Which three domains of human development were discussed? Which developmental psychologist is associated with each?

7. Be familiar with the cognitive and social developmental tasks that developmental psychologists believe are associated with each of the developmental periods outlined in Table 3-2.

8. Be familiar with each of the suspected impacts of psychological maltreatment at the developmental periods, as outlined in Table 3-3.

9. Compare and contrast the concepts of critical period and sensitive period. What are the implications of using each?

10. Be able to discuss what is meant by a strengths-based perspective.

11. What conclusions drawn from the literature are or are not consistent with the projected impacts we developed based upon developmental theory? Be familiar with what the research indicates.

12. Be able to define defensive independence, and discuss Rohner and Rhoner's thoughts about how this can happen.

13. Be able to discuss what has been learned at the Minnesota Mother-Child Interaction Project. What four types of maltreatment did researchers find in their sample? How did the maltreated children compare to others with respect to their development? Which form of maltreatment, if any, resulted in the most serious impacts?

14. What do systemic or ecological approaches propose about the causes of child maltreatment? What three levels of explanation are we interested in? What kinds of influences operate at each level? Be able to reproduce and explain the model developed by Garbarino et al. (1986). Define environmental context and family context.

15. Be able to discuss the cultural and social influences that are believed to contribute to the impacts of maltreatment. Be familiar with any research cited.

16. Be able to discuss the family or small group influences that are believed to contribute to the impacts of maltreatment. Which four factors did family therapist Virginia Satir suggest are important?

17. Be able to discuss the individual-level influences that are believed to contribute to the impacts of maltreatment. What parent characteristics

are important? What, if any, child characteristics or factors are important? Be familiar with any research cited.

18.   Be able to discuss the concept of resiliency. What does it say about human potential and problem solving?

19.   What is retrospective analysis? How can it lead to false conclusions about the relationship between an undesirable outcome and prior life experience?

20.   When we include the concept of resiliency, what can we say about the relationship between human potential, experience, and the destructive impact of maltreatment?

21.   Discuss what we mean by child neglect. What is "neglect of neglect?" Why is child neglect a serious matter? What are the possible reasons for our inattention to the problem? What are the possible social costs of neglecting neglect?

22.   Be able to define child neglect and be familiar with each of the categories of neglect, giving examples for each.

23.   Be fully familiar with failure to thrive syndrome (FTT). What is it? How do we assess when it is present? What do we think causes it? What are some of the risk factors specifically associated with FTT? What are the long-term effects of FTT? What treatment approaches have been used to deal with it?

24.   Be familiar with all risk factors associated with neglect. What is the anger turned inward hypothesis? How does it relate to depression? How does depression relate to child neglect? What is the apathy-futility syndrome? What are the eight components in the apathy-futility syndrome?

25.   What are fetal alcohol syndrome and fetal alcohol effect.

26.   What are the resiliencies or compensatory factors associated with child neglect? In the context of child neglect, name those factors that seem to be most promising in terms of reducing risk.

SUGGESTED READING

Brassard, M. R., Germain, R., & Hart, S. N. (Eds.). (1987). *Psychological maltreatment of children and youth.* New York: Pergamon Press.

This is a classic in the field. It is a wonderful anthology that has chapters written by a number of authorities. The position taken in this book is that psychological maltreatment is at the core of all forms of child maltreatment. Building on this idea, it devotes chapter after chapter to discussing the relationship between psychological maltreatment and the other specific forms of abuse.

Garbarino, J., Guttman, E., & Seeley, J. W. (1986). *The psychologically battered child.* San Francisco: Jossey-Bass.

This is another classic in the field and should be read by anyone and everyone who has an interest in psychological maltreatment. Not only do the authors help the reader understand what it is but they provide some guidelines for assessment and suggest approaches to prevention and intervention.

Pillari, V. (1991). *Scapegoating in families.* New York: Brunner/Mazel.

 This is one of the few books on the market dealing with psychological maltreatment that can be read by client or clinician. Based upon the clinical experience of the author, it is filled with examples.

Polansky, N. A., Chalmers, M. A., Buttenwieser, E., & Williams, D. P. (1981). *Damaged parents: An anatomy of child neglect.* Chicago: University of Chicago Press.

 One of the few works devoted to a neglected topic: child neglect. In this classic work, Dr. Polansky identifies several behavior patterns associated with neglectful parents. One, which he calls the apathy-futility syndrome, he says fits many of the women he saw in poverty-stricken Appalachia.

CHAPTER GLOSSARY

Anger turned inward hypothesis
A theory proposing that clinical depression is caused by turning internalized anger against oneself.

Apathy-futility syndrome
A syndrome, or conglomeration of associated signs and symptoms, proposed by Polansky to describe a category of neglecting parents. Characterized by a loss of hope (the belief that any efforts are futile), emotional numbness, desperate interpersonal relationships (described as "clingy"), and a resulting lack of competence in dealing with important areas of life.

Cognitive development
A specific area of study within the general field of developmental psychology. The term *cognitive* literally refers to thinking. Jean Piaget was a pioneer in the field who based much of his theory on the observation of his own daughter. His ideas continue to be influential. A key component of his theory is that our ability to think is a progressive process in which we learn in stages.

Corrupting
The process that occurs when the child is mis-socialized, or is encouraged to participate in inappropriate activities, such as the use of drugs, gambling, or promiscuous sex. Associated with this idea is that the caregiver is either neglectful of the child's need to be protected from this type of activity or else derives some vicarious satisfaction from the child's behavior.

Critical periods
In developmental psychology, the idea that specific developmental tasks need to be accomplished during specific stages of development or else might never be mastered.

Defensive independence
A term used by researchers Rohner and Rohner (1980) to refer to a strategy used by people who have been psychologically maltreated of isolating themselves from others, despite their true need for them, to protect themselves from further mental injury.

Degrading/ devaluing
The term used to describe what happens when the child is criticized, stigmatized, humiliated,or made to feel inferior.

Denying essential stimulation
Refers to depriving a child of loving and sensitive caregiving. Can include being detached and uninvolved, having only limited and superficial interactions with the child, and failing to express affection and love for the child.

Emotional abuse
A term used by Dean (1979) to refer to a pattern of emotional attacks or neglect that injures children emotionally and becomes a dominant theme in their lives.

Emotional assault   A term used by Dean (1979) to refer to individual attacks on the psyche of the child. Can be hurtful but is not necessarily considered abuse unless it is part of an ongoing pattern that becomes a dominant issue in the child's life.

Emotional neglect   A term used by Dean (1979) to refer to acts of omission in which the adult fails to attend to the emotional needs of the child.

Environmental context   One of three main domains in the Garbarino et al. (1986) ecological model. The environmental context includes all the social influences that operate within a society.

Exploiting   What happens when a child is used to meet the needs or desires of the caretaker. In extreme cases this could involve making the child sexually available to others for monetary gain.

Failure to thrive syndrome   See Nonorganic failure to thrive.

Family context   One of three main domains in the Garbarino et al. (1986) ecological model. The family context includes all the influences (values, beliefs, rules) that operate within a family.

Fetal alcohol effect   Physical and psychological disturbances caused by the mother's use of alcohol during pregnancy. Signs and symptoms are said to include behavior problems, academic difficulties, and difficulty concentrating, among others.

Fetal alcohol syndrome   A syndrome first observable in infancy in which the child has certain characterological deformities and/or other anomalies caused by the mother's use of alcohol during pregnancy. Some of the symptoms, such as mental retardation, can be severe.

Isolation   The process of severely restricting the child's ability to interact with others outside the family. In extreme cases the child might be locked in a room or confined space.

Moral development   A specific area of study within the general field of developmental psychology. Lawrence Kohlberg was a pioneer in the field. He believed that, just as individuals develop cognitively and socially, they develop morally as well. Proposed different levels of moral development, some more advanced than others. Suggested that the way to determine moral development is to determine how individuals solve certain moral dilemmas. His ideas continue to be influential.

Nonorganic failure to thrive   A syndrome, or cluster of signs and symptoms, in which the child is markedly below size. Specific criteria include that the child's weight or height is below the third percentile. Organic or biological causes have been ruled out, and the child is able to gain weight briefly when separated from his parent or parents.

Operational definition   A definition in which an abstract concept is broken down into steps, or operations, that can be observed. For example, an operational definition for *empathy,* the concept that refers to the ability to understand how another sees a situation, might be operationalized as accurate paraphrasing.

Psychological abuse   An act of commission, perpetrated by an adult on a child, that causes, or can cause, injury to the child's psyche. An active form of psychological maltreatment that harms because the adult frustrates the child's attainment of his or her psychological needs.

Psychological maltreatment   The preferred term in this text to denote injury or potential injury to the individual's psyche caused by a pattern of specified acts of commission or omission, which do not fall into one of the other categories of maltreatment.

Psychological neglect	An act of omission, perpetrated by an adult on a child, that causes, or can cause, injury to the child's psyche. A passive form of psychological maltreatment that harms because the adult fails to meet the child's psychological needs.
Rejection	What happens when the child is pushed away and made to feel unacceptable and unworthy.
Resiliency	A term used in developmental psychology and the human services to refer to the ability of individuals to do well despite difficult life experiences.
Retrospective analysis	A form of analysis in which a person's prior life experiences are analyzed in light of what happened to them later. For example, you might look for things that happened in a person's history to explain why they are schizophrenic. Because so many other factors might come into play, this form of analysis can often lead to faulty conclusions about causes.
Sensitive periods	A contrasting word to "critical periods." Whereas a critical period implies that certain developmental tasks must be learned during a certain period or else will never be learned, a sensitive period implies that there is an optimum period during which tasks should be mastered, though they can also be mastered later.
Sensitivity	A term used by Kaufman and Zigler (1989) that refers to the ability of a theory to correctly identify those who will abuse.
Social development	A specific area of study within the general field of developmental psychology that concerns itself with how human beings learn to behave with other human beings. Erik Erikson was a pioneer in the field. He believed that each of us goes through a series of developmental crises in which we either succeed and develop well or have one of a number of issues that remains unsettled.
Strengths-based perspective	A way of looking at human problems from the point of view of strengths or abilities rather than deficits.
Terrorizing	What occurs when a child is verbally assaulted and threatened. As a consequence the child's behavior is governed by a sense of fear.

CHAPTER

CHILD SEXUAL ABUSE

The Problem   Models of Victimology and
The Victims   Emerging Trends

It's only been in the last 20 or so years that we as a society have begun to wake up to the problem of child sexual abuse. Now that we have, as if swinging on a pendulum, we seem to have gone from slumber to preoccupation. Who has not heard vivid descriptions or discussion of sexual abuse experiences on one of the many TV talk shows? In the professional arena, one authority suggests that the issue of child sexual abuse has gone from being nearly nonexistent to sparking a semiautonomous speciality within the mental health field, getting more research dollars than all other forms of abuse combined.

While we have now roused to the issue, we still don't fully understand it. In this chapter we will start by taking a look at the enigma of child sexual abuse. Although there is still much we do not know, one thing we seem to have figured out is that most child sexual abuse is perpetrated by people close to the family, if not members of the family itself. Contrast this to the real but more rare instances of brutal, sexually motivated attacks on children by strangers. We will open by discussing and contrasting these two. The drama associated with brutal attacks perpetrated by strangers can startle us to action, but when we think that this is the typical pattern of child sexual abuse, it can perhaps also overshadow the problem.

In this context we'll be taking a look at how professional beliefs about childhood sexual fantasies may have contributed to our having had a blind eye to this issue. We will try to answer the question, How big is the child sexual abuse problem? In this regard we will be reviewing some of the available data, but we will not restrict our exploration to numbers. We also want to pay attention to the impact on the children themselves. We will probe social, cultural, and family factors that seem to contribute to the problem. We will explore the treatment of victims, including taking a look at philosophies of treatment that seem to hold promise for providing a framework in which recovery can take place.

THE PROBLEM

The following incident really happened; this is the kind of brutal attack that can shock us into an awareness of one of our most crucial social problems, child sexual abuse. A nine-year-old boy was riding his bicycle through a neighborhood park. A recently released sexual offender was in the park looking for just such a victim. No one else was within earshot. The man grabbed the boy from his bicycle. He brutally assaulted and raped the boy, severed his penis, and left him lying there, bleeding. Released sex offender Earl Shriner was the perpetrator and Boy X was his victim.

Incidents like the one described above are any parent's worst nightmare and perhaps an important reason why, for so long, so much emphasis was placed on cautioning children not to talk to strangers, as if it were lurking strangers we really had to worry about. These incidents rivet themselves into our psyches and cause fear; they also tend to reinforce our preexisting stereotypes of offenders. The image of the offender as the dirty-old-man-in-a-raincoat was for a long time the image we had of sexual offenders. When the whole field of child sexual abuse was beginning its revival, one of its pioneers wrote extensively about the myths surrounding the sexual offender stereotype (Groth, et al., 1982). Perhaps it's still the image some people have about offenders, but most of us now seem to understand a disturbing reality about child sexual abuse: that it is most commonly perpetrated by trusted people, people whom the child knows, often a family member.

Contrasting these two distinct classes of abuse, stranger and in-family child sexual abuse, points out how challenging it is to study and understand the problem. When we take a closer look at offenders in Chapter 6, we will explore this issue in greater depth. For now we can simply say that, while each type seems very different, both classes involve the sexual exploitation of children. Perhaps because of these perceived differences, we have felt forced to choose one or the other representation in our own belief systems. In deciding how to think about child sexual abuse, we as a people seem to have conceptualized it, until fairly recently, more in terms of the old stranger-perpetrator stereotype. We've already suggested one possible reason for this: many cases of stranger assault are so horrible that they are hard to forget. Another might be that acts of child sexual abuse are so at odds with what we believe about the people who are close to us. To even imagine that they might perpetrate an act of sexual abuse requires an attitude toward them that is foreign to the kinds of relationships we have with them. In modern-day self-help jargon, we loosely call it "denial" when we find psychological ways to avoid accepting such an emotionally threatening idea.

Professional and Societal Neglect of the Issue

It may also be true that the professional mental health community itself contributed to society's denial of the problem. In Chapter 1, we briefly discussed how the ideas of Sigmund Freud may have played a role. Freud was the first 20th-century mental health professional to identify child sexual abuse as a mental health problem. In his early work with clients, he recognized traumatic events in childhood, especially child sexual abuse, as being directly related to the development of significant psychological trauma (Wong, 1989). He used the term *hysterical neuroses* to describe very remarkable syndromes he believed were caused by such trauma. Symptoms could be as severe as psychologically induced blindness, paralysis, or loss of hearing. In our own time the **hysterical neuroses** would be categorized as **conversion disorders** (American Psychiatric Association, 1994). As present-day critics point out, Freud did not stick to his original position for long (Masson, 1984; Rush, 1977). Freud's early theory, called the **seduction theory,** was not well received by his contemporaries. In fact, one source suggests that the majority of Freud's female patients reported being molested by their adult relatives when they were children (Phillips & Frederick, 1995). These same relatives were people who traveled in Freud's social and professional circles. It was not until he reformulated his ideas that his work received acceptance. His reformulated theory involved changing a significant premise. As you recall, Freud originally proposed that children were subjected to real sexual abuse and that this violation caused significant trauma. His new theory suggested that children's conflict over their own sexual fantasies toward a parent causes the trauma. The reformulation became the most famous of all Freudian theories: those of the **Oedipus** and **Electra** complexes. In the Oedipus complex, Freud asserted that at a certain point boy children become sexually interested in their mothers; in the Electra complex, girl children have similar sexual fantasies about their fathers. It is easy to see the implications—attention is shifted from the behavior of the adult to the supposed sexual fantasies of the child.

When the seduction theory was rejected by his contemporaries, one could argue that the refusal to accept the possibility that children were being sexually victimized constituted a form of **denial**, a concept Freud himself developed. He described denial as an unconscious defensive process whereby we keep ourselves from being aware of psychologically threatening truth, usually involving sexuality.

It would be an understatement to say that Freud's reformulated theories influenced the development of what has become the modern mental health field. It would be far more accurate to say that his ideas sparked a revolution. Freudian ideas caught fire in continental Europe, and by the 1920s they were taking root on the American continent as well. With the rising of totalitarian regimes in Europe during the 1930s, psychoanalysts and other members of the intelligentsia began fleeing Europe, finding haven in the United States and other democratic countries. Freudian beliefs found their way into the human service infrastructure, contributing to the thinking of countless human service providers—providers who might have been inclined, as a result, to have believed that children's allegations of sexual abuse might really be expressions of their own fantasies.

If Freudian theory has been abused, then the damage done was this: for a long time, sexually abused children were not believed. Freudian theory, while generally not taken as literal truth any longer, is far from dead, however. It is still highlighted in virtually every introductory psychology text. It also continues to be taught in the standard text (Wong, 1989; Kaplan & Sadock, 1989) that, to this day, is used to train new generations of psychiatrists who, as members of an elite class, will exert considerable influence.

While I believe it's important to note how flaws in Freudian theory may have affected the perceptions of mental health professionals, I think it's also important to acknowledge the significant contributions made by Freud's ideas. Freudian theory elevated the issue of sexuality, and childhood sexuality, in the public consciousness and also raised awareness about the influence of early experiences on human development. In fact, the seed of our modern-day reawakening to the problem may have actually been at least partially contained within a social phenomenon spawned by Freudian thought.

Rediscovering Child Sexual Abuse

The term **Zeitgeist**, roughly translated as "spirit of the times," conveys a sense of shared attitudes, beliefs, and values common to people living in a particular place and time. If an earlier Zeitgeist included certain beliefs about children's sexual fantasies, and attitudes such as "Children should be seen but not heard," then the Zeitgeist of the last decade of the 20th century includes acceptance of widespread child sexual abuse as a social phenomenon. The pendulum has swung. Not only have we come to believe that child sexual abuse is real but we have also come to accept that it is more common than we ever imagined.

How is it that child sexual abuse reemerged in the social consciousness? Some suggest that the shift began when the women's movement became a force in American society and women began speaking out for the first time, not just about the inequality between men and women but also about the abuses women suffered when they were children. Add to this a "psychologically oriented" pop culture, and we have heightened sensitivity to the issue. Interestingly, it was Freud himself, by creating the discipline of psychoanalysis, who ushered in the "psychological age" in which we live. Mental health disciplines and the practice of psychotherapy, the present-day heirs of the psychoanalytic movement, have become ever-growing social institutions in our society, being applied to an expanding array of social problems, not the least of which is family abuse. Families and family relations, "dysfunctional" or otherwise, have thus become the subject of extraordinary popular and professional interest. As reflected in the comments of luminaries in the field, by the late 1970s and early 1980s the public and professional communities alike were paying sober attention to the issue of child sexual abuse (Finkelhor, 1992; Haugaard & Repucci, 1988). Advocates and activists were speaking out, funding for research was more available, and an assortment of professionals from a variety of helping professions gave birth to this emerging field. Then a new Zeitgeist, one of skepticism about the rising number of allegations about sexual abuse, seems to be emerging in the mid-1990s.

How Big Is the Problem?

How big is the problem of child sexual abuse? This leads us into an area that can be confusing and frustrating for students. We've heard lots in the media and the professional literature about the extent of child sexual abuse. Estimates of how many girls and boys are victimized abound. When students start to examine the issue, however, they soon learn that it's not so simple. Studies differ in their research methods, the population they sample, and how they define abuse. As a consequence, they often arrive at different results—a predicament that social scientists call a *reliability* problem. By its very nature, child sexual abuse is an activity that is perpetrated in secret, and this makes it tough to get a true reading of its magnitude. Interpreting the research requires the ability to accept a certain amount of ambiguity while at the same time asking the hard questions that might ultimately lead to greater understanding. The hope is that, as a result of ongoing research, we will eventually have knowledge that is both *reliable* and *valid*.

In an effort to gain an understanding about the extent of the child sexual abuse problem, professionals in the field sometimes like to explain their attempts to measure the problem by using the analogy of the iceberg. From a distance we might not even see the tip of an iceberg, but the further down below the water level we go, the better we see its true extent (see Figure 4-1). The part of the iceberg that is above water can be thought of as the known and reported cases. Just below this is an area that represents known abuse that doesn't show up in official statistics. Perhaps the largest area of the iceberg relates to abuse that is known only by the victims and perpetrators. Scholars point out that, for a long time, we thought child sexual abuse was a rare occurrence; but when we began hearing quotes like, "One in four girls

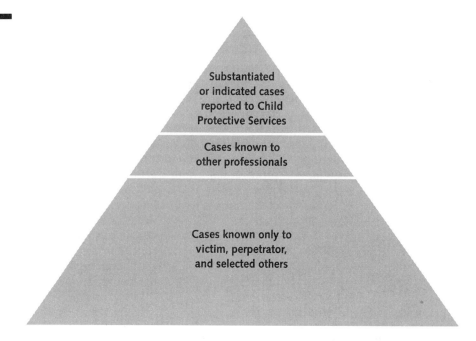

FIGURE 4-1
The Child
Sexual Abuse
Iceberg

and one in nine boys will be sexually victimized," we opened our eyes with shock at the apparent scope of the problem. It was as if we awoke in the middle of a deep sleep to the jolt of striking our proverbial iceberg.

Studying this iceberg is fraught with challenges (Peters, et al., 1986) and is best approached with respect. Researchers tell us it's difficult to do and the results need to be evaluated carefully. As we've already said, definitions of abuse, the populations sampled, and the methods of research vary from study to study and investigator to investigator. It is now fairly well understood that these differences do influence the results of the research (Finkelhor et al., 1990; Finkelhor, 1994).

Incidence

The "tip of the iceberg" is what we can actually see. As discussed in Chapter 1, new cases reported each year are referred to as the *incidence*. Until 1986 the American Humane Association published the official summary of reported abuse under contract with the government (Peters et al., 1986). After that, child protective reports from all states were reported to the National Center on Child Abuse and Neglect (NCCAN) and entered into the National Child Abuse and Neglect Data System (NCANDS). Congress eliminated funding for NCCAN in the 1995 session, and at this writing its future is uncertain. As summarized by NCCAN (1995a, 1995b), there were slightly more than 1 million **substantiated** or **indicated** cases of abuse in 1993, and these estimates suggest that about 14% of these cases involved child sexual abuse. Based on this information, we can estimate there were about 140,000 substantiated or indicated cases of child sexual abuse reported in 1993. *Substantiated* cases are those cases in which local authorities feel they have sufficient information to conclude that abuse has occurred. *Indicated* cases are those in which local authorities have strong reason to suspect that the abuse has actually occurred but lack sufficient evidence to justify making a determination that it is substantiated. The substantiated and indicated reports of child sexual abuse represent the tip of our iceberg. Most researchers now believe that incidence reports represent just a fraction of the number of actual cases. We know from studies of adults that victims of abuse are often reluctant to report their abuse (Finkelhor, et al., 1990). The vast majority of adult survivors indicate they never told anyone, let alone a member of the professional community. Simply stated, child victims of sexual abuse may not feel they can disclose for many reasons. Children who are currently experiencing child sexual abuse at the hands of an adult are likely to be either under the influence of these adults or else dependent upon them for their physical or emotional needs. For obvious reasons, we can't expect offenders to voluntarily come forward. Others, even professionals, who know of the abuse, despite mandatory reporting laws, are also sometimes reluctant to report it.

Prevalence

Going to a deeper level of our metaphorical iceberg, just below the water line, we can try to get at those cases that are known to professionals but that failed to make it into the official statistics. The National Incidence Studies (NCCAN, 1981; 1988) attempt to do precisely this, measuring cases known to professionals in addition to the reported cases. Using a representative sample of 29 counties throughout the United States, results from the second National Incidence Study estimate about 2.5 cases of known child sexual abuse per 1000 children (Landes et al., 1993). If we apply these rates to the population of children under 18 years of age, we should be able to make a somewhat up-to-date projection about known cases. Since there are approximately 67,500,000 children under 18 in the United States, we can project that there were in the neighborhood of 168,750 known cases.

Incidence figures and estimates of known cases still don't give us a picture of the entire iceberg. This leads us to our next question: "How, then, do we estimate the true extent of child sexual abuse?" We know that victims often don't tell until much later, if ever, and offenders rarely come forward. So, if we can't sample the population of children currently being victimized, what do we do? One way is to develop **prevalence estimates** by sampling the adult population and asking them about experiences of sexual abuse in their childhoods.

There are several well-known studies that take this tack, but before we look at them, a few cautionary words are in order. First of all, prevalence rates among the current generation of children may be different from times past. Second, retrospective studies, as mentioned previously, have problems because of distortions that can occur in memory, and it is unfeasible to try to independently verify such recollections. This situation, coupled with the variables in research methodology, produces a range of estimates. This doesn't imply that one researcher's results negate the others; hopefully, it simply reflects on the current state of the art, the complexity of the task, and the inherent difficulties in even attempting to do prevalence estimates.

That often quoted phrase, "One in four girls and one in nine boys will be sexually abused," is based on a prevalence estimate. In order to know how reliable and valid such estimates are, we have to know where they come from. David Finkelhor is regarded as one of the most credible authorities in the field, and he and his associates are known for both the clarity of their work and their integrity. They point out that the one-in-four statistic was repeated so often that we accepted it as fact, even though we'd forgotten where it had come from (Peters et al., 1986). They suggest that the origins of this particular statistic can probably be traced to the famous Kinsey study (Kinsey et al., 1953) of women's sexual experiences (Peters et al., 1986). With regard to the sexual abuse question, the Kinsey study merely asked respondents if they had ever been approached by or had sexual contact with an adult male before reaching adolescence. About 24% of their respondents answered the question "yes," hence, the famous one-in-four statistic.

Prevalence estimates will vary depending on how sexual abuse is defined. The definition used in the Kinsey survey is very broad indeed; it could include everything from being inappropriately touched with clothes on to rape. Over 50% of these cases involved only contact with an exhibitionist. Other more recent studies approach the question in a similar way, yet usually try to operationalize their definitions and be more specific.

Finkelhor (1979) developed criteria for defining child sexual abuse that is often used by other researchers who attempt to replicate his work. He categorizes an act as child sexual abuse if any sexual contact occurs: (1) between a child less than 12 years old and someone at least 5 years older or (2) between an adolescent 13 years old or older and a person at least 10 years older. Using this definition, his study found that about 19% of women and 9% of men experienced some form of sexual abuse. Approximately 20% of the cases involved noncontact types of abuse, either exposure to an exhibitionist or being solicited. If these experiences were excluded, 15% of women could be considered to have been victims. We should note that this study was based on a sample of 796 male and female college students. A number of other studies based on college student samples have also been done. Those reviewed by Hauggard and Repucci (1988) get rates of abuse that range from 7.7 to 22% for females and 3.1 to 5% for males. The low figures seem much less dramatic than our one-in-four figure, yet even these are not small in terms of the absolute number of people who have been affected. If we apply even the most conservative prevalence estimates to the U.S. population, we can project that nearly 10 million females and almost 400,000 males who live in this country have been sexually abused.

The prevalence estimates based on college samples intuitively seem low. Briere (1992) comments that the prevalence rate is generally considered to be 20 to 30% for women and about half that for men. One of the criticisms of studies that use college samples is that they aren't representative of the population as a whole. Since we believe child sexual abuse can have an impact on cognitive, emotional, and social development, it's not unreasonable to speculate that it could interfere with a person's ability to succeed in school and go on to college. If this is the case, we would expect smaller numbers of sexual abuse victims on college campuses.

Some studies with noncollege samples do yield higher prevalence rates. Diana Russell did one study, now regarded as a classic, using a random sample of over 900 adult women in San Francisco (Russell, 1983). Her results indicated that about 38% of these urban women had experienced some form of sexual abuse (involving actual contact) by the time they were 18 years old. Finkelhor (1984b) did a study based on a representative sample in Boston. The rates of sexual abuse in this study, however, were nowhere near as high as those reported by Russell; about 15% of women and 6% of men had experienced sexual abuse. As you can see, there's a fairly widespread difference in the results of these two studies, both of which were conducted in large metropolitan areas. One possible explanation is that the rates for Boston and San Francisco are truly different; another is that their results were influenced by the methods they used or how they defined child sexual abuse. According to Finkelhor (1984a), Russell's questionnaire was more extensive, and there seems to be some evidence that such questionnaires are more likely to jar recognition. Another factor, however, is again one of definition. Russell's study defined acts as sexually abusive even if perpetrated by peers. Finkelhor's definition, on the other hand, required that there be at least a five-year age span (ten years if the victim was at least 13) and that the individual considered the act abusive. Using a nationally representative sample, Finkelhor and colleagues (Finkelhor, et al., 1990) conducted a survey using a broad definition of sexual abuse based on the respondent's perception and four broad screening questions. The results of this study suggest that as many as 27% of females and 16% of males experience sexual abuse. Interestingly, it also found much higher rates on the West coast than in the East, possibly helping to explain the gulf between the results of earlier studies.

Relevance of incidence and prevalence estimates

"Okay," you might be saying, "if the very figures researchers have come up with differ and need to be qualified, what does this say about our level of knowledge?" What it might be saying is that we don't yet have all the answers. Perhaps we never will. As Finkelhor (1984a) reminds us, sexual abuse by its very nature is hard to study. When we try to do prevalence estimates, we are, after all, trying to fathom that portion of our iceberg that only victims and perpetrators often know about. Researchers are approaching the problem from a variety of angles, using different definitions, different methods, and different samples. Perhaps this furthers the cause of social science. If all researchers approached it the same way, we would have more consistency, but we might not learn as much. Rather than try to pin down a specific number, Finkelhor suggests that, at least for now, we should think in terms of ranges. We can't say with certainty that one in four girls or one in ten boys, for example, will be sexually abused; we probably can say, however, if current trends continue, that we project between 8 to 38% of girls and 4 to 15% of boys may be abused by the time they are 18. While this range seems to be broad, it is also consistent with the international figures that are now beginning to come in. Finkelhor (1994), in a review of a number of studies done in other countries, found ranges that are very consistent with those reviewed here for the United States.

THE VICTIMS

Numbers seem to depersonalize a subject as grave as child sexual abuse, and they certainly don't tell the whole story. Most students are somewhat curious about the statistics, but what they usually want to know about are the people involved, especially the victims. Mere statistics associated with incidence reports or prevalence rates just don't seem to help when it comes to understanding the victims at a personal level.

Basic Information about Victimization

At this point in the chapter, we will begin to concern ourselves with understanding victims, or survivors, of child sexual abuse. We will examine the impact of a number of factors on victims, including the relationship between victim and perpetrator, the extent of abuse, and the frequency of abuse. But we first need to take care of some unfinished business. In order to speak more meaningfully, we need a working definition of child sexual abuse. It might also be helpful at this point to take a brief look at a few recent statistics that describe the range of sexually abusive behavior imposed on children and who the perpetrators are in relationship to the victims, and to attempt to get a better idea about the frequency of occurrence once a child becomes the object of abuse.

Definition of child sexual abuse

While definitions of abuse vary, including those in studies cited in this text, it might still be helpful to have a working definition of child sexual abuse here. While children can be tricked into **cooperating** with sexual acts, they can never truly **consent** to such acts, because an informed consent implies that the child has an understanding of the consequences. All sexual contact between a child and an adult is therefore defined as child sexual abuse. It is slightly more complicated to define sexual abuse when it involves children who engage in sexual activity with other children. Recognizing that some experimentation may be normal, an age difference of at least five years, while arbitrary, is now generally accepted as the demarcation line to differentiate experimental activity from abuse (Monteleone et al., 1994). If force or intimidation is used, however, it should always be considered abuse regardless of the age difference. (Finkelhor, 1985, cited in Landes et al., 1993).

Severity of abuse

Child sexual abuse exists on a continuum that varies considerably. It involves the abuse of a position of responsibility, or status as an older person, and the use of the child in order to satisfy the older person's sexual and power needs. Behaviors that are considered sexually abusive range from exposing private parts and viewing the child in a state of undress to **fondling, fellatio** (oral contact with the male genitalia), **cunnilingus** (oral contact with the female genitalia), **interfemural intercourse** (often called *dry intercourse*—rubbing the penis between the legs or buttocks without penetrating a body opening), vaginal or anal **intercourse**, inserting objects in body parts, acts of mutilation, and **sexual exploitation** (involving the child in pornography or prostitution) all the way to **sadistic abuse** or torture, **ritualistic abuse** (cult-inflicted abuse), and even murder. For discussion about the Satanic ritual abuse controversy, see Box 4-1.

Let's take a look at a summary breakdown of types of abusive activity reported in a recent national study (see Finkelhor et al., 1990, Table 1, for raw percentages by types of activity). This study is based on a representative national sample; the reader needs to interpret these statistics carefully, however, because the authors themselves acknowledge that the definitions for their screening questions were very broad. The authors also comment that, while their results in most areas are consistent with previous studies, the figures for intercourse or attempted intercourse are much higher than in other studies, and that this is probably a result of the broadness of definition. For females, the results suggest that about 51% of the abuse involved fondling, about 38% actual or attempted intercourse, 8% exhibitionism, and very small amounts of other kinds of abuse. For males, the results of this same study suggest that about 60% involved actual or attempted intercourse, 28% fondling, and 6% exhibitionism. The use of force was reported by about 19% of the females and 15% of the males (see Finkelhor et al., 1990, Table 4). Other very serious forms of child sexual abuse, such as stranger abductions and the use of children in pornography and prostitution, seem much less well documented (Landes et al., 1993). They appear to be more rare or difficult to research and thus may be less likely to show up in studies such as that of Finkelhor and his colleagues (1990). Citing estimates of the Office of Juvenile Justice and Delinquency Prevention, Landes et al. (1993) estimate that between 52 and 158 children are abducted by strangers each year.

BOX 4-1   The Satanic Ritualistic Abuse Controversy

Ritualistic abuse becomes a "hot" issue. While ritualistic abuse, and especially Satanic ritual abuse, has become a hot issue, complete with talk show attention, it is not without controversy. On one side of the debate, mental health professionals report dramatic accounts of Satanic ritual abuse (SRA) of their clients (Gould & Cozolino, 1992; Shaffer & Cozolino, 1992).

The crux of the controversy. On the other side of the debate, critics raise concerns that therapists may actually be creating a climate of hysteria, one in which mental health professionals actually manufacture cases of ritualistic abuse that never existed before their clients came in for therapy. Sherrill Mulhern (1994) looks at this phenomenon from a social and historical perspective and suggests that there are some striking similarities between the modern-day campaign, which alleges that there is a sizable Satanic conspiracy, and the demonic hysteria and witch hunts of centuries ago. Jeffrey Victor (1992) likens what has been happening to a "moral crusade," one waged by some segments of the mental health field, some fundamentalist clergy, a few law enforcement Satan hunters, and a few members of anticult volunteer organizations.

A case example. To demonstrate what can happen when such a crusade builds up steam, Victor (1992) profiles a case that occurred in England after social service personnel participated in some ritualistic abuse training sponsored by their American counterparts. The story began when a six-year-old boy told his teachers stories involving black magic and the killing of babies. Child Protective Services intervened, placed the children in foster care, and the police conducted an investigation. When the case reached the courts, there was no evidence to support the allegations. The judge returned the children and criticized the social service department and police for unnecessarily traumatizing them.

Commonalities of reports and lack of objective evidence. To support their case, those who say that reports of Satanic ritualistic abuse are real point out that cases from diverse locations tend to be remarkably similar (Shaffer & Cozolino, 1992) and are consistent with the very severe nature of the symptoms of their clients. Critics argue that this may have resulted because of contact between therapists who have attended "trainings" and workshops sponsored by the very moral crusaders who started the commotion in the first place (Lanning, 1991; Victor, 1992). While the debate has not been settled, those who say that allegations of widespread Satanic ritualistic abuse are real are faced with some significant problems. One law enforcement veteran says he initially tended to believe these reports but says that the utter lack of physical evidence, the difficulty in committing a large-scale conspiracy crime, and human nature (natural intergroup conflicts that arise in any organization) make this possibility extremely unlikely (Lanning, 1991). An extremely well-regarded expert on trauma abuse recovery and treating clients with dissociative disorders agrees (Putnam, 1991).

Relationship between
victim and perpetrator

Finkelhor's research (see Finkelhor et al., 1990, Table 3) also suggests that, for both males and females, the victims regarded their perpetrators as being authority figures in 49% of the cases and the offender was in some way known to them in 60% of the cases. Finkelhor suggests that friends represented 13% of perpetrators of boys and 85% of girls, cousins 5% for both males and females, uncles 5% for males and 14% for females, and siblings in 1% of cases for males and 2% for females. Grandparents, stepparents, and parents were not reported by the males in this national study as being sexual abusers, but females reported that grandparents were perpetrators in 2% of cases, stepparents 3%, and biological parents 3%.

Frequency of abuse over time

If the Finkelhor research is representative (see Finkelhor, et al., 1990, Table 3), the vast majority of sexual abuse involves single incidents—73% of the cases involving boys and 64% of those involving girls. In 17% of cases involving boys the abuse went on between one month and one year; for girls, the figure was 19%. Sexual abuse persisted for more than a year in 8% of the cases involving male victims and in 11% of those involving female victims.

Impact of Child Sexual Abuse on Victims

Child sexual abuse is an experience that can have a profound impact, but survivors respond in diverse ways. Some function at extremely high levels, excelling in professions or other important areas. The status, prestige, and money associated with professional success can be a way of compensating or can simply be a way of being and feeling competent. Others respond differently, perhaps developing chemical dependency problems or having other kinds of severe adjustment difficulties. That this diversity exists seems fairly clear; what we don't know, with any reasonable degree of certainty, is why some individuals have less obvious problems and go on to lead highly productive and creative lives, while others seem to develop very obvious and crippling difficulties. (See Box 4-2.)

In medicine and psychiatry, healers look for observable signs of illness or injury and also pay attention to the symptoms or complaints of the patient or sufferer. Physical signs and symptoms of child sexual abuse are often few and far between, however; so we'll be focusing on the emotional, behavioral, and psychological signs and symptoms often associated with abuse.

Please take note that, while abuse can influence the development of certain signs and symptoms, other causes can account for these signs and

BOX 4-2 The Stories of Susan & Hilda

The following case examples have been significantly changed in order to protect the identities of the people we'll call Susan and Hilda.

Susan is a 40-year-old woman of Scottish origin who sought counseling because of emotional problems she associated with her mother's recent death. She complained of feeling both angry at her mother and guilty. She said the anger was not because of her mother's dying but seemed to be related to the sexual abuse that was perpetrated by her stepfather for many years. She said she'd always somehow blamed her mother for bringing this man into her life and didn't realize that she'd not let go of it until after her mother's funeral. In all other areas in Susan's life, she is a success. She has three children and a husband who cares about her. She is a successful businesswoman who has advanced to management in a large insurance company.

Hilda is a 32-year-old Arizonan. She's married to a man she feels very good about but is generally troubled nevertheless. She has great difficulty being intimate with her husband, has mood swings, occasional problems with anger, is often confused about her life, and has been unable to hold down a job for any length of time. She has been in therapy for some time now, with a primary focus being on both her current adjustment and an extensive history of emotional, physical, and sexual abuse by her biological father. She loves her children and often expresses wonder that her husband and children remain committed to her despite her many emotional problems.

symptoms as well. They are not conclusive, or exclusive, indicators of sexual abuse alone. (We will discuss this issue in greater detail when we talk about indicators.) I should also mention that a fairly large number of victims fail to develop significant symptoms at all. With these cautions in mind, we can say that the range of signs and symptoms we might see, or which might be experienced by victims, is fairly extensive and could include the following (American Psychiatric Association, 1994; Briere, 1992; Browne & Finkelhor, 1985; Monteleone et al., 1994; Steinberg & Westhoff, 1988; Sgroi, 1982; Summit, 1983):

- Problems with concentration
- Nervousness
- Irritability, mood changes
- Withdrawal
- Wetting or soiling (especially in children who have been potty trained)
- Regressive behavior; e.g., thumb sucking

- Trouble getting along with others
- Problems with emotions (numbness or excitability)
- Personality changes
- Problems with depression or anxiety, sleep disturbance, loss of interest in things or activities that were previously enjoyable, change in eating patterns (loss of appetite or "nervous" eating, low energy)
- Posttraumatic symptoms (nightmares, fearful reactions possibly related to reexperiencing trauma, heightened physiological arousal [easily startled, jumpy], hypervigilence [seeming "on guard"])
- Impaired sense of self
- Distortions of thinking
- Relationship problems
- Avoiding certain kinds of situations or people
- Use of substances or activities to reduce stress
- Sexualized behavior; e.g., compulsive masturbating, precocious sex play (or, in adults, sex avoidance)
- Ritualized behavior such as bathing
- Feeling depressed or profoundly unhappy
- Self-mutilating behavior
- Suicidal thoughts or attempts
- Dissociation, possibly to include "multiple personalities"

The exact relationship between the experience of sexual abuse and how it affects its victims isn't well established (Haugaard & Repucci, 1988; Sheldrick, 1991). There are gaps and inconsistencies in our knowledge base (Finkelhor, 1986a; Haugaard & Repucci, 1988) as well as our professional orientations. More and more we are moving away from trying to explain phenomena like this with single-cause explanations. It may very well be that it's not just one factor that determines how a child sexual abuse victim will cope and adapt, but a combination of factors. Among the most common ones associated with impact and later adaptation include the following (Beitchman et al., 1991; Beitchman et al., 1992; Berliner, 1991; Browne & Finkelhor, 1986; Elliot & Briere, 1992, cited in Briere, 1992; Finkelhor, 1979; Fromuth & Burkhard, 1989; Haugaard & Repucci, 1988; Ziveney et al., 1988):

- Degree or level of abuse
- Frequency
- Closeness of the relationship between perpetrator and victim
- Amount of violence or threat used
- Length of time during which the abuse transpired
- Age of perpetrator

- Age of victim when abuse began
- Existence of social and emotional supports
- Family structure
- Psychological makeup and adjustment prior to abuse
- Reactions of others after disclosure
- Making a court appearance

While we don't know conclusively, some pioneers in the field suggest three factors that seem to be the most likely suspects when it comes to explaining the causes for the victims' trauma (Browne & Finkelhor, 1986; Berliner, 1991). These are the severity of the abuse, the degree of closeness in the relationship between the victim and perpetrator, and the length of time over which the abuse occurs. Earlier in the chapter, we reviewed some recent findings about what kinds of abusive behavior children experience, who the perpetrators are, and how long it lasts (Finkelhor et al., 1990). This study is consistent with others in saying that most abuse is not as extreme as intercourse, is seldom perpetrated by a father or stepfather, and is usually a single incident. When the abuse is extensive, is perpetrated by a person the child should be able to trust, and goes on for a long time, common sense seems to tell us that we can expect the impact to be much more devastating.

Indicators of Abuse

At an earlier time in the study of child sexual abuse, many so-called indicators of abuse would be listed to help with identification and even substantiation of abuse. Many of the indicators are similar to the list of victim impacts surveyed above. Unfortunately, as it turns out, what were often hailed as indicators of sexual abuse were really indicators of stress (Conte, 1991) or other disturbance, such as depression. While it seems true that many victims of child sexual abuse exhibit signs and symptoms of stress and other disturbances, it is also true that many children who are not sexually abused exhibit identical signs and symptoms. The strongest individual behavior signal of possible sexual abuse is age-inappropriate sexual knowledge and behavior. Children don't learn this from playing doctor. Indicators should not be taken as evidence that child sexual abuse has occurred; they can, however be a signal to observant adults that something might be wrong and worthy of general exploration. In a similar vein, there may be indicators of possible family dysfunction (Satir, 1988): an arbitrary or rigid rule system that does not respect the individuals under it; communication that is dishonest, vague, and indirect; lack of respect for the self-worth of family members; and lack of social connections outside the family. If there are problems in these areas, it might mean there's a problem. It then becomes important to further explore what this might mean. Perhaps the strongest family signal of possible abuse is excessive jealousy on the part of a male caretaker about the social or dating behavior of a child in the family. Sexually abusive parents sometimes become quite possessive.

MODELS OF VICTIMOLOGY AND EMERGING TRENDS

When we talk about signs and symptoms, we are operating from within a particular human service model, or framework, that professionals often refer to as the medical model. Maybe you've already heard the term. This is a very well established and respected framework, based on medical principles, that traces its roots in psychiatry as a branch of medicine through Freud and before. The model has some advantages, as well as some potential pitfalls. One of the pitfalls is that, by accepting a medical framework, clinicians might fall into treating clients as if they are "ill," forgetting that the illness is connected to living and breathing human beings. To some degree, this overemphasis on illness, or **pathology,** is understandable, since the mental health field deals with some very debilitating problems, and it's easy to get bogged down. It doesn't, however, always serve our clients well—victims of abuse who are likely to have already suffered blows to their sense of self. In this section we'll be exploring several models of **victimology,** or models that attempt to understand victims and hopefully find ways to be of real help. Some of the ideas reviewed are new to the field, and others have been around for a while. You'll probably notice that certain illness-oriented terms, such as **disorder** and **syndrome,** weave themselves into the fabric of various models. This is part of our **culture of helping.** I also ask you to keep in mind that, just because a model has been developed, it doesn't necessarily mean the model should be taken as absolute fact. To do this is to **reify** it, that is, to turn an idea into a truth. Let's face it, some models do a better job representing reality than others. Time is the ultimate test.

The Medical Model

The signs and symptoms we discussed previously represent the first stage of intervention by physicians—diagnosis. Let's take the example of a private medical practice. If you had an ailment of some kind, you might go see your family doctor. Any physician would be interested not only in the presenting signs and symptoms of your ailment, perhaps developing a "problem list," but also in having a full medical history. Once all this is done, the physician organizes the information and develops a diagnosis that would relate to a specific illness, disease, or injury. If the physician is very sure about what's wrong, he or she might make an outright diagnosis. If not quite so sure, the physician may make a provisional diagnosis and seek to validate it in an ongoing process that could involve monitoring or further testing. The treatment, or intervention, will correspond to the diagnosis, along accepted lines. Much as physicians would be asked to evaluate for suspected child physical abuse, mental health professionals are asked to render opinions about the signs and symptoms that suspected child sexual abuse victims present and whether or not they are consistent with abuse.

Psychiatric Diagnosis

The accepted "authoritative work" when it comes to diagnosis in psychiatry is the *Diagnostic and Statistical Manual,* fourth edition (American Psychiatric Association, 1994). Beginning with the publication of the third edition of the manual in 1980, efforts were made to objectively describe each disorder according to recognized patterns of signs and symptoms, without reference to any particular theoretical orientation. The fourth edition (known as the DSM-IV) does not contain any specific diagnosis for sexual abuse victimization, though it does provide a way to "code" and include this experience. While the clinical experience of many mental health professionals suggests that severe and catastrophic childhood experiences, such as child sexual abuse, can contribute to the development of specific **mental disorders**, the DSM-IV does not provide for a way of classifying specific abuse-related disorders. Many patients do, however, have sufficient symptoms to warrant a diagnosis. Now we will briefly summarize some of the most common disorders diagnosed in persons who have experienced child sexual abuse and other forms of severe childhood psychological trauma. The criteria for diagnosing each of them is based on the DSM-IV.

Posttraumatic stress disorder

Posttraumatic stress disorder is a recognized disorder caused by exposure to situations that would be experienced as traumatic by almost anyone. Posttraumatic stress disorder, or PTSD, is a disorder that didn't make the *Diagnostic and Statistical Manual* until the third edition arrived on the scene in 1980. It was originally used to describe disturbance among a large number of Vietnam veterans, who seemed to suffer from a number of related symptoms connected with their wartime experiences. Since then, it has come to be applied to people who develop symptoms in response to other traumatic experiences, such as auto accidents, torture, kidnapping, and sexual abuse. In addition to a **traumagenic** event, symptoms include **intrusive reexperiencing** (through such things as flashbacks and nightmares), **avoidance** of events, situations, or people that trigger the reexperiencing, and **hyperarousal** (vigilant scanning of the environment, sleep disturbance, jumpiness, and so on). The symptoms must last more than a month and may be of short duration (less than three months), chronic (more than three months), or have delayed onset.

Acute stress disorder

According to the DSM-IV, acute stress disorder is a disorder in which the person develops anxiety, dissociation, or other symptoms that occur within one month of exposure to one of the stressors associated with posttraumatic stress disorder. The factor that distinguishes acute stress disorder from PTSD is that it surfaces within four weeks of the event and persists for no longer than four weeks. If symptoms persist for longer than four weeks, the DSM-IV indicates that diagnosis for PTSD should be considered. One other feature of this diagnosis that differs from PTSD is the presence of **dissociative symptoms**, whereby a person separates, or splits away, from experience. They can include numbing, detachment, absence of emotional responsiveness, reduction of awareness, a feeling that an experience isn't real, a feeling of personal detachment, and amnesia about important aspects of the trauma. (It should be noted that, just because dissociative symptoms are not included within the criteria for PTSD, it does not mean that persons with PTSD don't also have dissociative symptoms.)

Dissociative disorders

There is an entire class of disorders called the **dissociative disorders.** Rather than to catalog each of them separately, I'd like to survey them as a group. According to the DSM-IV, "The essential feature of the Dissociative Disorders is a disruption in the usually integrated functions of consciousness, memory, identity, or perception of the environment."

Perhaps the most extreme, and famous, form of dissociative disorder is called **dissociative identity disorder.** Formerly known as **multiple personality disorder**, it involves the development of a number of distinct, autonomous or semiautonomous personalities. As with other forms of dissociation, it develops as an attempt to cope with overpowering stress and trauma and can be seen as a way to psychologically manage extreme levels of anxiety. Dissociative identity disorder is now well recognized as being closely linked to extreme forms of child sexual abuse. Some authorities suggest that as many as 90% of people diagnosed with this disorder have experienced extreme forms of child abuse, invariably involving sexual abuse. (Later in this chapter, we'll be looking at a case example and discussing it in more depth.)

Other dissociative disorders include **dissociative amnesia** (loss of memory, usually about traumatic events, too extensive to be normal forgetfulness), **depersonalization disorder** (chronic feeling of being separated from one's mind or body, but having normal awareness of reality), and **dissociative fugue** (sudden travel away from home, confusion about identity, and loss of memory about one's past).

Dissociative disorders seem to be related to **hysterical neuroses**, a term first coined by Freud to describe such phenomena as the development of physical symptoms in response to trauma. In the field of psychiatry, this was officially classified as "Conversion Disorder, Dissociative Type" right up to the present time, and what are now called dissociative disorders seem to be closely related in important ways. In fact, dissociative disorders were called "Conversion Disorders, Dissociative Type" for a brief period of time, which points to how closely related these two phenomena were once thought to be.

Mood disorders

Mood disorders span a range that runs from depression to mania. Many people have at least a commonsense notion of what **depression** is. Clinically, a **major depressive episode** includes a number of signs and symptoms we refer to as **vegetative symptoms.** Having already read about the major signs and symptoms associated with child sexual abuse, you will probably recognize many of the symptoms on this list. They include the following: depressed mood, loss of ability to experience pleasure and diminished interest in activities, appetite changes (usually involving weight loss but could entail weight gain), sleep disturbance (inability to sleep or constant sleeping), fidgetiness or dulling of psychomotor responses (lack of body movement), fatigue and loss of energy, feelings of worthlessness or guilt, inability to think and concentrate, ongoing thoughts of death, and suicidal thoughts (American Psychiatric Association, 1994). In order to qualify for diagnosis, the symptoms must cause clinically significant distress or impairment that cannot be accounted for by other disorders.

A **manic episode** is at the other end of the continuum. It is characterized by a time when there is an abnormally "elevated, expansive, or irritable mood" (American Psychiatric Association, 1994). Symptoms include inflated self-esteem or **grandiosity,** decreased need for sleep, talkativeness or **pressured speech,** racing thoughts or **flight of ideas, distractibility** (attention easily diverted), increased goal-directed activity or **psychomotor agitation,** and excessive involvement in risky, pleasurable activities (e.g., binge buying, promiscuity, foolish investments, gambling). As is also the case with depressive episodes, the manic episode must be severe enough to cause significant impairment and must not be caused by other factors (American Psychiatric Association, 1994).

If an individual meets the criteria of diagnosis for a depressive episode at least once, they are said to have a **major depressive disorder.** Many of us are familiar with the term *manic-depressive illness,* which refers to a disorder in which the person experiences extreme shifts in mood, from depressed to elated or agitated. The American Psychiatric Association (1994) no longer uses this term. Persons who meet the criteria for a manic episode at least once may meet criteria for **Bipolar I disorder,** which usually occurs alternately with major depressive episodes. Mental health professionals diagnose **Bipolar II disorder** when the person has had a hypomanic episode (less severe than a full manic episode). Disorders that are less severe than either major depressive disorder or bipolar I and II disorders include **dysthymic disorder** (a low-grade chronic depression) and **cyclothymic disorder** (a mood swing disorder less severe than a bipolar disorder). It is fairly common to find a large number of abuse survivors among patients who have mood disorder diagnoses. Symptoms associated with depression are one of the most commonly associated kinds of mental health problems reported by survivors of all kinds of abuse. If you refer to the long list of signs and symptoms associated with victim impact outlined earlier in the chapter, you will find that many symptoms appear on that list as well as in the diagnostic criteria for mood disorders, especially those associated with depression.

Personality disorders

The **personality disorders** are a category of mental disorders that relate to patterns of personality characteristics that are inflexible and maladaptive (American Psychiatric Association, 1994). Important psychiatric authority suggests that the personality disorders probably develop in childhood and adolescence as a response to conditions growing up (Perry & Vaillant, 1989). Perry and Vaillant (1989) suggest that the behaviors associated with the personality disorders are ways of trying to cope with or adapt to overpowering and dysfunctional life circumstances. Because abuse is such a powerful environmental condition, it is a suspect in explaining the development of personality disorders among persons who were abused. The attempts at coping work to some degree but become ingrained and rigid patterns over time. When individuals enter adulthood, they carry these same behaviors with them, where they are not appropriate. Whereas the behaviors were once adaptive, they are now maladaptive because they interfere with the person's adjustment. Because the symptoms are perceived by the individual as adaptive, and a means of coping, they are not experienced as unpleasant. Others who come in social contact with the person, however, often experience their behavior as disagreeable. When signs or symptoms of disorder are not experienced by the individual as unpleasant, they are referred to as **ego syntonic**. This is in contrast to **ego dystonic** symptoms, which are experienced as unpleasant. Persons with personality disorders do not experience their primary personality disorder traits as ego dystonic, but they do experience the social consequences of their behavior, including rejection and isolation, as unpleasant. Many professionals believe that persons with personality disorders, first of all, don't go to therapy, and if they do, they are unmotivated to change because the symptoms are ego syntonic.

Quite a high number of clinicians who work with abuse survivors report behaviors that are quite consistent with those associated with various personality disorders. Vice versa, clinicians who work with personality disorders indicate a high rate of abuse among their patients.

There are several specific personality disorders, with different types of symptoms. The personality disorder most often associated with prior abuse is the **borderline personality disorder**, which is characterized by unstable emotionality and anger, black-white thinking, unstable and intense interpersonal relationships, identity confusion and disturbance, impulsivity, suicidal and self-mutilating behavior, feelings of emptiness, and temporary periods of paranoid ideation or dissociation in response to stress.

Diagnostic Labeling and Child Sexual Abuse

The brief reviews above are not intended to cover all of the possible psychiatric diagnoses that might be associated with abuse. They are simply the most common. The clinical data seem to be fairly strong for a connection between child sexual abuse and the dissociative disorders. While it seems that many victims of abuse suffer from depressive symptoms and many others suffer from PTSD, a clear-cut, cause-and-effect relationship has not been established. Recent research is inconclusive about the connection between child sexual abuse and any specific diagnoses or a potentially new diagnosis that might conceivably be called something like *post sexual abuse syndrome* (Beichman et al., 1992). Clinicians should probably continue to diagnose patients with the diagnostic classifications that are appropriate to their signs and symptoms. We should not assume that all abuse victims should be classified with a particular diagnosis (or any diagnosis, for that matter) unless it is justified by their signs and symptoms. Clearly, however, a disproportionately high number of patients in **clinical samples,** or that group of people who are being seen in mental health settings, have been sexually abused.

A criticism of a diagnostic model of understanding victims is that, by focusing on diagnosis, we imply that people who have been victimized are "ill" or "sick." While sometimes patients experience relief at having a name to put on their troubles, labels can also have a negative effect. Sociologists tell us that, when individuals are labeled, they tend to behave in ways that are consistent with the label they've been given. Both the labels, *ill* and *sick,* have negative connotations. When considering a diagnostic, medical model I think we want to consider both the possible relief for the individual that can come from getting an explanation as well as the stigmatization, or potential negative impact on self-esteem, that the label can bring.

The Four-Factor Traumagenic Model

One of the best-known models for thinking about the impact of child sexual abuse is the **four-factor traumagenic model** developed by Finkelhor and Browne (1986). It's very different from psychiatric diagnosis in that the model isn't so interested in diagnosing, or labeling, clusters of signs and symptoms as it is in trying to understand the **dynamics,** or processes, involved.

Finkelhor and Browne identify four factors that they believe are the keys to understanding the impact of child sexual abuse on victims:

- Traumatic sexualization
- Betrayal
- Powerlessness
- Stigmatization

They concede that the model could be applied to other kinds of trauma, but suggest that it is the distinctive combination of these four factors that makes the impact of child sexual abuse unique. By applying the four-factor model to specific cases, they say, the model can be used to help explain what's going on and possibly assist in developing a better treatment plan.*

Traumatic sexualization refers to the sexualization that occurs in response to the sexual abuse. As a result of being **groomed** into participating in sexual activity, what happens to the child's sexuality? Finkelhor and Browne suggest that in such cases where the child is more active in the abuse, the child may become sexualized beyond his or her developmental maturity. This might explain why some children have an inappropriately advanced knowledge of sexual matters or attempt to engage other children in such sophisticated forms of sexual behavior as oral sex. Other children might try to avoid sex and sexuality altogether because of the fear and trauma they associate with it. While

---

*Adapted, with permission, from "The Traumatic Impact of Child Sexual Abuse," by D. Finkelhor and A. Browne, 1986, *American Journal of Orthopsychiatry, 55,* 530–541. Copyright © 1986 American Orthopsychiatric Association, Inc.

seemingly the flip side of the coin, it's the same coin. As adults, traumatic sexualization might help explain both the reported promiscuity of some survivors and the inability of other survivors to enjoy normal adult sexual relations.

Betrayal refers to the feelings and beliefs that result when important people betray the faith and trust the child places in them. For an innocent child, this experience teaches the lesson that you can't trust others, even people you should be able to trust. Finkelhor and Browne point out that victims experience betrayal not only from the perpetrators of abuse but by others. Once the abuse is disclosed, others sometimes cause further harm when they turn their backs on the victim, through not believing, blaming the child, or focusing on what the child has done.

Finkelhor and Browne suggest that *powerlessness* occurs when the child's will or ability to choose appropriately is taken away. This includes violation of the child's right to his or her own body and personal integrity. Through trickery, coercion, or force, the will of the perpetrator is imposed on the child. Once caught up in the process, the child is in a difficult place with no easy choices. This loss of personal integrity and ability to choose is worse when there is severe abusive behavior and fear.

Finkelhor and Browne use the term *stigmatization* in a way similar to our discussion of the term as a possible consequence of psychiatric diagnosis and labeling, but for them it also involves belief about the self based on the judgment of self and others. Even when disclosure has not occurred, the child is likely to have some kind of evaluation of what is going on and what the social norms are. The child may not feel able to seek clarification and guidance from adults because of the secrecy. Without that guidance and support, the child may become isolated and imagine all kinds of meaning about the self as a result of the sexualized relationship with the older person. When disclosure has been made, others may be less than empathic and sensitive to the significance of the child's plight. They may actually say and do things that make the victim acutely aware of his or her changed status and negatively affect the child's **self-efficacy**, or positive sense of self.

The four-factor traumagenic model is a conceptual model that is a way of thinking about and organizing what we think about child sexual abuse. Whether or not these are *the* four factors involved in the negative impact of child sexual abuse is a question for research, not one we have the answers to now. As the authors point out, however, this is an approach that makes sense at an intuitive level; it seems to be helpful in organizing our thoughts and beliefs and perhaps in assisting with future research and innovations in practice.

One group (Patten et al., 1989) has integrated the four-factor model with a PTSD conceptualization into a distinct approach to working with abuse victims. In their model, Patten and colleagues assume that the posttraumatic symptoms are actually necessary attempts to deal with one or more of the traumagenic factors identified by Finkelhor and Browne (1986). The treatment involves alternating the "processing" of whatever traumatic issue needs work with recuperative rest periods called *respite*. This process of working through the trauma proceeds through five treatment stages suggested by Figley (1985): (1) catastrophe, (2) relief and confusion, (3) avoidance, (4) reconsideration, and (5) adjustment.

Abuse-Related Accommodation:
An Emerging Model

Perhaps one of the most exciting developments in the area of family abuse is a shift in how we view its victims. In times past, many mental health professionals may have been guilty of **pathologizing** victims; in other words, excessively focusing on their "illness" or "dysfunction." At first blush this may seem like a small point, but just to bring it home, think of the most awful experience in your life and now imagine what it would be like if you and others defined who you are on the basis of that experience. Viewing the behavior and symptoms of survivors as adaptive is not something we've emphasized much in the past. It is, however, the perspective of a new generation of more client-oriented philosophies of victimology that are now emerging, such as that of John Briere (1992). Briere suggests that clinicians who pathologize their clients or deprive them of self-determination are unlikely to be especially helpful.

Briere (1992) proposes a philosophy of treatment intended to be more beneficial. A central principle is that we should think of the client as a **survivor**, not a victim. He points out that these are "individuals who have persevered despite often extreme childhood traumas and later abuse-related difficulties." This approach is more **phenomenological**—that is, centered on the person's own subjective experience of reality rather than the reality of outside experts. It assumes that survivors are striving for growth, and in this context, Briere regards the signs and symptoms of abuse as **functional**. In other words, what we've labeled as signs and symptoms of pathology are considered *functional* expressions of the survivor's attempts to accommodate, both to the past abuse itself and to the abuse-related problems that developed later. This is an important concept. By accepting it, Briere suggests, there are at least three implications for how we understand our clients: (1) their behavior is active and **pragmatic** (or practical) rather than passive and symptomatic; (2) because the behavior is functional, it is not easy to give up; and (3) because the behavior is an adaptation to real-life events, it can inform us about the client's past or current experience.

The coping mechanisms of clients can look very dysfunctional to us, but can make perfect sense to the survivor. Let's take a few examples: substance abuse, gambling, workaholism, fits of rage, promiscuity, self-destructive behavior, manipulativeness, dissociation, and amnesia. Substance abuse makes intuitive sense; if you feel bad, you can take a drug to self-medicate. Self-destructive behavior, like cutting your body with a razor blade or making a suicide attempt, doesn't make such obvious sense. Briere points out, however, that sometimes what a survivor is trying to do is to mask the unbearable emotional pain with bearable physical pain. For a survivor who has difficulty feeling at all, perhaps because of emotional numbing, cutting is a crude way to feel something. Numbing itself seems to be a natural and logical response. If you have unbearable emotional pain, what better way to deal with it than to numb it out or anesthetize yourself. Trauma-induced amnesia, or blocking of conscious memory, can be a way of avoiding having to deal with whatever has occurred. All the other types of behavior men-

More awareness about child sexual abuse can help give us the courage to deal with it.

tioned can, in a similar vein, "function" or "work" to protect the psyche of the individual involved.

In the next couple of paragraphs, we'll be looking at some examples. Rather than to operate from a diagnostic point of view, we'll try to focus primarily on problem behaviors.

Let's say we have a client who cuts on her arms with razor blades, threatens to commit suicide, and verbally attacks those who try to help her. Lest you think this is an unusual client, I assure you that this is the kind of client clinicians know only too well. Often the survivors of abuse, clients like this will tell you, if you listen, that the self-inflicted physical pain caused by the razor blade hurts less than the psychic injuries caused by years of abuse. Psychiatrically, such a person is often diagnosed with borderline personality disorder. This is a dreaded disorder for many mental health professionals because of the intensity of the problems and the high amount of energy and skill required to work with it.

Perhaps one of the most interesting strategies or adaptations is that of dissociation. As we discussed previously, *dissociation* is a psychological way of distancing the self from overwhelming emotional or psychological stress. Who among us has not pushed unpleasant thoughts or feelings out of consciousness as a way of coping? We can think of this as a mild form of dissociative response. An extreme form is identified as dissociative identity disorder in the DSM-IV. Formerly called multiple personality disorder, dissociative identity disorder is intriguing to just about anyone already fascinated with the mind. The phenomenon of multiple personalities is described in such popular books as *When Rabbit Howls, Sybil,* and *Three Faces of Eve.* While controversial, experts acknowledge valid cases of multiple personality as dramatic, and quite incredible. The phenomenon exemplifies

---

BOX 4-3   The Many Faces of Rachael

In the interest of confidentiality, the following case has been fictionalized to protect the identity of any dissociative patient, but it is based on phenomena observed in real cases.

Rachael is a 31-year-old African American woman who was referred to a mental health clinic near Ft. Benning, Georgia, after her release from a nearby psychiatric hospital where she had been for the previous six weeks. She explained that she'd had a "nervous breakdown," and was suicidal. As a result of therapy, it was learned that Rachael had been the victim of very extreme abuse, some of it sexual, that began when she was a very little girl. She had been molested by a number of people over the years, and once she was pushed over an embankment after a rape and left for dead.

After several weeks in therapy, Rachael's therapist noticed some very dramatic and remarkable mood shifts, some of which involved complete changes in personality. One day Rachael's mood shifted during the therapy session, and she acted surprised at being in the office. She denied that her name was Rachael, claiming to be Ezmirelda. After a period of time, and evaluation by other mental health professionals, Rachael was diagnosed as having what was then called multiple personality disorder. Therapy proceeded for several years and over sixty separate alter identities were documented and confirmed. Therapy was often difficult for Rachael, since it involved remembering things that were horrible when experienced the first time. Over time her various alters got to know one another, and while her life has never been easy, her "system" of personalities became better organized and she (that is, her core personality) eventually learned to function in most situations without calling up one of her alters. She has a family and wants others to know that she's "normal," except that she had learned to cope by creating other personalities to do some of the things in life that are difficult for her.

---

adaptation to extreme forms of abuse, usually sexual, which results in the creation of one or more "alter" personalities (American Psychiatric Association, 1994; Bryant et al., 1992; Phillips & Frederick, 1995; Putnam, 1989). Applying Briere's principle that the client's coping strategy can inform us of their experience, we would certainly assume that any trauma extreme enough to cause a person to split into more than one personality would be very powerful indeed. This seems to be borne out by clinicians who specialize in working with this kind of problem, who describe from their clinical cases the horror recounted by their clients in therapy.

As in the case of Rachael, outlined in Box 4-3, child sexual abuse can have a profound and life-changing effect on people's lives. What we can miss in a case such as this, however, is the significance of these symptoms. Developing numerous alter personalities might seem, on the face of it, abnormal or aberrant. Admittedly, it looks extreme, yet it can also demonstrate how remarkable are the ways that human beings adjust in order to cope with even the most horrifying childhood experiences. When we think about it, developing alter personalities, many of whom often have special skills and abilities, is an amazingly ingenious and creative adaptation to extraordinary life events.

To describe the process of how this happens, Briere suggests that abuse survivors adapt in three stages: (1) initial reactions to traumatization, (2) accommodation to ongoing abuse, and (3) long-term elaboration and secondary accommodation. The kinds of things included in stage 1, initial reactions, are things like traumatic stress reactions, changes in how the child goes through the stages of development, the experience of painful feelings, and changes in the way the child thinks. According to this model, these things occur because the trauma-producing event overpowers the individual's normal coping abilities. The trauma is greater than the individual's psychological resources and external supports (network of family, friends, and others). Traumatization and crisis results; but as the crisis subsides, the child enters stage 2—accommodation. During this stage, the child finds whatever ways possible to adapt in order to cope. According to Briere, the goal at this stage is to increase safety and/or decrease pain during victimization. During stage 3, long-term elaboration and secondary accommodation, the victim integrates the trauma as well as coping strategies and behaviors that help the child survive; however, these can get in the way of enjoying a more full life later on.

According to Briere (1992), abuse survivors can develop psychological problems in one or more of seven areas: (1) posttraumatic stress, (2) cognitive distortions or thought distortion, (3) altered emotionality, (4) dissociation, (5) impaired self-reference, (6) disturbed relatedness to others, and (7) avoidance. As you can see, most of these represent behaviors or problems that can be associated with specific disorders contained in the DSM-IV or that are included in other models. What the abuse-focused model advocated by Briere does is provide a coherent explanation in a model that makes intuitive sense.

Current State of the Art in Victimology

The abuse-related accommodation model sketched by Briere (1992), with its humane attitude toward survivors and its focus on the functional aspects of symptoms, represents a more parsimonious model and could be a harbinger of an "abuse-related accommodation disorder." While the scientific evidence to support a clear-cut relationship between abuse and existing disorders is lacking, more parsimonious models may assist with establishing better diagnostic criteria.

Curiously, the current state of the art when it comes to understanding victims seems to have come almost full circle—back to ideas similar to the ones Freud first proposed. We believe that children are subjected to sexual abuse at the hands of older people, that the abuse is sometimes severe, and that it can trigger traumatic reactions. Even at an intuitive level, this just makes common sense. Freud was interested in patients who developed physical impairments, such as blindness, because of trauma. Today, mental health professionals seem more interested in the relationship between abuse-induced trauma and an assortment of psychological reactions and adaptations. These can be as minor as sleep disturbance, irritability, and withdrawal; as severe as terrorizing flashbacks; and as extreme as the development of multiple identities within the same individual.

CHAPTER SUMMARY

We began this chapter by challenging our assumptions about sexual offenders, and trying to square the contrast between two types of offenders that exist in our midst: the sexual predator and the offender who is our grandfather, our neighbor, or just another kid at school. We explored how our perceptions may have helped us avoid having to deal with this issue and how the mental health field itself may have at one time turned its back on the issue because of its inability to face it. While we acknowledged how difficult it is to get accurate figures, we reviewed the most recent available figures about the number of new cases reported each year as well as prevalence estimates about the number of those who have been affected by child sexual abuse. In this regard we took note that, because child sexual abuse occurs in secret, it is very hard to get a true reading.

We also discussed issues related to both victims and offenders. When we talked about victims, we took a look at what the research indicates about who molests them, what they do, and how long they do it. Next we explored the ways in which victims have been affected by abuse. We learned that there are many possible effects of abuse and many people who, for unknown reasons, seem to avoid negative consequences. Indicators of abuse have always been of interest to those who want to identify victims so they can intervene, but we stressed that this must be approached with caution because so-called indicators of abuse are also indicators of stress, depression, or anxiety. For this reason, "false positives" are a real possibility. We reviewed several models that attempt to understand victims. One of these is the medical model, which tends to look at victims in terms of signs and symptoms; and in this regard, we summarized some of the most widely used diagnoses associated with victims. Two other models were also explored: the four-factor traumagenic model, and an emerging abuse-related accommodation model.

LEGAL AND ETHICAL CONCERNS:
CRITICAL THINKING QUESTIONS

1.   Child sexual abuse is a disturbing problem. While we may not want to deal with the issue. it is a reality we should probably come to grips with.

If you learned that a child you knew had been victimized, how do you think you should deal with it? If it happened last month? If it happened 20 years ago? If the suspected perpetrator was a family member or friend?

2.   A number of authors have commented that Freud may have altered his theories in response to professional, social, and political pressures. How should an aspiring professional balance the desire to be successful with a commitment to science and truth? How would you deal with it if you felt the truth conflicted with a popular view or trend?

3.   There is an old expression that goes like this: "There are liars, damn liars, and statistics." Researchers and professionals sometimes want to prove a point and use statistics to do it. What responsibilities do professionals have to accurately report statistics without slanting them? What if they feel passionately about the issue?

4.   Medical personnel and mental health professionals are often asked to confirm sexual abuse. What do you do if you do not feel able to give a competent opinion? Would you treat a request by the police differently than you would a request by a defense attorney? What obligations do you have to the victim? To society? To the accused?

5.   Allegations of child sexual abuse may trigger crises in the families of the victim and the accused (if it is a different family). How should a helper approach each?

6.   We now know that indicators of abuse are often really no more than indicators of disturbance. How should you handle a situation when such indicators are present and you suspect abuse?

7.   There are a number of models that can be used to understand and explain what happens to victims. If a colleague, or even another person you know, claimed that one point of view was the right one, how would you deal with the person?

8.   Psychiatric diagnoses are often given to victims of abuse because they have significant disturbance. What are the ethical considerations?

9.   In the past, mental health professionals have emphasized the problems of abuse survivors rather than their strengths. This has been called *pathologizing*. What do you think of this? How should we relate to abuse survivors?

_____

SUGGESTED ACTIVITIES

1.   Determine if your community has a unit in the police department and prosecutor's office that specializes in child sexual abuse cases.

2.   In your community, locate as much literature about sexual abuse as you can.

3.   Select at least one book on child sexual abuse and read it critically. Be willing to ask hard questions. What issues surface as you examine the work carefully?

REVIEW GUIDE

1.   Be able to discuss the reawakening in our society to the problem of child sexual abuse.

2.   Be able to discuss the issues of denial, professional denial, and societal denial of child sexual abuse.

3.   Discuss the development of Freudian concepts in relation to child sexual abuse. In this regard, be familiar with the following concepts: Oedipus complex, Electra complex, denial, hysterical neuroses, conversion disorders, and seduction theory. Be familiar with the controversy over the suppression of seduction theory.

4.   Be familiar with the concept of Zeitgeist. Discuss it in the context of how we deal with social problems like child sexual abuse.

5.   Be able to define *validity* and *reliability*. Discuss why these concepts are important in the social sciences.

6.   Be able to define *incidence* and *prevalence*. What is the difference? What are the most recent incidence estimates on child sexual abuse? What are the most recent prevalence estimates on child sexual abuse? How do definitions of abuse and research methods influence these estimates?

7.   Identify and define the range of sexually abusive activities. What do we know about the kinds of abuse perpetrated? Who does it? How long does it typically last?

8.   Be able to describe the ways in which child sexual abuse can impact its victims. Discuss what indicators of abuse are. Be able to explain why indicators should be interpreted cautiously.

9.   Be able to define what the medical model is. Discuss it, what it means, and the implications of using it.

10.   Discuss the concept of psychiatric diagnosis as applied to victims of abuse.

11.   Identify the signs and symptoms of each of the psychiatric disorders that are often associated with victims.

12.   List each of the models that attempt to describe victims of sexual abuse. Be able to discuss these models, and explain the major terms and concepts in each.

13.   Be able to articulate the philosophy of treatment advocated by Dr. John Briere. What does it mean to say the approach is phenomenological? What does it mean to say that signs and symptoms are "functional?"

SUGGESTED READING

Briere, J. N. (1992). *Child abuse trauma: Theory and treatment of the lasting effects.* Newbury Park, CA: Sage Publications.

A highly intriguing book that describes a philosophy of treatment that places the client's view at the center and that interprets signs and symptoms as attempts to cope and adapt. Written for the clinician, the book outlines innovations in treatment based on its client-centered philosophy.

Finkelhor, D. (Ed.) (1986). *A sourcebook on child sexual abuse.* Newbury Park, CA: Sage Publications.

A classic. A scholarly, though clean and readable, book that touches on a variety of important issues: high-risk children, review of research about abusers, impact of child sexual abuse, and a discussion of what we need from new research.

Haden, D. C. (Ed.) (1986). *Out of harm's way: Readings on child sexual abuse, its prevention and treatment.* Phoenix, AZ: Oryx Press.

An edited anthology of some of the most readable, and informative, short articles about child sexual abuse. Out of print, but still available at some libraries.

CHAPTER GLOSSARY

Avoidance
A concept employed to describe one of the classes of psychiatric symptoms associated with posttraumatic stress disorder. In this context, the person avoids situations that might trigger uncomfortable feelings, flashbacks, or nightmares.

Betrayal
One of four major issues believed by Finkelhor and Browne (1986) to be important for understanding child sexual abuse victimization. Refers to emotional trauma caused by the betrayal of a person the victim should have been able to trust.

Bipolar I disorder
A psychiatric disorder characterized by extreme mood swings. Involves one or more manic or mixed episodes, which usually accompany major depressive episodes.

Bipolar II disorder
A psychiatric disorder characterized by extreme mood swings. Involves one or more major depressive episodes, accompanied by one or more hypomanic episodes.

Blockage
One of four major issues believed to be important for understanding dynamics of child sexual abusers, described in review of Araji and Finkelhor (1986). It refers to blocks to appropriate sexual outlets.

Borderline personality disorder
A recognized psychiatric disorder, believed to develop in childhood and adolescence. Its chief characteristics are emotional instability, intense interpersonal relationships, and dramatic, sometimes destructive, behavior.

Clinical samples
A sample drawn from those people who are receiving treatment for emotional or mental health reasons.

Consent
An agreement on the part of a person who, by virtue of their status as an adult and their ability to understand the potential consequences of their decision, has the capacity to do so.

Conversion disorder
A phenomenon in which a person who experiences psychological trauma converts the trauma, for instance, into a physical symptom or a psychological symptom such as memory loss.

Cooperation
In the field of child sexual abuse, this refers to the ability of child victims to go along with abuse without truly "consenting," since children are not mature enough to give consent.

Culture of helping
The beliefs, values, norms, and ways of behaving that are part of a "culture" in which human service professionals practice.

Cunnilingus
Oral-genital contact involving the female sexual organ.

Cyclothymic disorder
A mental disorder that involves mood swings that are not as severe as in bipolar disorders.

Denial

A concept developed by Freud that denotes an unconscious process by which a person is able to exclude from consciousness realities that are too psychologically threatening.

Depersonalization disorder

A dissociative disorder in which the person feels that events that are really happening to him or her are happening to someone else.

Depression

A psychological disorder involving profound sadness and characterized by a number of "vegetative symptoms," such as sleep disturbance, feelings of hopelessness, loss of interest, and lethargy.

Disorder

In the mental health field, a disturbance characterized by specific psychological signs and symptoms.

Dissociation

A psychological process whereby a person cuts the self off from traumatic experiences, thoughts, memories, or feelings.

Dissociative amnesia

A type of dissociation that involves loss of memory.

Dissociative disorders

A class of psychiatric disorders, recognized by the DSM-IV, that involves dissociative processes.

Dissociative fugue

A dissociative disorder characterized by a sudden moving away and starting life with a new identity, with loss of memory about the previous life.

Dissociative identity disorder

A dissociative disorder characterized by having more than one personality or identity.

Dissociative symptom

Any symptom in which the person prevents traumatic experiences, feelings, or thoughts from entering consciousness.

Distractibility

A characteristic whereby the person is easily distracted from the current or intended focus.

Dynamics

A psychiatric or psychological expression that refers to the interaction of people, events, and circumstances.

Dysthymic disorder

In the DSM-IV, a long-term mood disorder characterized by depression, but which has signs and symptoms that are less severe than in major depressive disorder.

Ego dystonic

Experienced by the person as unpleasant and undesirable.

Ego syntonic

Not experienced by the person as unpleasant or undesirable.

Electra complex

A theory proposed by Freud in which he hypothesizes the secret desire of female children to possess their fathers sexually.

Fellatio

Oral-genital sexual act that involves oral contact with the male sex organ.

Fondling

Touching a child sexually, often including sexual parts, but not involving any type of oral-genital contact or intercourse.

Four-factor traumagenic model

A model developed by Finkelhor and Browne (1986) that postulates four types of sexual trauma: traumatic sexualization, betrayal, powerlessness, and stigmatization.

Functional

In the emerging abuse accommodation models, the view of "dysfunctional" signs and symptoms as "functional," meaning they were adopted as an attempt to cope with the abuse.

Grandiosity

In psychiatry, an unrealistically elevated sense of self-esteem in which individuals believe themselves to be superior to others or even take on pretensions of importance.

Grooming	In the study of child molestation, the process whereby the perpetrator gradually introduces more and more sexually explicit activity and prepares the child for the intended sexual activity.
Hyperarousal	One of the classes of symptoms of posttraumatic stress disorder that involves extreme sensitivity to environmental stimuli, for instance, jumping at the sound of a noise.
Hysterical neuroses	A type of mental disorder, hypothesized by Freud, in which the individual develops physical symptoms in response to trauma.
Indicated abuse	Child abuse that is suspected and believed true, though the investigating authorities lack sufficient evidence to say it is substantiated.
Intercourse	Sexual contact that involves the insertion of the male sex organ into an orifice of another person's body, e.g., anus or vagina.
Interfemoral intercourse	Sometimes referred to as *simulated intercourse* or *dry intercourse* because the active party inserts his penis between the legs. Some perpetrators engage in interfemoral intercourse so as to prevent injuring the vagina and hence not leave evidence.
Intrusive reexperiencing	One of the categories of symptoms in posttraumatic stress disorder that involves involuntary reexperiencing of traumatic events through such processes as flashbacks or nightmares.
Major depressive episode	An episode recognized in the DSM-IV that is characterized by profound depression or sadness.
Manic episode	An episode recognized in the DSM-IV that is characterized by excited or elevated symptoms such as inflated self-esteem, grandiosity, invulnerability, impulsive behavior (binge buying, gambling, promiscuity, etc.), psychomotor agitation, and irritability.
Mental disorder	A psychiatric disorder that involves characteristic signs and symptoms and that interferes with the person's ability to function.
Multiple personality disorder	A term used in previous versions of the *Diagnostic and Statistical Manual of Mental Disorders* (American Psychiatric Association, 1980; 1987), now referred to as dissociative identity disorder. Characterized by the presence of more than one personality or identity.
Oedipus complex	A theory proposed by Freud in which he hypothesizes the secret desire of male children to possess their mothers sexually.
Pathologizing	The interpretation of the victim's reactions to their victimization as "illness," "sickness," or "pathology."
Pathology	In medicine or psychiatry, a state of illness or disease.
Personality disorder	A class of psychiatric disorder believed to develop as a response to experiences in childhood or adolescence, characterized by rigidity. It is believed that the symptoms are experienced as ego syntonic. Some mental health professionals regard these disorders as troublesome and hard to work with.
Phenomeno-logical	A philosophical or clinical orientation that emphasizes the subjective experience of the individual.
Posttraumatic stress disorder	A disorder recognized in the DSM-IV that is characterized by the presence of a trauma-inducing experience, intrusive symptoms, avoidance of situations that trigger intrusive symptoms, and hyperarousal.
Powerlessness	One of four types of trauma hypothesized by Finkelhor and Browne (1986), characterized by a sense of loss of control or the ability to make choices for oneself.

Pragmatic	Practical; with immediate utilitarian value.
Pressured speech	A psychiatric sign in which the person seems to have enormous pressure or energy behind their speech. The speech seems driven, rapid, and sometimes unending. Qualitatively different from talkativeness.
Prevalence estimates	Estimates about the total number of people in the population who have a particular characteristic; in the case of child sexual abuse, an estimate of the number of sexual abuse victims.
Psychomotor agitation	Psychomotor behaviors, such as fidgetiness, nervousness, and so forth.
Regression	A Freudian concept that refers to moving backward from one level of psychological development to a level that is characteristic of an earlier level.
Reify	A term used to denote the process whereby we begin to treat certain ideas or models as if they exist in reality, regardless of whether or not there is empirical evidence to support this belief.
Ritualistic abuse	Abuse inflicted on children by adults as part of certain cult religious practices.
Sadistic abuse	Abuse that involves the use of pain, torture, or even death.
Seduction theory	A theory originally proposed by Sigmund Freud that attributed severe psychological symptoms to actual sexual abuse by an adult or caretaker.
Self-efficacy	Also called *self-worth* or *self-esteem*. Belief in the self as viable and worthy.
Stigmatization	A sociological term, adopted in the abuse field, which denotes negative social reaction to a person because of what has happened to them or has been done to others.
Substantiated abuse	Child abuse that has been found by the appropriate investigating authority to be valid.
Survivor	A term used as a substitute for victim because it implies that the person has found ways to cope and is not truly controlled by the harmful experience.
Syndrome	In medicine and psychiatry, a cluster or grouping of signs and symptoms that cause suspicion that they may be associated with a specific disease or disorder.
Traumatic event	An experience in a person's life, often life threatening, that is sufficiently emotionally charged to stimulate a strong reaction in the person—a necessary feature of posttraumatic stress disorder and acute stress disorder.
Traumatic reexperiencing	A psychological process associated with posttraumatic stress disorder or acute stress disorder whereby a person traumatically reexperiences difficult events in his or her life; for instance, through having flashbacks or nightmares.
Traumatic sexualization	A fixation on sexual matters caused by traumatic sexual experience, which can be expressed as either overinvolvement or complete avoidance.
Vegetative symptoms	Symptoms associated with clinical depression: disturbance in appetite, sleep, loss of energy level, loss of interest in usually pleasurable activity, disturbance in sexual appetite, and sometimes suicidal or homicidal thoughts.
Zeitgeist	A sociological term referring to the overall moral and intellectual character of an era in time; literally means "spirit of the times."

CHAPTER 5

CHILD MALTREATMENT: INVESTIGATION, THE COURTS, AND INTERVENTION

Reporting Suspected Child Maltreatment

Child Protective Services Investigation and Interviewing procedures

Risk Assessment

Initial Intervention by CPS

Juvenile Civil Court Action—Dependency Proceedings

Social Service Intervention

Child Abuse and Criminal Proceedings

False Memory/Repressed Memory Controversy

Problems, Issues, and Trends In Intervention

This chapter is devoted to discussing the things we can do to deal with child maltreatment. It will include discussions about reporting, investigation, risk assessment, court involvement, intervention, and prevention of all types of child abuse and neglect. We won't focus on each specific form of maltreatment or review all the indicators of maltreatment, since this is covered elsewhere in this text. We will, however, touch on them when it's relevant. I have included a review of court proceedings as they relate to child maltreatment since the courts really do have the power to intervene on behalf of kids. In this vein, we will survey the role of juvenile court as well as the adult criminal and civil courts. Since there are a number of controversies associated with child maltreatment intervention, we will also explore these whenever relevant. Some of these include the reliability of the testimony of young victims, the admissibility of hearsay evidence, the influence of interviewing methods on a child's testimony, and the retraction, or recanting, of allegations of abuse. We will also discuss treatment interventions. Since no two cases are exactly alike, the kind of intervention or treatment is likely to vary along a number of dimensions. The range of approaches could, and usually does, include a combination of different interventions and treatments: providing supportive services to the parents (such as a home aide, intensive in-home therapy, counseling, parent effectiveness training, and parent support groups), removing the child, making a referral to law enforcement, and, in certain difficult cases, terminating the parents' rights, thereby making the child available for adoption. At the close of the chapter, we'll also get a chance to talk about some bright spots and innovations.

REPORTING SUSPECTED CHILD MALTREATMENT

As discussed in Chapter 2, the Child Abuse Prevention and Treatment Act of 1974 requires all states and territories to enact laws that require professionals to report suspected child abuse. Psychologists, therapists, social workers, physicians, nurses, counselors, teachers, foster parents, and an array of other professionals are often included in the catalog of "mandatory reporters." Some states require all citizens to report. Generally, reports are made to the state-designated **child protective services** (CPS) agency, sometimes a state governmental agency and sometimes county or local. Many states have toll-free numbers, staffed 24 hours a day, seven days a week, that citizens and professionals alike can call. Not only do states have mandatory reporting laws but the laws protect people with immunity when making reports in good faith, even should the allegations turn out to be incorrect (Sagatun & Edwards, 1995). Many states also permit the name of the person who makes the report to remain anonymous, if so requested. Neighbors and family members often opt for anonymity, while professionals are often very open with their clients about their professional obligation to report any suspected maltreatment.

Common categories of people who report include teachers, school counselors, neighbors, family members, therapists, and parents of other children. When the case is called in, the social worker on the other end of the line will typically take down whatever information is provided and ask for enough clarifying details to prioritize the case for investigation. If the immediate risk to the child seems low it may be given a low priority, whereas cases in which the child seems to be in imminent risk will get a very quick response. Reporting laws vary to some degree from state to state, though in many states people concerned about the abuse of a child may satisfy mandatory reporting requirements by making the report to law enforcement. If there is immediate danger to the child, this is generally the preferred option. After the case is reported and the responsible child protective agency does an initial assessment, the next step is to investigate.

CHILD PROTECTIVE SERVICES INVESTIGATION AND INTERVIEWING PROCEDURES

Strategies for investigating reports vary from jurisdiction to jurisdiction because of a number of things: state laws, agency policies and procedures, the urban or rural setting, caseload size, staffing patterns, and so on. CPS workers will often make a face-to-face visit to the residence, though children are often interviewed at school for practical reasons. Workers want to determine if the allegations called in are true, if they constitute abuse, and the degree to which the child may be in danger.

In terms of determining if the child is being abused, Kathleen Coulbourn Faller, in a recent discussion about assessment, reminds us that when a child is physically abused or neglected, the child's physical condition and living environment often speak for themselves (Faller, 1996). She suggests that we commonly rely on medical expertise to distinguish accidental from non-accidental injuries. In practice, child protection workers generally try to get kids medically evaluated as soon as possible, not only to determine if abuse has occurred but also to protect them from any further harm that might result from the maltreatment. As discussed in Chapter 2, there are a number of physical indicators associated with maltreatment, and these often help medical experts discriminate accidental from non-accidental injuries. The presence of a number of fractures at different stages of healing is one of the classic tip-offs to what is referred to as the *battered child syndrome*. Marks left by objects such as extension cords and coat hangers are usually characteristic of the shapes of these objects (see Chapter 2). While not all CPS units have cameras, documenting the physical effects of maltreatment photographically is often extremely helpful for later use in court. In neglect cases, workers are looking for care of the home, availability of food, safety, adequate parental supervision of the child, cleanliness of the child, and adequate clothing. In assessing nonorganic failure to thrive, the medical expert will be looking at weight and height, ability to maintain a previously achieved weight, ability to maintain growth, and psychomotor development (see Chapter 3).

The dynamics, or workings, of child sexual abuse are different from those of physical maltreatment or neglect. In severe cases of sexual abuse, there may be detectable physical trauma to the genitals or anus (Monteleone, et al., 1994), but more often than not, any trauma will be of a psychological or emotional nature and therefore not easily detectable through a physical examination (Sgroi, 1982). Since physical evidence is rare and sexual abuse is something that usually occurs in secret, only two people generally know what happened: the victim and the perpetrator (Faller, 1996; Sgroi, 1982). Since the perpetrator is not likely to want to tell about the abuse, the most logical person to ask is the child (Faller, 1996). Whereas in cases of physical abuse or neglect a medical person would be asked to distinguish between accidental and non-accidental injuries based on the physical evidence, in child sexual abuse the expert we consult is usually a child protective services or mental health professional. What we are asking them to do is ply the tools of their trade—interviewing and assessment skills—in order to determine if child sexual abuse has occurred. If it has, we also want to know the extent of the abuse and the degree to which the child continues to be at risk.

Validated Interviewing Procedures

An **interviewing protocol** refers to a set of steps or procedures used to elicit information from suspected victims of child sexual abuse. At this point in time, there is no single set of accepted protocols in the field of child sexual abuse, though the **American Professional Society on the Abuse of Children** (**APSAC**) has published a set of general guidelines (1990). Advantages of adopting protocols include greater consistency across interviewers and the establishment of minimal professional standards; disadvantages include creating a de facto obligation on the part of practitioners to conduct all interviews in a particular way, making them vulnerable to attacks from adversarial attorneys.

While interviewing technique seems like a benign topic, the way professionals have conducted their interviews of suspected child sexual abuse victims has come under attack in recent years. Warren, Woodall, Hunt, and Perry (1996) discuss recent failed prosecutions and convictions that have been overturned because of potentially suggestive and coercive pretrial interview techniques. As a result, the efficacy of interviewing practices in the field has been called into question. It also probably points to the need to identify both good and poor interviewing practices.

While there is no single accepted protocol for interviewing suspected victims of child sexual abuse, there has been recent research that can serve as a guide for good practice. Using recent research as well as suggestions from experienced interviewers, L. Dennison Reed (1996) has developed some general guidelines she believes may increase the accuracy of interviews and reduce the risk of accusations about suggestive or coercive interview techniques. Box 5-1 summarizes these suggestions. Interestingly, most of these make a great deal of intuitive sense, are consistent with what we believe about good interviewing skills (Ivey, 1994), and now also have good support from the latest empirical research.

In their review of recent research, Warren and colleagues (1996) include two components that are not explicitly spelled out in our summarization of Reed's suggestions: first, establishing and discussing ground rules for the

BOX 5-1   Guidelines for Increasing Accuracy in Investigatory Interviewing

Setting

- Do the interview in a place where the child feels comfortable

Interviewer behavior and attitude

- Approach the interview with an open mind
- Be friendly and build rapport with the child before exploring for sensitive material

Clarify your expectations

- Emphasize being truthful and not pretending
- Be sure to tell the child you don't know much about the facts of the case
- Encourage the child to admit being confused rather than guessing
- Encourage the child to admit not knowing or not remembering rather than guessing
- Tell the child that when you repeat a question, it doesn't mean his or her previous answer was wrong
- Give the child permission to refuse to answer questions that are too hard
- Encourage the child to disagree with you and correct you when you make mistakes

Be thoughtful about how you ask your questions

- Keep in mind that you can mislead in any direction, depending on the nature of the suggestions
- Make your questions developmentally appropriate
- Avoid highly leading or coercive questions
- Avoid repetitive suggestions and interviews
- Begin with open-ended questions after a free narrative, then focused questions as appropriate
- Document relevant questions and responses

Attempt to corroborate

- When law enforcement is involved, every effort should be made to collect whatever material evidence there might be that might corroborate the child's testimony

Based on "Findings from Research on Children's Suggestibility and Implications for Conducting Child Interviews," by L. D. Reed, 1996, *Child Maltreatment, 1*(2), 105–120. Copyright © 1996 Sage Publications, Inc. Adapted by permission of Sage Publications, Inc.

child interview (though this can be inferred from the suggestions made in the section on clarifying expectations); and second, conducting a practice interview on a neutral subject. They suggest that such an interview can probably go a long way in helping the interviewer establish rapport prior to delving into sensitive issues, as well as helping the interviewer understand more about the child and the child's way of experiencing the world. Warren et al. (1996) quote one study (Sternberg, et al., 1996) which suggests that doing a well-conducted practice interview actually increases the information that the children provide later, during the abuse-focused part of the interview.

The Issue of Multiple Interviews

Based on new literature, it seems to be recommended that the number of child interviews be kept to a minimum. This recommendation may be based on the assumption that people who are unknown to the child will be doing the interviewing. This is not always the case. In systems with good service coordination, children who have been identified as victims of sexual abuse are often referred fairly quickly for therapy. I believe there are some real advantages to doing this, including the ability of a therapist to establish a relationship with the child and discuss the details of the abuse gradually over time. When a child can be enrolled in a program of therapy, it can also do much to minimize the negative impact of the abuse as well as provide a valuable support for the child as he or she experiences various aspects of the justice system.

Videotaping Interviews

Because of the highly charged legal atmosphere, videotaping interviews is another controversial issue. Some clinicians are concerned about a requirement to videotape all interviews for reasons of fairness. The argument in this camp goes something like this: "Other kinds of interviews done as part of investigation in the criminal justice system are not required to be taped, so why should we have a separate standard in child sexual abuse cases?" John Myers, a law professor and recognized expert on litigating child abuse and neglect cases, points out that there are advantages and disadvantages of taping interviews (1992). From a legal point of view, Myers indicates that one advantage is that the U.S. Supreme Court has ruled that videotaped interviews might be used to increase confidence in the child's disclosure (*Idaho v. Wright,* 1990, cited in Myers, 1992). Another key advantage is that, when interviews are done properly, the videotape itself makes it very difficult to attack the interview methods (Berliner, et al., 1992; Davies, et al., 1996; Myers, 1992). In addition to a number of other advantages, Myers (1992) points out that awareness about being taped may influence the interviewer to do a good interview. It can document exactly what the child reported, in addition to the child's emotional state, and it may reduce the number of intrusive interviews the child has to be subjected to.

There are also disadvantages of videotaping interviews (Myers, 1992; Sagatun & Edwards, 1995). As alluded to earlier, defense attorneys may find minor inconsistencies on the tape and try to use these to discredit disclosures. Since there is usually a great deal of information in any given case, showing the videotape without the rest of the context can distort. In addition, Myers (1992) suggests that videotaping is not always practical. It can make some children nervous. It is also a permanent record, one that may fall into the wrong hands.

The Use of Anatomically Detailed Dolls

Anatomically detailed dolls (sometimes referred to as *anatomically correct*) are dolls that include sexual parts, such as penises, breasts, and anuses. They have been used in a number of different ways to assist in investigating child sexual abuse allegations. The use of anatomically detailed dolls in these investigations is another "hot issue" (Faller, 1996; Myers, 1992; Sagatun & Edwards, 1995). In their discussion of the debate, Mark Everson and Barbara Boat (1996) point out that, because of controversies, evidence gathered through the use of anatomically detailed dolls has been banned in California courts and that both English and Dutch courts have ruled against their use. There seem to be four primary objections to their use (Boat & Everson, 1996; Everson & Boat, 1994, cited in Boat & Everson, 1996): (1) there is no accepted protocol for their use, (2) norms on how sexually abused and other abused children respond to them are not established, (3) they are sexually suggestive by their very nature, and (4) their use can encourage leading and suggestive questioning. Boat and Everson (1996) suggest that, based on the empirical evidence, there is generally no basis for the first three objections. They believe the fourth objection (that they can contribute to interviewer error) to be the most concerning.

Based on a review of guidelines, Boat and Everson (1996) have been able to identify five distinct uses of anatomically detailed dolls: as a comforter, an icebreaker, an anatomical model, a demonstration aid, and a diagnostic screen. In their research, they were trying to determine how anatomically detailed dolls are actually used and the extent to which the technique might be misused. They observed and coded 97 tapes of actual CPS interviews in a midsouthern state. Based on their own case experience, they coded these tapes and watched for "concerning behavior." This is their term for interviewer behavior that had the potential to elicit an adverse response. Their results suggested that interviewers used anatomically detailed dolls with a wide range of ages (2–12) and that they tended to be used most frequently as anatomical models and demonstration aids. They also reported that most interviews contained at least one concerning practice.

The use of anatomically detailed dolls continues to be an unresolved controversy (Faller, 1996; Myers, 1992; Sagatun & Edwards, 1995), though the professional consensus seems to be that they are an appropriate tool when used correctly by people who have been properly trained in their use (American Professional Society on the Abuse of Children, 1995a, Boat &

Everson, 1996; Faller, 1996). The American Professional Society on the Abuse of Children (1995a) has published a set of guidelines to this end. One especially important consideration is that it is clearly best to let the child describe the sexual behavior that has occurred *prior* to using the dolls to demonstrate the sexual activity.

Classic Work on Investigatory Interviewing

In addition to the empirically based guidelines summarized above, there is also a classic body of work, including that of Suzanne Sgroi. I don't think any student of child investigatory interviewing should complete their studies without learning of Sgroi's pioneering work, not only because she gave us the very concept of investigatory interviewing but also because of her heart and sensitivity to victims. Herself a physician, Sgroi has taken pains to take us into the child's world, a world that, for victims, also includes something called the *damaged goods syndrome* (Sgroi, 1982). This is when children come to believe that "because they were used sexually they're broken now . . . not good anymore." They often feel damaged and defaced. Sgroi teaches us that, by opening our hearts as well as our minds to understand the child's world, we are taking a step toward solving the problem, one that takes us away from clinical or scientific detachment and toward a more holistic and empathic acceptance of the patient.

In her classic handbook on child sexual abuse, Sgroi (1982) outlines an approach to working with child sexual abuse. The process in her model that would substitute for the physical examination of the general practitioner is investigatory interviewing. Sgroi suggests that investigative interviewing is perhaps the most important tool in **validating complaints**, or trying to determine the truthfulness of allegations, of child sexual abuse. She was among the first to outline a set of protocols to use when investigating cases of child sexual abuse. Among the suggestions Sgroi makes is that we learn to use the same words the child uses, that we understand that their sense of time may revolve more around significant events in their lives, and that it may be necessary for a skilled interviewer to meet with the child over an extended period of time in order to get an understanding of what has happened.

Another contribution made by Sgroi in her handbook (1982) is her guidance on doing **credibility assessments.** In a court of law, without physical evidence or other witnesses, the relative credibility of the only witness, the victim, is extremely important. Sgroi comments that determining the credibility of the alleged victim is a matter of belief. Based upon her experience, she suggests that credibility is strengthened when certain elements are present in the child's story (for example, being able to provide explicit details or describe methods the perpetrator used to gain cooperation, and so on).

As you can see, much of what Sgroi suggests (for example, an emphasis on building rapport with the client) is very consistent with the newer empirically based guidelines such as those previously outlined in Box 5-1.

RISK ASSESSMENT

Up to this point we've discussed some of the "basics" as well as some of the controversial issues associated with child maltreatment investigation and interviewing. We now turn to the issue of risk assessment. Once we have reason to believe that maltreatment has occurred, the worker is in a position of having to decide what to do about it. Workers know that there is always a risk that a child on their caseload could end up on the front page of the morning paper. It is every worker's nightmare. If the worker doesn't feel that immediate action is appropriate and fails to act, but something dreadful happens in that case, the worker is likely to get the blame. The reverse situation also seems true. If the worker acts expeditiously and removes the child from the home, he or she can be in for some serious criticism. I myself have seen a group of accused parents outside the courthouse with picket signs accusing child protective services of being like the gestapo, arbitrarily tearing their kids away from them. To top it off, not only are CPS workers put in a position where they can be criticized no matter what they do, or don't do, they are often faced with staggering caseloads, enormous pressures from the decisions they have to make on a daily basis, and, in recent days, dwindling resources because of more competition for the available tax dollars.

In this atmosphere, having to decide which cases to deal with first and what to do about them is an extremely precarious undertaking. It leaves many CPS workers feeling extremely uncomfortable. Perhaps as a result of these pressures, along with public demands for accountability in child protective services and a genuine desire to do a better job, there seems to be increasing interest in the whole area of risk assessment. One possible indication of this is that the American Professional Society on the Abuse of Children has devoted an entire issue of the *APSAC Advisor* to this topic (American Professional Society on the Abuse of Children, 1995b).

While there seems to be increasing professional interest in risk assessment, it isn't such a new thing. As Thomas Curran (1995) points out, CPS workers have been doing informal risk assessments from the beginning. They have relied on general policies, agency guidelines, and their own subjective impression of cases all along (Curran, 1995). From those earlier days when individual social workers used their own judgment, the use of formal **risk assessment instruments** (RAIs) has emerged. The vast majority of states now use some form of formalized risk assessment in CPS cases (Cicchinelli, 1995; Curran, 1995), some states legislatively mandate it. Among the earliest risk assessment instruments were simple checklists of factors that were believed to be associated with child maltreatment (Cicchinelli, 1995). There are now a wide variety of risk assessment models in use, with proposals that some of these be made available for use on computers (Sheets, 1996).

Cicchinelli (1995) describes the risk assessment models in use today as formalized methods of providing consistency in the risk determination process. He points out that one of the ways to distinguish among the variety of risk assessment instruments out there is by the way they were developed. Some were developed based on empirical research, called **empirically based models**, while others, called **consensus-based models**, are based on an agreement among child abuse professionals about the relevant risk factors. Cicchinelli (1995) also points out that the two are not necessarily exclusive, since many of the items included in consensus-based models have been shown by research to have some predictive value.

While it is nice to know that we seem to be developing the tools we need to do a better job in handling CPS cases, we have a long way yet to go. As Curran (1995) points out, "No instrument has passed both statistical validity and reliability, nor has a consensus been reached regarding even what level would be sufficient." In the present state of the art, there seems to be no clear evidence about which, if any, risk assessment instrument is able to predict either immediate or long-term harm to any given child. Curran (1995) points out that, based on the current state of the art, CPS workers do not have the training and tools necessary to conduct investigations that result in accurate and reliable assessments. Since decisions about removal of children from the homes of their natural parents are in part based upon the assessment of risk, there are some sticky legal issues at stake. Among substantiated child maltreatment cases, we may be able to identify the presence of certain risk factors perhaps as much as 90% of the time, retrospectively. But retrospectively derived risk factors have problems. Just as in research about intergenerational transmission as a risk factor (Kaufman & Zigler, 1987, 1989; Widom, 1989), we may be able to predict that a relatively small percentage of families, say 30%, with certain identified risk factors will actually become abusive. If we accurately predict 30% of the time, this also means we're likely to guess wrong the other 70%. If we remove a child in each of those cases, we will be unjustified 70% of the time. A parent whose child has been removed, based at least in part on the use of a formalized risk assessment instrument, could argue that to do so on such evidence impinges upon their rights as a parent.

This brings us full circle to the question of how we balance our desire to protect children from harm and the rights of parents to be free from undue interference. The field is still young, and research about the causes and risks associated with child maltreatment is complex. It seems at this stage that we don't yet have instruments that can reliably predict the level of danger a child is in. Even advocates of the use of risk assessment instruments concede that this whole process is enigmatic. In the final analysis, risk assessment tools cannot replace human judgment; they can probably only serve as a tool to be used by human beings as they attempt to weigh the child's safety and the societal goal of preserving families whenever possible.

INITIAL INTERVENTION BY CPS

Once a case of child maltreatment has been investigated, the CPS worker is in a position to make an initial determination of whether child maltreatment has in fact occurred. If the answer is "no," then the case can be closed and the file archived. Sometimes, when child maltreatment is not found but the worker believes there is risk to the child, the worker can offer voluntary services to the family, if services are available. The services could be referral to a clinic, a counseling program, or perhaps assistance with parenting or child care. If, on the other hand, the worker believes that there is sufficient evidence to show that child maltreatment has occurred, the worker has a different set of options. First of all, the worker will need to weigh the safety of the child versus the damage that might result as a consequence of other action the worker might take. In child maltreatment cases, it seems that some harm to the child and family will occur as a result of intervention; it is a matter of trying to decide what course of action will cause the least harm.

Even in cases where child maltreatment seems to be substantiated, there are a number of options available to the CPS worker, depending upon the laws of the state and the specific agency's policies. It is here where formal or informal risk assessment comes into play. Depending on state law, if the immediate risk to the child seems low, the worker might temporarily leave the child in the home but provide supervision until the matter can be heard in court. If the worker believes that there is immediate risk to the child, the worker, or law enforcement officer, is often empowered to remove the child immediately from the home and place the child in **temporary custody**, sometimes called **temporary care.** Most jurisdictions have temporary shelters or foster homes, sometimes called *receiving homes,* for such children. While the worker generally has the authority to take this step on a temporary basis, continued placement generally requires a court order. Since this marks the limit of what the CPS worker can do without court action, we will turn now to the involvement of the courts.

JUVENILE CIVIL COURT ACTION—DEPENDENCY PROCEEDINGS

As discussed in the previous section, a child can only remain in a temporary out-of-home placement for a limited time before a court hearing must be held, generally within 72 hours (weekends and holidays usually don't count). Hearings that deal with child maltreatment issues are generally heard in special courts that are most frequently called **juvenile courts**, but that sometimes go by other names such as family court (Bulkley, et al., 1996). The first hearing to be held after a child is removed from the home is the one to decide if the child needs to remain in temporary care. This is often referred to as the **shelter care hearing.** Since the parents' rights to custody of the child are in jeopardy, the parent or parents are usually entitled to be represented by an attorney. At the shelter care hearing, the question the judge generally needs to answer is, "Does the safety of the child necessitate that the child remain in an out-of-home placement?" After hearing evidence from all parties concerned, the judge will render a decision about the central question in the hearing and thereby order the child to remain in care or be returned to the parent, pending a court decision about whether or not child maltreatment has occurred.

When a worker makes the decision that there is sufficient evidence to believe that child maltreatment has occurred, in addition to either placing the child in care or allowing the child to remain home, the worker is generally required to file a petition with whatever court happens to have jurisdiction in that particular state. Petitions that allege child abuse or neglect are often called **dependency petitions.** When this takes place, many jurisdictions now have a program where a neutral third party is appointed to advocate for the best interests of the child. This person is sometimes referred to as a **court-appointed special advocate (CASA)** or **guardian ad litem.** Court-appointed special advocates are commonly volunteers. While some cases involving other forms of child maltreatment may find their way into these courts, the overwhelming majority of cases heard involve neglect or child physical abuse. Child sexual abuse cases may be heard if the children are at continued risk, but the offenses in child sexual abuse cases are often dealt with as criminal matters in the criminal courts. Dependency actions are considered to be civil proceedings.

While bruising or visible welts, or neglect, might result in CPS intervention, this kind of maltreatment usually does not result in additional criminal action, though it could. **Severe physical abuse,** those acts of maltreatment that threaten or cause serious injury or death, are another matter. In such cases, not only are the parents likely to face dependency proceedings but criminal charges as well. A finding of maltreatment by the juvenile court in dependency proceedings could result in the loss of child custody; conviction in criminal proceedings in the adult courts can result in jail or prison time. (We will discuss criminal proceedings in a later section.)

As suggested earlier, the court still has the authority to take some fairly drastic steps in dependency proceedings, such as removing the children or permanently ending the parent-child relationship. Because of this, the parents are generally entitled to legal representation at each step of the way. There are often a variety of separate hearings that are part of dependency proceedings. They attempt to resolve a number of important questions and issues. Is the child abused or neglected? Do we need to supervise what the parents do? Do we need to require the parents to change certain behaviors or solve personal problems, such as alcoholism, that interfere with their ability to care for their children? Should we remove the child from his or her caretaker? If we should remove the child, for how long should this be? Where should we place the child instead? None of these are easy questions, yet for the sake of at-risk children, the courts are compelled to try to deal with them.

States vary in their court rules; however, there are some consistencies. For one, these cases are generally heard by a judge alone and not a jury. Another point where there seems to be a fair degree of consistency is in the **standard of evidence** that is required to find that the child needs the protection of the state. That standard of evidence in dependency cases is usually called **preponderance of the evidence** (Sagatun & Edwards, 1995), meaning there is more evidence pointing to abuse or neglect than not. At the conclusion of the dependency hearing, the judge will make a decision about whether a dependency exists (that is, whether the child is dependent upon the state for protection). When this decision is made, it is often called a **finding of fact** and the hearing leading up to the decision a **fact-finding hearing**. Even after finding a dependency, however, there are other decisions that these courts must make, including the approval of the case plan. Hearings that decide what happens after a dependency has been ruled on are frequently called **disposition hearings**. At this hearing, the judge will generally listen to the recommendations of the CPS worker, and the special advocate or guardian ad litem appointed for the child as well as to the requests from the parents and other interested persons. Recommendations will usually be based on the needs and problems in the family and the options in the community that are available to address them.

Parents may be referred to Alcoholics Anonymous, a parent support group, parent effectiveness training, anger management counseling, psychotherapy, outpatient mental health services, employment services, or any number of other programs, depending on their needs. Sometimes decisions about what the program for the parent will look like is left to the social service department of the state; other times it will be specified by the court, depending upon the laws of the particular state. Similar decisions need to be made on behalf of the child as well. Where the child will be placed (relative's home, foster home, specialized foster care program, residential placement) and what kind of services the child will receive also need to be decided. Visitation, whether supervised or unsupervised, is another part of the case plan. Sometimes the details of the case plan will be heard at a separate hearing, to be held within a short period of time after the dependency ruling has been made.

Review hearings are held at specified intervals after the disposition of the case. The purpose of these hearings is to evaluate the progress made by the child and his or her parents. Federal law (P. L. 96-272) requires states to take certain steps to safeguard the rights of children and their parents when a dependency has been established and out-of-home care is required (Bulkley et al., 1996). One of these requirements is that reasonable efforts be made to provide sufficient services so that out-of-home placement can be prevented or kept to a minimum (Bulkley et al., 1996). While there are variations from state to state, generally the first review hearing will occur in six months or less, and every six months thereafter (Bulkley et al., 1996; Sagatun & Edwards, 1995). If needed family changes have been made, children can be returned home. Sometimes the dependency continues to be in force, and the social service department supervises the case even after the child is returned home to ensure that the child is safe prior to ending the dependency and, hence, the authority of the juvenile court in the case.

In addition to the questions surveyed earlier, there is at least one more that the juvenile courts must rule on any time a child is removed from home and placed in out-of-home care: that of what the **permanent plan** for the child's placement should be. Court hearings to decide on a permanent plan are required to be held within 18 months, under federal law (P. L. 96-272)

(Bulkley et al., 1996). Usually, the permanent plan for a given child or family is supposed to provide the family with the supervision, support, and structure they need until they are able to care for the child independently. The sad reality, however, is that with some families it is never reasonable to expect them to be able to do this. When this is the case, an alternative permanent plan such as long-term foster care, guardianship, or adoption may be appropriate. The requirement to develop a permanent plan for each child in care recognizes a very important consideration: children have a need for security in their lives. One way to accomplish this is through adoption, but in order for this to be an option, the child must be legally free. This means that the parents have either agreed to adoption or else their parental rights have been ended by the courts. A criticism of our current process is that the system takes so long to get to this point that children's lives are permanently harmed. Young children sometimes linger in temporary foster homes until they reach school years or beyond. As the years tick by, children are at risk of having significant problems in bonding when a permanent family is finally found for them (James, 1994; Jewett, 1978).

When the social service department or agency exhausts its intervention options and finally decides that it is not reasonable to expect that the parent will ever be able to care for the child, it can initiate legal proceedings that can permanently end the parent-child relationship. When the courts consider permanently severing the parent-child bond, a special type of court proceeding, often called a **termination proceeding**, is initiated. While dependency cases are decided based upon a preponderance of the evidence, the standard of evidence required in termination proceedings is much higher, depending upon the state called "clear, cogent, and convincing." If, after listening to all the evidence, the court agrees with the social service department, it can legally and permanently dissolve the parent-child relationship. For the child there may be other proceedings in order to finalize guardianship or adoption, but for the biological parents this is generally the end of the line insofar as it concerns their relationship with the child.

SOCIAL SERVICE INTERVENTION

Once it is established that the child needs the protection of the courts and that abuse or neglect has occurred, then the social services department is usually given the authority to supervise the case, place the children, and take whatever intervention steps it feels necessary. In the past, most of our intervention efforts have gone to try to correct or alleviate whatever problems the caretakers had that seemed to be getting in the way of being able to adequately parent their children. If alcohol or substances were involved, the court order would often mandate a treatment program. If the courts believed the problem was one of parenting skills, it might order the parent to take parenting classes. If the court believed the parent had an anger man-

Children's Protective Services exists to investigate suspected cases of maltreatment, provide families with what they need to function better, and protect children from abuse.

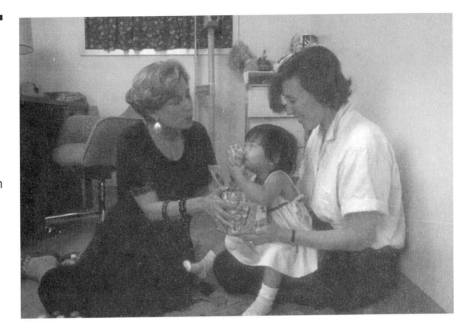

agement problem, it might order a counseling program to help correct it. In addition, support groups such as Parents Anonymous, Alcoholics Anonymous, or Narcotics Anonymous were made a part of the parent's program. Sometimes other supportive services such as chore services were offered. The children were sometimes left in the home, with periodic supervision, and sometimes removed. When removed, the young children were often placed in temporary or long-term foster care placements. Older children, especially those with serious emotional or behavior problems, might be placed in group homes or residential treatment facilities.

CHILD ABUSE AND CRIMINAL PROCEEDINGS

In most instances of child maltreatment, the case will be handled exclusively in the juvenile court as a dependency matter; however, certain serious cases are also referred to the adult courts for criminal prosecution. The kinds of cases most likely to be referred to the adult criminal courts include cases of intrafamily child sexual abuse, and physical abuse and neglect cases in which a child has been seriously injured or could have been injured as a result of parental action or negligence. When a child maltreatment case finds its way to the adult criminal courts, the rules and procedures will generally be the same as for any other serious criminal matter. In physical abuse cases, there is likely to be physical evidence as with any other serious assault; however, in child sexual abuse cases, this may not be true. As discussed previously, there will frequently be little or no physical evidence. As a result, a great deal hinges on the perceived truthfulness and credibility of the only witness, the alleged victim.

Coordinated Response and Law Enforcement Investigation

When a case is referred to law enforcement, the responsible law enforcement agency, whether federal, state, county, or municipal, will have jurisdiction to conduct a law enforcement investigation. Since other agencies and professionals are likely to be involved, there has been a greater emphasis in recent years on increased coordination between law enforcement and others, such as child protective services, medical professionals, and child mental health personnel. Some communities have developed formal and informal response teams made up of individuals from each of the disciplines or agencies involved. Lanning (1996) suggests that a multidisciplinary approach has many advantages: "Each discipline performs a function for which it has specific resources, training, and experience." In the military, for instance, family advocacy programs are a mandated part of each branch of the service. These programs are required to coordinate a number of professionals for the investigation and response to family maltreatment complaints that take place on military installations, or involve military personnel. In addition, all branches of the U. S. military have law enforcement investigatory agencies, such as the Army's Criminal Investigations Division (CID), the Naval Investigative Service (NIS), and the Air Force Office of Special Investigations (AFOSI). Each of these agencies participates in family maltreatment case management teams, which include family advocacy personnel as well as child care, legal, social work, mental health, medical, and nursing personnel, and a number of other disciplines and activities.

Law enforcement has particular expertise in investigating criminal behavior as well as questioning and interrogating suspects. Social service and mental health personnel may be more skilled at forming therapeutic relationships with children and understanding the particular difficulties they may be experiencing as a consequence of the maltreatment. Medical personnel, especially when equipped with additional specialized training, are able to detect and diagnose the effects of trauma, sometimes being able to provide law enforcement with physical evidence.

In addition to greater coordination between law enforcement and other key participants, in many communities specialized law enforcement units have been organized to deal with certain kinds of cases, such as child sexual abuse. When such units exist, they have more specialized training and experience; they may also be in a position to work with other law enforcement agencies, such as the U.S. Postal Inspectors and U.S. Customs, in investigating cases or even conducting "sting" operations. The Postal Inspection Service is a little-known agency, but one with a great deal of experience in investigating distribution of child pornography in the mails. Many pedophiles (people who have a sexual preference for children) have an interest in child pornography and, amazingly, as attested to by the customs seizures and postal investigations, there seems to be a market for it. With advances in technology, new methods of distributing pornography or making contact with minors for sexual purposes are becoming available. In a recent well-publicized development, a group of subscribers to the commercial on-line service, America Online, were arrested for distributing child pornography over the Internet. In any child abuse case where federal law has been violated, it is often advantageous to have federal law enforcement participation, since federal courts frequently have much stronger sentencing options than are available in state courts.

Prosecution of Criminal Cases

As with law enforcement investigation, prosecution of child abuse cases seems to have improved considerably. Some jurisdictions have established specialized units, or at least designated deputy prosecutors, to handle these cases. As is also true in the domestic violence field, many prosecutors' offices have now hired victims' advocates. In child sexual abuse cases, specially trained interviewers who work for prosecutors' offices are often provided to interview suspected victims. Some innovative communities have this person interview the child in a room with a one way mirror in order to allow the process to be videotaped and/or observed by others, including law enforcement, child protective services, and mental health personnel. Sometimes these interviews occur in specialized units established in major hospitals, where the child can also have any necessary specialized medical exams performed by medical personnel sensitive to the issues.

Once the prosecutor is convinced that there is enough evidence to prosecute, the next step is to file a complaint (in some jurisdictions called an information) formally charging the alleged offender with a crime (Sagatun & Edwards, 1995). If the suspect has not already been arrested, an arrest can be made at this time. The next steps are **arraignment** (or grand jury indictment), **preliminary hearing, plea bargaining, plea, pretrial motions, discovery, trial** (if a not-guilty plea is made), and **sentencing** if the defendant is found guilty (Myers, 1992; Sagatun & Edwards, 1995).

The initial court appearance generally takes place within a very brief period of time, especially if an arrest has been made. At this time the accused person is informed of legal rights (Myers, 1992; Sagatun & Edwards, 1995), including the right to be represented by an attorney. Bail may also be set at this hearing if the person is detained. The preliminary hearing follows sometime later, at which time the evidence is reviewed and the case dismissed if it does not look like a trial should be held (Myers, 1992; Sagatun & Edwards, 1995). Plea bargaining refers to a process whereby prosecutors offer reduced charges or sentencing recommendations in exchange for a guilty plea by the accused. At the arraignment the accused person is formally informed of the charges and given an opportunity to enter a plea (Myers, 1992). Other hearings may be held in order to consider pretrial motions by either or both sides (Myers, 1992). Discovery refers to the process by which the defense and, to a lesser degree, the prosecution are entitled to information the other might have (Myers, 1992; Sagatun & Edwards, 1995). This could include the right to copies of reports, interview transcripts, inspection of the evidence, and so on in order to prepare for the trial. At the trial the accused person has the right to a jury, which will ultimately decide on guilt or innocence. The standard of evidence required for conviction in a criminal case is that of **beyond a reasonable doubt.** If the person is found guilty at the trial, sentencing follows some time after this, usually after a presentencing report has been prepared detailing relevant aspects of the person's history, circumstances, strengths, problems, and so on.

Testimony in Criminal Cases

The most potentially valuable testimony in a child sexual abuse case is that of the victim. However, it is often difficult to get good testimony from victims for a number of reasons. First of all, many victims have extremely ambivalent feelings about the perpetrator, especially if it is a family member or another person they feel close to. Regardless of everything else, children may understand enough of what's going on to know that their testimony could hurt the perpetrator. Another reason why children may have difficulty wanting to testify is out of fear, especially if the perpetrator is someone they see as very strong and powerful or when the perpetrator has used intimidation to keep the victim quiet. In addition to this, the credibility of victims, especially very young victims, has come under attack because of the perceived limitations of children. The overall legal term used to describe the ability to testify in a meaningful way is **competency.** Until fairly recently, most jurisdictions presumed children below a certain age (10–14) not to be competent, requiring the judge to determine this on a case-by-case basis (Bulkley et al., 1996). Questionable areas included the ability to communicate about their experiences, the capacity to accurately remember, the capacity to distinguish between fact and fantasy, vulnerability to suggestion, understanding the difference between truth and lie, and an appreciation of the importance of telling the truth (Bulkley et al., 1996; Myers, 1992). Now, a sizable number (but still a minority) of states accept new rules of evidence that establish a presumption of competency of *all* persons (Bulkley et al., 1996; Sagatun & Edwards, 1995). What we now believe is that, with children above about 3 or 4 years of age, it is fairly clear they are able to provide good testimony (Bulkley et al., 1996).

Tainted victim testimony

As alluded to earlier, the way children are interviewed has come under increasing scrutiny in recent years, and even child advocates acknowledge that there have been at least some problems. More recently, there have been challenges to the credibility of victim statements, based on allegations of suggestive interview techniques. In a recent article in *Child Maltreatment,* John Myers (1996) discusses a turn of events that portends to have a significant impact on criminal trials. That development is the creation of something called **taint hearings.** Taint hearings have been created as a result of a New Jersey Supreme Court concern about the investigative interviewing in the *Michaels* case (*State v. Michaels,* 1994). As Myers (1996) puts it, "The court ruled that defective interviewing can utterly destroy a child's credibility." What the New Jersey court did as a result of their concern is rule that a defendant may request a pretrial hearing to challenge investigative interviews. An appeals court threw out the conviction of Margaret Kelly Michaels on 163 counts of sexual abuse alleged to have occurred at the Wee Care Nursery School, and the matter eventually ended up in the New Jersey Supreme Court.

Hearsay Evidence

Most of the time **hearsay evidence** (the testimony of a person about what someone else said happened) is excluded from criminal trials. This is often excluded for good reason. We all know that the details of what a person said can get distorted when it's filtered through third parties. In child abuse cases, however, there are exceptions to the rule of **hearsay exclusion,** or the policy of keeping hearsay evidence out of a trial.

One exception is called the **excited utterance exception.** In this situation, if someone has a shocking experience, what they say has happened to them when in an excited state can be testified to in court by someone who heard the utterance (Bulkley et al., 1996, Myers, 1992; Sagatun & Edwards, 1995). Because of the circumstances, it is regarded as trustworthy. Another exception to the hearsay exclusion rule, which often applies in child abuse cases, relates to **statements made to professionals providing diagnosis and treatment** for the child (Bulkley et al., 1996, Myers, 1992; Sagatun & Edwards, 1995). It is assumed that, because the professional is there to diagnose and treat what is wrong with the person, the person is likely to be truthful. While originally intended for medical personnel proper, this exception has been commonly extended to mental health professionals who might interview a child victim. The testimony of the professional about such statements could be introduced under this exception to the hearsay rule even if the child does not or cannot testify. A third exception to the hearsay rule is called the **residual exception,** which is invoked when there appears to be a comparable degree of trustworthiness in the statement but it does not fall under the other exceptions (Bulkley et al., 1996; Myers, 1992; Sagatun & Edwards, 1995). Finally, there is the **child abuse hearsay exception,** which has been passed into law in a number of states for the specific purpose of permitting hearsay evidence in child abuse cases (Bulkley et al., 1996).

Testimony by interviewers

Interviewers often shoulder a great deal of responsibility in child abuse cases because they often testify as to what has been reported to them by the victim.

This is an area not without concern, as some interviewers have been accused of using coercive or suggestive interview techniques. The primary concern is that highly vulnerable people can be prone to suggestion, and in response to suggestive interview techniques, can give false statements (Faller, 1996; Myers, 1996; Reed, 1996). In a short discussion that includes the topic of defense tactics, Myers (1992) suggests that, until fairly recently, a common defense strategy was to attack the credibility or competence of the witness. Now, he suggests, a more common tactic is for the defense attorney to attack the interviewer. The most vulnerable place for this attack is in potentially coercive or suggestive interview strategies or improper use of anatomically detailed dolls in child sexual abuse cases. Current recommendations for the use of anatomically detailed dolls are that the dolls be used as aids to help the child explain what has happened *after* the child has already made a verbal disclosure (American Professional Society on the Abuse of Children, 1995a).

Making sure that the interview process begins with an open-minded attitude and follows the guidelines summarized in Box 5-1, as well as those promulgated by the American Professional Society on the Abuse of Children (1990), can probably go a long way toward preventing intentional or unintentional suggestive interviews from happening in the first place.

Expert testimony

Medical and mental health professionals may testify in criminal court on child abuse matters, with certain limitations. According to Myers (1992), the expert has to have sufficient knowledge, skill, and background to be able to assist the court. Usually experts have advanced professional degrees, but sometimes a person without them who has special experience or understanding can qualify to testify as an expert witness.

Examples of what the expert could testify to might include consistency of signs and symptoms with the battered child syndrome or shaken infant syndrome (Myers, 1992), the presence of physical or psychological indicators of various forms of possible maltreatment, characteristics of child abuse and neglect (Sagatun & Edwards, 1995), why children don't report abuse or delay in doing so (Bulkley et al., 1996), or the consistency of the alleged abuser's story with known causes (Myers, 1992).

The expert cannot offer an opinion about whether the victim is telling the truth or if the perpetrator committed the offense, since these are decisions reserved for the trier of fact (either the judge or jury) (Myers, 1995; Sagatun & Edwards, 1995).

Child sexual abuse
accommodation syndrome

In Chapter 4, we took a look at what a number of experts had to say about the impact of child sexual abuse on victims. Roland Summit (1983) may have been the first to try to develop a model to explain some of the confusing behavior victims sometimes engage in, especially their reluctance to report and their retractions of allegations after initial disclosure.

Summit (1983) tells us that part of his motivation for developing the model was to undo some of the harm being done to children by the distrust and disbelief in their disclosures. He made a comparison between how the disclosures of child sexual abuse were being received and how those of adult rape had previously been encountered. He comments that the public attitude about rape victims didn't turn around until Burgess and Holmstrom (1974, as cited in Summit, 1983) developed and published a model for recognizing, understanding, and explaining the reactions of victims, including reluctance to report it and later recantations. Summit argues that we need a similar turnaround in public attitude toward victims of child sexual abuse.

Summit (1983) developed a model, which he called the *child sexual abuse accommodation syndrome*. He indicates that he based the validity of the model on statistically validated assumptions about prevalence, age relationships, and role characteristics in child sexual abuse cases, as well as clinical observations and feedback from numerous participants in various trainings. The model outlines five categories in the syndrome:

- Secrecy
- Helplessness
- Entrapment and accommodation
- Delayed, conflicted, and unconvincing disclosure
- Retraction

Summit explains that secrecy is a necessary condition for the abuse to occur. A feeling of helplessness results because of an imbalance in power between the child and the adult and contributes to an atmosphere in which the abuse can occur without the child being able to control it. Entrapment and accommodation is a critical part of the model and perhaps a harbinger to some of the work now going on. Summit (1983) suggests that "the healthy, normal, emotionally resilient child will learn to accommodate." The child cannot control the abuse and learns to adapt as a way to survive psychologically, emotionally, and perhaps physically. As you will soon see, interpreting what the child does to survive in light of adaptability and resilience is a hallmark of an emerging newer approach to victimology. According to Summit, the delayed, conflicted, and unconvincing disclosure will usually only occur in response to family conflict and perhaps a breakdown in accommodation mechanisms. The child may be likely to retract the allegation later because of ambivalence, guilt, and a sense of obligation to preserve the family.

While Summit developed this model in 1983, it has only recently entered center stage. As we already mentioned, Summit's intent was to provide a framework for understanding the victim's behavior, including delayed reporting and retraction. Apparently, at least some expert witnesses and attorneys had been introducing the syndrome in court to support their views. Its validity as a bona fide medical concept was challenged and the Kentucky Supreme Court ruled to disallow it, throwing out convictions in cases where its use was even suspected (Summit, 1992a). In the judicial system, any medical procedure or test must pass muster as a valid tool in what is called a **Kelly-Frye hearing.** The child sexual abuse accommodation syndrome did not pass this test. While Summit decries the Kentucky Supreme Court decision (1992a; 1992b), he acknowledges that the term *syndrome* may have been an inappropriate title, since in lay terms it could be taken to imply it is a recognized psychiatric disorder, which it is not (in order for it to be considered a valid disorder, it must be listed in the official DSM-IV). He also acknowledges that the concept probably had been abused by attorneys on both sides (Summit, 1992a).

Summit (1983) attempted to take what was known about child sexual abuse victimization, both clinical and research, and frame it in a way that would help us understand the child's behavior, including initial secrecy and later retractions. Despite prior misuses of the model, he suggests that it should continue to have a place in judicial proceedings. When the child's credibility and character is attacked by the defense, he points out, it may be appropriate to introduce the syndrome, or other expert opinion, to help "rehabilitate" the child's testimony (Salter, 1992; Stewart & Young, 1992; Summit, 1992b). Despite the recent controversy about the child sexual abuse accommodation syndrome, perhaps the most significant thing to keep in mind when reviewing this model is that it explains the behavior of victims as an attempt to accommodate to a disastrous situation.

Inadmissibility of perpetrator profiles

While attempts to develop psychological profiles of child sexual offenders have a long history in professional efforts to understand this phenomenon (see Chapter 6), prosecutors are not allowed to present expert testimony to show that a defendant in a case fits any such profile. Myers (1992) points out that a fundamental part of American law is that a person cannot be convicted as a result of personality or psychological characteristics. One of the things we now believe about sexual offenders is that they are a much more diverse population than was previously believed, and there doesn't seem to be any single "typical" sexual offender or set of characteristics (see Chapter 6). Myers says, "No psychological test or device reliably detects persons who have sexually abused children or are likely to do so. Thus, under the current state of scientific knowledge, there is no profile of a 'typical' child molester" (Myers et al., 1989, as cited in Myers, 1992, p. 143)." Myers (1992) comments that, since there is no typical profile, there is no basis for expert testimony describing one.

Not only does it seem that we do not have valid and reliable profiles of offenders but it is also possible that the profiles that have been developed also describe people who turn out not to be offenders. As in the domestic violence field, however, it may be that there are some distinguishing features of types of offenders. The psychological instruments that have been developed might be better used to assist us in understanding offenders once convicted of their offenses and to help determine what we should do with them.

Clearly, some may be too dangerous to be in the community, while others may be appropriate for community treatment options (see Chapter 6).

Sentencing

Once the accused adult has been found guilty of an offense against a child, the next step in the legal process is **sentencing.** In juvenile courts prosecuting adolescent offenders, a similar step is often called *disposition.* Depending upon the state and the options available to the judge, a presentence investigation may be completed by a court representative, usually a probation officer. The purpose of the report is to familiarize the judge with the offender's background, history, problems, strengths, and anything else that may assist the judge in deciding on the sentence of the offender. The trend in recent years seems to be toward more consistency in sentencing, so much of the discretion a judge may have previously had is now frequently more limited. Given some latitude in sentencing options, judges are faced with the same position as the rest of society. Should they act to try to do something to help the offender overcome the problem or should their primary concern be protection of the community? In the context of child sexual abuse cases, we will be discussing this dilemma in greater depth in Chapter 6.

FALSE MEMORY/REPRESSED MEMORY CONTROVERSY

While we might not think of civil court actions by adult survivors as intervention per se, it is nevertheless a step that people who have been affected by child maltreatment take for themselves. It is also tied to one of the most controversial aspects of what's happening in the field today.

Currently, one of the most contentious debates is focused on adults who say they were abused as children. No one will argue that abuse has not become a matter of great concern over the last 30 years. Based on the many prevalence studies discussed in this text (see Chapters 2, 3, and 4), it also seems that a substantial number of adults living today have experienced maltreatment in one form or another during childhood. Perhaps because of the increased awareness as well as the rise in popularity of psychotherapy, a number of adults are now talking about their experiences; not only this, but some have filed civil suits against parents and other caretakers who they say abused them when they were children. As a consequence, a number of legal and social issues have come to the fore.

At the core of the discussion is whether memories of abuse that an adult becomes aware of are repressed, true memories that have come to light or whether they arise as a consequence of the spirit of the times and highly suggestive techniques used by therapists. On one side of the issue are those who assert that large numbers of people have been victimized as children and that such maltreatment is sufficiently traumatic to cause them to dissociate, or block out, its memory. As a result of life experiences or going into therapy, this side suggests, these memories rise to the surface and the person becomes aware of them again. Included on this side of the debate are well-known sociologist Linda Williams and the authors of a popular self-help book for survivors of abuse, *The Courage to Heal.* On the other side of the debate are those who claim that, in the present social atmosphere, many therapists unwittingly encourage their clients to believe they were abused, even when they do not initially remember it. These critics assert that when therapists are biased they communicate this to their clients, who, over the course of time, begin to believe they were abused. Most prominent among these critics are psychologist Elizabeth Loftus and an organization known as the False Memory Foundation.

The debate is much more than merely academic. Virtually all states have a **statute of limitation** on the amount of time that can elapse between the occurrence of an offense and when it is prosecuted. If the time lapses, no criminal case can be brought against the offender. In recent years people have become more aware of issues of abuse, and some have wanted to hold their parents or other caretakers accountable. Since these cases are "old," and because witnesses and evidence have evaporated, even serious cases cannot be prosecuted in criminal courts. In civil courts, some changes have occurred so as to allow a person who has been injured by maltreatment as a child to file suit as an adult. In a very nice review of the topic, Inger Sagatun and Leonard Edwards (1995) point out that most courts have adopted a **discovery rule**, some a **delayed discovery rule**, whereby a person has a specified period of time between the time they discover, or should have discovered, that the abuse or injury occurred and when a suit is filed (Sagatun & Edwards, 1995). Sagatun and Edwards indicate that the courts have identified at least two types of cases. One involves people who knew they were abused but did not understand that their psychological problems resulted from it. Another involves those whose trauma caused them to unconsciously repress the memory of the abuse. The courts have agreed to be more lenient in their interpretation of the statute of limitation with the second type, but generally not with the first. If the courts decide to allow the suit to be filed, the merits of the case will be a matter for a judge or jury to decide, and a great deal will hinge upon their belief in the reliability of the testimony and memory of the plaintiff and any corroborating evidence that may still exist.

Another kind of suit has been brought against therapists involved in working with survivors of childhood abuse. The accused family members have become upset with therapists who they say are unscrupulous in fostering false beliefs in their children, thereby alienating them from the affections of their adult offspring.

The discussion so far leads to a couple of important questions. Do people who have been severely maltreated sometimes dissociate traumatic memories? Do some therapists subtly or not so subtly make suggestions to their clients, which lead them to believe they were abused when they were not? It seems that the answer to *both* questions may be yes. Debra Poole and her colleagues (Poole, Lindsay, Memon, & Bull, 1995) review the recent research and also conduct their own research on the beliefs and practices of doctoral-level practitioners in two countries. On one side of the issue, they report on the work of Spanos (1994), who was able to use hypnosis to get clients to report memories of past lives and, with very mild suggestions, was able to influence exactly what those memories would contain. On the other side of the issue, Sagatun and Edwards (1995) report on an interesting study done by Williams (1994). Williams located over 120 women with documented histories of sexual victimization, interviewed them as adults, and found that about one-third had no memories of their abuse. Of those who did remember, about 20% of them reported that at one time or another in their lives they could not remember the abuse. Interestingly, a disproportionately high number of these women suffered from abuse by a family member, the type of abuse we would expect to be more traumatic.

So far our discussion tells us that victims of maltreatment sometimes repress memories of maltreatment and that therapists can influence their clients to believe false suggestions. The next question is, "Do therapists conduct their work in such a way that this actually happens?" In order to try to answer this question, Poole and her colleagues (1995) surveyed 1,300 doctoral-level clinicians in the United States and Britain. What they found is intriguing. Some highly trained clinicians believe they can spot abuse victims even when they deny having been abused. A number of clinicians use a variety of techniques (hypnosis, age regression, dream interpretation, guided imagery, use of family photographs, interpreting physical symptoms, and so on) to try to help their clients remember, and they often claim to be successful. They also found that these discoveries can have a profound, adverse impact on the relationships of these clients with their parents.

Poole and her colleagues express concern about their results, since a sizable number of even very highly trained clinicians seem willing to use techniques that are suggestive. This is not to say there is no place for such techniques as hypnosis; only that these techniques should be used with great care. Other recent research suggests that less well educated, "frontline" CPS workers are not doing interviews that conform to new research-based guidelines (Warren, et al., 1996). On the other side of the coin, I believe the vast majority of therapists make it a point to be very open in how they do their interviews and to work with what the client actually brings into the office, allowing the client's story to unfold naturally. Most clinicians I know agree that we should be careful not to plant suggestions about what might have happened. Rather, most seem to believe we should suspend any preconceived ideas we might have and listen carefully to what the clients themselves tell us about their experiences. This is clearly what the child abuse professional community is saying (American Professional Society on the Abuse of Children, 1990; Faller, 1996; Reed, 1996).

PROBLEMS, ISSUES, AND TRENDS IN INTERVENTION

In preceding sections, we have looked at legal interventions in child maltreatment cases, and we also have briefly reviewed some of the common approaches to providing services in such cases. While the usual approaches provide at least some measure of immediate relief, there are many concerns about our current system. We now take a look at some of the contemporary problems and issues, trends in providing services, and emerging ideas and innovations.

Traditional Interventions

Of immediate concern in most cases is the physical and psychological condition of the kids. It is fairly common to try to provide counseling or therapy for kids in this situation, and the research seems to indicate that receiving this kind of supportive service is effective in buffering the impact of maltreatment (see Bensley & Meengs, 1996, for discussion of several reviews of the research). Some states offer assistance to all crime victims through a fund established for this purpose. Most children nationwide who are placed outside the home are eligible for Medicaid services. Therapeutic day programs, which combine care, support services, and sometimes even parent training are also often available, especially for younger children. Because of the trauma of a court trial, many children, especially sexual abuse victims, are often familiarized with what happens in court and are given emotional support so that any trauma associated with a trial can be minimized. While there are usually at least some services available to help children with the immediate problems associated with maltreatment, most children in this situation require longer-term assistance.

State-Funded Care: Problems and Issues

One of the first reactions people often have when they hear about typical child welfare cases is that we should immediately pull the children out of the abusive homes and put them in decent homes. This is easy to say, but when it comes to actually doing it, we often come in contact with some hard realities. For one, we can naively assume that we have something better to replace the dysfunctional home with. While we sometimes get lucky and find the right placement for a child, the need is much greater than the available resources. Another reason is that the children coming into the system often have incredible needs. Maltreated children don't usually have simple problems. If they did we would probably already have learned to solve them. The fact is that maltreatment has some serious emotional and behavioral consequences and there are usually a multitude of issues that go with each case. School problems, relationship problems, aggression, sexual acting out, and problems

BOX 5-2   Model Programs for Foster Parents

We have been asking foster parents to take on some of the toughest challenges imaginable. Children entering care come from the most difficult of circumstances: horrific abuse, family environments that often include severe child maltreatment, substance abuse, crime, and prostitution. In addition to all the other issues associated with maltreated youth, we ask foster parents to be there for them as their cases weave through the court system. This also means dealing with all the emotional and behavioral ups and downs that go with it. While we ask for the moon from foster parents, we rarely provide them with all the tools they need.

At the national level, some really good training programs have been developed, one being Fosterparentscope, a 60-hour training. One unique program is offered at Pierce College, a community college in Tacoma, Washington. In addition to offering Fosterparentscope in collaboration with the state's child and family services division, Pierce offers an advanced training program for foster parents, which leads to a one-year certificate or a two-year degree in foster-parent education. Foster parents begin with Fosterparentscope and an introductory psychology course and then take coursework in a variety of other specialized areas, such as human development, family disruption, behavior management, abuse in the family, chemical dependency and the family, culture and identity, team building, and self-care. Upon completion of their training at Pierce, foster parents become professionals in their own right and often qualify for more advanced studies at four-year universities.

being able to live in a "normal" family are all too common. Yet another reason we have such a difficult time meeting the need is that we ask a lot of foster parents and all too often burn them out. With the very troubled children we often ask foster parents to take, we probably need to provide them with much more support if we're going to keep them and keep them healthy. This includes having enough social workers available to give support and provide the foster parent with more extensive training and preparation, respite care, and a feeling of inclusion as part of the helping team (see Box 5-2).

The Family Preservation/Child Protection Controversy

High-quality programming requires financial support; and while "throwing money at problems" doesn't necessarily solve them, many of the things we believe need to be done in order to provide high-quality care for maltreated kids require funding. While most agree that money shouldn't be the primary concern when the welfare of children is at stake, the political debate about government funding and the extent to which government should be involved do seem to be factors influencing the debate about services for kids and families. Perhaps the most central issue in child welfare policy today is reflected in the debate about **family preservation** versus **child protection** (Berliner, 1993; Gelles, 1993b). Not only does the issue of cost come into play in this debate but some of the most important policy questions and considerations are raised as well. Shortly we will discuss some of these issues, but first we should declare what each side of the debate is saying. Proponents of the family preservation approach argue that we should be doing whatever we can to try to preserve or keep families together; advocates of the child protection position contend that we should be putting greater emphasis on doing whatever we need to do in order to make sure kids are safe.

One of the key advantages of the family preservation effort is that it is much less costly than out-of-home care. But apart from the issue of dollars, the family preservation versus child protection debate involves philosophy, strongly held beliefs about the value of the family, and concern for kids. One of the arguments raised in support of the family preservation model is the potential damage that can be caused by putting kids in out-of-home placements (Melton, 1990; Wolfe & Jaffe, 1990, both as cited in Wolfe, 1994). As a colleague of mine says, "We know we're going to cause damage when we pull a kid out of his or her home, but sometimes we just have to weigh how much damage we're willing to inflict against the potential damage that can be caused by leaving the kid at home." Some of the damage that can occur within the child welfare system results from the lack of having a permanent home. As you read earlier, the current legal system requires a lengthy process before we can terminate a parent's rights, and this often means that kids linger for years with their lives on hold. Another problem we have is finding enough good homes for all the kids who need them, and even when we are able to find good substitute homes for kids, there's no guarantee we'll be able to keep them there. As we already mentioned, many of the kids we tend to place come with a myriad of problems, and this makes it very difficult to keep them in a placement.

It takes incredible stamina on the part of foster parents to be able to work through the kinds of problems many of these kids bring with them. For this and numerous other reasons, kids are shuttled from one placement to another far too often, in what I sometimes call the "bouncing kid" phenomenon. When considering this, bear in mind that each disrupted placement tends to take its toll, often contributing to escalating psychological damage and other problems. While prevention of placement has usually been the primary outcome objective of the family preservation model, results of controlled studies do not necessarily show significant differences when this model is used (see Pecora, et al., 1992). One of the criticisms of the model is that it emphasizes placement outcomes too much. Pecora, Whittaker, and Maluccio (1992) note that newer research is looking at other outcomes, such as parent, child, and family functioning. They report on studies that suggest significant successes for the model in these areas (see Box 5-3).

BOX 5-3　A Family Preservation Model

One approach to providing intensive in-home intervention to at-risk families is called the homebuilders model (Kinney, Haapala, Booth, & Leavitt, 1991). One of the things that happens when services are provided using this model is that a therapist, or team of therapists, will go into the home, almost camp out there, and provide services for an almost open-ended number of hours within a given time frame, sometimes for as much as six weeks or more. Practical, skills-oriented interventions are often used, and when the families need additional services, the worker or therapist is able to act as a liaison with other service providers to get them. Recognizing that out-of-home care is not always a good option, one state that uses this model, and a slightly less intensive adaptation of it, is attempting to reduce these placements with its use. "Success rates," measured in terms of preventing out-of-home placements, are reported to be quite high. On the down side, if children are inappropriately left in abusive homes, the risk of serious injury or death is an ever-present possibility.

On the other side of the debate, there are some equally powerful arguments, the safety of the child being first and foremost. As exemplified by the Eli Creekmore case (see Chapter 1), Richard Gelles (1993b) points out that 30 to 50% of children who are killed are killed by a parent or caretaker *after* child protective services has gotten involved. This not only suggests that family preservation services are not effective but that, by engaging in them, we sometimes actually endanger children's lives. Another argument is that there are many successful children who have benefited from out-of-home placements and have gone on to lead happy and productive lives. Gelles (1993b) points out that kids do not necessarily need their biological parents, but they do need to develop an attachment during a sensitive developmental time (see Chapter 3), somewhere between 4 and 10 years of age. He implies that if child protective services engages in trying to preserve hopelessly dysfunctional families during this time, it will be too late for some kids by the time the child welfare system places them outside their biological home. Another argument is that, because family preservation programs have now gotten political support, we are making major dollar investments in these programs without good evidence that they are actually effective (Blythe, 1994, as cited in Bensley & Meengs, 1996; Gelles, 1993b; Wolfe, 1994).

As with so many issues, the question may not be whether we should try to preserve families or to protect kids, but rather when to protect and when to try to preserve. As Gelles (1993b) indicates, family preservation efforts may be appropriate in up to 65 to 70% of the cases, but inappropriate for the others. The family preservation versus child protection debate points out the unresolved questions in the field of child welfare. Child maltreatment as a field is relatively young, having its roots in the "child-saving" movement that began in this country about a hundred years ago. Intervention practice can probably be better described as an art rather than a science, and there are those who describe our early efforts as "trial and error" (Wolfe, 1994). While we still have a long way to go in terms of both research about causes and intervention, we may be at the point in the development of the child maltreatment field where we can begin to look at patterns, synthesizing what we've already learned.

An Overview of Intervention Approaches

There are many approaches, and types of programs, that attempt to resolve problems associated with child maltreatment, and from a distance this diversity may look somewhat random; however, each effort can be seen as an attempt to solve part of the problem and as a step in the development of the field. In order to get an overall sense of this development, we may want to take an overview. There are now any number of reviews that try to take a "big picture" look at the various approaches to prevention and intervention (see Bensley & Meengs, 1996; DePanfilis, 1996; Hay & Jones, 1994; Wekerle & Wolfe, 1993; Wolfe, 1987, 1991, 1994). Based on a cursory review of the various approaches, it seems that there is increasing recognition of the complex interaction of societal, family, and individual factors, consistent with the systems or ecological orientation emphasized in this text. The field also seems to be moving in the direction of greater coordination and integration of services. While we could organize the summary of the various approaches in any number of ways, we will follow the macro-meso-micro framework we've adopted throughout this text.

Macro level interventions—
the broad social and cultural approaches

As discussed elsewhere (see Chapters 1, 2, 3, and 4), there are a number of risk factors associated with child maltreatment at the macro level. These include cultural attitudes about the authority of parents and the value of children, acceptance of corporal punishment as a child-rearing tool, cultural beliefs about the appropriateness of violence (including in the media), poverty, unemployment or underemployment, educational opportunities, lack of access to health care, availability of child care, social isolation, and neighborhood characteristics. While there has been a great deal of work done at the family and individual levels in terms of child maltreatment intervention, programs and policies to combat broad societal-level concerns such as poverty are almost nonexistent (Hay & Jones, 1994).

The one major federal program specifically aimed at trying to see to it that all children receive a minimum level of economic support, **Aid to Families with Dependent Children** (AFDC), was begun under the Franklin D. Roosevelt administration and has been under attack for some time. The program, most commonly known as "welfare," has been seen in many quarters as ineffective. The 104th Congress passed legislation reforming the program and President Clinton signed the bill into law in August, 1996. The two factors often associated with the difficulty of being able to get off welfare are the availability of child care and medical insurance. AFDC recipients are eligible for Medicaid insurance for their children. A woman wanting to get off welfare faces the loss of medical insurance for her child, minimum wage earnings, and high child care expenses. The educational and work training aspects of welfare-to-work programs, such as those in Wisconsin, may hold promise if once the mother is in the work force, the medical and day care needs of the children are addressed.

While most of the antipoverty programs of the Lyndon B. Johnson administration have not survived, one of them, the **Head Start program**, has. It attempts to provide educational and social enrichment to at-risk kids. While children attend Head Start in groups with other kids, the program is not really intended as day care.

Meso level interventions—
family and relationship based approaches

Social and family relations also seem to be important factors that can either increase or decrease the risk of child maltreatment. Marital discord and relationships characterized by the use of intimidation and coercion are often associated with abusive and neglectful families (Wolfe, 1985, 1994). Some estimates suggest that the co-occurrence of child maltreatment and domestic violence may be as high as 40 to 45% (Straus & Gelles, 1990, as cited in Wolfe, 1994). Social isolation is commonly associated with family dysfunction and child maltreatment (DePanfilis, 1996; Wolfe, 1994).

Interestingly, Wolfe (1994) could identify only one controlled study that focused on the use of family therapy to address the issues of maltreating families (Brunk, et al., 1987). The results of this study suggest that family therapy can be effective in assisting with a number of factors associated with maltreatment and may be superior to others in terms of helping with parent-child relationships.

DePanfilis (1996) has conducted a review of social support models and has identified seven different intervention models that address the issue of the social isolation of maltreating families: (1) network assessment, (2) multiservice models, (3) individual support, (4) parent education and support, (5) self-help groups, (6) social skills training, and (7) therapeutic day care. Both DePanfilis (1996) and Wolfe (1994) comment that, while providing social support is extremely popular in many communities, there is not a great deal of research demonstrating its utility in reducing child maltreatment. With the current state of the art on research, the social support model should probably be seen as a promising approach that still needs more study. For at-risk kids, on the other hand, there is probably no protective factor cited more often than having a positive relationship with at least one supportive adult.

With respect to mother-child relationships, there are a number of intervention approaches, including during pregnancy, after birth, and during early childhood (Wolfe, 1994). Prenatal efforts seem to focus primarily on prenatal care as well as the use of substances (for example, alcohol, tobacco, and other drugs) that can be harmful to the developing child. Clinic as well as visiting nurse services can assist the mother in becoming better able to care for the developing child and can also act as a social support, thereby reducing the risk of abusive behavior. Based on his review of a large number of studies, Wolfe (1994) suggests that intensive home visitations of the mothers of children under age three seems to be a significant help. Bensley and Meengs (1996) comment that the results of the research on whether this approach is actually effective in preventing child maltreatment is inconclusive.

Earlier in this section, we briefly introduced the in-home services, or intensive family preservation, model. While the evidence does not seem clear-cut about the effectiveness of these kinds of services, they do provide something in addition to trying to keep families united; that is, increased social contact with someone outside the family system. In-home family workers are often qualified in family therapy and may be particularly well positioned not only to assess at-risk families but also to provide support that may ultimately reduce the risk of further maltreatment. One of the strategies often employed by in-home family preservation programs is teaching communication and problem-solving skills to both kids and their parents. One possible drawback to the model is that it invariably allows for intervention only within a relatively short period of time, usually from 30 days to 12 weeks. As research on this model continues, I hope that a more extended version is included for study and that outcomes other than preventing placements are more fully investigated.

Micro level interventions with maltreating parents

When professionals interested in child maltreatment began to study the phenomenon, one of the factors often investigated was the characteristics of the perpetrator. One of the early assumptions about abusive parents was that they are more likely to have psychopathology, especially personality disturbance. While there seem to be some characteristics that are frequently associated with abusive parents (increased life stressors, inadequate social support, low self-esteem, and depressive symptoms), there has been no success in finding consistent profiles that accurately characterize offenders (Kinard, 1996). Wolfe (1994) identifies four factors associated with the issues of offending parents: (1) symptoms of emotional distress, (2) emotional reactivity to child provocation, (3) inappropriate expectations of children, and (4) negative lifestyle and habits (for example, substance abuse, prostitution, and so on).

Traditional approaches to working with maltreating parents have included social casework and often individual psychotherapy, presumably because of the assumption that they have psychiatric disturbance. Wolfe

(1994) points out that, while they often have maturity problems and may be more likely to have limited learning abilities, they do not necessarily have psychiatric problems. For this reason, traditional psychotherapy may not always be the treatment of choice.

The programs that seem to have the greatest amount of validation from the research are those that focus on teaching parents new behaviors and skills (Bensley & Meengs, 1996; Wolfe, 1994). Wolfe (1994) divides these into three basic types: (1) **behaviorally oriented programs** that help parents improve their parenting skills, (2) **cognitively oriented programs** that help parents with awareness and coping, and (3) **cognitive-behavioral programs** that attempt to assist with both parenting skills and the ability of parents to cope. Wolfe (1994) reports that these approaches show generally good results. He also notes that they have their limitations, chief among which is their inappropriateness for those parents who do have significant personality or psychiatric disturbance (Wolfe, 1994). Bensley and Meengs (1996) suggest that some behavioral approaches have shown effectiveness in improving parenting behavior but that the overall effects on maltreatment are still unknown. Their review of studies (for example, Graziano & Diament, 1992; Patterson & Fleischman, 1979; Patterson, et al., 1982; Stoolmiller, et al., 1993; Wolfe, et al., 1988) indicates improved parent-child interactions, more positive child management techniques, better stress management, reduced child abuse potential, and reduced child aggression.

Micro level interventions with maltreated children

The controlled research on the helpfulness of psychotherapy for maltreated children seems to show that it is moderately to highly effective in helping abused kids and that the gains that maltreated kids make may be long lasting (Bensley and Meengs, 1996). Building on the success of therapy for kids, several teams suggest the need for developing integrated models (Friedrich, 1996) or abuse-focused treatment approaches that vary depending upon the type of maltreatment experienced by the child (Chaffin, Bonner, Worley, & Lawson, 1996; Crittenden, 1996). As referred to elsewhere in this text (see Chapters 4 and 7), Briere (1992, 1996) has put together a very simple yet elegant model that focuses on adaptations to maltreatment, different types of impacts likely to be experienced, and approaches to working through the trauma.

Other approaches to working with maltreated kids include specialized therapeutic day treatment programs for preschool-aged kids (Bensley and Meengs, 1996; Wolfe, 1994), agency-based or school-based support groups for school-aged maltreated kids, and comprehensive therapeutic foster care programs. Both therapeutic day treatment programs and therapeutic foster care are often very comprehensive in their scope and are used in some of the more severe or difficult cases. Therapeutic day treatment programs, for instance, while they provide a safe and nurturing environment for the kids, typically also work with parents, individually or in groups, to provide them with support, therapy, and education. In comprehensive therapeutic foster care programs, therapy services might be available for the kids, their parents, and the families "in house." They might also provide intensive case management services, in which a case manager who works with everyone else in the system (for example, therapist, parents, foster parents, state or county social worker, the court, the school) acts as a troubleshooter and coordinator of services.

Services for child sexual abuse victims are likely to be somewhat specialized. In addition to the response teams set up in many communities to handle these kinds of cases, victims are often provided with specialized psychotherapy. Because of the additional trauma associated with the legal process, many programs now try to minimize the trauma by familiarizing the children with the courtroom and providing them with lots of support and encouragement (Wolfe, 1994). In terms of prevention, educational programs about child sexual abuse in the schools are probably the single most common approach. While assessments of what kids learn seems good even after periods of time, there is no reliable research to tell us whether the risk of sexual abuse among these children is lowered (Bensley & Meengs, 1996).

On the positive side of intervention

We know that there are many children who are what we call "at risk" and that many of them are likely to have significant problems in their lives as a result. So far our discussion has primarily centered on interventions after the damage is done or with at-risk kids and families. It is the perception of many that the system as we know it is "broken." One concern circulating among the public and in various quarters within the professional community is that the problems are so overwhelming and that we focus so much on reacting to crises that we never get around to accomplishing positive outcomes. However, there are some bright spots and innovations.

One of the bright spots is naturally occurring; that is, while many at-risk kids develop significant problems, some grow and flourish despite the odds. For the past 20 years or so, a small group of researchers has taken an interest in this phenomenon (Norman Garmezy at the University of Minnesota and Michael Rutter in England are two that come to mind). The hope is that, if we can identify those other factors that get the at-risk kids past their hurdles, we might be able to design interventions to help hurt kids succeed instead of merely helping them overcome specific problems.

In the Hawaiian Islands on the island of Kauai, a long-range study was begun over forty years ago (Werner, 1989a, 1989b, 1992, 1993, 1995). This is a very interesting study for a number of reasons. For one, it turns out that Kauai is an ideal place to do this kind of study—there is a stable population that doesn't move too much, services are comparable to those offered on the mainland and elsewhere, there is a great deal of cultural diversity, and the island is small enough that it is possible to study all the kids born there. For the year 1955, the study had a cohort of 698 children, of which 201 were identified as being at "high risk" (defined as having four or more risk factors by age two). Two-thirds of these in fact developed significant problems by the time they reached adulthood. A full third, however, did very well. As Werner (1989a) puts it, they "grew into competent young adults who loved well, worked well and played well." When the odds were against them, how is it this could happen?

Werner and her colleagues identified a number of protective factors that enabled the resilient kids of Kauai to resist stress. Those factors, identified throughout the children's lives, included positive temperaments, high activity level, low degree of excitability and distress, and high degree of sociability. Observers reported that the children tended to be alert, responsive, and curious, their teachers found them to be able to concentrate and have good problem-solving skills, and they were able to form a close bond with at least one caretaker; if not a parent, a substitute from within or outside the family. Overall, they were also able to develop an informal support network outside the family. Were we to synthesize the protective factors identified in the **Kauai Longitudinal Study**, they would include an easy-going temperament, a supportive caretaker, a positive outlook and attitude, the ability to concentrate and engage in problem solving, and the ability to form constructive interpersonal relationships.

Because of the stable population, Werner and her colleagues were able to track the children at intervals for years after initial contact. In comparison to other kids at high risk, and even kids at low risk, the resilient group did extremely well in their lives. Werner indicates that, because of this study and what they were able to learn as a result, many positive changes occurred in Hawaii's children's service system.

While not necessarily directly related to the Kauai Longitudinal Study, one of the most promising programs developed to date also hails from Hawaii. The following description is based on the summary contained in the review by Bensley and Meengs (1996). It is called the **Healthy Start program.** This program is an ongoing program in the state of Hawaii in which families are screened at the hospital for risk factors associated with child abuse. The goal is to provide home visiting services to all families identified as being at high risk. Since, due to funding limitations, the researchers could not study all communities, they compared matched sets of about 1,353 high risk families, one set receiving home visiting services and the other not. The results suggest that the rate of abuse for the families who received services was 1.9%, compared to 5.0% for the others (U. S. Department of Justice, 1995, cited in Bensley & Meengs, 1996).

Since many people are frustrated and concerned about the quagmires in the existing system, there seem to be stirrings of interest in exploring new, and potentially more effective, ways of doing things. Some of this interest has sprung from an effort of the National Council of Governors Planning Advisors, which selected ten states to participate in a family policy academy to work on strategies for reforming their state systems (Family Policy Council, 1995). The states, for their part, selected senior-level officials to participate in the academy, generally heads of major departments in state government. The participants in turn went back to their states to help lead attempts to change and reform their systems. Two driving forces seem to underlie this movement: the desire for systemwide reform and a concern about outcomes, or getting positive results from what we do (S. Watson, Family Policy Council, personal communication, September 18, 1996). In the social sciences, there is now greater recognition that protective factors or resiliencies can indeed play an important role in buffering children from the negative impact of even the most dismal of life circumstances (see Chapters 2 and 3). In an attempt to achieve system reform and better outcomes for kids, at least one of the broad state initiatives includes an emphasis on finding ways to enhance protective factors and minimize the risk factors associated with maltreatment and family violence.

CHAPTER SUMMARY

In this chapter we discussed investigation, interviewing, risk assessment, court involvement, and intervention efforts. Included in this discussion was a brief synopsis of investigation and a review of the use and abuse of interviewing techniques. In this context, we surveyed issues surrounding the use of anatomically detailed dolls in sexual abuse investigations and the practice of videotaping interviews. We introduced the concept of investigatory interviewing and reviewed the classic work of Suzanne Sgroi. We briefly touched on risk assessment and risk assessment instruments, as well as some controversies that surround their use. We also took a look at the role of child protective services in legal intervention and the kinds of juvenile court proceedings that occur in child abuse and neglect cases. We discussed the kind of options available to the courts when findings of maltreatment are made. We also covered some of the resources available in the social welfare system.

Before discussing criminal prosecution, we briefly touched on law enforcement investigation and coordination with other players in the network. Adult criminal proceedings are very different from juvenile court dependency cases, with a criminal conviction potentially resulting in a prison sentence. We reviewed the various steps and hearings in the process of criminal court prosecution. We discussed the potential stress on child victims and controversies about alleged suggestive interview techniques. We spoke about hearsay exceptions, which permit into evidence things the victim has told others about the abuse. In addition, we addressed some other controversial issues, including the use of the child sexual abuse accommodation syndrome, in criminal court cases.

The last type of legal proceeding we discussed was the filing of civil lawsuits. Issues in some of these cases have gotten a lot of attention because sometimes suits are filed years after the alleged abuse and sometimes after the person has been in therapy. We reviewed evidence on both sides of the false memory/repressed memory debate, in which one side claims that memories are really responses to suggestions by therapists and the other side insists that these memories are real.

After reviewing the various legal interventions, we turned to a discussion about some of the problems, issues, and trends in child maltreatment intervention. We noted that the traditional approaches are very hard on all involved, and we also explored some of the difficulties in getting good foster care and adoptive homes for maltreated kids. Since there is debate in the field about the relative merits of placing kids outside their homes versus trying to keep them safe in the home, we also reviewed some of the professional discussion about "family preservation" as opposed to "child protection." We then moved to a review of intervention approaches at the societal, relationship, and individual (macro-meso-micro) levels. We concluded our discourse on a positive note, talking about some of the innovations being explored, including an emphasis on supporting the strengths and resiliencies of kids.

LEGAL AND ETHICAL CONCERNS: CRITICAL THINKING QUESTIONS

1. How can a professional balance the commitment to safeguard confidential information with the legal requirements to report maltreatment?

2. As a professional, what is more important ethically: to get disclosure on suspected maltreatment or to do a really open and nonsuggestive interview? Is there a conflict?

3. If you had videotaped an interview in which you had inadvertently used suggestive interviewing techniques, would you conceal the presence of that tape in order to prevent a potentially guilty person from "getting off?" What would you do if you learned a colleague had done this?

4. Do you think it is ethical to testify that when you appraised the victim's statement you believed it was credible? What does the law permit?

5. Is it ethical to advocate in court that a child not be returned home, substantially on the basis of the results of a formal risk assessment instrument? Why or why not?

6. How does one balance the need to protect a child and prevent undue interference with the parents' right to bring up their child?

7. Hypothetically, you are working on a case where you believe it's hopeless to expect the parents to ever be able to care for their child. You have the child in a wonderful foster home, and they want to adopt. The law says you must take reasonable steps to reunify the family. How can you balance the rights of the parents with the potential damage that will be caused by delaying termination of parental rights? What if the only reason the parent cannot care for the child is mental retardation? Is this discrimination?

8. Hypothetically, you are working with a child as a helping professional, and the child is needed to provide testimony in order to gain a conviction. You believe that the child will be harmed emotionally by going through with testimony. What should you do?

9. There are certain exceptions to the rule that hearsay evidence must not be introduced in court. Do you think allowing these exceptions infringes upon the rights of a defendant? Why or why not?

10. The child sexual abuse accommodation syndrome has been used to explain how and why victims adapt as they do. This includes keeping the secret and recanting. What issues arise by using this syndrome in court?

11. As a society we are becoming very angry with people who sexually abuse children. Should society try to treat sex offenders or punish them? Always? Why or why not

12. The false memory/repressed memory debate continues to rage. People on one side say therapists are planting suggestions, while those on the other side say anger about "false" memories is nothing more than backlash. What are the legal and ethical issues here? Please explain.

13. The family preservation/child protection debate is also ongoing. It seems true that we damage kids when we bring them into the child welfare system. It is also true that, when we don't intervene, kids get hurt. What should we do? Why? Please explain.

14. We have a limited number of dollars and a great many maltreated kids. Do we spend the money to help the kids who have already been hurt, or do we spend the money to try new and different ways to solve the problem? Why? Please explain.

SUGGESTED ACTIVITIES

1. Most jurisdictions have risk assessment procedures. Find out from your local children's protective service how they determine risk. Do they use a particular risk assessment instrument or do they operate from general guidelines or state-established criteria? How are neglect cases prioritized in comparison to physical abuse or sexual abuse cases?

2. Courts have to make sensitive decisions about how to intervene in cases of child physical abuse and neglect. Contact your local court administrator or judge and find out how this is done in your community.

3. Select at least one book on child physical abuse or neglect. Read it, and evaluate it critically and honestly.

4. Contact your local police department, sheriff's office, CPS agency, or prosecutor's office and find out what kind of coordinated efforts exist (or don't exist) in your community for investigating child sexual abuse cases.

5. If you have a children's hospital in your area, find out if they have a sexual assault unit. If they do, give them a call and see what information you can get about what they do.

6. See if you can identify a professional who interviews victims of sexual maltreatment. See if the person is able to give you an interview. Find out what kind of interview techniques the person uses when interviewing kids suspected of being sexually abused.

7.   Contact your local juvenile court and find out if they have a CASA or guardian ad litem program. Give them a call and find out how they go about trying to help kids.

8.   Select an abuse case that has hit the newspapers or TV in your area. Start keeping a journal or scrapbook on developments in the case. Check with the courts and perhaps make a point to sit in on any hearing open to the public.

9.   Contact your local children's services unit and find out about the foster parent program in your area. What does it take to become a foster parent? What training is provided?

10.   Find out if there is a local foster parent organization in your area; if there is, see if you can get the name and number of a contact person. Give them a call and see if they'll give you an interview.

REVIEW GUIDE

1.   Be able to discuss mandatory reporting, including who such reports are made to, typical categories of professionals required to report, liability protections for those who report, and how cases are typically prioritized.

2.   Be able to briefly outline basic issues in Child Protective Services investigations as discussed in the chapter. Generally, how does a CPS worker go about trying to determine if cases are substantiated or not?

3.   Be familiar with how an interviewing protocol is defined, and be able to discuss advantages and disadvantages of either adopting a formal interviewing protocol or not.

4.   Be fully familiar with the interviewing guidelines, including those proposed by L. Dennison Reed (see Box 5-1). Be able to identify two additional recommended practices suggested by Warren and colleagues (1996).

5.   Be able to discuss the pros and cons of doing multiple interviews with victims. Discuss when you might want to do multiple interviews and when this might be an intrusive and countertherapeutic practice.

6.   Discuss some of the issues associated with the controversy over videotaping interviews. Discuss advantages and disadvantages of the use of videotaping.

7.   Be familiar with the controversy over use of anatomically detailed dolls in child sexual abuse investigations. What are the four primary objections to their use? Which seem valid? Invalid? What are the advantages and disadvantages of using them? When does the American Professional Society on the Abuse of Children say is an appropriate time and way to use them?

8.   Be familiar with some of the main contributions of Dr. Suzanne Sgroi.

9.   What is risk assessment? Be able to discuss the two primary reasons to do risk assessment, as discussed in the text. Which reason is used by the

greatest number of jurisdictions? What are the stakes, on each side, when doing risk assessments? What are risk assessment instruments (RAIs)? What two types of risk assessment instruments were described in the text? What are the problems and controversies over the use of RAIs?

10.   Be familiar with steps a CPS worker might take as part of an initial intervention. What authority does the CPS worker have? What is temporary custody or temporary care?

11.   Be able to describe and discuss court action related to child abuse and neglect. What is a common term used to describe court action related to abuse and neglect? Define all terms. Distinguish between juvenile, criminal, and civil courts. Distinguish between civil proceedings in juvenile court and criminal proceedings. Which applies to abuse and neglect proceedings? What questions do the courts try to answer in abuse and neglect proceedings? Be familiar with the various hearings that occur in child maltreatment cases. What is permanency planning? What are the issues surrounding permanency planning and termination proceedings? Be familiar with the standard of evidence required in both dependency actions and termination proceedings. What kinds of treatment options can the court ask parents to participate in, should a dependency be established?

12.   Be able to describe the range of service options available once the courts establish that a child needs protection.

13.   Be familiar with criminal justice aspects of child maltreatment cases. What are coordinated services? What are the advantages of a coordinated team effort? In addition to criminal investigation and prosecution, what specialized services are sometimes available through the prosecutor's office? Be able to identify and describe each of the hearings or steps in the criminal prosecution. What does the expression "beyond a reasonable doubt" mean? What does competency mean in the context of a criminal trial of child maltreatment? What is tainted victim testimony? What is a taint hearing? What is hearsay evidence, when is it excluded, and what are the exceptions to excluding it? What are the common attacks on interviewers by defense attorneys? What is an expert in the context of a criminal trial? What can experts testify to? What can't they? What is the child sexual abuse accommodation syndrome? When can it be admitted, if ever?

14.   What are the basic elements in each position of the false memory/repressed memory debate?

15.   In the context of civil proceedings for damages, what is a statute of limitation? What is a discovery rule? A delayed discovery rule? What is the evidence supporting the validity of repressed memory? Of false memories and the influence of suggestion? What risk is there that CPS workers might sometimes be using suggestive instead of nonsuggestive interviewing techniques?

16.   Be familiar with what the traditional interventions are in child maltreatment cases. What are the general problems and issues associated with providing state-funded care?

17. Be familiar with each position of the family preservation/child protection controversy. What evidence is there to support each?

18. Be familiar with the interventions and types of programs discussed at the macro, meso, and micro levels. (For example, what is AFDC? The Head Start program? What seven different types of social support models does DePanfilis [1996] identify? What kinds of interventions are used to help parent-child relationships? To assist with parenting skills?) What three types of programs does Wolfe suggest as having value in terms of working with maltreating parents? When might the use of these approaches be inappropriate?

19. What does the research say about the effectiveness of therapy for child victims of maltreatment?

20. In addition to therapy, what other approaches were identified in the chapter for working with maltreated kids?

21. Be able to discuss some of the positives when it comes to intervention. Be familiar with the discussion about the Kauai Longitudinal Study. Discuss the implications of research about resiliency. Be able to discuss the Healthy Start program.

SUGGESTED READING

Briere, J., Berliner, L., Bulkley, J. A., Jenny, C., & Reid, T. (Eds.). (1996). *The APSAC handbook on child maltreatment.* Thousand Oaks, CA: Sage Publications and the American Professional Society on the Abuse of Children.
   An edited handbook, available in paperback, with chapters written by experts on various aspects of child maltreatment. Section topics include psychosocial treatment, medical aspects, legal aspects, preventing and reporting, and organization and service delivery. The American Professional Society on the Abuse of Children is a new, but growing, organization of professionals who concern themselves with the problem of child maltreatment. This handbook represents a significant contribution by members of the society to address this issue.

Calof, D. (Ed.). *Treating Abuse Today.*
   I have included this reference, though it is neither a book nor a specific issue of a journal, because it represents a unique kind of resource. It is a small, but growing, periodical geared specifically to people working with child abuse and adult survivor issues. The editor is a renowned figure in the field of treating clients with dissociative disorders. Information about the magazine can be obtained by writing: Treating Abuse Today, Clinical Training Publications, 150 Nickerson St., Suite 209, Seattle, WA 98109.

Goodman, G. S., & Bottoms, B. L. (1993). *Child victims, child witness.* New York: Guilford Press.
   This is a scholarly, but highly readable, book that focuses on children as witnesses in legal proceedings. Discusses the role of development in memory, use of anatomical dolls, the effects of questioning techniques, how to interview, preparing children to testify, and testing children's evidence, among many other issues.

Jewett, C. L. (1978). *Adopting the older child.* Harvard, MA: Harvard Common Press.
   This is another classic. It is one of the first and best regarded books about the problems associated with older kids in care. Not only does it movingly discuss the needs of older

kids but is candid about the challenges in attempting to provide them with permanent homes. This is a "must read" for anyone involved in the long-term care system.

Myers, J. E. B. (1992). *Legal issues in child abuse and neglect.* Newbury Park, CA: Sage Publications.

A very concise book, written in a clean style, which does an excellent job in familiarizing the reader with how the legal system works when it comes to child abuse and neglect cases. Discusses the balance between confidentiality and reporting requirements, reporting laws, expert testimony, cross-examination and impeachment of witnesses, and lawsuits against professionals.

Pecora, P. J., Whittaker, J. K., & Maluccio, A. N. (1992). *The child welfare challenge.* New York: Aldine de Gruyeter.

A very thorough and helpful book dealing with many important aspects of the child welfare system. Discusses child abuse and neglect from the standpoint of understanding the role of social policies and emphasizes "family-centered" practice. In addition to providing an overview of each of the major types of maltreatment, this book, unlike many others, takes the next step and discusses what to do about the issues. In this vein, the authors review virtually every form of intervention: family-based services, foster care, adoption, and group care.

Sagatun, I. J., & Edwards, L. P. (1995). *Child abuse and the legal system.* Chicago: Nelson-Hall Publishers.

A fairly comprehensive, though easy-to-follow, book about the legal system and child abuse and neglect cases. Includes a nice discussion about history, an overview of types of maltreatment (with summary of indicators), discussion about the roles of various professionals, the legal response to maltreatment, children in court, and some emerging issues in the field.

CHAPTER GLOSSARY

AFDC	Acronym for Aid to Families with Dependent Children.
Aid to Families with Dependent Children	A federal program, first begun in the Franklin D. Roosevelt administration, that provides a support payment for eligible children in order to meet their basic needs. More commonly known as welfare.
American Professional Society on the Abuse of Children	The largest interdisciplinary professional society in the United States for those who work with maltreated children and their families.
APSAC	Acronym for American Professional Society on the Abuse of Children.
Arraignment	A court hearing in a criminal court proceeding in which the defendant is officially notified of the charges against him or her.
Behaviorally oriented programs	One of three types of programs identified by Wolfe (1994) as being effective. In this approach, the behavior is the exclusive focus of intervention.
Beyond a reasonable doubt	The highest level of proof possible, generally required only in criminal cases.
CASA	Acronym for court-appointed special advocate.

Child abuse hearsay exception An exception to the rule, which usually excludes other than direct testimony, that permits what children have said to others to be introduced into evidence in criminal proceedings.

Child protection When used in the context of the family preservation/child protection debate, refers to an emphasis being placed on protecting the child from further harm rather than keeping the family together.

Child Protective Services (CPS) A term used to describe the agency of a state or territory whose job it is to investigate complaints of child maltreatment and to take necessary steps to protect the child.

Civil proceedings A type of court proceeding, which, while it can affect the lives of individuals named, cannot impose jail or prison sentence. Child abuse proceedings to determine if a child needs protection or placement are civil in nature.

Cognitive-behavioral programs One of three types of programs identified by Wolfe (1994) as being effective. In this approach, both the behavior and internal coping abilities and strategies are emphasized.

Cognitively oriented programs One of three types of programs identified by Wolfe (1994) as being effective. In this approach, the internal coping abilities and strategies are the exclusive focus of intervention.

Competency In child abuse legal cases, this term refers to the ability of the child to be able to testify in a meaningful way, including the ability to understand, to communicate, and to know that he or she should tell the truth.

Consensus-based models When used in the context of discussion about risk assessment instruments (RAIs), this term refers to the inclusion of risk factors in assessment tools on the basis of general agreement about their importance.

Court-appointed special advocate A person appointed by the juvenile court to act as an advocate for the child's best interests in dependency matters.

Credibility assessment When used in the context of child sexual abuse investigations, this term refers to the formal or informal process whereby the believability of the child's statement is evaluated.

Criminal proceeding A type of court proceeding that is criminal in nature and can result in the imposition of a jail or prison sentence.

Delayed discovery rule A rule adopted in civil court proceedings, which says that a person who was sexually victimized as a child has a specified period of time after remembering it to file a suit.

Dependency actions A type of civil legal proceeding called to establish the need of a child for the protection and supervision of the court.

Dependency petition A formal legal document filed by the responsible social service agency that alleges maltreatment and the need of the state to protect the child.

Discovery A term used to refer to the process in criminal court cases whereby the prosecutors are required to turn over to the defense all information they possess and, to a lesser degree, whereby the defense must turn over information to the prosecution.

Discovery rule A legal doctrine that says that the statute of limitations in civil cases does not commence until a victim discovers, or should have discovered, the injury.

Disposition hearing A formal hearing in child maltreatment dependency cases, held after the court has ruled that the child was abused and needs protection, at which the judge decides what services will be offered and what will be required of the parents.

Empirically based models	When used in the context of risk assessment instruments (RAIs), this term refers to the inclusion of risk factors in assessment tools on the basis of their reliability and validity, as established by scientific research.
Excited utterance exception	An exception to the usual rule that excludes second-hand testimony, whereby others may testify about something that another person says in an excited state, for instance, after having suffered from a trauma.
Fact-finding hearing	In the context of juvenile court dependency proceedings, the type of hearing that establishes the truth or falsehood to allegations of maltreatment and the need for state protection for a child.
Family preservation	When used in the context of the family preservation/child protection debate, refers to the emphasis on trying to keep the family together whenever possible.
Finding of fact	In the context of juvenile court dependency proceedings, the actual ruling that establishes the truth or falsehood of allegations of mistreatment and the alleged need to protect the child.
Guardian ad litem	A person appointed by the court to act on behalf of a child. Sometimes used in juvenile court dependency proceedings to act as an advocate for the best interests of the child.
Head Start program	One of the few surviving programs of the Lyndon B. Johnson administration's War on Poverty. Provides an enriched social and educational program in a group setting for kids identified as being disadvantaged or at high risk.
Healthy Start program	A program initiated in Hawaii whereby all kids born in the state are assessed in the hospital for risk of maltreatment. Those identified as being at risk receive home visiting services, which research suggests is effective in preventing maltreatment.
Hearsay evidence	Testimony from one person about what another person says happened, which is offered to prove the truth of the matter at hand.
Hearsay exclusion	The court rule that generally excludes hearsay evidence.
Interviewing protocol	A set of steps or procedures to follow when conducting an interview, especially in child sexual abuse investigations.
Juvenile courts	Courts that have jurisdiction to hear cases involving children and youth.
Kauai Longitudinal Study	A study of a group of children born on the island of Kauai in the 1950s, done over a 40-year time span, that looked at their risk factors and how they actually did.
Kelly-Frye hearing	A hearing held to prevent fact finders (that is, judges or juries) from being misled by the "aura of infallibility" that may surround unproven scientific methods.
Permanency planning	A term used in the child welfare field that refers to the establishment of a permanent plan for a child in terms of parents and a home.
Permanent plan	A plan required under federal law in which the goal for permanent care of a dependent child is established.
Plea bargaining	A process of negotiation between the prosecutor and the defendant's attorney over what charges will be brought against the defendant if he or she agrees to plead guilty.
Preliminary hearing	A hearing to determine if the evidence is sufficient to proceed with a trial.
Preponderance of the evidence	A standard of evidence establishing that, in order to reach a ruling that could be adverse for a person, there must be more evidence that something has happened than not.

Pretrial motions Motions made to the court in order to resolve selected legal issues before trial.

Residual exception An exception to the rule excluding hearsay evidence, which allows for the admission of statements not covered by other exceptions so long as they are also trustworthy.

Review hearings Formal hearings in dependency cases where the judge reviews the efforts of each of the parties and evaluates what progress has been made.

Risk assessment instrument (RAI) Usually, a form or test of some kind used to assist child protective service investigators in making their decisions about steps to take in a case.

Sentencing A formal hearing held in a criminal case in which the decision is made about what will happen to the defendant who has pleaded or been found guilty.

Severe physical abuse Acts of maltreatment that threaten or cause serious injury or death.

Shelter care hearing A formal hearing held in dependency cases at which the judge decides if the child already in care needs to remain there or if a child not in care needs to be placed.

Standard of evidence The standard by which a decision in a legal matter is decided. In criminal cases the standard of evidence is "beyond a reasonable doubt," but in dependency cases it is the much less rigorous "preponderance of the evidence."

Statements made to professionals providing diagnosis and treatment One of the exceptions to the hearsay exclusion rule, whereby what a child says to medical personnel, including clinical social workers, is permitted to be told in court by the professional. This exception is permitted because what is told to a person diagnosing and treating for a problem is generally considered reliable.

Statute of limitation A legally established time limit on the amount of time that can elapse before legal action can no longer be brought against a person.

Taint hearings Special hearings held to determine if faulty interview procedures were used in order to obtain the statement of a child, usually in cases involving child sexual abuse allegations.

Temporary care See Temporary custody.

Temporary custody In the context of child maltreatment, the process by which children's protective services can temporarily take custody of a suspected maltreated child and place the child outside the home.

Termination proceedings Legal proceedings to determine whether the parent-child relationship shall be permanently ended, thereby ending all parental rights to make decisions on behalf of the child. The standard of evidence required is often much higher than for other types of child welfare hearings in which the stakes are not so high.

Trial A legal proceeding in criminal cases during which the guilt or innocence of a defendant is decided. Argument, testimony, and evidence are generally presented by opposing sides.

Validating complaints The process by which a Child Protective Services worker, or other appropriate personnel, attempts to assess whether claims of maltreatment are true, usually in child sexual abuse cases.

CHAPTER

SEXUAL OFFENDERS

Types of Offenders

Psychiatric Diagnosis and Sexual Offenders

Profile Models

The Four-Factor Offender Model

The Addiction Model

A Special Class of Offenders: Children and Adolescents

Concluding Comments about Sexual Offenders

Intervention and Treatment

For most people, the subject of sexual offenders can be strangely intriguing and abhorrent at the same time. In this chapter, we will explore this topic with an eye toward trying to achieve a better understanding. If you want simple answers, you probably won't find them here. This is a very complex area, one that has been the subject of intense study by professionals in the field. We will be discussing several different models, each of which should give you some idea as to professional thinking on the topic. While knowledge has increased when it comes to this phenomenon, there is much we still don't understand.

Although not all child sexual abuse occurs within a family context, a full 60% of perpetrators are known to the victim, and 49% of them are authority figures, such as a parent or stepparent (Finkelhor, et al., 1990). For a number of reasons, it would be very difficult to separate those offenders who only commit sexual offenses against family members, so we will deal with sex offenders generally in this chapter.

While we usually think of sex offenders as being adults who prey on children, many sexual offenses are committed by young people. In our attempt to understand offenders, we will also take a look at the issue of youthful offenders. Since much of the professional opinion is that most offenders begin to exhibit problematic sexual behavior by their teen years or early adulthood, it makes sense to try to fathom this population. There is also another reason why we may want to understand this type of offender: if we can effectively intervene with this group early on, we might prevent them from becoming "hardened" sexual offenders in later life. When we explore the issue of the youthful offender, we will revisit some of the same questions we ask when studying adult offenders, but we will do so with the understanding that they may differ in important ways.

Each of the models we will discuss tries to answer the central question of this chapter: "Why do sexual offenders do what they do?" Since the models are likely to be unfamiliar, you may find yourself a little overwhelmed at first. I encourage you to think about the concepts, question the ideas, and try to grasp the basic ideas of each model. Once you've gone through several of them, you may find that all the information seems to flow together. Don't worry too much about it at first. Take your time. Go back and review each model and be sure to compare and contrast them. Ask yourself in what ways are the models similar, and in what ways are they different? How does each contribute to our understanding of why offenders do what they do? We always want to return to this question. A related question is: "Once we have a working idea about why offenders do what they do, what can we do to change it?" With all this in mind, I want to encourage you to be open in exploring the models, to review whatever beliefs and feelings you already have on the topic, and to think critically. I also hope that, as a result of this process, you will challenge existing concepts and models and pose new questions of your own.

After going through the various models that try to help us understand offenders, we'll turn our attention to intervention and treatment. Of all the issues you're likely to come up against when dealing with this issue, the question of whether we should treat sex offenders or simply treat them like criminals will be central. In this context, we will be taking a look at criminal justice interventions as well as approaches to try to help offenders overcome their aggressive and compulsive behavior. As part of this discussion we will briefly introduce a couple of cases that have attracted some national attention. Since we've already discussed the process of criminal prosecution in Chapter 5, we will pick up the discussion at the point at which the offender is sentenced. In terms of treatment, we will briefly review both community-based approaches and programs developed within correctional institutions. We will also be discussing some new federal and state initiatives aimed at trying to tackle this problem, including the civil commitment of offenders who are believed too dangerous to ever be released to the community.

Now that we've taken care of some of the preliminaries it's time to start discussing that group of people who sexually abuse children. Before getting into the meat of the subject, however, it may be helpful to take a look at your current beliefs about sexual offenders.

Now I'd like to invite you to participate in a short exercise. Take a moment and imagine what a sexual offender is like. One good way to do this is to write a paragraph or page on what you think sexual offenders are like. Okay, what did you come up with? Were I to ask everyone reading this text to share their images, I venture to guess that I'd get quite a variety of responses. Some might describe a sexually motivated serial killer. Someone else might describe a lonely adult man who lurks near the schoolyard waiting to molest an unsuspecting child. Another might describe a close family friend or uncle who seduces children within the extended family. Sexual offenders exist who conform to each of these images. The point here is that there is no single description of the sexual offender. This also means that, just in terms of describing sexual offenders, it is more complex than we might first imagine.

TYPES OF OFFENDERS

People who sexually abuse children are a diverse group. You probably already have a pretty clear idea that a very large number of offenders are known to the victim (see Chapter 4). Virtually all research says that identified offenders are overwhelmingly male. They are often friends of the family, neighbors, caregivers, relatives, and sometimes even parents or stepparents of the children themselves.

What are the varieties of sexual offenders? How do they differ from each other? What makes them tick? These are all questions most of us want answers to. In terms of types of offenders, we can identify at least the following major categories: **sexual predators, ritualistic abusers, sex ring abusers, exploiters, rapists,** and **molesters.** *Sexual predators* are individuals who seek out victims, stalk them, and ultimately offend against them. Some of them are referred to as **sadistic offenders** (Lanning, 1987) because these particular offenders seem to derive pleasure from causing injury or inflicting pain (see Box 6-1).

Ritualistic abusers are individuals who abuse a child sexually as part of a ritual, sometimes within the context of a cult or group. *Sex ring abusers* also act as part of a group but do not necessarily use ritualism nor are they necessarily sadistic. *Exploiters* are people who use children in sexual ways for the purpose of gaining financially (Davidson & Loken, 1987). This usually amounts to using the victim in prostitution or child pornography. One pioneer in the field distinguishes between child *rapists* and *molesters* according to how the offender gets the victim to comply (Groth, 1982). Child *rapists* get compliance through the use of force or threat of force; child *molesters* get their victims to cooperate through trickery or enticement (Groth, 1982).

The descriptions and definitions of abusers introduced here are just that—descriptions. It is a **typology,** or system of naming. And while it begins to give us a framework for categorizing abusers, it doesn't explain abusers or

---

BOX 6-1   The Life and Death of a Sexual Predator:
The Case of Wesley Allen Dodd

On November 11, 1992, PBS presented a special *Frontline* episode that profiled the case of Wesley Allen Dodd, a man who molested and killed three little boys in 1989 before he was finally caught. While Wesley Dodd's family was not close, and his mother and father eventually divorced, there was really nothing specific in his background that anyone could point to as the cause of his behavior. He was a quiet youth who stayed to himself much of the time and didn't really get in a lot of trouble. A high school band teacher described him as a very cooperative youth whom he could always count on to follow through on commitments.

While on the outside Wesley Allen Dodd didn't attract much attention at school or home, he began exposing himself to children when he was 13 years old. By the time he was 15, he had been arrested for the first time and confessed to six or seven sexual crimes involving as many as 20 children. When he was in his early twenties, he was brought to court in Idaho on charges of molesting a boy and received a ten-year sentence. Apparently because of an incomplete pre-sentence report and making a "good appearance" in court, the sentence was commuted to one year in county jail, of which he served only about four months. When released he went to Seattle, where he attempted to abduct another child. He admitted that this time he intended to also kill the boy. He was convicted of a fairly minor crime and served only a brief amount of time before being released again. While Dodd had been referred for sex offender treatment several times during the years, he never followed through and "fell through the cracks" of the criminal justice and children's services systems. By his own admission, he had molested as many as 100 children by the time he was finally stopped. His sexual predatory behavior ultimately ended in the deaths of three children. The last one he brought home and molested for several days before finally hanging and killing him. Dodd reported that the plans of killing the children began to turn him on more than molesting them. He confessed and was given a sentence of death, which he refused to fight. Dodd was finally executed himself, by hanging, at Walla Walla Prison.

Based on *Monsters Among Us* (video), by M. McLeod (Director) and D. Fanning (Executive Producer) for "Frontline" November 10, 1992, WGBH Education Foundation and Oregon Public Broadcasting.

---

their motivation. A number of mental health professionals and researchers have attempted to do this, and we will review some of their ideas and models. First, however, we will briefly discuss the issue of the psychiatric diagnosis of sexual offenders and review some DSM-IV diagnoses that, under certain circumstances, can be directly or indirectly applied to sexual offenders.

PSYCHIATRIC DIAGNOSIS AND SEXUAL OFFENDERS

At the outset, we should probably clarify the role of the mental health diagnosis in cases of child sexual abuse. Acts of child sexual abuse are violations of social norms and the law, even if the offender also happens to have a diagnosable disorder. The individual continues to be responsible for his behavior despite meeting the criteria of a psychiatric diagnosis (if in fact the criteria fit), except in extremely rare circumstances (such as in the case of a severely psychotic or brain-impaired individual whose impulsive behavior can be at least partially explained as being a consequence of a brain dysfunction). Having a diagnosis in no way absolves perpetrators of responsibility for their behavior, and many mental health professionals and professional organizations take the position that it is a crime—not a mental disorder—and refuse to treat the sexual offense behavior.

In the classification system of the DSM-IV, there is no specific diagnosis for sexual offenders per se. While the popular feeling may be that people who molest children must be "sick" or "psychotic," the simple fact that a person has committed an act of child sexual abuse does not necessarily mean that the person has a diagnosable disorder. The DSM-IV only has a few distinct diagnostic categories that can be directly applied to sexual offenders, and then only under certain circumstances. These include **exhibitionism, frotteurism, pedophilia, sexual sadism,** and **voyeurism** (American Psychiatric Association, 1994). *Exhibitionism* could be used as a diagnosis for individuals who exhibit their sexual parts to anyone, including a child. It is a disorder characterized by recurrent, intense, sexually arousing fantasies, urges, or behavior that involves exposing oneself to an unsuspecting person. *Frotteurism* has some of the same qualities but involves touching or rubbing against a nonconsenting person. *Pedophilia* is a DSM-IV disorder that involves recurrent, intense, sexually arousing fantasies, urges, or acts that center on sexual activity with prepubescent children. In order for a person to be diagnosable with this disorder, the offender must be at least 16 years old and more than five years older than the victim. Mental health professionals usually think of pedophiles as people who have an exclusive sexual preference for children; there are many others who may commit a sexual offense against a child yet who do not necessarily prefer children sexually. *Sexual sadism* is described as intense, recurrent, sexually arousing fantasies, urges, or acts that focus on inflicting physical or psychological suffering on a victim, either adult or child. *Voyeurism* involves intense fantasies, urges, or acts focused on observing unsuspecting people in a state of undress, disrobing, or engaging in sexual activity. The intended target of this activity could be a child.

There is also at least one diagnosis that might indirectly apply to some perpetrators of child sexual abuse: **antisocial personality disorder.** This diagnosis applies to people who engage in behavior, sexual or otherwise, that utterly disregards the rights and integrity of other human beings. They do so coolly and without feelings of remorse. This tends to be a lifelong pattern that includes a number of other diagnostic criteria, such as a tendency to be highly self-centered and have a lack of empathy for others. People with this disorder are popularly known as *sociopaths* or *psychopaths,* though no such diagnoses with these names actually exist in the DSM-IV. The reader should be cautious in how to interpret the significance of this diagnosis. Some sexual offenders may meet the diagnostic criteria for this disorder though many others do not. Likewise, many who do meet the criteria are not sexual offenders

It may be helpful to remember that there is not necessarily a direct relationship between sexual offenses and psychiatric diagnosis. The DSM-IV attempts to synthesize known signs and symptoms into specific diagnoses. It is a descriptive system that attempts to be "theory neutral." As such, it doesn't focus on trying to explain the behavior as much as to serve as an empirically valid way of naming and describing it. It is up to others to try to explain it, and so we turn now to a selected review of theories that attempt to do this.

PROFILE MODELS

The Fixated-Regressed Profile Model

A. Nicholas Groth is regarded as a pioneer both in treating and researching sexual offenders. Based on his clinical experience with sex offenders incarcerated at a state correctional facility, he and his colleagues developed a model to describe and explain sex offenders (Groth, Hobson, & Gary, 1982). This is probably the best-known, and perhaps most often cited, model in the sexual abuse area.

First of all, Groth and his associates distinguish between rapists and molesters, as cited previously, according to the method of gaining the compliance of their victims, through actual or implied force, trickery, or enticement. Within the molester category (those who trick or entice their victims), they further differentiate between two types, **fixated** and **regressed**, and suggest that both their profiles and motivations for offending are distinct from each other.

Groth and his colleagues (1982) believed that *fixated* molesters are essentially insecure and immature perpetrators who seek out victims who pose no emotional threat to them. They are **pedophiles;** that is, their primary sexual orientation is toward children. Groth and his colleagues suggest that, in addition to having a primary sexual attraction to children, pedophiles meet the following profile: their pedophilic interests usually begin by adolescence; offending is not triggered by stress; the behavior is persistent and compulsive; offenses tend to be thought out ahead of time; the offender identifies with the victim (and can relate to the victim at the victim's level); targets of abuse are usually male; they tend not to relate to people their own age sexually (often don't marry or have significant adult relationships); they tend not to be involved in substance abuse; they are developmentally immature; and their offenses represent maladaptive adjustments to life (Groth, et al., 1982). Essentially what Groth and his associates are saying is that the fixated molester sees himself as being at the level of the child in his own mind. To everyone else, it looks as if a big person is involved with a little one; but the offender really pictures himself as being little, like the child. In this model, one of the things that is suggested is that the offender is fixated and attracted to little boys because he himself may have been molested at approximately the same age as his victim. In this scheme the offender is trying to resolve his own traumatization, albeit at an unconscious level. These offenders, according to Groth et al. (1982), often relate very well to children and may seek careers or vocations that give them the opportunity to be involved with children. This is the kind of molester who is also likely to have multiple victims over the course of his career.

The other kind of molester in the Groth model is the one he refers to as the *regressed* molester. According to Groth et al. (1982), this kind of molester sees himself quite differently and has very different motivations for his behavior. In contrast to the fixated molester, the regressed molester is sexually oriented toward women his own age and the molestation is a **regression;** that is, the molester may seek out a young girl for sex as a substitute for an adult female. Rather than picturing himself as psychologically little like a child, he elevates the child in his mind to being at his level. Groth suggests that the first incident is usually triggered by some sort of stress. He also suggests that, rather than being a fixed, compulsive pattern, the impulses to offend wax and wane. Groth and his colleagues offer the following other features of the regressed molester's profile: sexual contact with a child often coexists with adult sexual relations; the offense often involves the use of alcohol; they tend to have a more normal lifestyle than the fixated molester, though they seem to have somewhat immature peer relationships; and, according to Groth et al. (1982), the sexual offending is an attempt to cope with specific life stresses.

If you look carefully at the Groth model, and if you have a grounding in Freudian theory, you may recognize fixation and regression as being Freudian concepts. The idea of fixation relates to an arrest or blockage in normal psychosexual development, whereas regression suggests that the perpetrator has developed somewhat normally yet regresses because of stress in life.

There are some problems with the Groth model. While it was a pioneering effort, it was based upon an unusual sample: incarcerated offenders. Although states now seem to be more aggressively pursuing jail terms for offenders, at the time this model was developed, judges may have been more likely to send those offenders to prison who perpetrated the most heinous offenses, looked more deviant, and less normal. The second possible problem with the model is that it is based on a particular theoretical orientation, the Freudian psychoanalytic model. Within the social sciences there remain unresolved problems associated with Freudian theory. For one, social scientists point out, it is hard to test empirically. Freudian theory seems highly speculative, making assertions about the nature of our psychic life without any clear basis in science. From a practice point of view, many clinicians note that offenders are much more diverse in their "profiles" than the two categories suggested by Groth and his colleagues. The results of some fairly recent research testing Groth's idea (Simon, et al., 1992) demonstrate fairly persuasively that rather than there being two distinct types of molester (a bimodal distribution), there are many. What emerges from the data is a continuum with a broad range of offender types and offender behaviors.

While there are problems associated with the fixated-regressed dichotomy, it is still used as a model for describing offenders. Students of family maltreatment are probably well advised to be familiar with it, since there are many professionals who either build on it or make reference to it in their own work.

The Situational-Preferential Profile Model

Dietz (1983) developed a model that is somewhat similar to that of Groth et al. He also describes two basic types of molesters: **preferential** and **situational.** In addition, Dietz and his colleagues (1983) add several subtypes of molesters that are not included in the Groth model. A distinction between this model and Groth's is that it is relatively "theory neutral"; that is, it describes the variety of offenders without reliance on any particular theoretical orientation, such as Freudian theory. Preferential molesters in Dietz's model are like Groth's fixated offenders; situational molesters are much like Groth's regressed molesters.

Dietz describes four types of *situational* molesters: **regressed, morally indiscriminate, sexually indiscriminate,** and **inadequate.** The *regressed* molester in this scheme is much like Groth's regressed offender. He uses children as a substitute for a preferred adult partner. The *morally indiscriminate* offender in this model is just generally an abuser of people, who is willing to abuse children, sexually or otherwise, if they are nearby. This is the type of abuser who lacks much of a conscience. The *sexually indiscriminate* abuser, unlike the morally indiscriminate, restricts his abuse to the sexual arena. His motivation according to Dietz is experimentation. The *inadequate* molester has some sort of physical or mental defect. This might be mental retardation, psychosis, or an organic brain disorder of some kind. In this model, the motivation is one of impulse and opportunity. They may find children approachable and easy to use to meet their own sexual desires.

In addition to the four types of situational molesters, Dietz (1983) identifies three types of *preferential* molesters: **seductive, introverted,** and **sadistic.** The *seductive* molester is somewhat similar to Groth's fixated molester. He is able to identify with children and engage with them and prefers them sexually. According to Dietz, he is likely to have a career or interests that involve him with children. The *introverted* molester in this model prefers children sexually but lacks the skill to seduce them. According to Dietz, he might marry someone with children or have his own as a way to have access to children. The *sadistic* molester is the kind of dangerous molester who might abduct, torture, and perhaps ultimately kill a child.

The situational-preferential model developed by Dietz solves some of the problems inherent in Groth's fixated-regressed model. For one thing, it accounts for the greater variety of offenders that clinicians report in their practices. It is also more theoretically neutral, which seems to be an advantage since the validity problems surrounding Freudian theory have not been resolved. Being theory neutral may, however, also be a limitation since the model merely attempts to describe known types of offenders and does not attempt to explain them.

Cautions on Using Profile Models

Profiles are intriguing, possibly because we believe that, by the use of profiles, we might be able to identify offenders. A limitation of virtually all profile models, however, is that, while they may describe offenders who have certain characteristics, they fail to take into account other individuals who have these same characteristics yet who do not commit sexual offenses. The legal system, which must concern itself with issues of justice, has implicitly taken note of this problem by not allowing profile evidence to be considered when deciding on the guilt or innocence of an accused person. According to Myers (1992), given the current state of scientific knowledge, there is no reliable profile of the "typical" sexual offender, and, hence, no basis for expert testimony in court describing such profiles. An accused person may not be convicted on the basis of fitting a particular profile.

THE FOUR-FACTOR OFFENDER MODEL

In terms of trying to understand and explain the behavior of sexual offenders, Finkelhor (1986b) notes that in the past researchers attempted to isolate single factors, such as having been sexually victimized, to explain the development of sexual abusers. He acknowledges that there is a great deal of variability in offenders. For instance, with regard to the theory that being victimized may cause one to victimize others, he points to research that seems to indicate that only 30 to 60% of identified offenders had themselves been sexually victimized. Finkelhor suggests that more than one factor is probably needed to explain how and why sexual offenders develop as they do. In an attempt to shed some light on this, he and his colleague, Sharon Araji, developed a four-factor model to describe sexual offenders (Araji & Finkelhor, 1986).

The four-factor model is based on a survey of the available research and literature about sexual offenders. Araji and Finkelhor (1986) not only reviewed the current theories about why certain individuals become sexual offenders but attempted to assess the amount of scientific support these theories have. They point out that most theories for explaining child sexual abusers can be categorized according to four factors (Araji & Finkelhor, 1986). These factors are seen by Araji and Finkelhor as being complementary, rather than competing, explanations for why certain individuals develop pedophilia. (They use this term to denote anyone who develops a sexual interest in children.) The four factors are

- Emotional congruence
- Sexual arousal
- Blockage
- Disinhibition

Emotional congruence is a term used to express the idea that sexual offenders, for some reason, feel more emotionally comfortable with children. In their review of the literature, Araji and Finklehor identify several theories that can be included under this umbrella. The ideas that molesters are arrested in their psychosexual development, are emotionally immature, have low self-esteem, or are narcissistic are all theories that had been proposed to explain pedophilia (Araji & Finkelhor, 1986). Based on a review of research, Araji and Finkelhor conclude that there does appear to be some support for the idea that offenders may be immature and have low self-esteem.

Sexual arousal in the context of child sexual abuse refers to the sexual excitement or arousal that offenders feel toward children. We might think of this as sexualization to children. Araji and Finkelhor review a number of proposed explanations for how this could happen. These include early sexual experiences with other children that leave an imprint, confusing parental and erotic feelings, and exposure to child-centered erotica. Araji and Finkelhor report that a solid, and reliable, body of research supports the idea that child sexual offenders, especially molesters, have a heightened arousal preference for children. It also seems that there is more victimization in the childhoods of people who later become sexual offenders.

As the name implies, *blockage* refers to barriers that get in the way of getting normal sexual needs met for the offender. Araji and Finkelhor (1986) describe two different types: **developmental** and **situational.** *Developmental* blockages include, for instance, a failure to develop the ability to relate to appropriate potential mates in a mature way. *Situational* blockages might be such circumstances as marital conflict, or the birth of a child, that blocks the spouse from being available sexually. Their review of the research also shows that many sexual offenders may feel inadequate and may have trouble relating to adult females and possibly to adults in general. They found other research that suggested many offenders seem to experience high amounts of anxiety about sex. They also found support for the idea that some offenders, especially incest offenders, seem to suffer from frustrations in their love relationships. An unavailable partner was often an issue for them.

Araji and Finkelhor (1986) point out that a number of theories about sexual offenders deal with the issue of *disinhibition*. Their review suggests that disinhibition factors, while they do not cause the molesting, may contribute to it. They note that the literature contains several disinhibiting factors, including impulse control deficits, senility, mental retardation, alcohol and substance abuse, and incest avoidance failure. They conclude that there seems to be good evidence to implicate substance abuse and to support the idea that an incest avoidance mechanism may break down among stepfathers.

There is probably no single explanation. Finkelhor (1986b) suggests that we might be well advised not to adopt any single-factor model. Instead they propose we adopt a multi-factor model. The four-factor model developed by Araji and Finkelhor seems capable of serving as a framework. In this way it can function as a kind of "template." The four-factor model suggests that there is a complex relationship between a number of factors. What remains to be done is articulate what the dynamics are.

THE ADDICTION MODEL

In the spirit of the times, a popular explanation for much compulsive and dysfunctional behavior is addiction. A number of self-help groups have become organized using methods and principles that were first developed by the Alcoholics Anonymous organization. AA is famous for developing what is called a **twelve-step program** of recovery. Addictive, compulsive behaviors around which 12-Step groups have developed include eating, gambling, buying, shoplifting, and sex. Patrick Carnes is a psychologist who worked with sexual offenders for a while before going to work at a hospital serving people with chemical dependency problems. The hospital branched out into other areas and ultimately established a sexual addiction program. As a result of his prior experience and his work there, Carnes developed a model that attempts to explain sexual compulsivity from an "addictions" point of view (1983; 1989).[*]

In this model, Carnes describes four basic parts of an **addictive system:**

- Belief system
- Impaired thinking
- Addiction cycle
- Unmanageability

Carnes suggests that the *belief system* includes false assumptions, myths, and attitudes about sexuality that reinforce *impaired thinking*. The

---

[*]From *Out of the Shadows*, by P. Carnes. Copyright © 1983 Hazelden Educational Materials.

delusional thinking system then insulates the addict from reality. A four-phase *addiction cycle* repeats itself, and in the end the addict's life becomes *unmanageable*.

The four distinct phases of the **addiction cycle**, according to Carnes, are

- Preoccupation
- Ritualization
- Sexual compulsivity
- Despair

Carnes asserts that the "addict" abuses and is dependent upon sex much like an alcoholic is dependent upon alcohol. He describes *preoccupation* as a trancelike state in which the addict is engrossed in sexual fantasy. *Ritualization* involves the use of specific rituals or behaviors that tend to intensify the arousal. *Sexual compulsivity* is the actual sexual behavior, that Carnes says is the end goal of preoccupation and ritualization. After orgasm is *despair,* a time in which the addict feels hopeless and without control.

Carnes proposes that with each sexually compulsive act the pattern becomes a more ingrained part of a dysfunctional life. In a similar way as is described within the chemical dependency field, Carnes describes levels of addiction. With alcoholism, the movement from less severe to more severe is known as the **progression** of the disease. Carnes identifies three levels: The first level contains many behaviors that, for most of us, would be considered a normal expression of our sexual identity. Carnes suggests that for the addict, however, this behavior too has a compulsive, driven, and ultimately unsatisfying character. Examples of level two include voyeurism or exhibitionism. Level three examples include rape and child molestation.

While the preceding discussion is a bare-bones representation of the addiction model, one important aspect of the model that isn't apparent in this sketch is the model's family systems emphasis. Carnes suggests that sometimes there are interlocking compulsive patterns among various family members, especially a spouse who might become a co-addict. The addictive behavior in this model starts as an attempt to satisfy a basic need or to feel good but ends up spiraling downward into a desperate and dysfunctional lifestyle. As an alcoholic uses alcohol in a misguided effort to cope, so it is with the sexual addict, Carnes suggests. As briefly outlined in Chapter 1, Carnes (1989) reviewed research that suggests that adolescents from families that function in the extremes are more at risk of becoming sexually abusive than those from more balanced family systems.

The addiction model developed by Carnes attempts to explain the dynamics of sexually compulsive behavior and suggests there may be interlocking patterns that involve others in the family. The model offers an intriguing model with the concept of sexual addiction at the core. It does not as yet have a body of research to support its interesting assertions.

A SPECIAL CLASS OF OFFENDERS: CHILDREN AND ADOLESCENTS

The problem of youthful sexual offenders is an important one. Youthful offenders don't necessarily fit any stereotype of child molester, yet they commit a substantial proportion of all sexual abuse offenses, ranging from minor sexual experimentation to very serious, and severe, maltreatment, as in the case of Caleb W. (see Box 6-2).

One recent review suggests that about 20% of all rapes and 30 to 50% of all molestations are committed by juvenile males (Barbaree, et al., 1993). A number of professionals who have looked at the histories of adult sexual offenders suggest that a substantial number of them began offending when still juveniles (cited in Barbaree, et al., 1993). If we really hope to do something about the problem of child sexual abuse, it seems to be in our best interest to look seriously at offenders in this age group.

The very issue of children committing sexual offenses is tricky, since we don't generally think of children and juveniles as being capable of committing crimes the same way we do with adults. Juvenile courts in fact are officially concerned with the welfare of minors. In ancient Rome, persons were assumed to have the capability of knowing right from wrong, in legal parlance **mens rea** (also known as capacity), at age 12, and hence could be held accountable for their behavior (Cox & Conrad, 1991). Between the ages of 8 and 12, the burden of establishing capacity was on the prosecution. Below age 8 it was assumed that the child could not be responsible. As discussed earlier, some sexual experimentation between children is considered normal, so distinguishing experimentation from molestation becomes an issue. While many definitions of child sexual abuse require that there be at least a five-year age difference unless coercion is involved (American Psychiatric Association, 1994; Finkelhor, 1979; Monteleone, Gloze, & Bly, 1994), some suggest that a significant maturity difference between the children would be a more appropriate guideline. Legal definitions vary from jurisdiction to jurisdiction, and in serious cases it is possible even to refer a case to the adult courts for prosecution.

Barbaree, Hudson, and Seto (1993) note that the same diversity that exists among adult offenders also holds for youthful sexual offenders. There is also research to suggest that some of the same issues suspected as contributing to the problems of adult offenders are also present among juveniles. These include low self-esteem, social isolation, and poor social skills as well as other serious behavior and family problems (Barbaree, et al., 1993). As with adult offenders, a higher number had themselves been victimized than those in the general population. As is true for adults, fewer had been victimized, 19 to 54%, than we might have expected if we had assumed that being sexually victimized causes people to become victimizers (Barbaree, et al., 1993).

BOX 6-2   "No treatment for Caleb W.": The Story of a Juvenile Offender

---

On July 11, 1991, ABC broadcast a segment of PrimeTime that highlighted the case of Caleb W., who was then 15 years old. The report indicated that Caleb began molesting children when he was 12 years old, including his younger brother. His behavior included not only sexual contact with children but threats with weapons and violence as well. The case drew national attention after Caleb's mother, Deborah Butler, had hidden Caleb from state authorities and appeared on camera telling anyone who would listen that something was wrong. She said that she felt her son had a serious problem and that the state was not providing him with adequate treatment for his sexual offense problem.

The matter had come to a head after Caleb was charged with a second series of sexual offenses. He had previously served six months at a state institution, which did offer treatment of sexual offenders. After the second series of charges, which involved the rape of two teenage girls, he was placed in the care of the children's services division. They placed Caleb at a boys' ranch that specialized in work and reforestation but did very little in terms of providing a sexual offender program. Caleb's mother charged that she felt her son could become like convicted child molester and murderer Wesley Allen Dodd without help. In an interview with Jay Schadler of *PrimeTime,* Caleb agreed that he had actually committed more serious sexual offenses than had Dodd at the same age. Dodd, who was also interviewed, said he thought the state was neglecting Caleb's need for help the way it had ignored his own problem.

Caleb was ultimately returned to state custody, but the details of follow-up treatment are unknown.

Based on *For His Own Good* (video), by M. Malkovich (Producer) and P. Nichols (Editor) for "PrimeTime" July 11, 1991, ABC News.

One way of looking at youthful offenders is to regard them as **sexually reactive children** (Gil & Johnson, 1993). One team of professionals has developed a continuum that describes four groups of children according to their level of sexualization (Johnson & Feldmeth, 1993): normal sexual exploration (Group I), sexually reactive (Group II), extensive mutual sexual behaviors (Group III), and children who molest (Group IV). In this continuum, normal exploratory play (Group I) involves children who are of a similar size and age who engage in voluntary exploration that often has a playful character. In Group II, the children's focus on sexuality is comparatively out of balance. Johnson and Feldmeth suggest that, with sexually reactive children, their genitals become the central organizing principle in their development. They further propose that many children in this group have been sexually abused or else live in families where there is an imbalance of

If we can learn to work effectively and quickly with youthful offenders we may be able to stop the cycle.

sexual stimulation. They also indicate that children in this group tend to experience shame and guilt about their sexuality. Children in Group III engage in extensive, and almost compulsive, mutual sexual activity. These children lack emotion about sexuality. In the final group on the continuum, Group IV, the children actually engage in extensive sexually abusive behavior involving sophisticated sexual activities, such as oral, anal, or genital intercourse, use of force or coercion, and the use of objects in the sexual activity. In terms of their emotional state, Johnson and Feldmeth characterize these children as cool and detached, utterly lacking in empathy or remorse for their victims.

As is the case for adult offenders, many youthful offenders have been victimized, many have painful social deficits, and many have troubling family experiences. What we don't understand is why other children with these same kinds of issues don't "act out" sexually. As Barbaree, Hudson, and Seto (1993) point out, we don't yet have good, controlled studies to answer this question. Since many of these youth are at risk of joining the ranks of adult offenders, it seems this is a good area to invest in, if we have the clinical and political will to do so. Large numbers of youth are being adjudicated in the juvenile justice system, and many others are being removed from their homes and placed in residential facilities or specialized foster care programs; yet it is not clear when we take these steps that we are also ensuring that the sexual offense behavior is adequately addressed.

CONCLUDING COMMENTS
ABOUT SEXUAL OFFENDERS

The two cases highlighted earlier in this chapter, those of Wesley Allen Dodd and Caleb W., have come to public attention largely because they are so extreme. While it is probably true that cases like these catch our attention and influence our image of sexual offenders, such cases are fortunately in the minority. Because of the nature of these crimes and the devastating consequences to the victims and their families, this is a very serious problem; yet these types of molestations are extremely rare in comparison to the overall number of cases that are reported. Stranger abductions of children for sexual purposes are relatively rare, probably somewhere in the range of 200 to 300 (Finkelhor, et al., 1992). This compares to approximately 140,000 cases of *reported* sexual abuse (NCCAN, 1994, 1995b, 1996). Sexual offenders are a varied group composed of individuals with different backgrounds, motivations, and vastly different offending patterns. As has so often been said, the trick is to figure out who can be helped and who can't.

The whole topic of sexual offenders is an emotionally charged issue, but also an important one, since as a society we have important policy decisions to make about how to address this problem. When it comes to treatment for sex offenders, the popular perception is that it doesn't work and we should just lock them up. However, while the research isn't conclusive, it seems that recidivism rates for offenders isn't as high as we might fear (Finkelhor, 1986b; Smith, 1995), depending, of course, on the kind of offender we're talking about. The recidivism is likely to be quite different for, say, a sadistic pedophile than for a one-time situational offender.

INTERVENTION
AND TREATMENT

As a result of increasing awareness about the issue of sexual offenders and sensitivity to the need to do something more, a number of initiatives have taken place at the federal level, as well as in a number of states and localities.

Federal Initiatives

While many people think of state laws when they think of child sexual abuse law enforcement, the federal government has actually been fairly active in this area. In Chapter 5, when we discussed abuse treatment and intervention, we noted that the U.S. Postal Inspector and the U.S. Customs Service lead the effort when it comes to investigating the importation and distribution through the mails of child pornography. As we noted earlier in this chapter, pedophiles represent the type of sexual offender most likely to commit multiple acts of molestation and the type most likely to produce, distribute, and collect child pornography. On August 24, 1996, President Clinton announced in his weekly radio address that he would sign a new crime bill. With the signing of the new legislation, the federal role in trying to control child sexual abuse was broadened considerably.

The new legislation not only tightens the controls on the importation and distribution of child pornography but also expands federal jurisdiction in the area of child prostitution. For some time now we've been aware that some U.S. citizens who are pedophiles travel to certain Asian and third-world countries where they can procure child prostitutes. The addition of a new section to Title 16 of the federal criminal code now makes sexual contact with kids in foreign countries a violation of federal law, an offense that could result in prison sentences of up to ten years.

While the addition of so-called sex vacations to federal statutes is significant, the legislation also includes a new act in the U. S. code: the **Crimes against Children and Sexually Violent Offender Registration Act.** This is coming to be known as the federal version of **Megan's Law**, named after Megan Kanka, who lived in Hamilton Township, New Jersey. Megan was killed in 1994 by a neighbor who had a history of committing sex offenses against children. The Kankas did not know of his history and therefore were not able to take precautions to protect their daughter. Shortly after the murder, New Jersey passed the original Megan's Law, which permitted law enforcement to warn the public of the presence of known sex offenders. The new federal legislation requires all states to enact laws that compel **sexually violent predators** to register with their local law enforcement agency and that allow local law enforcement authorities to warn their communities about released offenders. The legislation defines the types of offenses that qualify as sexually violent, and imposes a penalty on states that do not comply: loss of 10% of federal funds that would otherwise have been awarded under the Crime Control and Safe Streets Act of 1968.

The new act also establishes a national **Missing and Exploited Children's Task Force**, composed of representatives of the Federal Bureau of Investigation, Secret Service, Bureau of Alcohol, Tobacco, and Firearms, U.S. Customs Service, U.S. Postal Inspection Service, U.S. Marshal's Service, and the Drug Enforcement Administration. The official purpose of the task force is to make the combined, coordinated services of the major federal law enforcement agencies available to state and local governments in the investigation of the most difficult missing children's cases.

State Initiatives

Even prior to the federal initiatives described above, a number of states had passed legislation toughening criminal sanctions for serious offenders, requiring convicted offenders to register with local law enforcement. Some states enacted violent sex predator laws that permit the state to place dangerous predators in secure treatment centers for indefinite periods of time.

Lucy Berliner and colleagues Schram, Miller, and Milloy (1995) point out that once before, beginning in the 1930s, states enacted sexual psychopath laws, based on the assumption that we might be able to treat offenders and thereby make them safe to be in the community. They also point out that, because of a lack of effectiveness of the programs that were created and a concern about the constitutionality of indefinite commitments, many of these laws were ultimately repealed. This tide seems to be shifting, however, and states are reexamining the need to commit potentially violent offenders.

After some particularly heinous sexual crimes, Washington was one of the first states to enact new legislation. This legislation permits the state to petition the court to declare a previously convicted sexual offender a sexual predator, thereby giving the state the authority to retain the person in a treatment facility until it is deemed that he no longer poses a significant risk. The Washington law was struck down by the federal district court on grounds that a new law was being applied to a previous offense, that the person was put in double jeopardy, and that it violated federal due process requirements (*Young v. Weston,* 898 F. Supp. 744, W. D. Wash 1995). California and a number of other states, including Kansas, have subsequently passed similar legislation. The United States Supreme Court handed down its decision on this case on June 23, 1997. The court determined that sexually violent predators can be held if they are considered mentally abnormal and are likely to commit new crimes (Associated Press, 1997). This decision has immediate application to the five states that currently have sexually violent predator laws and can be expected to influence the enactment of such legislation in other states.

Local Initiatives

As discussed elsewhere in this text (see Chapter 5), many local communities have come to recognize many of the coordination problems and gaps in how they investigate, prosecute, and intervene in sexual abuse cases. Some moderate to large-sized communities have developed special law enforcement and prosecutorial units to handle these cases, and there often seems to be increasing emphasis on collaboration and coordination among law enforcement, social services, mental health, and child protective services in these cases (Lanning, 1996; Walsh, 1996). Also see Chapter 5 for a discussion of coordinated investigation and treatment programs for victims.

Overview of Sex Offender Treatment

The whole issue of offender treatment is an extraordinarily sensitive one. Many people are so angry about the fact that sexual abuse and sexual offenders even exist that the whole idea of providing treatment, on first blush, seems ludicrous. However, on a practical level, providing programs seems to be a necessary commitment. Even were we to give all offenders lengthy prison sentences, we know that most will eventually be released back into the community. While the question of whether we should treat sex offenders or punish them remains unsettled, that we should do something to reduce the incidence of child sexual abuse is apparent. Berliner and her colleagues (1995) point out that the criminal justice system itself is uncertain about whether to treat or punish offenders, but they conclude that it is probably necessary to have treatment programs.

Whether to use a treatment program, or prison, or both in any given case depends on a number of factors, including prior criminal history, the nature and severity of the offense, the level of community and family support the person has, and the degree to which the court feels the offender is a good candidate for a community-based treatment program as well as community concern and the discretion of the judge. Offenders with more extensive general criminal histories who are otherwise seen as being a greater risk to the community seem more likely to be sentenced to prison, whereas those who behave more like average citizens may be more likely to be given a community treatment program (Berliner, et al., 1995). An encouraging note is rung by the conclusions of Berliner and her colleagues (1995), who indicate that judges seem to fairly accurately assess low- and high-risk offenders, correctly giving them either community programs or sending them to prison. Berliner et al. (1995) point out that in the majority of cases where a conviction occurred, probation was imposed about two-thirds of the time. Even in those cases where a convicted offender was placed on probation, a specialized offender treatment program was not required about 30% of the time. For offenders sentenced to prison, participation in sex offender treatment programs is not generally required. While there is a trend to develop high-quality sex offender treatment programs in correctional institutions, there is still a lack of such programs, even in those institutions with large sex offender populations.

Does Sex Offender Treatment Work?

The public perception is that the vast majority of sexual offenders reoffend and that they are at such high risk that we shouldn't take chances with them. Because of the seriousness of some very well known cases, this concern is understandable. Since we are using sex offender treatment programs to help us deal with the problem, and since we are being asked to invest in such programs, we probably want to know if such programs are, in fact, effective. Even before we get to the issue of effectiveness, per se, there are a couple of related fundamental questions we need to ask. First of all, is it safe? Secondly, is it likely to reduce the risk of future offenses?

Since there is always a certain amount of recidivism among offenders, the answer to the first question would have to be that some degree of risk exists—it is never 100% safe to treat offenders in the community. Our second question is easier to answer. A group of researchers in Eugene, Oregon, conducted the first extensive review of offender recidivism in 1989 (Furby, et al., 1989), and Gordon C. Nagayama Hall from Kent State University did a metanalylis, or study of studies, on recidivism in 1995. Nagayama Hall's analysis included all studies done since Furby and her colleagues completed their 1989 study. Furby and her colleagues (1989) comment that, because of certain inherent difficulties in doing research in this area, it was difficult to determine if offender programs were effective in reducing the risk of a reoffense. Using only rigorously conducted empirical studies that included control groups, Nagayama Hall (1995) did find a difference between treated and untreated offenders: 19% of those completing programs later committed additional offenses, compared to 27% for those who did not. While the final analysis rests on 12 rigorous studies, Nagayama Hall believes the results to be robust, and they seem to tell us that treatment can at least reduce the risk of a reoffense.

While the difference between 19% and 27% recidivism may not seem large, when dealing with a problem as difficult as this, it can be extremely important. Scientifically tested treatment programs are a relatively new phenomenon, and as with any relatively new approach, the effectiveness of intervention is less potent when learning to deal with the problem rather than later after much more is known. Marshall and Eccles (1991) use the analogy of cancer treatment. When we were first learning to treat various forms of cancer, the methods we used were relatively ineffective, and a diagnosis of cancer was almost considered a death sentence. As the medical profession has advanced in its ability to treat cancer, we've learned that treatability not only depends on the form of cancer but on the various tools available for combating it.

Not only does it seem that there is a difference between the recidivism rates of treated and nontreated offenders, but the characteristics of the offender, the length of follow-up, and the type of treatment also seem to make a difference in recidivism rates (Nagayama Hall, 1995). With regard to types of offenders, we know that some offenders are at extremely high risk to continue in a pattern of repeated offenses. Dr. Art Gordon, a well-known figure in the field, suggests that while 80 to 90% of offenders do not reoffend, perhaps 10 to 20% of repeat offenders will account for the lion's share of reported reoffenses (personal communication, July 18, 1996).

Nagayama Hall's analysis (1995) suggests that, while offenders treated in both institutional and outpatient settings did better than their untreated counterparts, those in outpatient programs seemed to fare better, though Nagayama Hall notes that institutionalized offenders are likely to be higher-risk/more serious offenders to begin with. Length of follow-up seemed to distinguish between effective and less effective approaches to therapy, with the results of effective programs showing up well after five years, whereas the results of less effective programs seem to wear off after that time (Nagayama Hall, 1995). Nagayama Hall points out that since offenders seem to be at continued risk for reoffense even after 20 years, this is an important distinction. Since there seem to be differences between so-called effective and less effective therapies, what are they? Broad traditional talking approaches to therapy and strictly behavioral approaches seem less effective than cognitive-behavioral or hormonal approaches (the use of such antiandrogen substances as cyproterone acetate, medroxyprogesterone acetate, or even castration). Neither hormonal nor cognitive-behavioral approaches seems superior to the other (Nagayama Hall, 1995). Other research suggests that incest offenders may be less likely to reoffend than pedophiles (Berliner et al., 1995; Marshall & Barbaree, 1988). Indications are that incest and molestation offenses may respond to the cognitive-behavioral approaches, which deal with these offenses as at least partially sexually motivated, whereas rapists may need programs more tailored to issues of power and control (Marshall & Eccles, 1991).

Comprehensive Treatment Approaches

Most programs that specialize in the treatment of offenders do not claim to "cure" offenders, only to treat them as part of an overall effort to minimize the risk that they will reoffend. This is often called a **relapse prevention model** (Murphy & Smith, 1996; Pithers, 1990; Pithers et al., 1988; Pithers et al., 1989; Pithers, 1996; Research and Statistics Branch, Correctional Service of Canada, 1991). Many high-quality programs that treat sexual offenders, especially those reviewed by Nagayama Hall (1995), integrate a relapse prevention orientation, as well as behavioral or cognitive-behavioral techniques, into a comprehensive program. Behavioral techniques are aimed exclusively at changing behavior, while cognitive-behavioral procedures target specific behavior but also try to work with the thinking patterns and feelings of the person. The various techniques usually target specific risk factors associated with sexual offense behavior. Some programs also use hormone therapy to reduce deviant urges. The specific techniques will be discussed in greater detail below.

Before a client is accepted into a program, he usually undergoes an assessment or evaluation. When programs receive referrals from the courts, they have an obligation to notify the court if they do not believe they can work with the individual safely and effectively. While doing an intake or assessment is routine in the mental health field, it takes on added significance when working with sexual offenders. We have previously discussed that sexual offending is usually considered first and foremost a criminal activity, and that whatever mental health diagnosis a person might have would usually not take precedence. The sexual offender assessment is often done at the request of the courts or probation officer to determine the suitability of the person for the program as well as the risk to the community at large. In addition, programs usually want to assess the level of psychopathology of the individual, the risk factors involved, the family and community support that may enhance the person's chances of making a good adjustment, the amount of empathy the offender has for the victim, the level of remorse, the motivation to change, and the willingness to be honest about their behavior (Berliner et al., 1995; Murphy & Smith, 1996).

One of the problems in connection with sexual offenders is their tendency to deny or minimize their responsibility for what they've done. When they admit to their actions and accept responsibility, it is generally taken as an indication of commitment and a marker for reduced risk to reoffend. Treatment programs, therefore, usually will not rely solely upon the statement of the offender but will want victim statements, police reports, and firsthand information from others who know of the offender's patterns of behavior. Many programs employ **polygraph examinations**, sometimes called "lie detector tests," as part of their evaluation procedures.

Depending on the expertise of the staff, programs may also employ a number of psychological assessment instruments in order to get a sense of the person's personality and pathology (see Table 10.2, Murphy & Smith, 1996, for a list of commonly used instruments). Many programs also use an instrument called a **penile plethysmograph** in order to test the sexual arousal pattern of the offender. Penile plethysmography includes a flexible gauge, which measures the strength of the male erection, and a recording device, much like that used on a polygraph device, to record the level of arousal of the offender. Typically, the assessment team displays sexually explicit photos, videos, and audio recordings and records the offender's responses. The ratio of arousal to deviant versus normal sexual stimuli is often used as an indicator of the level of the offender's deviancy (Freund & Blanchard, 1989).

Assessments can often tell us about deviant and normal sexual arousal patterns (Freund & Blanchard, 1989), the presence or absence of a mental or personality disorder, personality characteristics, and a number of other things. What they can't do is tell us whether any given offender has committed a specific offense. As has been mentioned previously, the courts have consistently found that psychological testimony about profiles has been consistently ruled out of bounds in criminal trials. Consistent with rulings by various courts, the state of the art is such that assessments cannot tell us if an individual defendant is guilty or innocent of the crime he is charged with.

When the court has made a ruling about the guilt of an individual and makes a referral to treatment, or when a nonadjudicated client volunteers for treatment, the next step, treatment, can begin. Since we now know that offenders vary markedly along many dimensions (Marshall & Eccles, 1991; Murphy & Smith, 1996), sophisticated treatment approaches will usually try to individualize the program to the offender as much as possible. While good programs are generally individualized, there are also a number of common themes that are well known in the field. Murphy and Smith (1996) summarize these elements as follows:

- Confronting denial
- Identifying risk factors
- Decreasing cognitive distortions
- Increasing victim empathy
- Increasing social competency
- Decreasing deviant arousal
- The offender's own victimization (if applicable)

As discussed earlier, models that have been evaluated as being more effective include cognitive-behavioral or hormonal approaches to treatment (Marshall & Eccles, 1991; Nagayama Hall, 1995). Cognitive-behavioral approaches commonly begin with an educational element, the demonstration of specific skills, and opportunities to practice new skills and demonstrate mastery in role-play or practice situations. In certain educational circles, these components are sometimes referred to as "tell," "show," and "do." The goals of this kind of treatment might include increasing comfort in relating to members of the opposite sex, managing angry feelings, or increasing self-esteem. Among the things therapists might do as part of the process is to encourage, coach, or facilitate discussion, depending upon the client's level of ability to deal with a particular topic area. Cognitively oriented aspects of treatment may also help the client face his distorted thinking patterns and learn new ways to think about himself and others. This might involve changing distorted views about sexuality. As pointed out by Murphy and Smith (1996), group treatment is probably the most common modality for therapy. In terms of working with offenders, it has at least a couple of advantages. For one, it is economical, and for another, groups can be extremely effective at identifying and confronting offenders about denial and minimization. Groups can also provide a great deal of support and acceptance for a person who might have a great deal of shame about his behavior and who wants to change.

Behavioral techniques that have been used with offenders include aversive therapies, covert desensitization, and covert resensitization. Aversive therapy means associating something unpleasant with the deviant idea, like asking an offender to wear a rubber band and snap it each time a deviant thought comes into his mind. Ammonia vials are also sometimes used for this purpose. Covert desensitization might include asking the offender to think about deviant thoughts while playing a tape about some awful consequence that would befall him for acting on the idea. Covert resensitization would include asking the client to learn to become aroused to appropriate sexual stimuli (for offenders who do not have this type of arousal).

Murphy and Smith (1996) also comment that family therapy is also sometimes used in treatment, especially in cases that involve incest. Interestingly, some families where incest has occurred desire to remain united, and working with such families is extremely controversial. One world-famous team of strategic family therapists, Jay Haley and Cloe Madanes of the Family Therapy Institute of Washington, D.C., have done some pioneering work using family therapy techniques with families in which incestuous abuse has occurred, where the therapy is done in collaboration with court personnel (Madanes, 1990). Madanes, in particular, has worked out a very specific set of steps for working with these families, and they report good results. However, without comparing their results with families who do not receive this form of therapy, it is difficult to determine how they compare to the relatively low recidivism rates that occur naturally in cases of incest abuse. While the answers to these questions do not seem clear, I think the work of Madanes and Haley might deserve more attention than it has gotten so far in the child sexual abuse professional community.

A criticism of the approach is that, by doing therapy with both victim and offender at the same time, it puts the victim in an uncomfortable position. Some believe that this kind of family therapy unwittingly tells the family that something about the family, rather than the behavior of the offender, is the cause of the abuse. They contend that this takes responsibility away from where it ought to be and tends to blame the victim.

Hormonal therapies include the use of castration (which therefore reduces the body's natural production of testosterone), **cyproterone acetate**, and **medroxyprogesterone acetate**, which is often known as **Provera** or **Depo Provera**. All three of these methods, based on the research, seem effective in reducing the risk of reoffenses (Marshall & Eccles, 1991; Nagayama Hall, 1995). To my knowledge castration is never used without the consent of the offender, and while there has been popular snickering about the use of this method with offenders, one of the studies reviewed by Nagayama Hall (1995) suggests that the recidivism rate can be extremely low (3%) when used. Cyproterone acetate and medroxyprogesterone acetate are both **antiandrogens**, or substances that reduce the production of male sex hormones. Most recent research seems to confirm the perception that they are effective in reducing deviant impulses, and improve the chances that an offender will not offend again (Bradford & Pawlak, 1993a, 1993b; Cooper, 1995; Emory, et al., 1992; Kiersch, 1990; Maletzky, 1991). They need to be administered on a regular basis, however, or they wear off. Nagayama Hall points out that one of the disadvantages of using antiandrogens, especially medroxyprogesterone acetate, is that it not only reduces the deviant sex drive but the normal sex drive as well, and this often means that some offenders will refuse to continue to use it. The conditions of probation are likely to vary considerably, and some judges may not require that an offender submit to the use of antiandrogens for any number of reasons. Hormonal therapies are probably most often used in conjunction with other more interpersonal or psychologically oriented approaches to treatment.

Treatment is not the exclusive province of the mental health or medical professional, and case management seems to be an important aspect of any program. When offenders are referred to community programs, close coordination between the treatment provider and court personnel, especially the probation officer, is extremely important. The provider and "PO" depend on each other, and it is always advantageous when a trusting and collegial relationship exists. Steps need to be taken to protect the offender from being placed in a tempting situation and to protect any potential victims. Pithers (1991) outlines two basic dimensions to relapse prevention: (1) external supervisory element, and (2) internal self-management. The external dimension includes the monitoring of risk factors associated with offending behavior. This could include the use of pornography, the use of alcohol or other chemical substances, living in proximity to children, and so forth. The internal factors the offender needs to learn about include the identification of his own *"red flags,"* decision making, and developing strategies for coping with and avoiding high-risk situations. Beyond what happens at the treatment program, the offender will need to make some significant changes in his daily life. This might include changing jobs, if employment involves contact, moving out of the home, and so on (Murphy & Smith, 1996).

Outpatient programs should not be restricted to offenders who were sent there in lieu of prison. Perhaps one of the most important things we're learning is that releasing convicted offenders to the streets without supervision and further treatment may be a mistake. While it may be costly for governmental jurisdictions in terms of dollars, in the long run it may have the potential to prevent the creation of new victims. For offenders who are released on parole, continued monitoring that includes participation in a program seems to make a great deal of sense. Arthur Gordon and his colleagues (Gordon, Holden, & Leis, 1991) point out that postrelease treatment models are an extremely important part of any program that accepts a relapse prevention model of treatment.

CHAPTER SUMMARY

This chapter has focused on sexual offenders. We noted that the topic of sexual offenders is itself difficult, not simply from the standpoint of trying to understand but also because of our emotions about one of the most reviled groups in society. We surveyed some of the issues related to sexual offenders and explored four models that try to explain them: the regressed-fixated profile model, the preferential-situational profile model, the four-factor offender model, and the addiction model. While it may be intriguing to imagine that we might be able to develop some sort of psychological profile of sexual offenders that could ultimately lead to an understanding of what "makes them tick," we noted that it might be wise to be cautious any time we try to use a profile model. The case of Wesley Allen Dodd is a case in point, since he is an example of the most dangerous type of offender, the sexual predator, yet there was nothing very specific in his background, except an escalating pattern of sexual behavior, that would distinguish him from many average citizens. Profiles are in some ways like stereotypes, and stereotypes, while sometimes containing a grain of truth, are often off the mark. In addition to looking at various descriptions of offenders, including possible reasons for their behavior, we also took a look at a special class of offender: children and adolescents who molest. In this connection, we highlighted the case of one very serious adolescent offender, Caleb W. The issue of youthful offenders is especially important since we believe that most adult offenders begin their careers in late childhood or early adolescence. If we wish to prevent sexual abuse, the common wisdom seems to be that we should try to target younger perpetrators.

After discussing the general topic of sexual offenders, we turned our attention to intervention and treatment. We noted that there have been several recent initiatives at the federal and state levels, including passage of a federal version of Megan's Law, legislation that requires offenders to register with local law enforcement. Other aspects of the federal legislation include provisions making it illegal for Americans to go overseas for so-called sex vacations that involve the sexual exploitation of children in foreign countries. In addition, the recent federal legislation establishes the Missing and Exploited Children's Task Force at the national level. State initiatives include laws passed in several states that allow for the indefinite detention of sexual predators for treatment. One such case has been challenged on constitutional grounds and was upheld by the U.S. Supreme Court.

In many respects the public may be much more supportive of strong laws targeted against sex offenders than they are of treatment programs. While this sentiment is understandable, it also seems clear that we also need treatment programs. Even when we do incarcerate offenders, wise policy might dictate that we also provide treatment. One group of researchers has conducted a study that includes looking at what courts actually do with offenders. It was found that a large number are placed on probation, most of whom are also required to participate in a treatment program. We looked at one very common question: "Does sex offender treatment work?" and concluded that, based on the most extensive research of controlled studies, it seems that well-designed programs do reduce the risk of reoffenses. We noted that the research also tells us that programs that are cognitive-behavioral in orientation or use hormonal treatment seem to do better than more traditional approaches. We concluded the chapter with an overview of treatment methods currently in use.

LEGAL AND ETHICAL CONCERNS: CRITICAL THINKING QUESTIONS

1. Sexual offenders are part of a class of people whom others have strong emotional reactions to, yet they are a diverse group. How should we relate to people who have been identified as sexual offenders? What should we do in regard to distinguishing between types of offenders, if anything?

2. At least two profile models have been developed that attempt to categorize sex offenders. What are the problems with profile models? When should we use them? When shouldn't we?

3. The study of sexual offenders is an emotionally challenging area. What are your thoughts about why it may be important? Do we have a responsibility to try to help them change? Should we be primarily interested in the protection of the community?

4. The available literature suggests that children and adolescents commit a substantial amount of the child sexual abuse. How should we distinguish between youthful offenders and adults? Should we treat them differently? Should we remove them from the community? Will our actions make them better or worse? What kind of treatment should we give them, if any?

5. New laws are now on the books in several states that permit the indefinite civil commitment of sexual offenders whom correctional authorities believe are still a risk. What are some of the legal and ethical issues that surround depriving people of their freedom on the basis of what they might do in the future?

6.   Based on recent research we are now fairly certain that hormonal therapies, which could include the use of certain antiandrogen chemicals as well as castration, seem effective in reducing the risk of future offenses. What do you think about requiring offenders to undergo treatment that will not only reduce deviant sexual urges but will also impair their ability to engage in normal sexual activity?

7.   Well-designed sex offender treatment programs seem to be effective. We often sentence offenders to prison, yet we do not offer treatment programs at many prisons. Are we partly responsible when they reoffend if we fail to provide them with services while they're in prison?

SUGGESTED ACTIVITIES

1.   Find out what, if any, special laws there may be in your state or community dealing with sexual offenders. Find out what these laws have to say.

2.   Consult with several professionals in your community who regularly deal with sexual offenders. Find out how they get their referrals. How do they go about treating offenders? What are their opinions about why sexual offenders do what they do? Do they feel treatment is successful? If so, under what conditions?

3.   Contact local law enforcement agencies and find out if they have a special unit devoted to sexual offenses. Try to determine if the local law enforcement agency has any special procedures they use when investigating child sexual abuse cases.

4.   Try to find out what kind of partnerships exist between law enforcement, child protective services, and other service providers in your community. Are these relationships informal or do specialized teams exist for investigating child sexual abuse cases?

5.   By consulting with the prosecutor's office, try to determine an estimate of the number of accused sexual offenders who are convicted of their offenses. For those who are convicted, what consequences did they face for their behavior?

6.   Consult with corrections agencies in your state. In addition to confinement, what programs are available to assist convicted sexual offenders to stop their behavior?

7.   Can treatment programs or mental health professionals advise courts on the guilt or innocence of a defendant in a sexual abuse case? Why or why not? Please explain.

REVIEW GUIDE

1.   Discuss why it seems to be both intriguing and abhorrent to study sexual offenders. Review the various categories of sexual offenders outlined in the text. Define each.

2. List each of the psychiatric diagnoses discussed in the text that are sometimes associated with sexual offenders. Compare these diagnoses with the types of offenders discussed. Are all offenders diagnosable in the DSM-IV?

3. List the four primary offender models summarized in this chapter. Be able to define each of the major terms and concepts associated with each.

4. Compare and contrast the two profile models introduced. Be able to describe each of the types of offenders defined in the two profile models. How did a theory both help and hurt one of these profile models?

5. Discuss the four factors that Araji and Finkelhor (1986) believe can be used to help understand child sexual offenders. Be able to describe each of these four factors.

6. Discuss the addiction model of Patrick Carnes. What is the addictive system? What is the addictive cycle? What is the difference? What are the model's strengths and weaknesses? Be able to discuss the three levels of addiction and what "progression of the disease" means.

7. What are the differences between youthful offenders and adult offenders? Does the literature suggest any distinctions in their characteristics? Why is it more difficult to define a youthful child sexual abuser?

8. Be able to discuss the four groups identified by Johnson and Feldmeth. What kind of sexual activity distinguishes each group from the other?

9. Be able to discuss the concept of sexually reactive children.

10. Be familiar with each of the federal, state, and local initiatives for dealing with child sexual abuse, as discussed in the text. Know what the federal Megan's Law does. What is the Missing and Exploited Children's Task Force? Be familiar with the legal cases dealing with the civil commitment of sexually violent predators that are now working their way through the courts.

11. What kinds of factors are likely to come into play when a court tries to decide if a sex offender should be put on probation or sent to prison? What percentage of offenders get put on probation? How many of them are required to undergo sex offender treatment?

12. Does sex offender treatment work? What does the research say about this? What do we mean when we say "reduced risk"?

13. What do we mean by "relapse prevention model"?

14. What kinds of treatment are typically included in so-called high-quality programs? Be able to discuss each type.

15. What common themes do Murphy and Smith (1996) say are generally included in high-quality programs?

16. Be able to discuss what is involved in the evaluation of a sex offender for acceptance into a treatment program. What kinds of methods or procedures are likely to be used? What is a polygraph examination? A penile plethysmograph examination?

17.   Be able to identify what behavioral and cognitive-behavioral treatment techniques are. Be able to identify examples of each.

18.   Groups are often used in the treatment of sex offenders. What are the advantages of this?

19.   When is family therapy likely to be used as a treatment alternative? What are the controversies that currently surround its use?

20.   Be familiar with the hormonal therapies. What substances are being used? What do they do?

21.   Be able to discuss why it seems to be important to have coordination between the probation/parole officer and the treatment provider.

22.   What are the two dimensions to relapse prevention? What does each include?

SUGGESTED READING

Carnes, P. (1983). *Out of the shadows.* Center City, MN: Hazelden Educational Materials.

Carnes, P. (1989). *Contrary to love.* Center City, MN: Hazelden Educational Materials.
Two related popular and readable books by the same author that outline an addiction model for working with sexual addicts, many of whom are sexual offenders. Contrary to Love also includes discussion of interlocking family dynamics, with information on the use of the "circumplex model" (FACES II) to understand family function and dysfunction.

Gil, E., & Johnson, T. C. (1993). *Sexualized children: Assessment and treatment of sexualized children and children who molest.* Rockville, MD: Launch Press.
An edited book by a group of writers and clinicians who have made a significant commitment to working with sexualized children and children who molest. Human and humane in their treatment of this thorny issue.

CHAPTER GLOSSARY

Addiction cycle   One of four components of the addictive system in the addiction model developed by Patrick Carnes. The addiction cycle has four parts as well: sexual preoccupation, ritualization, sexual compulsivity, and despair.

Addictive system   The overarching system that is the core of the addiction model developed by Patrick Carnes. Includes four parts: belief system, impaired thinking, addiction cycle, and unmanageability.

Antiandrogens   Substances that reduce or stop the production of male hormones.

Antisocial personality disorder   A recognized psychiatric disorder, believed to develop in childhood and adolescence. Its chief characteristic is utter disregard for the feelings or rights of others.

Belief system   One of four parts of the addiction system which is at the core of a model developed by Patrick Carnes. It is a concept that includes faulty assumptions, myths, and values.

Blockage
One of four major issues believed to be important for understanding the dynamics of child sexual abusers, described in the review of Araji and Finkelhor (1986). It refers to blocks to appropriate sexual outlets.

Crimes against Children and Sexually Violent Offender Registration Act
Federal legislation that creates Title XVII of Chapter 42 of the U.S. Code. Among other things, it establishes a national registry of child sex abusers, the requirement that states enact legislation requiring offenders to register with local law enforcement, and allows law enforcement to warn communities of offenders believed to be dangerous (see Megan's Law).

Cyproterone acetate
An antiandrogen substance that reduces the production of male hormones in an effort to reduce deviant sexual urges.

Depo Provera
See Medroxyprogesterone acetate.

Despair
One of four parts of the addiction cycle in the addictive model developed by Patrick Carnes. It is a concept that refers to a sense of utter hopelessness sexual addicts have about their behavior.

Developmental blockage
An inability to relate to appropriate potential sexual partners that occurs during the development of the child.

Disinhibition
One of four major issues believed to be important for understanding the dynamics of child sexual abusers, described in the review of Araji and Finkelhor (1986). It refers to the breakdown of normal inhibitions to sexual activity with children.

Exploiters
People who use children in pornography or prostitution.

Fellatio
Oral-genital sexual act that involves oral contact with the male sex organ.

Fixated molester
One of two categories of molesters in the Groth et al. (1982) model. The fixated molester in this model is a person who has never psychosexually matured and, as a result, only feels comfortable relating to children sexually.

Fondling
Touching a child sexually, often including sexual parts, but not involving any type of oral-genital contact or intercourse.

Frotteurism
A sexual deviancy recognized by the DSM-IV characterized by rubbing against or feeling unsuspecting people in a sexual way.

Impaired thinking
One of four parts of the addiction system that is at the core of a model developed by Patrick Carnes. Refers to the kind of deluded thinking that allows the offender to be insulated from the reality of his behavior.

Inadequate molester
A type of situational molester in Dietz's model who, because of a mental or physical defect, has to resort to the use of children in order to get sexual needs met.

Introverted molester
A type of preferential molester in Dietz's model who is shy and withdrawn and, hence, lacks the skills needed to seduce the children he prefers. As a result, it is believed that this type of offender selects strangers or very young children.

Medroxy-progesterone acetate
An antiandrogen substance that reduces the production of male hormones in an effort to reduce deviant sexual urges.

Megan's Law
A law first passed in New Jersey after Megan Kanka was murdered by a neighbor who had a history of committing sexual offenses against children. The law provides for registration of convicted offenders and authorizes local law enforcement to inform the community of the presence of dangerous offenders. As part of new federal legislation, the Crimes against Children and Sexually Violent Offender Registration Act, all states are required to enact similar registration and notification laws.

Mens rea   A legal term that refers to the capacity, or ability, to know right from wrong. In the field of child sexual abuse, it can be useful in determining when youthful offenders or mentally incapacitated offenders should be held accountable for their behavior.

Mental disorder   A psychiatric disorder involving characteristic signs and symptoms that interfere with the person's ability to function.

Missing and Exploited Children's Task Force   A task force of key federal agencies authorized by law to assist local law enforcement agencies in investigating certain difficult missing children's cases.

Molesters   A generic term used to describe a class of sexual offenders who trick or entice children into engaging in sexual activities with them.

Morally indiscriminate molester   A category of situational molesters in Dietz's model, who not only molest but are willing to violate the rights of others in any way they see fit.

Pathology   In medicine or psychiatry, a state of illness or disease.

Pedophilia   Both a technical and general term that applies to a type of sexual offender who prefers children to peers sexually. Is a paraphilia recognized in the DSM-IV.

Penile plethysmograph   A device, similar to a polygraph device. A flexible gauge is attached to the shaft of the penis and a graphing device records the level of arousal. The person being examined is presented with deviant and normal sexual stimuli in an effort to determine the ratio of responses to each.

Personality disorder   A class of psychiatric disorder believed to develop as a response to experiences in childhood or adolescence, which is characterized by rigidity. It is believed that the symptoms are experienced as ego syntonic. Some mental health professionals regard these disorders as troublesome and hard to work with.

Polygraph examination   A technique or procedure, sometimes called a "lie detector test," whereby a suspect is connected to a device that graphs body responses. The person is interviewed, and the time at which individual questions are asked and the time at which body responses occur are compared, with the goal of detecting when a person is being untruthful.

Pragmatic   Practical; with immediate utilitarian value.

Preferential molester   One of two major categories of molesters in Dietz's model. Characterized by a preference for children sexually, over adults.

Preoccupation   One of four parts of the addiction cycle in the addictive model developed by Patrick Carnes. It is a concept that refers to a trance state or mood whereby the addict is completely engrossed in sex.

Progression of disease   Refers to a concept in the chemical dependency field that has been adopted in the addiction model developed by Patrick Carnes. In the sexual abuse field, it refers to the progression of sexual addiction.

Provera   See Medroxyprogesterone acetate.

Rapist   A class of offender who uses force or the threat of force to gain compliance of the victim.

Recovery   A term used in the chemical dependency field that refers to the process by which the addict moves from addiction to health. Applied in a similar way to sexual addicts in the model developed by Patrick Carnes.

Regressed molester	One of two types of molesters in the Groth et al. (1982) model. The type of offender who has perhaps matured psychosexually but who regresses in response to situational stress. According to this model, such a molester usually turns to female adolescents or late latency age female victims.
Regressed situational molester	A type of "situational" molester in Dietz's model, often with low self-esteem, who turns to children as a sexual substitute for a preferred peer sex partner.
Regression	A Freudian concept that refers to moving backward from one level of psychological development to a level that is characteristic of an earlier level.
Relapse prevention model	A model, or theoretical frame of reference, which asserts that efforts to treat sexual offenders should be based on the premise that sexual offender treatment can only help manage the risk of future offenses, not cure sex offenders.
Ritualistic abuse	Abuse that is inflicted on children by adults, often as part of certain cult religious practices.
Ritualization	One of four parts of the addiction cycle in the addictive model developed by Patrick Carnes. It is a concept that refers to the use of specific behaviors in a ritualistic way as a means to enhance sexual arousal.
Sadistic abuse	Abuse that involves the use of pain, torture, or even to the point of causing death.
Sadistic molester	A category of preferential molester in Dietz's model who enjoys torturing or inflicting pain on child victims.
Sadistic offenders	A general expression that refers to certain sexual offenders who enjoy inflicting pain on their victims.
Seductive molester	A class of preferential molester in Dietz's model who seeks out, grooms, and seduces the child into sexual activity.
Sex ring abusers	A class of sexual molesters who, as part of a group of adults, molest children. It is believed that individual members of the group molest for varied psychological reasons facilitated by the dynamics of the group.
Sexual arousal	In addition to its generally understood meaning, in the four-factor offender model, the term refers to the ability of sexual offenders to be aroused by children.
Sexual compulsivity	One of four parts of the addiction cycle in the addictive model developed by Patrick Carnes. It is a concept that refers to the addictive sexual activity itself.
Sexual exploitation	The use of children in pornography or prostitution.
Sexual predators	Sexual offenders who seek out victims and stalk them, often inflicting great harm or even death.
Sexual sadism	Deriving sexual pleasure from inflicting pain on others.
Sexually indiscriminate molester	A class of situational molester in Dietz's model in which the molester will molest as part of sexual experimentation.
Sexually reactive children	A term used by professionals who work with children who molest other children. It is a way of conceptualizing the behavior as a response to victimization. According to Johnson and Feldmeth (1993), their genitals become the central organizing principle in their development.

Sexually violent predator   A new category of offender recognized under the Crimes against Children and Violent Offender Registration Act. Defined as a person who has committed a sexually violent offense and who has a mental abnormality or personality disorder that makes the person likely to engage in predatory sexually violent offenses.

Situational blockage   A situational blockage to gaining access to appropriate sexual outlets.

Situational molester   A category of molester in Dietz's situational-preferential profile model who is distinguished from other molesters not so much because of preference for children but because of circumstances.

Twelve-step program   Any program to help people recover from compulsive, addictive behavior that uses the principles embodied in the twelve steps of Alcoholics Anonymous.

Typology   A system of naming.

Unmanageability   One of four parts of the addiction cycle developed by Patrick Carnes. It refers to one's life being out of control as a result of compulsive sexual behavior.

Voyeurism   A disorder characterized by becoming sexually aroused by fantasies, urges, or behaviors that involve watching others in a state of undress or in sexual activity.

CHAPTER

DOMESTIC VIOLENCE

A Brief Look at the Historical Context

What Is Domestic Violence?
A Working Definition

How Common Is Domestic Violence?
Incidence and Prevalence

The Controversy about Male and Female
Domestic Violence

What Is the Impact of Battering on Its Victims?

The Cycle of Violence

Why Do Women Stay?

Explanations and Risk Factors

Classifying Perpetrators

Intervention

In this chapter we'll be exploring one of the most pressing and controversial issues of our day: domestic violence. While many worry about rising violence on the streets, it is more likely for a person to be affected by violence in the home. Although it happens at home, no one should be mistaken—this is a potentially lethal form of violence.

With the publicity that has been generated by such high-profile cases as that of O. J. Simpson and John Wayne Bobbit, the public has become intensely aware of this issue (see Box 7-1). So, as people who are striving to understand domestic violence, what do we make of this public hubbub? For one, we know the public has a greater awareness. Based upon our past experience with severe child neglect, sexual abuse, and the battered child

BOX 7-1   Two Famous Domestic Violence Cases:
O. J. Simpson and John Wayne Bobbit

The criminal prosecution of O. J. Simpson, the famous retired football hero, was broadcast live to millions. As the case unfolded, we learned what the prosecution thought his motivation was: O. J. Simpson killed his former wife, Nicole, as the ultimate act of dominating and controlling her, part of a pattern of domestic violence. Those who watched the proceedings heard the 9-1-1 call made by Nicole, and testimony about prior abusive incidents. While Simpson was ultimately acquitted of criminal charges, the trial certainly riveted the issue into our social consciousness. In a wrongful death civil suit filed by the families of Ron Goldman, one of the victims, and Nicole, Simpson was found to be responsible for the deaths.

The John Wayne Bobbit case is another example of a publicized trial where the issue of domestic violence played a central role. John Wayne Bobbit's wife, Loreena, cut off her husband's penis while he slept, claiming that she had been repeatedly forced to have sex with him against her will and that she was an abused wife. Because of her claim of mental impairment caused by the abuse, she was found not guilty of the crime but was briefly placed in a psychiatric treatment program.

syndrome, we can probably conclude there is an opportunity for a favorable change in public attitudes. After all, it's during such times when changes in public attitudes seem to occur. We might also conclude, for whatever reason, that people are now more interested. It is my hope that, because of this heightened interest, there is now greater opportunity to educate.

A BRIEF LOOK AT THE HISTORICAL CONTEXT

Sometimes when you want to figure out where you are and where you want to go, it's nice to take a look at where you've been. However, there's no way that in a short historical overview we could possibly do justice to the topic of woman abuse. The history of the maltreatment of women is long. Paleopathologists have found 2,000- to 3,000-year-old female mummies with skull fractures, which they believe derive from woman abuse (Dickstein, 1988, cited in Hampton & Coner-Edwards, 1993). Gelles and Cornell (1990) comment that in ancient Rome husbands and fathers had nearly absolute power over women (just as with children) that included the right to chastise, divorce, and even kill. According to Lenore Walker (1979), a true pioneer in the battered women's movement, the patriarchal religious structure of the times supported this oppressive pattern. Specific citations in the Bible (Gelles & Cornell, 1990) and the Koran (Landes, et al., 1993) make references to men's rights to rule their women, and these citations have been used to justify the use of violence by men against women.

In their review of the history, Landes, Siegel, and Foster (1993) discuss the socially approved domination of women by men, which continued after the Roman era right up to the present day. Following Roman times, things improved a bit for women: men were still allowed to beat women, but they couldn't any longer kill or permanently maim them. Within the religious and social context of the day, men continued to be the masters in their homes and were seen as teachers and protectors of women. When verbal methods didn't work, they were allowed to use nonlethal physical means (Landes, et al., 1993).

This tradition of permitting physical discipline to control women became part of English **common law**, as codified by Blackstone in 1768 (Gelles & Cornell, 1990; Gelles, 1992). Lenore Walker (1979) reintroduces us to one such common law principle. In her groundbreaking book, *The Battered Woman,* she reminds us of the **rule of thumb.** Most of us have heard the expression but few of us have probably taken the time to trace its origins. It is a reference to the common law principle that permitted men to beat their wives so long as they didn't use a rod thicker than the circumference of their thumbs.

Wife beating remained an accepted part of English common law until 1829 (Landes, et al., 1993), but persisted in the United States until the latter part of that century. In the United States, a Mississippi court established a legal precedent in 1824 by ruling in *Calvin Bradley v. the State* (46 Mississippi 1824) that the "reasonable" physical "chastisement" of women by their husbands was permitted (Gelles, 1992; Landes, et al., 1993). This precedent stood until 1871, when an Alabama court found in *Fulgham v. the State* (46 Ala 143–148) that a married woman has as much right for protection under the law as anyone else (Gelles & Cornell, 1990; Landes, et al., 1993). In the same year, a Massachusetts court made a similar ruling (Gelles & Cornell, 1990). Discrimination against women, however, continued. According to one reference on human services and the law, discrimination against women was enforced in nearly all aspects of public and private life until 1871, when the Supreme Court began to reverse it (Brieland & Lemmon, 1977). In 1883 Maryland became the first state to enact legislation to make wife battering against the law (Davidson, 1978, as cited in Gelles & Cornell, 1990).

While women's rights may have gotten greater recognition in the courts beginning in the 1870s, women were still second-class citizens. Their power and influence within the society continued to be severely restricted. The Fifteenth Amendment to the U.S. Constitution granted voting rights to former slaves in 1867 but not if they were female. It wasn't until passage of the Nineteenth Amendment to the U.S. Constitution, in 1920, that women gained the same right.

While women did ultimately achieve the right to vote, the increase in political power did not stop the woman abuse or the second-class status of women. At the opening of the decade of the 1980s, Richard Gelles (1980), an extremely prolific writer in the family violence field, did a classic review of the family violence literature. He comments that, while interest in the issue of child abuse became ignited following publication of the trailblazing child abuse article, "The Battered Child Syndrome" (Kempe, et al., 1962), scholarly and popular interest in the area of woman abuse was virtually nonexistent.

According to Gelles (1980), it was in the 1970s that we saw a dramatic rise in attention to issues of family violence. Gelles suggests that it was another pioneer in the field, Murray Straus, who called attention to the fact that the women's movement was one of the social forces that had brought the issue of family violence to the public's attention. Straus had also pointed out that one of the first major books dealing with domestic violence had been written by Del Martin in 1976. Martin, it should be pointed out, had organized and chaired the NOW (**National Organization for Women**) task force on battered women (Gelles, 1980). Carden (1994), in an important new review of the literature, suggests that the women's movement was one of three powerful movements that contributed to the dramatic social changes of the period, the other two being the civil rights movement and the child advocacy movement. It was still an uphill battle, however, since public attitudes continued to accept abusive behavior between family members, behavior which would not be tolerated were they to occur between strangers (Gelles, 1974; Steinmetz, 1977; Straus, et al., 1980; all cited in Gelles, 1980).

Public indifference to the plight of abused women was not new. What was new was that a new movement had emerged—a movement that cared deeply about this issue. In the 1970s concern about abused women began to be expressed in grassroots drives to establish shelters for battered women. Erin Pizzey is credited with founding the first known battered woman's shelter, Chiswick Women's Aid, in London, England, in 1971 (Gelles & Cornell, 1990; Landes, et al., 1993). In the fall of the same year, A Woman's Place opened in Urbana, Illinois, soon followed by Rainbow Retreat in Phoenix, Arizona (Landes, et al., 1993). By 1985 there were about 780 shelters operating nationally, and by 1994 there were an estimated 2,000 shelters, transition houses, and programs for battered women, serving two-thirds of all counties in the country (Carden, 1994).

The establishment of programs for abusers followed those for victims. The first program to treat abusers in the United States, EMERGE, was opened in Boston in 1977 (Carden, 1994; Edleson & Tolman, 1992). One wouldn't necessarily expect battered women's advocates to be involved in establishing perpetrator programs, yet they are credited with just this. A large number of perpetrator treatment programs were established and operated in association with shelters (Carden, 1994). Carden (1994) comments that battered women's advocates noticed early on that as many as half their clients eventually returned to their abusive partners. Carden (1994) suggests that part of the motivation of people involved in the shelter movement was to prevent further abuse and reduce the risk that other women would be abused. In contrast to a relatively large number of shelters for battered women, however, the number of perpetrator programs was low in comparison. We should also note that, whereas the **National Coalition against Domestic Violence** had a national registry of programs, there was no equivalent registry of perpetrator programs. With new laws demanding the arrest of perpetrators, and with the increasing emphasis of the courts to require perpetrators to participate in specialized programs, this seems to be changing. These programs have proliferated and are now estimated to number in the hundreds (Edleson & Tolman, 1992).

WHAT IS DOMESTIC VIOLENCE? A WORKING DEFINITION

I'm temporarily putting the term "domestic violence" in quotation marks because we could use it to apply to all forms of family maltreatment. It does, after all, literally mean violence that occurs in the home. To do so, however, would misrepresent our topic since, in today's society, most of us correctly understand the term to refer to aggression that takes place in intimate relationships, usually between adults. While the term that is preferred in this chapter is domestic violence, the topic is sometimes referred to as "spousal abuse," "marital violence," "conjugal violence," "wife abuse," "partner abuse," and a number of other terms. We may use these terms in the text pretty much interchangeably, but not the terms **domestic violence** and **battering.** We will reserve the use of the term *battering* for the most serious forms of domestic violence—violence which includes severe physical assault or risk of serious injury.

Definitions serve to help us describe whatever it is we're trying to understand. Susan Schecter and Ann Ganley (1995) have developed one of the most elegant definitions of domestic violence around:

A pattern of assaultive and coercive behaviors, including physical, sexual, and psychological attacks, as well as economic coercion, that adults or adolescents use against their intimate partners. (p. 10)

Implicit within this definition are three basic criteria that Schecter and Ganley (1995) suggest we should consider when we define domestic violence:

- The relationship context of the violence
- The function the violence serves
- The specific behaviors of its perpetrators

BOX 7-2   Marital Rape

The whole concept of marital rape is controversial. As discussed earlier in this text, sexual violence can be one means by which one marital partner can exert dominance and control over another. On the other hand, the concept of marriage often includes vague ideas about marital rights and obligations. These were codified into English law by Lord Matthew Hale in the mid 17th century (Barnett, et al., 1997; Small & Tetreault, 1990; Whatley, 1993). Until fairly recently, these rights and obligations were part of the law (Whatley, 1993). As a consequence, laws designed to protect innocent people from rape by strangers could not be applied to violent sexual assault by one's marriage partner. In a recent review of state laws, Mark Small and Pat Tetreault (1990) inform us that there are three different varieties of "marital exemptions." One category of these exemptions completely protects husbands from being charged with the rape of their wives.

Laws that do not protect wives from the violent sexual assaults of their husbands are only part of the problem. As of 1993, only two states continued to give absolute exemption from prosecution to husbands against marital rape charges, yet marital rape continues as a significant domestic violence problem (Whatley, 1993). In his review of the literature on marital rape, Whatley suggests that marital rape is more likely to occur in relationships where other forms of domestic violence occur. Marital rape is often an expression of rage and aggression. Consistent with the definitional model of domestic violence adopted in this text, it can be viewed as a way to maintain dominance over one's partner. One team of researchers classified women who were victims of forced sex into three types (Finkelhor & Yllo, 1982, cited in Whatley, 1993). These include one category of women who are generally, and extensively, abused. A second category involves victims who have sexual conflicts with their partners. Sadistic sexuality is implicated in the third type.

Schecter and Ganley (1995) go on to enumerate the specific coercive behaviors referred to in their definition. They group them into three basic types of assault (physical, sexual, and psychological), plus economic control, and give us a virtual laundry list of behaviors in each category. Any and all of these forms of coercion can be used to control another person. Perhaps the most extreme example of how sexual behavior can be used to control and humiliate one's domestic partner is that of marital rape (see Box 7-2).

Examples of specific things perpetrators do in the physical and sexual categories of assault are fairly self-evident, but those in the psychological category don't always immediately come to mind and might do with a little further discussion here. Within the psychological assault category, Schecter and Ganley include the following:

- Threats of violence and physical harm
- Attacks against property or pets (assaults aimed at hurting things the victim cares about)
- Emotional abuse (repeated verbal attacks aimed at degrading, humiliating, and injuring the sense of self)
- Isolation (separating victims from their support system and preventing "reality checks")
- Use of children (hurting and controlling the victim through the use of those the victim cares most about)

The definitional model used by Schecter and Ganley (1995) places significant importance on the reason why the perpetrator behaves the way he does—to control—and this seems to be at the heart of what domestic violence is (see Figure 7-1).

Although the definition suggested by Schecter and Ganley (1995) seems to be an extremely helpful way to look at domestic violence, we should clarify one area before we consider it as part of our working definition. While power and control appear to be at the core of the perpetrator's motivation, we will reserve the term *domestic violence* for those cases where physical force or threat is at least one element. It seems possible for a person to be in an extremely controlling relationship yet one that is not violent, in the way we usually think of violence, that is, involving the use of physical force. We know, for example, that child psychological maltreatment can sometimes exist on its own without physical maltreatment (see Chapter 3). Do we want to classify the use of extremely controlling patterns of behavior that does not involve physical or sexual aggression as domestic violence? To do so does not seem to enhance our working definition. Therefore, the term **adult psychological maltreatment** will be used to refer to those cases where physical or sexual force or threat is not an element.

So, for the purposes of this chapter, the working definition of domestic violence we will adopt looks like this:

A pattern of coercive behavior, which must include physical aggression or threat, commonly accompanied by other forms of controlling behavior, that adults or adolescents use against their intimate partners.

There are just a few additional points we should make about domestic violence before we move on. First of all, we often think of domestic violence as being something that happens between a husband and wife. The fact is that couples in which domestic violence is involved need not be married, and frequently aren't. In a recent evaluation of perpetrator treatment programs, for instance, over half of the perpetrators were not married (Gondolf, 1996). Similar findings are reported for women in shelters (Gondolf, et al., 1991, as cited in Gondolf, 1996). Not only this, but it also seems that they frequently don't even live with each other (Gondolf, 1996).

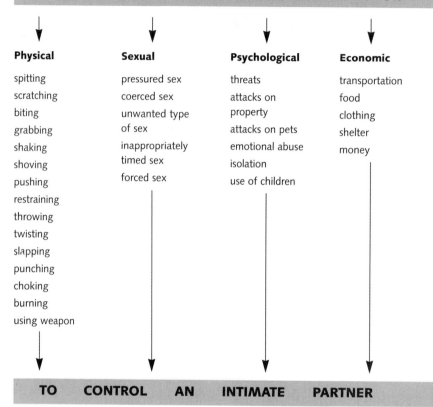

THE ABUSE OCCURS WITHIN A RELATIONSHIP CONTEXT IN WHICH PERPETRATORS USE SPECIFIC BEHAVIOR

Physical	Sexual	Psychological	Economic
spitting	pressured sex	threats	transportation
scratching	coerced sex	attacks on	food
biting	unwanted type	property	clothing
grabbing	of sex	attacks on pets	shelter
shaking	inappropriately	emotional abuse	money
shoving	timed sex	isolation	
pushing	forced sex	use of children	
restraining			
throwing			
twisting			
slapping			
punching			
choking			
burning			
using weapon			

TO   CONTROL   AN   INTIMATE   PARTNER

As our knowledge of domestic violence has grown, we've also learned that it isn't restricted to heterosexual couples. It exists in gay and lesbian relationships as well (see Box 7-3), and a healthy body of literature addressing issues of same-sex relationships is now beginning to develop (Coleman, 1994; Hamberger, 1994; Letellier, 1994; Lockhart, et al., 1994; Renzetti, 1995).

Domestic violence can also include violence in dating relationships, sometimes called **courtship violence** (Gelles & Cornell, 1990). In recent years we've come to recognize that this form of domestic violence is a significant problem, including among teenagers (see Box 7-4).

The final clarification we need to make about our definition is very, very important: domestic violence frequently occurs after a relationship is over. Many professionals and advocates tell us that victims are at the greatest danger when trying to get out of a domestically violent relationship or after separating (Browne, 1987; Campbell, 1992, as cited in Schecter & Ganley, 1995;

BOX 7-3   Domestic Violence in Gay and Lesbian Relationships

There seem to be at least two mistakes that can be made in reference to domestic violence and gay or lesbian relationships. One is to assume that domestic violence doesn't exist in gay and lesbian relationships. While we have been paying attention to the problem of domestic violence for some time, recognizing it in gay and lesbian relationships is relatively new (Lockhart et al., 1994; Renzetti, 1995). Even within activist circles it may have been overlooked, since feminist theory assumes unequal power distributions between men and women to be central to understanding domestic violence (Letellier, 1994).

A second possible mistake we can make is to assume that the dynamics of domestic violence in gay and lesbian relationships are identical to those that occur in "straight" relationships. Patrick Letellier (1994) points out that the dynamics may be quite different. He suggests that gay men may be more likely to fight back in response to being hit, because this is the way men are socialized. He also suggests that even men who are clearly abused may be more likely to see their abuse as "mutual combat" since they are more likely to hit back. Letellier goes on to suggests that, as a result of seeing their situation this way, gay men may be less likely than women to seek help. Another problem is that networks of resources for battered men, such as those in place for battered women, do not exist.

Claire Renzetti (1995) suggests that lesbian women may also be less likely to seek help than their heterosexual counterparts. In her research, she notes that lesbian women tend not to seek help from hot lines and women's shelters, and that when they do, they tend to view the help they get as not very helpful. She maintains that we are at about the same place today with the problem of lesbian battering that we were 20 years ago with domestic violence in general.

Edleson & Tolman, 1992). Newspaper or television accounts of the recently divorced abuser who returns home, kills his former spouse, children, and finally himself are unfortunately all too common.

HOW COMMON IS DOMESTIC VIOLENCE? INCIDENCE AND PREVALENCE

In contrast to the issue of child abuse, which has mandatory reporting laws in all 50 states, there is no such uniform reporting requirement for cases of suspected domestic violence. While some states and jurisdictions may have enacted requirements for key professionals, such as physicians and social

BOX 7-4 Courtship Violence and Date Rape

We can think of domestic violence as abuse that occurs in the context of a relationship, whereby perpetrators use specific behaviors to control their intimate partners (Schecter & Ganley, 1995). As summarized in Figure 7-1, these can include a variety of strategies, including belittling, intimidation, physical force, and sexual assaults. While we often think of adult marital relationships, this definition can and does encompass both courtship violence and date rape. Dating and courtship, a form of relationship in itself, provide the context for establishing more long-term relationships and as a precursor for marriage (White & Koss, 1991). Kathryn Ryan (1995) has identified at least two characteristics of wife-battering men that were also associated with courtship violence: threats and verbal abuse.

Courtship violence.   In order to estimate the extent of courtship violence, Jacquelyn White and Mary Koss conducted a survey using a nationally representative sample of nearly 5,000 college men and women. They found that approximately 40% of both men and women engaged in violent behavior, most often involving threats to hit, pushing, grabbing, and shoving. Jealousy, denial of sexual favors, and drinking are commonly cited reasons for the behavior. Taking note that preparation for marriage occurs in the context of courtship, White and Koss suggest that American families are likely to continue to experience a significant amount of marital violence. The extent of more severe forms of courtship violence is uncertain, though Gelles and Cornell (1990) estimate its range to be from 1 to 27%.

Date rape.   One of the most celebrated recent cases of date rape is that of William Kennedy Smith (Cowan & Curtis, 1994). Smith, the nephew of Senator Ted Kennedy, met the alleged victim in a Palm Beach, Florida, bar. She later said that he forced her to have sex with him after she accompanied him to his estate. While Smith was ultimately acquitted, this case brought the issue of date rape to America's attention (Cowan & Curtis, 1994). The estimates of how much sexual aggression occurs in dating relationships vary between 15 to 78% (Vicary et al., 1995). Actual date rape—forced sexual intercourse that occurs in the context of a dating relationship—is thought to occur more rarely (Vicary et al., 1995). Judith Vicary and her colleagues (1995) comment on the figures of Koss (1992), who suggests that about 5% of the women in their college sample had been raped during the previous year. Among adolescent girls, Vicary et al. (1995) report that 13% reported forced intercourse with a date. Another survey of high school students suggested that 1 in 5 report having experienced forced sex, but only half told of their experience (Davis et al., 1993). In this same study, 60% of boys found it acceptable in one or more situations to force sex on a girl (Davis et al., 1993).

workers, to report suspected domestic violence, the absence of a *national* mandate makes it more difficult to assess the extent of the problem.

As is also true with other facets of the family violence field, without controlled studies (which are difficult to do in this field), it is often very challenging to get really good information about the extent of domestic violence. Though there are clearly difficulties, it is also true that useful information exists. Richard Gelles, a true research pioneer in the field, tells us that when it comes to available data about domestic violence there are three primary types (Gelles, 1992, 1993a, 1995): clinical data and case studies, official reports, and self-report surveys. Each of these has its strengths (Gelles, 1992, 1993a, 1995). Clinical data, or case studies, can give us graphic, qualitative information about the experience of particular people. Official report data can provide us with measures of what is actually reported. And survey data can give us estimates of abuse within the general population based upon a sampling (the larger and more representative, the better). As the research methodology in the field is becoming more sophisticated, we are seeing research designs that also include comparison or control groups.

Not only does each type of available data have its strengths but also its limitations. None can give us everything we need. Clinical studies usually tell us about the most serious cases because they tend to be dramatic and stand out. Official report data only tell us about maltreatment that is actually reported, and we believe that only a fraction of actual abuse is ever reported. Survey data, even in large representative samples, relies upon the accuracy of the memories and perceptions of the people being surveyed; in the case of domestic violence, the men and women who are involved in it. And controlled experimental research often tells us only about a very focused area of investigation. Not only are there characteristic difficulties with each of these data types, but the definitions, methodology, samples of the people, and so on vary greatly from study to study. As a consequence of these differences the results often vary as well, making it difficult to compare one study to another.

One pair of national studies is unique in the domestic violence field because they were done with very large samples and conducted ten years apart. These are the **National Family Violence Surveys**, carried out by Murray Straus and his colleagues (Straus & Gelles, 1986; Straus & Gelles, 1990; Straus, et al., 1980). Their results yield survey data that have been used by countless investigators trying to plumb family violence. They are widely regarded as offering us among the best available information we have about abuse in the family. Because the surveys were done ten years apart, in 1975 and 1985, they can also help look at trends between one time and another. Using a now widely administered survey called the **Conflict Tactics Scale** (Straus, 1979), Straus and his colleagues interviewed a representative sample of families throughout the United States.

The incidence rates in the second survey averaged about 120 per 1,000 (incidence rates are usually reported in thousands), or 12% of couples reporting at least one incident of violence during the previous year. These included relatively "minor" types of assaults, such as slapping or pushing.

For serious incidents, or those likely to cause injury (for example, kicking, punching, biting, choking, or using a knife or gun) the overall rate was 63 per 1,000 couples, or nearly three and a half million.

Carden (1994) has done a fairly recent review. Her synopsis includes estimates from the 1990 **National Crime Victim Survey** (U.S. Department of Justice, 1992). The National Crime Victim Survey (NCVS) is an annual survey of about 60,000 homes conducted by the Bureau of the Census for the Justice Department (Gelles, 1995). One problem with this particular survey is that it asks respondents about "crimes," not necessarily about domestic violence. It is important to remember that people don't necessarily consider them to be the same. Based on this NCVS survey, there were an estimated 2.3 million crimes committed by family members or a person with whom the victim had an intimate relationship. Of those crimes, it was estimated that about 58%, or about 1.4 million, were committed by a spouse or ex-spouse. This is somewhat close to the 1.8 million estimate proposed by Van Hasselt, Morrison, Bellack, and Hersen in the *Handbook of Family Violence* (1988, as cited by Carden, 1994). We should take note that these estimates, as is also true of the results of the National Family Violence Survey, in no way approximate the number of actual reports, which is a much smaller number. There may be a lot of reasons why relatively few domestic violence incidents get reported compared to the number we estimate actually occur. One commonly suggested reason is that many victims are reluctant to report, because of wanting their relationship to be "okay," desiring to preserve the family, or fearing what the perpetrator might do.

One of the most important statistics in the field of domestic violence is literally a matter of life and death. They are the fatalities. The FBI maintains official crime statistics that include information on family homicides (Gelles, 1992). As discussed in Chapter 1, the FBI estimates that slightly more than 1,300 women are killed each year by past or present husbands or boyfriends (Federal Bureau of Investigation, 1985, 1991). In addition, approximately 800 men are killed by their intimate partners (Landes et al., 1993). Some suggest that over 50% of all female murders and 12% of all male murders are perpetrated by a past or present domestic partner (see Carden, 1994).

THE CONTROVERSY ABOUT MALE AND FEMALE DOMESTIC VIOLENCE

It is commonplace to hear quotes like, "95% of all domestic violence is perpetrated by men." Is it really true? According to one of the early pioneers in the field, there is no issue that has generated as much controversy as the question of whether there are a significant number of male victims of domestic violence (Gelles, 1995). At least a couple of authors have commented on very strong reactions to some of the rather startling findings of both the first and second National Family Violence Surveys. The results in question suggest that women may perpetrate violence against their partners as often, or perhaps even more often, than men. Landes, Siegel, and Foster (1993) note that some critics objected to the findings because they were contrary to those that would be expected based upon feminist theory. They also note that Straus and Gelles have consistently maintained that ignoring or covering up the research findings would do little to advance the cause of domestic violence victims or the field. In a discussion about the controversy, Gelles (1993a) describes the reaction to the early publication of the data (originally by his co-researcher Suzanne Steinmetz): "The reaction against these data was swift and emotional. Straus and Steinmetz were, and continue to be, subjected to vitriolic and personal attacks, including bomb scares and death threats."

In some sense the reaction may be understandable since the stakes are very high. If the results of the data are accurate, they fly in the face of what feminist theory proposes, and feminist theory has been influential, if not dominant, in guiding the domestic violence field. As a consequence, it has also been influential in determining social policy and how treatment programs are structured.

Just what are these controversial research results? In a recent report to the American Medical Association, Richard Gelles (1995) discusses them. In both the first and second National Family Violence Surveys (NFVS) the Conflict Tactics Scale was administered to representative samples of homes (the first with about 2,000 participants and the second about 6,000). The results, amazingly, did seem to suggest that women are as violent as men, and perhaps even slightly more so. Looking only at examples of violence that could conceivably result in injuries, the results of the first NFVS suggested that the rate of serious husband-to-wife violence was 38 per 1,000; the rate of serious wife-to-husband violence was 46 per 1,000. Ten years later in the second NFVS, the results indicated that husband-to-wife violence actually dropped slightly, to 34 per 1,000. The rates for women were essentially unchanged, 48 per 1,000.

These results really are startling, and the researchers themselves attempted to be very cautious about interpreting them. They wanted to see if there wasn't something they were missing. The possibility that the men themselves were minimizing and underreporting their abusive behavior was among the first possibilities that came to mind. Straus and his colleagues reexamined the data with the idea of testing this possibility. They did this by excluding reports from men and only reviewing the reports of women, about both their use of violence and that of their husbands. For severe violence, they found rates of 50 per 1,000 for men and 46 per 1,000 for women (Gelles, 1995). Not only did they get nearly the same results when they only looked at women's interviews, but Gelles (1995) comments that other studies were coming up with comparable results (see Straus, 1993).

How do we interpret these results in light of the common wisdom, that is, that men are the primary aggressors? Gelles (1995) points out that men are generally taller, heavier, and stronger than women. They are also more likely to have experience with weapons, through socialization or perhaps military experience, than women. As a result of the inequalities, Gelles suggests, we would expect that the violence men perpetrate would have a greater impact on victims than violence perpetrated by women (Gelles, 1995). Does research bear this out? The answer seems to be "yes." In a study of men and women who commit assaults, about 1.2% of them cause injuries compared to 0.2% for women (Brush, 1990, as cited in Gelles, 1995). In a review of the second National Family Violence Survey, Straus (1993) found the rate of assaults causing injuries to be 3.7 per 1,000 for men and 0.6 per 1,000 for women. The results of both these studies, then, conclude that assaults committed by men are at least six times more likely to cause injuries than assaults perpetrated by women.

We previously made a distinction between *domestic violence* and *battering,* reserving the latter term for "serious" cases, or those that can or do result in serious injury. This may be a good place to reintroduce that distinction into the discussion. Assaults committed by men are more likely to result in injury and, hence, men are far more likely to batter, the way we've chosen to define the word. The prevailing ideas in the field of domestic violence suggest that, as a result of a history of domination, greater strength and muscle mass, and the way men are raised or socialized, men have learned that they can batter women to control them, and they can get away with it. This leads us to the final questions in our discussion of this particular controversy: Do women use violence in self-defense? Do men use violence, as feminist theory suggests, as part of a pattern of domination and control?

As Gelles and his colleagues are quick to point out, surveys have limitations, not the least of which is their inability to determine the motivation for the violence. While the amount of violence men perpetrate against women, and that which women perpetrate against men, seems to be about equal in terms of the number of reported incidents, the quality of that violence and the reasons for using it are not distinguished. Gelles (1995) does suggest that when women behave violently, they frequently seem to do so in self-defense. He cautions, however, that some women behave violently for the same reasons men do; that is, out of a desire to control their mates or to express rage and frustration (Gelles, 1995). He points out that a limitation to the usefulness of the National Family Violence Surveys in answering this question, is that they don't assess any pattern, or escalation, of assaults throughout a relationship.

Often when women finally retaliate it happens after months or years of abuse. Firsthand accounts and case studies suggest that when women perpetrate violence, it is commonly in response to a protracted cycle of victimization (Browne, 1987; Browne & Williams, 1989). It is sometimes described as a last-ditch effort to somehow deal with an unending ordeal. Murray Straus (1993) points out that this pattern is commonly reported when women kill their spouses. Gelles (1995), in his discussion about female-perpetrated homicides, affirms that there may be significant, qualitative differences in homicides committed by men and women. Ann Goetting (1989) examined police reports on 84 cases involving individuals accused of having killed their spouses. Her assessment of the records seems to confirm that

---

BOX 7-5   Delia's Story

Delia is the survivor of severe domestic violence. She was also convicted of murdering her husband. Delia was a very young woman when she met her future husband and got married. She and her husband eventually had five children together, but all was not well. Delia's husband was not only abusive to her but assaulted and terrorized the children as well. He would laugh as he played Russian Roulette with the family with a loaded gun. A devout Roman Catholic, Delia sought help and advice from her family, but was told she needed to stay with him because they were married. Her priest told her she should try to do things better so her husband wouldn't get angry with her.

Despite running away, asking for help, and even getting a protection order, Delia could find no help. She ultimately killed her husband and served several years in prison before her case came to public attention, when there was an appeal to the governor for clemency. After highly publicized hearings, she was granted clemency and released. She now says she wants her story to help others.

Based on *Broken Vows: Religious Perspectives on Domestic Violence* (video), by J. Anton and M. M. Fortune (Executive Producers) and M. Garguilo (Writer-Director), Center for the Prevention of Sexual and Domestic Violence, Seattle, 1994.

---

when men killed women it was generally "offensive," whereas when women killed it was self-protective (Goetting, 1989). Gelles comments that there is fairly consistent anecdotal evidence suggesting that men who do ultimately kill their partners often stalk their victims (Wilson & Daly, 1992, cited in Gelles, 1995), and when they kill, in contrast to when women kill, they often kill not only their former spouses, but often the children as well.

WHAT IS THE IMPACT OF BATTERING ON ITS VICTIMS?

Delia's case, as outlined in Box 7-5, is among the most severe examples of domestic violence. Delia and her children had been terrorized for years by her husband. After unsuccessfully trying to deal with her situation, she ultimately killed her husband. By the time she reached this point, she felt she had exhausted all other sources of help. Such cases are controversial perhaps because we define criminals by what they do, not why they do it. What she did was never before part of her "repertoire" of behavior, and so we could think of it as one extreme example of the impact of domestic violence. The literature is replete with discussion about other effects of domestic violence.

The law enforcement community is becoming aware of how serious domestic violence is and is taking serious steps to attack the problem.

The physical consequences of domestic violence can be quite severe, up to and including loss of life, but women often tell us that the psychological impacts can be worse. In the remainder of this section, we'll be focusing primarily on the psychological or emotional impact of domestic violence. In this vein we'll begin with a brief discussion of some now classic ideas, reconsider these ideas in light of the current state of the art, and then turn to some recent thoughts and ideas about victimization and adaptation.

Lenore Walker, a pioneer in the battered women's movement, wrote a groundbreaking book in 1979 called *The Battered Woman*. Dr. Walker based her work on interviews with over 120 battered women; she coined the expression *battered woman syndrome* to describe the commonalities of abuse she found in the various women she interviewed. In this now classic book, Dr. Walker (1979) outlines a number of characteristics of the battered woman. These include

- having low self-esteem
- believing myths about battering relationships
- being a "traditionalist" (that is, traditional family values and sex role stereotypes)
- taking responsibility for the batterer's actions
- suffering from guilt but denying feelings of terror and anger
- seeming passive but able to manipulate environment in order to avoid further violence, including risk of being killed

- having severe stress reactions, with psychophysiological complaints
- using sex to establish intimacy
- believing no one will be able to resolve her predicament but her

In addition to these general characteristics, Walker (1979) discusses some of the psychological signs and symptoms that are often associated with the severe stress experienced by women in violent relationships. These include sleep disturbance, eating disturbance, and fatigue. In addition, Walker comments that many women in these circumstances suffer from a number of bodily, or somatic, complaints such as tension headaches, stomach problems, high blood pressure, allergies, and heart palpitations.

It seems common sense to think that living in a domestic combat zone could produce the kind of signs and symptoms described above. From a mental health point of view, these are consistent with mental health disorders recognized in the definitive manual of these disorders, the DSM-IV (American Psychiatric Association, 1994). Disturbance of sleep, appetite, energy level, and interest in being involved in activities, and subjective feelings of sadness are associated with mood disorders, particularly depression, and are a standard part of formal and informal mental status examinations done by mental health personnel (Kaplan & Sadock, 1989). Persons with palpitations sometimes have anxiety-related disorders (Kaplan & Sadock, 1989). Bodily complaints, headaches, and the like are frequently associated with stress and can sometimes actually be diagnosable as a "somatiform disorder" (Kaplan & Sadock, 1989).

Based on clinical reports, depression and anxiety are commonly associated with domestic violence victimization (Gelles & Harrop; 1989; Christophoulus et al., 1987, cited in Gelles & Conte, 1990; Hilberman, 1980; Hilberman & Munson, 1977; Schecter, 1983). Lest we overgeneralize and come to think that when these signs and symptoms are present domestic violence is also, we should be cautious because these same signs and symptoms are associated with other types of problems. We can, however, use them as indicators that something is not right and then explore more fully.

The reports of depression and anxiety so commonly found in women with domestic violence histories is clearly consistent with descriptions provided by Walker (1979), herself a qualified psychologist. As with other serious forms of family maltreatment (see Chapter 4), victimization is associated with another specific mental health disorder known as **posttraumatic stress disorder** (PTSD). This disorder originally came into the American Psychiatric Association's system for classifying mental disorders as a result of problems experienced by Vietnam War veterans. There are four basic components to PTSD:

- A traumatic event sufficient to cause a traumatic stress reaction
- Intrusive reexperiencing symptoms such as nightmares or flashbacks
- Symptoms associated with avoiding experiences that trigger unpleasant feelings or thoughts, and
- Hyperarousal or increased tendency to startle

PTSD is not the kind of disorder that excludes diagnosing for other disorders when it is appropriate to do so. It can, and often does, exist alongside other recognized mental health diagnoses. Victims of domestic violence might have depressive disorders, other anxiety-based disorders, somatiform disorders, and an array of other possible disorders.

Children Who Witness Abuse

We probably shouldn't discuss the impact of abuse without also discussing the impact on children. Many surveys suggest that approximately 20% of adults witnessed at least some domestic violence in their childhoods. Not only this, but it seems that about 50% of children in domestically violent homes are also victims of child physical abuse (Straus & Gelles, 1990). While the issue of child witnesses to domestic violence has not yet gotten the same kind of attention as other aspects of domestic violence, it is becoming a matter of increasing concern. Not only is there concern about the impact on the child's own life but that witnessing domestic violence might increase the risk of the child growing up to become domestically violent as well.

There are at least two major reviews of the literature that focus on child witnesses: Fantuzzo and Lindquist (1989) and a recent study by Kolko, Blakely, and Engleman (1996). This literature is by no means conclusive, but it seems fairly certain that children who witness domestic violence are at increased risk in one or more areas. Kolko and associates (1996) searched seven computer databases and found 29 articles that met certain selection criteria they had created (including each having a comparison group). They reported on results in five distinct areas of functioning: behavior, emotions, social adjustment, cognitive development, and physical (psychosomatic) problems.

The results of the Kolko et al. (1996) review seem to confirm that children who witness domestic violence are at increased risk for a variety of problems, especially disturbance in their emotional and behavioral functioning. They note that in the areas of social, cognitive, and physical development the results are not yet conclusive. They further comment that the literature generally supports the contention of social learning theory that some children (about 30%) learn to become violent by seeing it at home, but the majority (70%) do not (Kaufman & Zigler, 1987, 1989; Widom, 1989). As we will discuss when we talk about risk factors, we are becoming more concerned with understanding the conditions under which violence is learned intergenerationally, rather than *if* such learning occurs (Kaufman & Zigler, 1987, 1989; Widom, 1989; also see Chapter 2).

Toward a More Client-Friendly Approach to Understanding Victims

One of the most exciting developments in our understanding of victims is to appreciate how adaptive their responses to victimization can be. In times past, many mental health professionals have been guilty of "pathologizing" victims, excessively focusing on their pathology or dysfunction. The business of assigning diagnoses, including the PTSD diagnosis, for psychological problems has been a sensitive issue within the battered women's movement because of concern about its impact on the abused woman (Dutton & Goodman, 1994). Many victims have been told by their abusers that they're crazy, so to be given a psychiatric label can actually reinforce the message received from their abusive partners. In our previous discussion of child abuse, we talked about adopting more client-friendly attitudes toward victims of abuse (see especially Chapter 4). Some of these concepts may be appropriate to the issue of domestic violence as well.

One such concept is called **abuse-related accommodation**, which has been articulated by John Briere (1992), a psychologist who specializes in working with trauma victims. He suggests that, rather than focusing on the pathological aspects of a client's behavior, such as suicidal gestures, self-destructive behavior, or other acting out, we learn to work within the client's own subjective frame of reference. When we do, we can understand much of this behavior as a natural adaptation to the abuse—a way of trying to survive.

Briere (1992) suggests that PTSD can be a viable framework in which to understand abuse, but he expands and extends some of the basic concepts. As discussed earlier, PTSD has intrusive symptoms, avoidance symptoms, and increased arousal symptoms. Briere suggests that, in addition to these, there are a number of other adaptations that take place: distortions of thinking, altered emotionality (including depression and anxiety), and dissociation (disengagement, detachment/numbing, observation as opposed to experiencing amnesia, and other severe responses). He also proposes that there are certain behavioral and relationship adaptations. These include disturbed relatedness (problems with intimacy, altered sexuality, coming to believe that violence is "normal" in relationships, manipulativeness, antagonistic behavior, and aggression), avoidance (use of drugs or alcohol, suicidality), and other tension-reducing behaviors.

By looking at the clients' adaptation through their eyes, we are being highly respectful of their position. Problems previously described as signs and symptoms become functional attempts to adapt. By accepting this model, Briere suggests, we are also accepting three basic tenets: (1) the behavior of survivors is pragmatic (that is, it tends to work for the client); (2) because it has worked for the client, even behavior we think is dysfunctional isn't easy to give up; and (3) because the behavior is an adaptation, it can tell us something about what the client has been through.

While this model is borrowed from work about helping survivors of child abuse, much of it applies to all trauma victims. There are also some significant differences. For instance, we believe that some psychological problems, such as the development of personality disorders, form in childhood and adolescence. We would not expect these to emerge for the first time in adulthood. While adult victims might learn to dissociate, emotionally detach, or distance themselves from the psychological impact of abuse, they would be unlikely to develop multiple personalities, as might a very young child exposed to particularly heinous abuse.

Briere (1992) suggests that abuse survivors adapt in three stages. First, the person experiences a traumatic response, perhaps becoming fearful, anxious, hurt, betrayed, or abandoned. Briere refers to this as the **initial reaction.** The trauma-producing event overpowers the individual's normal coping abilities. It is greater than the individual's internal resources and external supports (network of family, friends, and others). If the person has been isolated and separated from family or friends, as often seems to happen in domestic violence, the person will be more vulnerable. Briere refers to the second stage in his model as **accommodation to ongoing abuse.** In an adult relationship the victim might try to smooth things over, find ways to avoid talking about touchy issues, or do things to pacify the abuser. According to Briere, the goal of stage two is to increase safety and/or decrease pain during victimization. The third stage is long-term adaptation to the trauma. Briere refers to this stage as **long-term elaboration and secondary accommodation.** It would be at stage three that the person's way of dealing with the world would undergo a change. The abuse becomes the central organizing theme in the person's life, and the victim fully integrates the trauma as well as coping strategies and behaviors.

The abuse-focused accommodation model advocated by Briere has been a useful model for working with children and adult victims of child abuse and might provide us with another framework for thinking about how victims of adult family violence adapt.

THE CYCLE OF VIOLENCE

One of the most intriguing contributions to the field of domestic violence is Lenore Walker's pioneering book, *The Battered Woman* (1979). Her description of the *cycle of violence* has become a particularly important component of our understanding of domestic violence. Based on interviews obtained from over 120 battered women, Walker developed this model for explaining the dynamics of violent relationships. She suggests that the physical violence itself is not a constant experience in these relationships but, rather, it waxes and wanes. She also suggests that by understanding the cycle we might learn how to stop or prevent it. Walker outlines three distinct phases within the cycle of violence:

- Tension-building phase
- Explosion or acute phase
- Calm, loving, respite phase (sometimes called the "honeymoon phase")

Walker (1979) describes the first phase of the cycle, the tension-building phase, as a time when everyone is "walking on eggshells." So-called minor abusive incidents occur, but these are all handled or managed by the victim.

In an effort to prevent overt battering, she might try to soothe the batterer, nurture him, and be compliant with his wishes. When she sees the potential for conflict, she finds a way to steer clear of the problem and stay on safe ground. She avoids becoming angry in response to his behavior, for she knows that to do so could be dangerous. She also makes excuses for the abuser as a way of keeping herself from having to face the reality of what is happening in her relationship. She might be willing to tolerate his minor abuses since she knows he is capable of much more severe violence. During this phase, the victim might feel that she has at least some control over the abuser's behavior. For his part, he feels entitled, but at some level also knows his behavior would not be tolerated outside the home. Knowing that his behavior is wrong, he fears that it will eventually drive his partner away, so he attempts to keep control of her through his abusive behavior. Walker suggests that it is at this time that he becomes insecure, excessively possessive, and jealous. As this phase in the cycle progresses, the ability of each to cope becomes stretched to the maximum.

When the tension reaches its climax, the explosion or acute phase is likely to occur. According to Walker (1979), the women she interviewed indicated that during phase two the batterer seemed to be out of control. It is this feature, being out of control, that distinguishes this phase from phase one, for both the victim and the perpetrator. Walker indicates that often the perpetrators seem bent on "teaching the spouses a lesson" during this phase. According to Walker's description, phase two is feared and dreaded by the victims, who might sometimes even do something to trigger it just to get it over with. To do so gives the victim at least some control over when it occurs. Walker suggests that the victim often knows what's going on during this phase and attempts to refrain from doing anything that might further antagonize the abuser, while the batterer often can't recount exactly what occurs during this phase. Walker further suggests that victims describe themselves as generally handling themselves fairly well during the acute phase. According to Walker, numbing out their emotions is common, and some are able to dissociate themselves from their bodies entirely, having the experience of watching as their bodies are being battered. When the attack is over, Walker suggests, both batterer and victim are often shocked at what has happened. If the police are going to be called, Walker suggests that it will usually be during the acute phase. Interestingly, she suggests that when the police do come, they are sometimes actually attacked by the victim. Walker explains this by suggesting that the battered woman knows that when the police leave, the violence is likely to escalate again, and that attacking the police officer is one way to demonstrate loyalty to the perpetrator.

Once the explosion has occurred, Walker observes, the tension built up during the initial phase is released. With the tension discharged, the perpetrator usually knows that he has gone too far. He is likely to be contrite, loving, and kind. Walker suggests that during this stage the batterer can be quite charming and loving to his partner. He is likely to express his sorrow and beg his partner's forgiveness, and may even be sincere. Walker indicates that it is during this time when the victim is the most likely to flee. If she does, the batterer is likely to ask his family and family friends, and perhaps even use the children, to convince her to return to him. Walker suggests that phase three can be a difficult time for the victim, since she is now experiencing the rewards of marriage. Helpers such as shelter workers, hospital staff, and court personnel are most likely to have contact with the victim during this phase, but she is torn. Those around her might be encouraging her to get out of the abusive relationship at the very time when she is able to experience relief, and perhaps even love, from her relationship.

Over the intervening years, many have suggested that the cycle-of-violence model may not be an exact representation of how domestic violence works in every case. Reflecting the evolving nature of the pattern, some suggest that we might have a clearer picture if we thought of it as a *spiral* of violence. A spiral not only has the circular patterns but depth as well. Perhaps the cycle is short-lived and relatively nonviolent at first. As it repeats itself it might take longer to cycle through, but the violence might also intensify as it becomes continually reinforced.

WHY DO WOMEN STAY?

The question, "Why do victims stay?" itself seems a little provocative because it presumes that battered wives do stay. This may or may not be a valid assumption; we certainly do hear from a number of surviving victims of domestic violence who get out of these relationships. Without being able to somehow poll all the domestic violence victims in the population, it seems difficult to even estimate how many victims stay in these relationships, and when they do, for how long.

Walker (1979) builds on some of the classic research done by psychologist Martin Seligman to explain why women stay even when it's painful. The term associated with this explanation is called **learned helplessness.** One of Seligman's classic experiments involved placing dogs inside a cage and administering electric shock. Initially the dogs would attempt to escape, but the cage was closed and escape was not possible. Once they learned that no matter what they did they would still get shocked, the dogs seemed to resign themselves to their fates. When this occurred they would remain in their cage, listless, and continue to be subject to the painful shocks, even after the cage door was finally left open. It then required direct coaching to get the dogs to leave the cage.

The application of this theory to domestic violence is obvious. In addition to learning that there is very little one can do, victims often become depressed or anxious. These emotional states can debilitate the victim, making it more difficult to take action. One of the symptoms of depression, in fact, is a loss of energy—energy that would be required to do all the things necessary to leave and reestablish elsewhere. Even this assumes that the victim has the means to take such steps. Unfortunately, during the course of the abuse, many become isolated from friends and family, often becoming financially or psychologically dependent on the abuser. Schecter and Ganley (1995) suggest a number of other reasons why victims remain in violent relationships. These include fear of the perpetrator, lack of other options, lack of employment and financial resources, being psychologically immobilized, cultural/family/religious beliefs that encourage the person to stay in the relationship, belief that the perpetrator might change, and her own belief that she may somehow be the cause of her own abuse.

EXPLANATIONS AND RISK FACTORS

There is probably no single explanation for domestic violence. None seems completely able to account for the complexity of the phenomenon. In this section we'll be looking at an array of factors and explanations in an attempt to understand this issue We'll be organizing these factors into the three-level model we have used throughout this text, consisting of the macro, meso, and micro levels.

With any issue that finally "catches" with the public, it seems that we hear all kinds of statistics; yet without good information, it's often hard to evaluate them. Hotaling and Sugarman (1986) comment that, since around 1980, there has been a virtual explosion of literature about domestic violence. They were concerned about the quality of some of this new research and indicated they wanted to separate out the literature that was actually useful. They also wanted to ensure that, if public policy was going to be based on research, it was based on good research.

Hotaling and Sugarman (1986) screened over 400 studies published in the professional literature. The criteria they used for inclusion in the final group included the following: the study had to include a comparison group; they had to evaluate their results using accepted statistical methods; and they had to include enough information about their procedures to ensure that only appropriate subjects for study were included (that is, that studies about perpetrators really included perpetrators and excluded people who were not perpetrators, and so on). The final group included 52 studies, using 333 measurements, for 97 separate risk markers. When at least 70% of the studies agreed about a risk factor, Hotaling and Sugarman labeled it a "consistent risk marker." When there was 30 to 69% agreement about a factor, they labeled it an "inconsistent risk marker." When less than 30% of studies agreed about a risk factor, they labeled it as a "consistent nonrisk marker." Whenever possible, the results of this analysis will be interjected into our discussion of explanations and risk factors at appropriate places. In addition, data from large national surveys, such as the National Crime Victim Survey and National Family Violence Surveys, as well as some of the newer literature, will also be included when it seems to contribute to a better understanding of the issue.

The Macro Level—
Broad Cultural and Social Factors

In the human service field, it is unusual for policy and practice to be strongly influenced by any single theoretical orientation, but this has happened in the area of domestic violence. Since Del Martin published the first book about domestic violence in 1976, feminist theory has become the dominant theoretical framework used to explain domestic violence. The key concept in this theoretical approach is **patriarchy**, a term used to denote the male-dominated nature of the culture in which we live. As you saw from our earlier discussion of history, the abuse of women has been accepted and condoned in our society throughout most of the past two millennia. In western European and North American societies, women continue to get less advantageous treatment than men. Within this theoretical framework, often called **profeminist**, it is believed that broad social and cultural attitudes contribute to the problem. From this frame of reference, the male batterer, socialized into the male role and position of dominance, feels entitled to control "his woman" and uses battering, sex, psychological abuse, and economic resources to coerce and control her.

Using the concept of patriarchy, then, we have a model with an overarching context in which to explain domestic violence. Is the profeminist position supported by literature? The answer seems to be a qualified yes. There is a clear historical tradition establishing the dominance of men and the subservience of women. As discussed earlier, there is also evidence demonstrating that women are injured by domestic violence far more often than men. There is also fairly convincing evidence that, when men use violence, they tend to do so in order to control women. When women become violent, more often than not, they tend to do so in self-defense. Can we say that the profeminist model explains all domestic violence? The answer seems to be a clear no. A number of other factors also play a role. The profeminist position does not adequately explain the unprovoked abusive behavior of an admittedly small group of female perpetrators (Gelles, 1993a, 1995). The profeminist position also has problems accounting for gay men who abuse other gay men and lesbian women who abuse other women in their intimate relationships (Letellier, 1994; Lockhart, et al., 1994).

So far our discussion about family violence has taken place in the context of the North American and western European cultural traditions. This negates and ignores the other cultural traditions in the world, not to mention the divergent cultures within our own society. In important ways, culture represents an unwritten set of rules about behavior, and these vary from culture to culture. By comparing cultures, we might be able to get a broader sense of how cultural rules influence a problem like domestic violence. One of the few cross-cultural studies about domestic violence (Levinson, 1981) is cited in Gelles and Cornell (1990). By reviewing the Human Relations Area Files at Yale University, Levinson (1981, cited in Gelles & Cornell, 1990) was able to compare the level of wife beating in a variety of cultures. Clearly, it is a rare activity in some cultures (Andaman Islanders, Copper Eskimo, Ifugao, Iroquois, Ona, and Thai), while it is common in others. This tends to confirm our contention that there are important differences that seem to play a role in determining the level of woman beating. In Chapter 1, we took a fairly close look at one of these cultural groups, the Iroquois. The respected roles women played in that culture, and the value placed upon their contributions, seems to have been a central reason for the low rates of woman abuse among the Iroquois people. Understanding patterns of behavior in cultures where domestic violence is rare might lead us to a greater appreciation of the role of culture and might shed light on how to reduce the problem of domestic violence in our own.

In addition to broad cultural factors, a number of other social and demographic characteristics seem to be associated with increased risk of domestic violence. The perpetrator demographic variables identified by Hotaling and Sugarman (1986) as "consistent risk markers at the macro level include low occupational status, low income, and low educational achievement. While it is widely reported that domestic violence perpetrators exist at all levels of society, those at the lower end seem to be at the greatest risk. The observations of other experts seem to confirm this. Gelles and Cornell (1990) comment that "irrespective of the method, sample, or research design, studies of marital violence support the hypothesis that spousal violence is more likely to occur in low-income, low-socioeconomic-status families."

The Meso Level— Family and Relationship Factors

At the family or relationship level, the most dominant theoretical framework could be called *systemic,* and is associated with the emerging specialty field of marriage and family therapy. As pointed out by Douglas Sprenkle, the editor of the *Journal of Marriage and Family Therapy,* there is no single "systems approach" (Sprenkle, 1994). He suggests that systems-oriented family therapists tend to conceptualize issues in a way that emphasizes the interrelatedness of the individual, the family, and the broader social context. These interconnecting relationships tend to be complex and perhaps more difficult to study. They have not been accepted within the mainstream of the domestic violence field to the same extent as the sociopolitical profeminist framework or individually oriented approaches to studying batterers. Jeffrey Edleson and some of his colleagues (Edleson, et al., 1991) found that there are relationship issues that seem to be associated with domestic violence, and they comment that there is probably a need to pay more attention to them.

While an emphasis on interrelationships has not been emphasized in the family violence field, Hotaling and Sugarman (1986) were able to identify and label some consistent couple or relationship risk markers that seem to come into play. These include frequent arguing, incompatible religious beliefs, and poor marital adjustment. Hotaling and Sugarman (1986) also note that being sexually aggressive toward one's partner and being violent toward one's children are consistently found when marital violence is an issue for the couple. Gelles and Cornell (1990) comment on early research, based on the National Family Violence Surveys, which indicates that families in which power is not wielded democratically are at increased risk of domestic violence. There was a slight increase in wife-to-husband violence when the woman was dominant and a significant rise when the man was. An unexpected result of Hotaling and Sugarman's analysis (1986) was to find that this is a consistent nonrisk marker, meaning that fewer than 30% of studies that looked at it found it to be associated with marital violence. Gelles and Cornell also suggest that families who are isolated are at increased risk. Finally, Gelles and Cornell (1990) review a significant body of research that suggests **status incompatibility** as a risk factor in marital violence. Status incompatibility can either mean the man has less status than his wife (in a male-dominated society) or else has much less than would be expected, given his level of education, experience, or family background. Hotaling and Sugarman (1986) were not able to find clear-cut results on status incompatibility.

The Micro Level—
Individual and Personality Factors

One of the most important theoretical explanations in the domestic violence field is that of **social learning theory.** In answer to the question, "How'd he get that way?" social learning theory essentially responds with, "He learned it!" Social learning theory proposes, in fact, that we learn all our social behavior as a result of what we observe (Bandura, 1973; Bandura & Walters, 1963). This theory is a behaviorally oriented one that uses concepts from behavioral psychology—in particular, that of **reinforcement**—though it makes some modifications. In social learning theory, the "observer" doesn't have to actually be rewarded or punished in order for there to be an increase or decrease in the probability of engaging in similar behavior. He or she can do so on the basis of **vicarious reinforcement** or **vicarious punishment**— that is, observing someone else being rewarded or punished.

At one time there seemed to be a public perception that victims may have "bought into" domestic violence. This idea seems to say that if a girl observes her mother being abused she finds a man like her dad and repeats the behavioral pattern of her mother. Are women who witnessed domestic violence as little girls really at greater risk? This, in fact, turned out to be the only risk factor Hotaling and Sugarman (1986) initially found in connection with victims. In a later reevaluation of the data from the first National Family Violence Survey, however, Sugarman and Hotaling were able to rule this out as a risk factor (see Carden, 1994). So, the answer to our question seems to be no. Since this was the only victim-related risk factor initially found by Hotaling and Sugarman (1986), and since this factor was ruled out, it seems that we can say there are *no* specific factors associated with the characteristics of victims that increase the risk of domestic violence. This is consistent with the profeminist view that domestic violence is a perpetrator-driven phenomenon.

The next logical group of people to ask about are the perpetrators. Do people who become batterers get that way by watching their fathers batter their mothers? In answer to this question, Hotaling and Sugarman (1986) found that one of the consistent risk markers is, in fact, having seen domestic violence at home when growing up.

Social learning theory seems to be a good explanatory framework for explaining how perpetrators learn to become violent, but it also has some problems. One of the most significant challenges to social learning theory is how to explain all those men who observed domestic violence and did not become perpetrators. Kaufman and Zigler (1987, 1988) did some pioneering work on intergenerational transmission, and they were able to estimate that it happens only about 30% of the time (see Chapter 2 for a complete discussion). This means that, in the other 70% of the cases, it does not occur. These findings do nothing to negate the associations found by Hotaling and Sugarman (1986), for we would expect an increased correlation in studies that examine this question. As Gelles and Cornell (1990) point out in their discussion of the topic, the 30% figure for child abuse contrasts to a 2 to 4% child abuse rate in the general population. Widom (1989) suggests, as mentioned previously, that the question isn't *if* intergenerational transmission occurs but rather *under what conditions* it happens. In order to answer this question, we probably need to understand the severity of the abuse, how often it occurred, and how long it lasted.

In addition to a history of witnessing domestic violence as a child, a number of other individual risk factors are associated with domestic violence. Hotaling and Sugarman (1986) identify the following as consistent risk markers: low occupational status, abuse of alcohol, low income, low in assertiveness, and generally low levels of educational attainment. In addition, age seems to be a factor. According to the studies looked at by Hotaling and Sugarman (1986), as well as data derived from the National Family Violence Surveys (Gelles & Cornell, 1990), people under thirty years of age seem to be at increased risk. Factors that Hotaling and Sugarman labeled as inconsistent risk markers, and that they believe *may* be associated with domestic violence, include having been abused as a child, unemployment, criminal arrests, and low self-esteem. They also identified one surprising factor as being a consistent nonrisk marker: having traditional expectations about sex roles.

In addition to social learning theory, there is another theoretical framework that has received some attention in the family violence field: attachment theory (see Carden, 1994). Based on the work of Bowlby (1980, 1984), this theoretical framework emphasizes the importance of how human beings form bonds with significant people, initially our mothers. These attachments can be strong and healthy if the person's psychological needs are met, or ambivalent or anxious if not. The bonding that occurs in such cases is sometimes called **anxious attachment** (James, 1994). If children grow up with an abusive caregiver, they might form what are called **trauma**

bonds (James, 1994). In the context of domestic violence, if people have insecure and ambivalent attachment problems, they may be particularly prone to heightened vulnerability both to abandonment and loss of intimacy. Abusive behavior, according to this view, can serve to maintain a "safe" emotional distance (Carden, 1994).

The concept of anxious and traumatic attachment may be an important theoretical position to consider. It may also be particularly relevant to the discussion that follows. Forming primary attachments and the ability to trust may be essential precursors to becoming healthy individuals and forming healthy personalities or, failing in this, to developing personality disorders. Hotaling and Sugarman (1986) suggest that the picture of perpetrators that emerges, based on their analysis of the literature, is consistent with the psychiatric diagnoses of borderline and antisocial personality disorders (see Chapter 4 for a discussion of these disorders). A recent study comparing batterers and a matched group of community volunteers found the batterers to have elevated borderline and antisocial personality characteristics (Else, et al., 1993). The summary of the literature reviewed by Hotaling and Sugarman (1986) portrays the perpetrator as a person who has experienced a violent childhood in which he has witnessed domestic violence and in which he may have been the object of abuse himself. Because of his difficulties he may be a person who had problems with school and, as an adult, may have low occupational achievement and may be more likely to be economically disadvantaged as a consequence. Hotaling and Sugarman (1986) also suggest that he may be at increased risk for having an arrest record and for violence problems outside the home.

CLASSIFYING PERPETRATORS

Despite years of trying to determine the "profile" of domestic violence perpetrators, it has been generally conceded that this is a diverse population and that no single profile emerges (Carden, 1994; Hamberger & Hastings, 1991; Saunders, 1992; Tolman & Bennett, 1990). There was a perception, however, that specific patterns did exist among perpetrators, and, ultimately, models that tried to characterize these patterns into **typologies** began to emerge.

Edward Gondolf (1988) developed one of the best-known batterer typologies. Based on interviews with over 500 women in shelters, he developed a typology that split perpetrators into three categories: **sociopathic**, **antisocial**, and **typical** batterers. The sociopathic group represents 7% of batterers, a group described as the most severely violent, who inflict the most injury, are the most likely to have committed crimes outside the family, the most likely to be abusive to children, and the most likely to have a severe alcohol or drug abuse problem (Saunders, 1992; Tolman & Bennett,

1990). The antisocial group is larger, representing about 41% of the sample. This group is the second most likely to cause severe injury and the most likely to use a weapon, but slightly less likely to have been arrested than those in the sociopathic group (Saunders, 1992; Tolman & Bennett, 1990). The last group in Gondolf's typology (1988) is the typical batterer, which is the largest group, representing 52% of the sample. These perpetrators are described as causing less serious abuse, are less likely to be arrested, and are more apologetic after battering incidents (Tolman & Bennett, 1990).

Kevin Hamberger and James Hastings (1988) developed a typology based upon personality tests of known batterers, relying especially on the Millon Clinical Multiaxial Inventory (Millon, 1983, as cited in Hamberger & Hastings, 1991). They also broke perpetrators into three categories, but based them on personality disorder characteristics. The first category is that which corresponds to the *borderline personality.* Those in this group are described as asocial, moody, and touchy. They are also characterized as being anxious, depressed, and having alcohol problems (Tolman & Bennett, 1990). The second category of perpetrators in the Hamberger and Hastings typology is of those whose characteristics correspond to *narcissistic and antisocial personality* disorders. Perpetrators in this category are described as highly self-centered individuals who tend to use others to get what they want. They tend not to give and take in relationships, but feel entitled and like to think they are right and others are wrong. The third category corresponds to *compulsive and dependent personality* types. Perpetrators in this category are described as tense and rigid individuals who try to ingratiate themselves with others and who lack self-esteem (Tolman & Bennett, 1990).

A third typology was developed by Daniel Saunders (1992). Based on an analysis of a number of variables (generalized violence, childhood victimization, severity of violence, psychological abuse, views of women's traditional roles, democratic decision making, level of conflict, anger toward partner, jealousy, depression, alcohol use, impression management, and background), Saunders was able to distinguish three "clusters" of abusers, which he called **Type 1, Type 2,** and **Type 3.** Saunders describes Type 1 batterers as "family only" aggressors. He suggests that these are the least likely to have been abused, were the most concerned with the opinions of others about them, and reported low levels of anger, depression, and jealousy (Saunders, 1992). They are also described as the most satisfied with their relationships, having the least marital conflict, and being the least psychologically abusive. Saunders describes Type 2 batterers as being "generally violent." He suggests they were the most likely of the three groups to be violent outside the home, use the most severe forms of violence, and have the most rigid ideas about the roles of men and women. They have high amounts of alcohol abuse, and arrests for drunk driving and other violence. Results of Saunders's analysis also suggests that they have "moderate" marital conflict compared to the other two types. Type 3 men, in Saunders's typology, reported the highest levels of anger, depression, and jealousy, and are described as "emotionally volatile" aggressors. They are reportedly less severely violent than the Type 2 men, but are the most psychologically abusive and the least satisfied in their relationships (Saunders, 1992).

Each of the three typologies discussed above offers us a way of distinguishing between types of offenders. There are clearly differences among these typologies, yet there are also some commonalities. Each typology describes a category of batterer who is unfeeling and impervious to the feelings of his partner and to the impact of his behavior. These individuals also seem more likely to have problems getting along in society. They are more likely to have an alcohol or drug problem and to have an arrest record. Another group of batterers seems more explosive and has severe problems with handling angry feelings, and may also have some alcohol problems. A third type may be slightly less destructive and more in control of his own feelings, but may also be more psychologically aggressive with his partner. While this comparison is not definitive, it at least gets us thinking about what is emerging in terms of our understanding of batterers.

One of the most exciting, and controversial, recent developments in the field is the discovery of physiological differences in the responses of some batterers. Neil Jacobson and his colleagues (Gottman, et al., 1995; Jacobson, et al., 1995) have done some rigorous new research in this area with profound implications. Like the typologists who preceded them, Jacobson and his colleagues were interested in studying severe batterers.

One of the things that makes this research different from the previous research is the methods they used. First of all, they spoke with both the batterers and their female partners. In addition to using similar instruments to those used in previous research, such as the Conflict Tactics Scale (Straus, 1979), they made direct measurements of the batterers' physiological responses when engaged in direct verbal conflict with their partners.

Those couples in which domestic violence was established were invited to come in to the lab for two interviews. In the first, they completed a series of questionnaires and a structured interview. In the second, the couple was interviewed together for a "communication assessment." A number of sophisticated physiological measures were made (see Gottman et al., 1995, for complete discussion of methods) while the couples were videotaped discussing conflict areas of their relationship. The data from the videotape and the physiological measuring equipment were synchronized. In addition, the couples were followed and reinterviewed two years later.

On the basis of this research, Jacobson and his colleagues (Gottman et al., 1995; Jacobson et al., 1995) were able to distinguish two types of severe batterers. They refer to them as Type 1 and Type 2, but to distinguish them from Saunders's typology, I will use the designations **Type I** and **Type II** here. The key distinguishing feature between the two is how their heart rates change. Type I batterers (about 20% of the sample) actually lowered their heart rate in response to conflict, rather than increased it as we would intuitively expect. Jacobson and his colleagues refer to the Type I batterers as **vagal reactors** since the vagal nerve is associated with the parasympathetic function of reducing heart rate (see Jacobson et al., 1995). The heart rate of Type II batterers (about 80% of the sample) increased as we would expect.

This key difference between the two groups—heart rate deceleration or acceleration—became a "marker variable" for a whole host of other variables, including severity of abuse, belligerence and contempt, violence outside the home, and having witnessed bilateral, or mother-to-father, aggression versus husband-to-wife aggression. Initially, Jacobson and his colleagues felt, based on the analysis of the Conflict Tactics Scale results, that the level of severity of battering was indistinguishable between the two groups (Gottman et al., 1995). On reevaluation of the raw data and modifying the procedures for evaluating it, however, it became clear that the kinds of battering behavior used by Type I batterers were much more severe; more Type I's threatened their wives with a knife or gun, used a knife or gun, or engaged in other serious abusive behavior such as kicking, biting, or hitting with a fist (Jacobson et al., 1995). This is consistent with the findings of Saunders (1992), who found that the most serious violence was not associated with anger. In addition to engaging in more serious types of abuse, Type I's were more belligerent and contemptuous toward their wives (Gottman et al., 1995). They were more likely to be more generally violent outside the home, toward friends, strangers, coworkers, or employers (Gottman et al., 1995). They were also more likely to be antisocial, drug dependent, and thought disordered (Gottman et al., 1995). One final conclusion is somewhat startling. After two years, there were no divorces or separations among the Type I batterers, whereas there was a very high rate among the Type II's (Gottman et al., 1995).

In terms of interpreting their results, Jacobson and his colleagues have arrived at a number of interesting conclusions. For one, they note that lowered heart rate has been observed by criminologists among criminal populations, though they interpret the reasons for it quite differently. The criminological view has been that a low base rate inclines them to seek excitement. What Jacobson and his colleagues are saying is that Type I's (the vagal reactors) lower their heart rate from base rate, suggesting that the lowered heart rate may be part of an attention-focusing process (Jacobson et al., 1995), perhaps making them more effective at intimidating and controlling their wives. In a plenary address at the annual meeting of the American Association of Marriage and Family Therapy, Jacobson (1993) likened their calmness during conflict to what happens to well-trained professional soldiers in combat.

There are some interesting issues that this new research brings to light. For one, we are forced to consider the possibility that the way batterers learn to be what they become may be contrary to how we've looked at it in the past. For instance, we've always assumed that batterers observe their fathers battering and repeat this in their own relationships. This may be true for Type II's, but vagal reactors seem more likely to have seen their mothers engage in serious conflict, thereby challenging these old assumptions. More research seems needed here. It also seems that the homes Type I's came from are much more violent generally. What does it mean that none of the wives of vagal reactors have left them? As Jacobson and his colleagues suggest, are they so under the control of their batterers they dare not leave?

Publicity surrounding this new research has gotten not only professional interest but public attention as well. In many ways, the research of Jacobson and his colleagues is consistent with much of the work already done on typologies; for example, there had been consensus for a long time that there is a group of batterers who are also violent outside the home. This research, which shows a type of batterer who often engages in other violent and criminal activity, suggests the need for increased dialog with, and extension of, research in the criminal justice field. This new research also seems to confirm a primary tenet of the field: battering is not necessarily about anger—it is about control. Type I batterers are not out of control when they engage their victims; they are very much "in control." Within the professional community, this has provided a focus for reexamination and reevaluation of what we believe about domestic violence.

INTERVENTION

The research of Jacobson and his colleagues (Gottman et al., 1995; Jacobson et al., 1995) also has implications for how we intervene. Type II's may have impulse control problems at home and problems handling their anger, and may need help here. Vagal reactors, on the other hand, may have too much control already. Providing them with anger management techniques may not make any sense, and could even make it worse.

There are probably a number of reasons why typologies might prove helpful to those interested in domestic violence, but the foremost among them has to be their usefulness in trying to stop the violence. It is possible that different types of batterers need different kinds of intervention, and that an approach that might be highly effective with one would prove disastrous with another. The "one-type-fits-all" mentality may not be the best way to work with domestic violence perpetrators. An approach that tries to match specific clients with an intervention that is most appropriate for them is called **client matching.** The new revelations about the Type I batterer should tell us that such an approach may be particularly prudent.

Jacobson and his colleagues reported on two types of perpetrators who commit very serious battery. In addition, there is another group of domestic violence perpetrators whose violence has not reached, or does not reach, this level. This may be the group that in Saunders's typology is called Type 1. In contrast to both groups reported on by Jacobson and his colleagues (Gottman et al., 1995; Jacobson et al., 1995), Saunders's Type 1's seem to have very low levels of violence (as confirmed by their partners) and may be very good candidates for relationship-oriented approaches to intervention (Saunders, 1992). Do we put them in a group with the Type I batterers described by Jacobson and his colleagues? With the Type II's? We'll get a chance to discuss some of these questions at greater length later in this section.

Services for Victims

Earlier in this chapter we noted that interest in the field of domestic violence was sparked by the women's movement (Carden, 1994; Gelles, 1980). The programs available to women today can trace their origins to these beginnings. Since those early days, grassroots coalitions against domestic violence have grown to the national level as well as having a presence in every state and the District of Columbia (Davis, et al., 1994). These coalitions, which advocate for women's programs, have spurred the development of laws, funding, and even specific programs to help battered women.

Intervention on behalf of women can be thought of as having two dimensions: (1) advocacy for social, political, and legal changes and, (2) direct services. In their review of this issue, Davis, Hagen, and Early (1994) comment that, in the past, direct services to battered women has been the more politically acceptable dimension to the public at large, yet these services alone are really not adequate to make the kind of major changes that will stop the oppression of women, including battering. Davis and colleagues (1994) in fact note that advocacy and direct services are not entirely distinct. Funding for direct services in large part depends on the political will to invest the dollars. Debra Kalmus and Murray Straus (1983) were interested in finding out what made the difference between getting programs for battered women or not getting them. The results of their research suggest that, regardless or how conservative or liberal, traditional or progressive a state happened to be, differences in the number of programs for battered women depended on how many women in the state were active in such advocacy groups as the National Organization for Women.

Coalitions against domestic violence that began as grassroots movements continue to advocate for political and legal change; they are also involved in fighting to get dollars to provide for direct services for battered women as well as collaborating with state agencies on how these programs are run (Davis et al, 1994). In terms of funding for programs, Davis and colleagues (1994) estimate that approximately one-third of services for battered women come from the federal government, one-third from the states, and one-third from private sources. They point out that there are several federal programs that currently assist in funding these services, including the Family Violence Prevention and Services Act, Victims of Crime Act, Title XX Social Services Block Grant, and Emergency Assistance for Families.

Of all the specific services provided to battered women, the first that comes to mind are the battered women's shelters. The first shelters began on a shoestring with voluntary labor and donated goods and services (Gelles & Cornell, 1990). As they have now become established, many operate with paid (or underpaid) staff and get state and federal dollars to operate, often through contracts or service agreements with their state social service departments (Davis et al., 1994).

Shelters vary in what they are able to offer but many have an assortment of services and programs. First and foremost is a safe place to stay. Other services include referrals to support groups, counseling, job training programs, financial assistance, and housing referrals. A key element seems to be helping the women with *self-efficacy,* or sense of a capable self. Some states have programs whereby victims of domestic violence can establish new identities with confidential addresses so as to escape the reach of their batterers. In such cases, the shelter staff can also assist the client by providing her with information on this program, including how to apply.

Women's advocacy has played a significant role in calling public attention to domestic violence as a major social issue. Well before highly publicized media cases came to light, women's advocates were in the trenches doing the hard work on behalf of battered women. Because of their advocacy, and increased public and professional attention to the issue, changes have begun to take place in how major social institutions respond to domestic violence. Two social institutions that perhaps have the most contact with severely battered women are health care and law enforcement.

The typical point of contact within the health care field is the emergency room. In the review of literature by Hampton and Coner-Edwards (1993), they note that as many as 1 in 10 women are assaulted by their partner each year, many women do sustain injuries, and, of those, 59% seek treatment at an emergency room. Partly in response to public attention and advocacy efforts, more hospital emergency rooms are establishing **protocols,** or standardized procedures, for assessing domestic violence, including asking the patients directly if this is going on.

Hospitals, especially in metropolitan areas, typically have medical social workers on call who can assist with assessing cases of suspected domestic violence and can provide patients with information about community resources for domestic violence and battered women's shelters. In addition to crisis intervention, one of the roles of the hospital social worker or crisis worker is to assist the victim in filing a police complaint and/or getting into a shelter. As noted earlier, victims are often at greatest risk when they decide to leave their partners. They know their batterers best and often have a good idea as to their level of risk. They should be asked. In addition, the worker should do a lethality assessment. Factors associated with high risk in perpetrators include threats of homicide or suicide, acute depression and hopelessness, having weapons, obsessiveness about their partner, rage, drug and alcohol intoxication, history of pet abuse, and access to the battered woman or her family (Harway & Hansen, 1994).

For those women who do not want to go into a shelter, they can also refer them to one of the many community support groups that are now coming into being. These are often run through shelters, nonprofit agencies, rape crisis centers, community mental health centers, churches, and hospitals. Regardless of whether the client decides to go to a shelter, the home of a friend or family member, or back home, it is wise to help the client develop a safety plan. This plan should include at least the following: ways the client can know when she's at the greatest risk, people she can call in a crisis, signals she might use with kids or neighbors to call the police, places where she can go, escape routes, identifying dangerous places in the house, dealing with weapons in the house, and having extra keys and an escape kit (important documents, papers, money, checkbook, and so on) (Register, 1993, cited in Harway & Hansen, 1994; Schecter & Ganley, 1995).

Law enforcement is often one of the services that a battered woman is likely to need. There has been a lot of discussion in the literature about previous attitudes among law enforcement personnel in dealing with "domestic disturbances" (Gelles, 1995; Gelles & Cornell, 1990; Hampton & Coner-Edwards, 1993; Landes et al., 1993). Many law enforcement agencies have now adopted **presumptive arrest** policies. This means that if they are called out on a domestic violence complaint, they will arrest the primary aggressor. Legal statutes preventing police officers from making arrests on misdemeanors they did not see have been removed (Davis & Smith, 1995), and many states have enacted legislation requiring arrest of the primary aggressor. A U.S. Attorney General's Task Force on Domestic Violence recommended arrest as the preferred response (Davis & Smith, 1995). In addition, there have been a number of lawsuits filed against police departments for failing to protect victims of domestic violence. Perhaps the best known of these is *Thurman v. City of Torrington* (595 F. Supp. 1521). The case involved Tracy Thurman, a battered woman who regularly called the police to protect her from her estranged husband. She was severely battered in 1983 and was left permanently injured (Gelles & Cornell, 1990; Hampton & Coner-Edwards, 1993; Landes et al., 1993). She settled for $1.9 million in damages, claiming that the police failed to protect her.

In addition to the compelling reasons for presumptive arrest policies discussed above, there is some famous and controversial research that suggests that arrests actually serve to reduce domestic violence recidivism. This research is known as the **Minneapolis Police Experiment** (Sherman & Berk, 1984). Police in two precincts in Minneapolis randomly assigned perpetrators to one of three experimental conditions: arrest, separation, or advice and mediation. Evaluation of follow-up data showed that those who had been arrested had the lowest recidivism rates of the three groups. When these results were published, they got a lot of attention, and as a consequence there was a dramatic increase in the use of presumptive arrests. Presumptive arrests became "criminal justice gospel" (see Berk, 1993). Perhaps because the implications are quite profound, the National Institute of Justice funded six projects to see if these results could be replicated elsewhere. The results of these replication projects, however, by admission of one of the original investigators (Berk, 1993), are showing no difference between the arrest condition and the other approaches. The principal investigator of the Minneapolis project has changed his position in response to the later research. Unemployed batterers actually seemed to become more violent following arrest (Sherman, 1992). For employed batterers with something to lose, it may have provided some incentive not to reoffend.

Despite the apparent failure of presumptive arrest policies to deter, most people in the field believe that presumptive arrests are an important tool. However, just as you can't do a tune-up on a car with just a gap gauge, you can't deal with domestic violence by using one tool. Because of an increasing number of arrests and many new victims coming into the system, battered women's advocates began to design and establish a new kind of program, called **community intervention projects**, or CIPs (Syers & Edleson, 1992). Often referred to as a "coordinated response" network, the CIPs were designed to change the way the criminal justice and social service systems respond to victims (Syers & Edleson, 1992). Just as many hospitals have medical social workers to help victims, prosecutors' offices are beginning to hire victim advocates to help the women they come in contact with.

Individual strategies that are integrated into a coordinated response include arrest, immediate notification of the CIP office, keeping perpetrators in jail long enough to get services for victims (including support groups and counseling for kids [Peled & Edleson, 1992]), vigorous prosecution, completion of presentence investigations by probation officers, sentencing, and deferring imposition of the sentence pending completion of a perpetrator treatment program (Syers & Edleson, 1992). In Lincoln, Nebraska, Steinman (1990) had attempted to replicate the earlier work of Sherman and Berk (1984) on mandatory arrest and found that, until the law changed to require that arrest be coordinated with other interventions, arrest actually increased the violence. Once other interventions were linked to arrest, recidivism went down significantly (Steinman, 1990). The overall results of research done by Syers and Edleson (1992) conclude that men who receive coordinated intervention seem less at risk to reoffend, though the results were not significant. We still need additional research.

Intervention with Perpetrators

In addition to the community intervention projects discussed above, there are two primary types of intervention approaches for working with men who batter: perpetrator groups and couples counseling (Tolman & Edleson, 1995). Often, as in the case of one group counseling example we will discuss, perpetrator programs probably work best as part of a coordinated community response. When it comes to treating batterers, however, there are many unresolved questions in the field and still no definitive answers.

As mentioned earlier, there has been an exponential growth in perpetrator programs since mandatory arrest efforts went into effect (Gondolf, in press). This dramatic increase in demand has sparked an increase not only in the number of programs but also in their variety (Gondolf, 1993). Since it is not possible to review the diversity of intervention programs in the space we have here, we will be looking at one of the first, and perhaps best developed, program to come on the scene. This program is often called the **Duluth Model.** In 1980, after publicity about a particularly savage domestic homicide, the community of Duluth, Minnesota, supported the efforts of the Duluth Abuse Intervention Project (a CIP) to make sweeping changes in how domestic violence was dealt with (Pence & Paymar, 1993).

An important part of those changes involved a change in attitude about the problem and the adoption of a philosophy that included an emphasis on accountability for the batterer. With the courts making a commitment to refer first-time offenders to treatment came the responsibility to develop a program (Pence & Paymar, 1993). The Duluth group brought in a number of experts, including staff from the very first program to be created, EMERGE, and developed what is now called the Duluth Model (Pence & Paymar, 1993).

The theoretical underpinnings of the Duluth Model are sometimes called profeminist or gender based. As discussed previously, a profeminist

FIGURE 7-2
Power and
Control Wheel

From *Education Groups for Men Who Batter,* by E. Pence and M. Paymar. Copyright © 1993 Springer Publishing Company, Inc, New York, 10012. Used by permission.

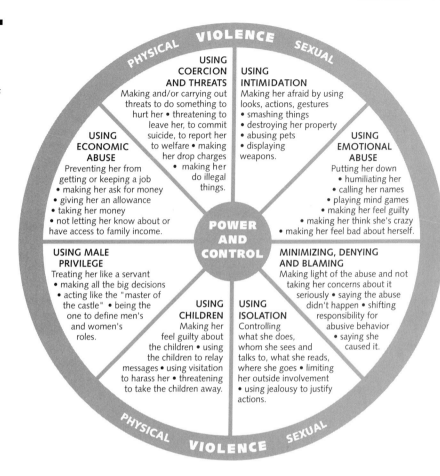

position takes the view that the violence of men against women is an extension and expression of the oppression of women generally. The curriculum is designed to change the existing power imbalance in the relationship between the batterer and his victim and to help the batterer learn to build healthier relationships with women. Consistent with the definition we adopted earlier in this chapter, the definition of domestic violence adopted in this model is one that emphasizes an examination of the means by which the abuser maintains his hold over his intimate partner. Elucidation of the "power and control" dynamic as well as examination of the methods used by the batterer to maintain his control are important elements of the Duluth program. These principles have been integrated into a diagram that has become quite well known in the field. It is called the **Power and Control Wheel** and is depicted in Figure 7-2.

FIGURE 7-3
Equality Wheel

From *Education Groups for Men Who Batter,* by E. Pence and M. Paymar. Copyright © 1993 Springer Publishing Company, Inc, New York, 10012. Used by permission.

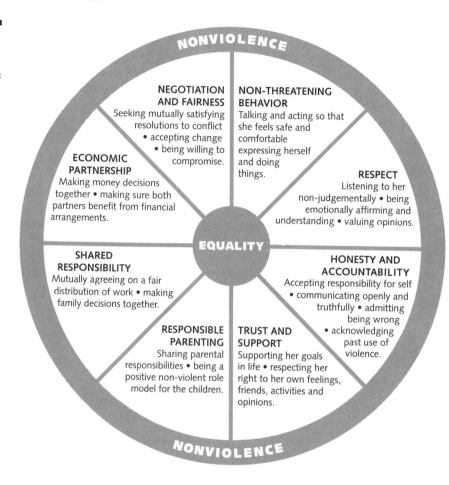

The Power and Control Wheel illustrates the existing pattern of domination and abuse we hope to end. A bias of the program is the view that men become the way they are because they learn it—culturally, socially, in the family, at school, in their neighborhood, and anywhere else. One of the tenets, or perhaps hopes, of the model seems to be that whatever can be learned can be unlearned, with the right motivation, information, and opportunity to integrate new behavior. This is very much in the tradition of the social learning perspective and is consistent with the **cognitive-behavioral school** of psychology. What we want men to learn in this model is how to relate to women in a more egalitarian way. This means turning the negative methods in the Power and Control Wheel into positive behaviors that contribute to mutuality and respect in the relationship. This idea has been integrated into a counterpart diagram called the **Equality Wheel,** depicted in Figure 7-3. Thus, getting from "power and control" to "equality" is the goal of the program.

Within this framework, the perpetrator focuses on five objectives: (1) to understand his behavior as a way to control, (2) to understand the causes of his violence, (3) to increase his willingness to change, (4) to become accountable, and, (5) to acquire the tools and practical information that will help him to change. The program and curriculum provide the structure for doing this. Eight themes are explored over a total of 24 weeks, which include nonviolent, nonthreatening behavior, respect, support and trust, accountability and honesty, responsibile parenting, shared responsibility, economic partnership, and negotiation and fairness.

A second approach to working with domestic violence is controversial in the field. Rather than treating men and women in separate groups, it emphasizes working with the couple together. It is controversial for at least a couple of reasons. It is felt by many that to treat the couple together, first, sends a message that the victim is partly to blame and, second, puts the woman at greater risk. Counseling of any kind can be stressful, and this is especially so for family counseling. These concerns about using a couples approach are largely based on anecdotal reports of women being battered after counseling for something they said or didn't say.

One of the best-known proponents of a couples approach is Peter Neidig. He and his colleague, Dale Friedman, have developed a treatment program for couples (Neidig & Friedman, 1984). They point out that most of the domestic violence programs that existed when they began emphasized rescuing the victim and separating the partners. They point out that most of the victims they interviewed wanted to stay in the relationship, if they could eliminate the violence. Others comment (see Carden, 1994) that even among women who go to shelters, many return to their partners even when shelter staff strongly discourage it. One argument for couples counseling is that they will often be together regardless of whether or not we provide them with couples counseling.

Neidig and Friedman (1984) adopt a very different philosophy from that of the profeminists, whereby they see the violence as springing from conflict in the relationship. They refer to this as the **interpersonal perspective**. In terms of determining who might benefit from their form of treatment, Neidig and Friedman (1984) suggest that couples counseling may be appropriate when the violence is an expression of conflict in the relationship. They suggest that violence exists on a continuum, and they refer to the two ends, or the poles, of this continuum as **expressive violence** and **instrumental violence**. They go on to suggest that expressive violence usually occurs in the context of gradually escalating conflict in the relationship. In this view, each partner plays a role in the escalation (though not necessarily equally). After a violent incident, according to Neidig and Friedman (1984), a period of remorse and sorrow follows. This, as you will recall, is consistent with the cycle-of-violence model proposed by Walker (1979). When the expressive violence repeats itself, according to Neidig and Friedman, it tends to become instrumental violence.

Instrumental violence is the purposeful use of violence as an instrument, or tool, for controlling one's partner (Neidig & Friedman, 1984). Neidig and Friedman also suggest that it is almost always perpetrated on the woman by the man and can accurately be called *wife battering*. These authors also tell us that a person who has seen or experienced violence as a child seems more predisposed to move quickly from expressive to instrumental violence. They go on to assert that in such cases provocation can be low and the process of escalation quite rapid. Neidig and Friedman (1984) agree that when dealing with instrumental violence, it is necessary for safety reasons to separate the couple and, if appropriate, refer the victim to a shelter. In military settings, where Neidig and Friedman have been active, it is often possible to have the perpetrator ordered to the barracks rather than removing the victim.

It is when the couple is still experiencing expressive violence that Neidig and Friedman (1984) believe the couples-oriented treatment model may be appropriate. As with the Duluth Model, they use a highly structured program built on cognitive-behavioral and social learning principles. They typically work with couples groups rather than individual couples, though there is an adaptation to this model (Mack, 1989) designed for use with individual couples. The Neidig/Friedman program covers a number of topics, including understanding dynamics, anger control, stress and violence, communication, and handling conflict, as well as handling jealousy, sex-role stereotyping, and marital dependency.

Perpetrator Treatment Issues

There are a number of reviews on the effectiveness of perpetrator treatment (Edleson & Tolman, 1992; Eisikovits & Edleson, 1989; Gondolf, 1993, 1995, in press; Hamberger & Hastings, 1993; Rosenfeld, 1992; Saunders & Azar, 1989; Tolman & Bennett, 1990; Tolman & Edleson, 1995). Based on the empirical research, it isn't clear cut, which, if any, approach to working with perpetrators is effective.

As also seems true in other family maltreatment areas, there appears to be a lack of standards and consistency in the domestic violence field. Gondolf (in press) points out a number of methodological shortcomings, which compromise the validity and reliability of existing program evaluations. These include low response rates, lack of control or comparison groups, and failing to adequately account for dropouts and uncooperative clients.

Despite this lack of reliability and validity in the treatment outcome research, there are some reasonable estimates about violence cessation outcomes. Richard Tolman and Jeffrey Edleson are among the best-known reviewers in the field. In one of the most current reviews of the literature, they indicate that, on the whole, we can probably say treatment works to some degree (Tolman & Edleson, 1995). They tell us that if we listen to what the partners say, there are successful outcomes in 50 to 85% of the cases. Gondolf, another prominent person in the field, estimates that cessation of violence occurs 60 to 80% of the time among program completers. While these generally positive estimates seem encouraging, we should also remember that, without comparing these results with people who don't get treatment, it is hard to know if we can attribute the results to the intervention or to something else. One longitudinal study (Feld & Straus, 1990, cited in Tolman & Edleson, 1995) shows a high cessation rate, even among participants who didn't get any formal treatment.

Despite the lack of definitive answers on recidivism, one program evaluation might be of interest to us, since we've already discussed the program it looks at. Melanie Shepard, a faculty member in the social work program at the University of Minnesota at Duluth, conducted a five-year follow-up of the Duluth Abuse Intervention Project (Shepard, 1992). This is the program that gave birth to the Duluth Model (Pence & Paymar, 1993). The study looked at the records of about 100 alumni of the program. Domestic violence data on assaults were collected from a number of secondary sources, including local law enforcement records on suspects, arrest records, state law enforcement records, and court records on protection order applications. Results suggested that when all these measures were counted as a reoffense, approximately 60% of the participants did not reoffend. About 22% of the participants, a figure similar to other reports, had a conviction for domestic violence after leaving the program. Shepard suggests that we may be making a mistake by looking at the program rather than the characteristics of the perpetrators themselves. This suggests that the results may have had more to do with characteristics of the perpetrators than the treatment program. She identified several risk factors. Substance abuse was one, as was having experienced severe violence as a child and having a prior conviction for any type of offense.

As we have already noted, couples counseling is controversial in the field. The prevailing view in the field seems to be that it is not the preferred mode of treatment (Gondolf, in press; Tolman & Edleson, 1995; Walker, 1995), but this is based more on philosophical grounds and out of concern for victim safety (a noble goal) rather than on the basis of clear conclusions drawn from the scientific evidence. In their review, Tolman and Edleson (1995) comment that recidivism rates reported in the evaluations of couples programs ranged from 15 to 100%, but remark that some of this research is of questionable value. Gondolf (in press) suggests that couples treatment is "not necessarily" as effective as a perpetrator group format and also comments that the characteristics of those who are referred to these programs seem to differ from those in the typical batterer group.

As reviewed earlier, it is recommended, even with group treatment for batterers, that treatment work be done as part of a coordinated community response. Informally, some professionals who work in a couples format report that support from the court and probation officer is critical to a successful outcome. Much of the work of Neidig and Friedman was done with military populations, where support from the command structure of the military was an essential element of the program. What we have not seen are evaluations of couples counseling efforts when these services are provided as part of a court-ordered or command-ordered program. Knowing if results can be achieved with this modality as part of a coordinated response could advance our current level of understanding about intervention effectiveness.

In concluding this discussion about the effectiveness of perpetrator treatment programs, we might want to draw a parallel to the medical field. If I were a cancer specialist and you asked me if there were any really effective treatments for cancer, I would probably say something like, "it depends on the kind of cancer." Maybe it depends on the perpetrator. We have noted that there is a strong suspicion that many batterers have personality disorders, and psychiatrists believe these to be very hard to treat (Kaplan & Sadock, 1989). When we discussed perpetrator typologies, we noted that there seem to be some distinct differences between types of perpetrators. Some are highly antisocial, have very troubled childhoods, and have substance abuse problems. They also have high recidivism rates and are a very high risk. Others seem more explosive and seem to crave support and validation. Still another type, the kind Gondolf (1988) called "typical," may be very different from the other two, and may be more treatable, and fortunately more common.

The new and exciting research being done by Neil Jacobson (Gottman et al., 1995; Jacobson et al., 1995), rather than contradicting these older typologies, seems to confirm their existence, pointing out that the most antisocial actually becomes more calm when violent. As Jacobson (1993) declares, "These guys don't have a problem with anger control, they have too much control."

One of the things we might start asking ourselves instead of "Does treatment work?" is "Under what conditions and with whom does it work?" Based on what we've learned, we might want to pay more serious attention to the assessment of batterers in order to determine perpetrator characteristics. If treatment outcomes are not as good as we want, we might ask ourselves, "Would the outcomes be better if we were able to match perpetrators with the most appropriate program for their type of difficulty?" While we don't currently have the data to answer that question, it seems to be an interesting one nevertheless. The most sociopathic perpetrator might be at very high risk regardless of what we do, but still might respond to a well-thought-out program. Perhaps the explosive type of batterer might do better with anger management techniques, support, encouragement, and monitoring. Perhaps the low-level perpetrator with relationship difficulties (more like the ones described by Neidig and Friedman) might be appropriate for couples treatment. Until we stop thinking of generic batterers, start differentiating between them, and begin conducting well-run clinical trials, we might never know. As Carden (1994) suggests, maybe it's time to be working toward developing an approach to treatment that integrates a number of theoretical perspectives and allows for the creative use of a number of tools.

CHAPTER SUMMARY

In this chapter we surveyed the field of domestic violence. We opened the chapter with a quick discussion about two high-profile domestic violence cases: O. J. Simpson and John Wayne Bobbit. We noted that, while these cases may have been "hyped," they did get the public's attention, thereby giving us an opportunity to educate. We noted that the abuse of women is nothing new, and took a short walk through history, especially in the western European tradition. Laws gave men the right to "correct" their women, and in the United States these rights weren't rescinded until late in the 19th century. In addition to the more remote history, we also discussed the emergence of the battered women's movement and changes in public and professional attitudes. We explored what we mean by domestic violence, noting that it is a pattern of behavior that involves one person using a variety of coercive strategies to control another. We reviewed the best available literature we have in order to try to determine how often it happens. We discussed the controversy about whether women also abuse men, and concluded that women are injured, or battered, much more often than men. We examined the impact of domestic violence on women. In addition, we took a very brief look at how the children are affected. Consistent with discussion in another chapter, we reviewed some ideas about a more client-friendly approach to understanding victims. We reviewed a couple of classic paradigms in the field, the cycle of violence and the model of learned helplessness. We also discussed reasons why women stay in abusive relationships. Within the context of the macro-meso-micro model, we explored ways of explaining domestic violence and reviewed some risk factors. We saved some of the more unsavory tasks for later in the text: a discussion of how to classify offenders (including some groundbreaking new research that seems to hold promise) and, finally, a look at intervention, both on behalf of the victims and with the perpetrators.

LEGAL AND ETHICAL CONCERNS: CRITICAL THINKING QUESTIONS

1. Philosophical points of view and social science empiricism (commitment to scientific method) sometimes come to different conclusions. If your strongly held philosophical view and the empirical evidence differed, how would you resolve this disparity?

2. Battered women's advocates are very concerned about the victims, and many feel that too much emphasis is being placed on perpetrators. How do we reconcile the need to intervene with perpetrators with the need for victim services?

3. A number of women each year kill their husbands, often after years of torture, but this is against the law. How do we reconcile respect for the law with the desperation of victims who kill their abusers?

4. Many women have been told by their abusers that they're crazy, yet it is often helpful to diagnose victims in order to get services for them. How can this be resolved?

5. Many children witness domestic violence, and this may put them at higher risk of becoming abusive themselves. How do we help these kids without labeling and stigmatizing them?

6. A number of typologies of perpetrators have emerged over the years. Some suggest that there are perpetrators who are at very high risk. How can

this information be used in a way that is ethical and fair in the criminal justice system?

7. There are some practices, such as presumptive arrests and group treatment for batterers, that we continue to use despite the inconclusive or negative empirical evidence. How do we justify this?

8. Some states have enacted perpetrator treatment standards that, for victim safety reasons, prohibit the use of family therapy with court-mandated clients. How can we balance victim concerns about safety while restricting the use of a treatment modality that might be helpful to certain "low-risk" couples?

SUGGESTED ACTIVITIES

1. Contact any local hospital you think might be likely to see domestic violence victims. Ask for the social work or social services department and arrange an interview with a social worker who works with domestic violence victims. Find out what services they provide and what services they can refer victims to.

2. Contact your prosecutor's office and determine what laws exist with regard to domestic violence. Is there any different handling of domestic cases as compared to other assaults? Do you have a community intervention project? Are there victim advocates assigned to their office? If so, see if you can arrange for an informational interview. Also, find out if your state has standards for perpetrator treatment programs.

3. Go through any current or back issues of your local newspaper, and see if you can find any homicide cases in which domestic violence seems to be a central issue. Do some additional research on the case, and perhaps even attend a trial. Write a paper on the results and either share it in class or turn it in to your instructor.

4. Contact your local public defender's office and determine if they have any cases involving women who have assaulted their abusers. Take a closer look at this case, and see how much information you can gather on it.

5. Go to your school library and conduct a search on the topic of domestic violence. How much information does your library have? How recent is it? Pick several books of interest to you and select a topic, research it, and write a paper on it.

6. Select one or more of the Suggested Reading selections, read it, and be prepared to discuss it.

REVIEW GUIDE

1. Be able to discuss how current high-profile media cases have increased interest in the subject of domestic violence.

2. Be familiar with the early history of woman abuse. This should include pre-Roman and Roman times. You should know what English common law said about it and how this became part of legal and social tradition

in the United States. Be familiar with major court decisions that relate to women's rights, as well as the Nineteenth Amendment to the Constitution of the United States.

3.   Be knowledgeable about the emergence of women's issues, including battered women, beginning in the 1970s. Know the key historical figures and what they did. How did this impact on attention to battered women's issues? Describe the development of shelters, battered women's coalitions, and perpetrator treatment programs.

4.   What three major components do Schecter and Ganley (1995) suggest should be included in definitions of domestic violence? What, if any, are the differences between such terms as "wife abuse," "woman abuse," "domestic violence," and "partner abuse"? How does this chapter differentiate between domestic violence and battering? What four types of coercive behavior do perpetrators use to control the other person? Be able to identify the examples of psychological maltreatment outlined in the chapter. Be familiar with Figure 7-1. What is the working definition adopted in this chapter? As discussed in the chapter, what else should we know to have a clearer picture of what domestic violence is (for example, marital status, courtship violence, sexual identity, and prior relationships)?

5.   Be familiar with the different types of data: Controlled studies, anecdotal data, official reports, and self report surveys. What are the strengths and limitations of each type of data?

6.   Be fairly familiar with incidence rates, especially NFVS rates of serious assaults, National Crime Victim Survey results on total numbers, and FBI crime statistics on male and female partner homicides.

7.   Be familiar with the various points in the debate about female perpetrators of domestic violence.

8.   Be able to identify the kinds of impacts experienced by victims of domestic violence. Be able to identify the characteristics of battered women as outlined by Dr. Lenore Walker. Be familiar with the signs and symptoms she suggests are associated with battered women. Be familiar with the kinds of psychiatric diagnoses that accompany them. Be familiar with the signs and symptoms associated with PTSD.

9.   What do we know about child witnesses of domestic violence?

10.   What is the philosophy of John Briere's approach to understanding trauma victims? What is abuse-related accommodation? What kinds of signs and symptoms, in addition to those in PTSD, might we find in a person suffering from abuse-related accommodation?

11.   Be able to describe each of the phases in the cycle of violence as outlined by Walker (1979).

12.   Be able to discuss why women stay in domestically violent relationships. Be sure to include the theory of learned helplessness, as well as the reasons suggested by Schecter and Ganley (1995).

13.   Be familiar with each of the macro, meso, and micro level explanations of domestic violence. Be familiar with the work of Hotaling and

Sugarman (1986) and be able to associate specific risk markers they describe with levels of explanation.

14. Be familiar with each of the perpetrator typologies discussed in the chapter. Be familiar with Jacobson and his colleagues and why their research may be so important to understanding perpetrators.

15. What two main types of services do Davis et al. (1994) describe? What sort of influence does it take to change state policies? What are common sources of federal dollars for programs? What kinds of services can shelters offer?

16. Be able to discuss each of the types of services for victims described in the chapter, including hospital services; community resources such as shelters, counseling programs, and support groups; presumptive arrest practices; and community intervention projects. Be able to describe the roles of the hospital social worker and prosecutor's office advocate.

17. Discuss how community intervention projects might be able to provide more than merely the arrest of the perpetrator. Are there differences in outcomes? What does the research say about the results?

18. What kinds of services are available for perpetrators? What two treatment models were profiled in the chapter? Be able to identify and discuss key components and the philosophy of each. Be familiar with the components of the Power and Control Wheel and the Equality Wheel. What is the controversy over couples counseling in domestic violence cases? What does the research say about the effectiveness of perpetrator treatment programs?

19. Be familiar with all terms and concepts highlighted in bold typeface.

SUGGESTED READING

Edleson, J. L., & Tolman, R. M. (1992). *Intervention for men who batter: An ecological approach.* Newbury Park, CA: Sage Publications.
This highly readable book outlines an ecological approach to working with batterers. This approach takes into account individual, family, immediate network, and broad social and societal influences that affect batterers and their families. The authors are considered pioneers and innovators in the field of batterer treatment.

Kurz, D. (1993). Physical assaults by husbands: A major social problem. In R. J. Gelles & D. R. Loseke (Eds.), *Current controversies on family violence.* Newbury Park, CA: Sage Publications.
For those interested in seriously exploring the controversy about whether women's violence to men is a social problem, this is one of two sources to put on the "must read" list (see Straus [1993] below for the other). Demie Kurz argues that the empirical research data fails to take into account the existing power inequality between men and women when stating that women's violence to men is a problem.

Neidig, P. H., & Friedman, D. H. (1984). *Spouse abuse: A treatment program for couples.* Champaign, IL: Research Press.
This is another highly readable book. Peter Neidig and Dale Friedman are the developers of this approach, which is often called the Neidig model. It diverges from other approaches to treatment in that it starts from the premise that couples may be

unlikely to stay apart and that we should not build a program that assumes they will be separated.

Pence, E., & Paymar, M. (1993). *Education groups for men who batter: The Duluth Model.* New York: Springer Publishing.

Within the pages of this book you will find a clearly stated description of the philosophy, methods, and goals of perhaps the best-known and accepted model of batterer treatment. The book takes what is often called a profeminist stand.

Straus, M. (1993). Physical assaults by wives: A major social problem. In R. J. Gelles and D. R. Loseke (Eds.), *Current controversies on family violence.* Newbury Park, CA: Sage Publications.

For those interested in seriously exploring the controversy about whether women's violence to men is a social problem, this is one of two sources to put on the "must read" list (see Kurz [1993] above for the other). Murray Straus examines the available empirical research and debates the use of this data with those who claim a feminist perspective.

Walker, L. (1979). *The battered woman.* New York: Harper Perennial.

Anyone interested in the field of domestic violence should read this book. It is a classic piece of work that has inspired many to do important work in the field. A surprisingly large number of people are familiar with one of the principal innovations of this book, the cycle-of-violence model. Walker also offers an explanation for why battered women seem to stay so often: the model of learned helplessness.

CHAPTER GLOSSARY

Abuse-related accommodation
A concept developed by trauma psychologist, John Briere, to describe the adaptations victims make to abuse. These include both immediate and long term, and can look dysfunctional to an outsider.

Antisocial batterer
One of three categories of batterers proposed by Edward Gondolf (1988), comprising 41% of his sample. The antisocial batterer is described as violent, but not as violent as the sociopathic batterer; this category of batterers is the most likely to use a weapon and somewhat less likely than the sociopathic batterer to be arrested.

Battering
A term used in this chapter to refer to the type of domestic violence that does or could lead to a serious injury.

Client matching
The process whereby we attempt to match clients to the most appropriate form of treatment for them.

Cognitive-behavioral school of psychology
A behaviorally oriented branch of psychology that concerns itself with outward behavior as well as the thinking and emotions of the subject.

Common law
Law based on custom and tradition, first codified in written form by Blackstone in 1768. Became an accepted part of United States law.

Community intervention projects
Projects in which the police, prosecutor, victim advocates, court, and treatment provider agree to work together and coordinate their services.

Conflict Tactics Scale
The most widely accepted survey instrument used for determining the presence of family violence. Criticized because it cannot determine intensity or the progression of violence, but still regarded as highly valid and reliable. Developed by Murray Straus (1979).

Courtship violence
Domestic violence that occurs within the context of a dating relationship.

Domestic violence   A form of family maltreatment in which one person in a past or present relationship uses threat or physical force, and any number of other coercive tactics, to control the other person.

Duluth Model   A batterer group treatment model based upon a profeminist philosophy, which incorporates principles from social learning theory and cognitive-behavioral psychology. Developed by the Duluth Abuse Intervention Project, it is regarded as perhaps the best-articulated perpetrator treatment program in the country.

Equality Wheel   A diagram used in the Duluth program that depicts the components of a more egalitarian relationship between intimate partners.

Explosion or acute phase   One of three phases in Dr. Lenore Walker's cycle-of-violence model. It is the phase during which built-up tensions explode and battering occurs.

FBI official crime statistics   Official statistics, including those on domestic homicide, maintained by the Federal Bureau of Investigation.

Honeymoon phase   One of three phases in Dr. Lenore Walker's model of the cycle of violence, which occurs after the explosive, or acute, phase and is characterized by apologetic and contrite behavior on the part of the perpetrator.

Interpersonal perspective   The term used by Peter Neidig and Dale Friedman to describe the importance they place on the interpersonal relationships among domestically violent couples.

Learned helplessness   A psychological concept borrowed by Dr. Lenore Walker to explain why battered women may be unable to leave their abusive relationships.

Minneapolis Police Experiment   A study on the effectiveness of arresting perpetrators of domestic violence, which initially indicated that arrest was effective in preventing further violence, but later was not replicated successfully.

National Coalition Against Domestic Violence   A national coalition that advocates for battered women and supports the activity of the state coalitions.

National Crime Victim Survey   Survey done with large representative samples (60,000 households) by the Bureau of the Census on behalf of the Department of Justice.

National Family Violence Surveys   Two studies conducted by Murray Straus and his associates using large samples, taken ten years apart. Regarded as among the best survey research done on family maltreatment.

National Organization for Women (NOW)   A large, national organization that emerged in the 1970s to promote women's rights. Credited with bringing public attention to the battered women's issue.

Patriarchy   A concept in feminist philosophy used to describe male domination of women.

Power and Control Wheel   A diagram used in the Duluth program that depicts the coercive strategies used by batterers against their intimate partners.

Presumptive arrest   The policy by which law enforcement officers arrest suspected primary aggressors in domestic disturbances. The rationale is that by doing this it will prevent further abuse and hold the perpetrator accountable.

Profeminist position   A treatment bias that accepts and integrates feminist theory and philosophy into treatment strategies.

Reinforcement   A concept in behavioral psychology that explains why behavior would be more likely to recur.

Rule of thumb	A principle of English common law that said a man could beat his wife so long as the rod he used was no bigger than the circumference of his thumb.
Social learning theory	A theory first developed in the second half of the 20th century, that asserts that we learn behavior by observing and imitating others.
Sociopathic batterer	One of three categories of batterers proposed by Edward Gondolf (1988), comprising 7% of his sample. The sociopathic batterer is described as the most violent and least feeling of all batterers and often has serious other problems including severe substance abuse, and criminal involvements.
Status incompatibility	A concept used to refer to a man who has less status than his wife in a patriarchal society or else not achieving as would be expected, given his family background, education, or experience.
Tension-building phase	One of three phases in Dr. Lenore Walker's cycle-of-violence model, which is characterized by tension that ultimately ends with the onset of the explosive, acute phase.
Type 1 batterer	A category of batterers in Saunders's typology, characterized as "family only" aggressors, the least likely to have been abused, the most concerned about the opinions of other's, with low levels of anger, depression, and jealousy.
Type 2 batterer	A category of batterers in Saunders's typology, characterized as "generally violent" aggressors. Saunders suggests that they are the most likely to be violent outside the home, use severe violence, and have rigid ideas about the roles of men and women.
Type 3 batterer	A category of batterers in Saunders's typology, characterized as "emotionally volatile" aggressors. Described as having the highest levels of anger, depression, and jealousy.
Type I batterer	One of two categories of severe batterers identified by Jacobson and his colleagues, who have been identified through direct research measures to have a *reduced* physiologic response to conflict. Strongly associated with greater violence, a more abusive family of origin, increased substance abuse, and an elevated risk of being violent outside the home. Sometimes called *vagal reactors*.
Type II batterer	One of two categories of severe batterers identified by Jacobson and his colleagues, who have been identified through direct research measures to have an *increased* physiologic response to conflict. Strongly associated with less violence, a less abusive family of origin, less substance abuse, and lower risk of being violent outside the home.
Typical batterer	One of three categories of batterers proposed by Edward Gondolf (1988), comprising 52% of his sample. The typical batterer is described as being less likely to be arrested and more apologetic and contrite after the abusive incident.
Vagal reactor	See Type I batterer above.
Vicarious punishment	A principle in social learning theory that describes how someone might be less likely to perform a particular behavior on the basis of watching someone else be punished.
Vicarious reinforcement	A principle in social learning theory that describes how someone might be more likely to perform a particular behavior on the basis of watching someone else be rewarded.

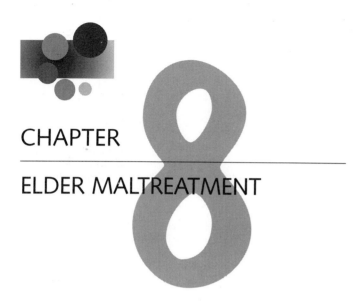

CHAPTER

ELDER MALTREATMENT

Historical Context

What Is Elder Maltreatment?

How Big Is the Problem?

What are the Indicators of Maltreatment?

What Is the Impact of Elder Maltreatment?

Explanations and Risk Factors

Efforts to Deal with Elder Maltreatment

The mistreatment of our older citizens has probably gotten less public and professional attention than all other areas within the family abuse field. In the sixties child physical abuse became a social priority; in the seventies, it was domestic violence; in the eighties, it became child sexual abuse, and elder abuse to a certain degree. However, elder maltreatment has never become a driving issue in the way these other areas have. As a consequence of the head start the other areas have gotten, some say that the field of elder maltreatment is 20 years behind when it comes to research and practice.

There is an old saying that goes something like, "Pay me now, or pay me later, but you will pay me." Neglecting this issue should not continue for a number of very important reasons. For one, the "baby boomers—those of us born in the years after World War II and in the fifties—like it or not, are in middle age now and will be hitting old age with a bang if we're not ready. Problems such as elder mistreatment will increase the demand for all kinds of services—medical, housing, and social. If problems with Social Security and health care insurance for the elderly (Medicare) are not resolved, the need for programs will happen at a time when the major social safety nets are themselves breaking down.

Despite the lack of attention to elder maltreatment, it isn't a small problem. Estimates vary, but most agree that between 500,000 and 1 million seniors experience abuse in the United States (see Landes et al., 1993). As we will see later in this chapter, to neglect the real physical, medical, and social needs of the elderly is a form of maltreatment. To neglect these real needs could make us, as a society, as guilty of maltreatment as those we will talk about in the pages to follow.

In this chapter we will take a very brief look at the history of elder abuse; explore the various types of maltreatment and their definitions; look at research that estimates the size of the problem; discuss explanations for abuse and risk factors; and examine how to identify the problem as well as ways to approach doing something about it.

HISTORICAL CONTEXT

The current perception is that formal human services for the elderly is a fairly modern phenomenon. To a certain extent this may be true. Before the Social Security Act was passed during the Franklin D. Roosevelt administration, there was no universal income insurance program for older Americans. Until passage of legislation in the Lyndon B. Johnson administration, there was no universal health care insurance for the elderly. These programs, while threatened, continue as the two primary sources of social supports for our older citizens.

If there is one population group within our society that epitomizes the modern social welfare system as many would like to envision it, it is the elderly. It is the only group that currently has both guaranteed income maintenance (Social Security) and universal health insurance (Medicare). In discussing this topic of elder abuse and neglect, we might want to give pause and explore what older people did before the time when they had income and health insurance. While we might have an image of families with affectionate relationships caring for each other, and members of a family, including the elderly, being able to count on their families for help, this idealized picture may not be very accurate for many.

It is true that we live in a far more complex world today than in times past, and perhaps because of some of this complexity, many people do not feel as connected as perhaps they once did. We can call the eighties and nineties the dawn of the information age. Prior to this, we had a period of rapid industrial growth that followed on the heels of the Second World War. Just before this came the Great Depression, which was characterized by high unemployment, soup lines, and shantytowns called "Hoovervilles." The late 1800s and early 1900s marked the height of the industrial age in our country. Dramatic shifts in population, usually from rural to urban, occurred then, as they have at many times in history when economic systems evolved and changed. Whereas in the beginnings of this country most people lived in rural circumstances, by the height of the industrial age most people lived in urban areas. With these shifts came a number of social problems: low pay and overcrowding, women and child labor abuses, and the development of urban underclasses, especially among the most recent to arrive or the most stigmatized.

The dawning of the industrial age, however, was not the first time in the western European tradition when such a population shift had occurred. In the closing days of the medieval period, there was a major shift in the economic life in Europe, and especially in England. Since in the United States we have borrowed many of our social and legal traditions from England, we'll take a closer look at this history. In the feudal system of the Middle Ages, peasants had lived on the land under the rule and protection of their feudal lords. The lords not only benefited from the labor of the peasants but, along with the church, were responsible for providing for their social welfare. Those without land of their own were dependent upon the largess of their lords, and those with land often had to be concerned about whether their heirs would be content to wait for them to die a natural death.

When the feudal system began to break down and commerce began to take its place, not only did people gravitate to towns and cities but numerous peasants were displaced from the land. They were no longer needed and often became too great a burden for their former lords. When this happened, not only did the serfs lose their "jobs" on the land but they lost their homes and the social protections previously provided by their feudal lords. Large numbers of these serfs became homeless and indigent when they were forced off the land. When these events unfolded, England experienced significant problems with crime and pauperism, and in order to deal with the social breakdown, Queen Elizabeth I enacted the Poor Law of 1601. The result of the act was that, for the first time, the poor and indigent were put under the protection of the crown. Following this came the Settlement Act of 1668, which required peasants to return to the parish of their births, where wardens of the poor would have charge of them.

This part of history marks the beginnings of the welfare state as we know it, and while it may have helped deal with the social problems that followed in the wake of these major social and economic changes, it was not completely benign. Some of the so-called "worthy poor" were supported in their own homes, but many more were forced into new institutions called workhouses, poorhouses, and almshouses. People placed in these "social welfare" institutions were segregated from their communities and were commonly torn from their families. To say that conditions in some of these institutions were harsh would be an understatement. There are historical accounts which describe how new residents would be whipped with the cat-o'-nine-tails. This kind of whip had a number of "tails," or lengths of leather, which often had bits of metal attached to the ends. They literally ripped flesh from the body and were intended to cause pain and leave a lasting impression.

The almshouse, poorhouse, and orphanage system, as it developed in England, was transported to America, and became part of the social welfare tradition of North America. Institutions that developed here included poorhouses, large mental hospitals, orphanages, and residential schools. It has only been in this century that some of the most pernicious and destructive impacts of these closed institutions have become apparent to us, leaving many with a negative view of institutional care in general. Most people who study elder maltreatment tell us, in fact, that among the greatest fears of elderly people, even those who have been chronically maltreated, is being placed in a nursing home or institution, and this brings us back to the present day. Individuals can't always meet their own needs, especially when their bodies give out or they run out of financial resources. Families and family members often can't do it either. And the institutions that have become integral to our social welfare system are often perceived as part of a solution that has turned into a problem. While most residential placements are probably very good, there are also a number of significant problems with many others.

Today many of us agree with elderly people that it is best to remain at home whenever possible. When it is not possible, we might need to recognize that institutions sometimes can do a better job. Some of the physical and social problems are beyond the abilities of families, and many other families are not willing to make the sacrifices that would be necessary to care for the elderly person at home. These problems are not so easy to tackle. If they were, maybe we'd have already solved them. There are significant challenges to meeting the needs of the elderly, whether in their own homes, the homes of family members, or in institutional care. As we will discuss, elder maltreatment occurs in each of these settings.

WHAT IS ELDER MALTREATMENT?

As is also true with other forms of family abuse, elder maltreatment is a complex phenomenon. No single definition can encompass its many aspects. It is usually divided into two broad categories and several specific varieties. The two broadest categories are **domestic elder abuse** and **institutional elder abuse** (Tatara, 1996). Domestic elder abuse differs from institutional abuse in that it is committed by a caregiver who has a special relationship with the abused elder person, such as an adult child, spouse, friend, or acquaintance. Institutional abuse occurs in a nursing home or other facility that is paid to care for the elderly person. In addition to these two broad categories, there is one other broad category called **self-neglect** (Tatara, 1996). As the name implies, self-neglect is a form of neglect in which an independent elderly person fails to care for their own needs. This is the most common type of case that elder maltreatment professionals hear about.

The terms *maltreatment* and *mistreatment* are often used pretty much interchangeably for "abuse," but the term *maltreatment* will be the preferred term in this chapter, since it can encompass both abuse and neglect. In addition to the three broad categories discussed above, there are a number of specific types of elder abuse. Most professionals in the field generally include the following categories: **physical abuse, sexual abuse, emotional or psychological abuse, neglect,** and **financial or material exploitation** (Tatara, 1996; Wolf, 1996), though lack of agreement about definitions has been a hindrance to evaluating the research. In addition, **abandonment** and **violation of basic human rights** are sometimes included as forms of maltreatment (Quinn & Tomita, 1986).

Physical abuse includes deliberate behavior that causes or can cause injury, pain, or impairment (Tatara, 1996; Tatara & Blumerman, 1996a; Wolf, 1996). Any type of unconsenting sexual contact with an elderly person is considered elder *sexual abuse* (Tatara, 1996; Tatara & Blumerman, 1996a). *Emotional or psychological abuse* is the willful infliction of mental or emotional anguish through threat, humiliation, intimidation, or any other verbal or nonverbal behavior (Tatara, 1996; Wolf, 1996). *Neglect* is the intentional or unintentional failure of the caregiver to fulfill the caregiving obligation (Tatara, 1996; Wolf, 1996). This can include the failure to provide adequate nutrition, personal hygiene, medication, physical aids and prostheses, and human contact. When it is done intentionally, as a way of controlling or influencing the elderly person, it is called **intentional neglect** (Vida, 1994), often referred to as **active neglect.** Examples might include deliberately withholding the elderly person's eyeglasses, dentures, walker, or other artificial aids. When the neglect results unintentionally it is called **unintentional neglect** (Vida, 1994), often referred to as **passive neglect.** *Financial or material exploitation* involves misappropriating the elderly person's personal property, money, or resources (Tatara, 1996; Tatara & Blumerman, 1996a; Wolf, 1996). This often includes such things as cashing the elderly person's social security check and taking the money, selling the person's stock portfolio, or even selling the person's home. It is not uncommon to hear of an older person who has been excluded from a home they signed over to an adult child. When an elderly person grants a power of attorney, any number of financial abuses can occur. *Abandonment* involves deserting a dependent elderly person. *Violation of basic human rights* is fairly self-explanatory. It includes violating the elderly person's right to liberty, to appropriate medical treatment, to use personal property, to worship as he or she wishes, to privacy, to complain, to vote, and to be treated with dignity and respect (Quinn & Tomita, 1986). (See Box 8-1.)

HOW BIG IS THE PROBLEM?

Again, as is true with others forms of family abuse, the research data we have about elder maltreatment is neither uniform nor clear-cut. What we have are estimates about the extent of abuse, and many suspect they are far lower

---

BOX 8-1   Two Examples of Elder Maltreatment

The following two cases are fictionalized vignettes based on profiles of abuse victims and reported cases.

Gloria is an 83-year-old woman whose husband died six years ago. She lives in her own home and is in reasonably good health for her age. Gloria's middle-aged son moved in with her about four years ago. He has lost a series of jobs, is not working, and often abuses alcohol and marijuana. Gloria has been brought into the emergency room several times with injuries that are inconsistent with the explanations given. She admits that her son has problems but says she doesn't want to get him in trouble.

John is a 78-year-old widower who has been diagnosed with severe Alzheimer's disorder. Occasionally he is assaultive and is often uncooperative. He is cared for by his middle-aged daughter, Sharon, who admits openly that she is stretched to the maximum of her abilities. She often has a hard time getting her father to bathe, gives up on trying to keep him fed, and is no longer consistent with giving him his medications. She has let her home go, and her father's physical condition is deteriorating.

---

than the true levels. Before we get down to the numbers, let's take just a few moments to review the kind of social science data we can draw on. We have official reports of abuses committed. As is also true with other forms of maltreatment, we suspect that official reports represent just the tip of the iceberg. We also have large representative sample survey data. These depend on the self-reports of the individuals who respond to them. When it comes to child abuse and domestic violence we have a number of good large surveys, including the National Family Violence Surveys conducted by Murray Straus and his colleagues (see Chapters 2, 4, and 7). It was not until Pillemer and Finkelhor used some of the same research methods in 1988 that we had a similar survey that examined elder abuse and neglect. In addition to official reports and large survey data, we also have various research projects about elder abuse, the best of which have comparison, or control, groups.

Official reports in the area of elder abuse are somewhat difficult to get since there is no single federal standard and definitions vary from state to state. We've had mandatory reporting in child abuse for some time (see Chapter 2), yet we don't yet have universal reporting laws for dependent adults. All jurisdictions have some sort of legislation dealing with elder abuse (Wolf, 1996), yet only 42 have laws that require professionals to report the abuse of dependent adults (Tatara & Blumerman, 1996c). Reports are also handled differently depending on whether they occur at home or in an institution. Reports of abuse of the elderly in out-of-home care are handled by a network of people working in a program called the **Long-Term Care Ombudsman Program.** Since there is no standardized reporting system in or collection center for the ombudsman program, we don't currently have reliable estimates of institutional maltreatment (Tatara, 1996). Data about domestic elder maltreatment is better. It is reported to the **National Center on Elder Abuse** (NCEA), which has more standardized procedures. As a result, we may have a fairly accurate estimate of reported domestic maltreatment.

The NCEA estimates there were 241,000 reports of domestic elder maltreatment in 1994 (Tatara, 1996). As is also true in child welfare, about half of these were substantiated (Wolf, 1996). The substantiation rate was estimated to be approximately 60% for 1994, yet this estimate is based on reports that include self-abuse. Because of inconsistencies in reporting by state Long-Term Care Ombudsman programs, it is difficult to estimate the incidence of institutional maltreatment; but in 1994, 176,590 individuals filed complaints (Administration on Aging, 1996b). The National Crime Victim Survey put out by the FBI does not report on elder abuse, though it does makes estimates about the number of elders who were victims of crime. In the only study that attempted to do for elder maltreatment what the National Family Violence Surveys did for other forms of family maltreatment, Karl Pillemer and David Finkelhor (1988) surveyed a sample of about 2,000 non-institutionalized elderly people in Boston. Based on this survey, they estimated that 32 elderly people per 1000 experience elder maltreatment. This translates to slightly over 3%. The most common form of abuse in this study was physical abuse (20 per 1000), followed by chronic verbal aggression (11 per 1000), and then neglect (4 per 1000). Some national estimates conservatively estimate that from 500,000 to approximately 1 million elderly people in this country are subject to abuse (Boudreau, 1993; Landes et al., 1993). Tatara and Blumerman (1996c) of the National Center on Elder Abuse estimate that the figure is between 820,000 and 1.86 million. Other estimates approach 2 to 2.5 million, but are generally believed to be inflated (Landes et al., 1993). One of the difficulties, still not resolved, with data about elder abuse is that many of these abuses seem to be perpetrated by other elders (Pillemer & Finkelhor, 1988), that is, their spouses. The question then is raised whether this kind of abuse is best considered domestic violence or elder maltreatment.

When we look at the official reports, the picture of elder abuse that emerges is somewhat different from that reported in the groundbreaking work of Pillemer and Finkelhor (1988), which was then replicated in Canada and Great Britain (Ogg & Bennett, 1992; Podkieks, 1992, both cited in Lachs & Pillemer, 1995). Of the *reported* cases of abuse, the figures look considerably different. For 1994, in about 37% of cases of reported abuse the perpetrator was an adult child, compared to spouses, who comprised about 15% of the total (Tatara & Blumerman, 1996b).

What is the most common form of elder maltreatment? The most recent data reported by the NCEA indicates that the most common form of reported domestic maltreatment is neglect, which amounted to 58.5% of reports for 1994 (Tatara & Blumerman, 1996a). This was followed by physical maltreatment, 15.7%, and then by financial or material exploitation at 12.3%. Reported cases of emotional or psychological maltreatment of the elderly accounted for only 7.3% of the total, and sexual abuse of the elderly was an extremely small proportion of the total.

When trying to reconcile research results that seem to be saying different things, we probably need to take a look at the kind of data we're comparing. The large sample survey done by Pillemer and Finkelhor (1988) and the Canadian and English replication studies were based on large representative survey samples. This kind of information is likely to give us an overall picture of elder abuse in the country. The cases reported by the states to the NCEA are likely to be smaller in number, but perhaps more serious, since the maltreatment might tend to be more serious before someone would be willing to call in a report. The rates of neglect that show up in the large sample surveys and the rates of *reported* maltreatment are very disparate. Survey reports suggest that neglect is far less frequent than physical maltreatment or even financial exploitation, yet the amount of neglect reported by the states to the NCEA suggests just the opposite. The reported cases seem to be a subset of a bigger sample, and unreported cases may be somewhat different from those that are reported.

WHAT ARE THE INDICATORS OF MALTREATMENT?

The impact of elder abuse, as with virtually every aspect of this issue, has not been assessed to the same extent as other forms of maltreatment. For one thing, there are so many different types of elder maltreatment that it's difficult to paint the effects with a single broad brush. In addition to other things, we can probably expect the impact to depend on the type of maltreatment. The reader might want to be cautious about confusing *indicators* (which may or may not be related to maltreatment) with *proof*. Some of the same signs and symptoms can have different causes, and often indicators simply mean that *something* is wrong. Determining specific causes takes more in-depth investigation.

Behavioral Indicators of Elder Abuse

As with many circumstances in which a person becomes distraught, an elderly person may have signs and symptoms of depression and anxiety. These can include (Kaplan & Sadock, 1989):

- Disturbance of sleep (much more or less than normal for the person)
- Disturbance in eating (either an increase or often a loss of appetite)
- Loss of energy and lethargy
- Subjective feelings of depression, anxiety, or disturbance
- Loss of interest in things the person normally enjoys
- Isolation and withdrawal

Other behavioral indicators can include the following (Administration on Aging, 1996a; Lachs & Pillemer, 1995; Quinn & Tomita, 1986):

- Frequent visits to the emergency room
- Numerous changes in primary care provider
- Delays in seeking medical assistance
- Easily startled or frightened
- Agitation or trembling
- Hesitancy to speak openly
- Implausible or vague explanations (for example, "she fell")

Indicators of Suspected Physical Abuse

As with other forms of abuse, there aren't always clear physical indicators, although with physical abuse the indicators may sometimes be more apparent among the elderly. Signs and symptoms are similar to those that appear in child abuse cases. When significant indicators are present in any area, concerned individuals may want to explore more fully to determine if the elderly person is being abused, neglected, or exploited. When abuse has occurred, any of the following may be present:

- Friction burns around wrists and ankles, around chest, and under arms. (These sometimes occur if caregivers tie up older persons to keep them restrained [Administration on Aging, 1996a; Quinn & Tomita,1986].)
- Bruises from hitting, shoving, slapping, pinching, or kicking
- Skin discoloration
- Burns, especially if they leave a characteristic pattern that could be indicative of deliberate infliction
- Fractures, sprains, lacerations, and abrasions

Injuries that are inconsistent with the reports of the primary caretaker are always suspicious, as are numerous injuries in varying degrees of healing (Quinn & Tomita, 1986). As is also true in the case of children (see Chapter 2), subdural hematomas and retinal hemorrhaging are possible consequences of severe shaking.

Physical Indicators of Neglect

There are a number of physical indicators of neglect. Some of the most common are listed here:

- Severe malnutrition or dehydration
- Blood levels that are inconsistent with medication compliance reported by primary caretaker (Lachs & Pillemer, 1995)

- Decubitus ulcers (or bed sores) that have not been cared for
- Poor hygiene
- Skin rashes
- Skin pallor and sunken eyes
- Lack of eyeglasses, hearing aids, dentures, and so on
- Untreated injuries or medical conditions
- Poor housing conditions and uncleanliness (lack of clean linen, poor housekeeping, and so forth)

Indicators of Financial or Material Exploitation

Indicators of financial or material exploitation may be less likely to be identified since health care and human service providers may be unaccustomed to interviewing about financial resources (Quinn & Tomita, 1986). Quinn and Tomita (1986) review a number of indicators of possible financial exploitation:

- Unusual activity in bank accounts
- Bank statements stop arriving at elder's home
- Elder is given documents to sign that elder does not understand
- Care of elder is less than elder can afford
- Lack of amenities when the elder can afford them
- Caregiver is excessively interested in the elder's finances
- Recent acquaintances acting as if they are very close to the elder
- Elder is isolated from others, especially other members of the family, old friends, and other social contacts
- Promises of lifelong care given to elder
- Elder being asked to deed over home or other significant resources
- Signatures don't match
- Lack of appropriate financial management plan
- Implausible explanations about management of elder's finances

Seniors also seem to be at risk for financial exploitation by non-caregivers who work their way into the elders' confidence and then swindle them. These, however, are difficult to determine based on the National Crime Victim Survey (U.S. Department of Justice, 1994). While the elderly are generally the least likely age group to experience crime, according to the NCVS, they are more at risk of crimes motivated by economic gain, such as larceny, burglary, and auto theft. Since we are talking about reported crimes, we are probably referring to economic crimes perpetrated by non-intimates.

WHAT IS THE IMPACT
OF ELDER MALTREATMENT?

While there seems to be a great deal of interest in the impact of maltreatment on children and adult women, there is very little in the literature about the impact of maltreatment on elderly people. While we don't have clear answers as to why, the implication of this omission seems to be that the future impact of maltreatment on the elderly isn't seen as being as important, possibly because of the perception that the elderly are at the end of the life cycle. This omission is probably unintentional, though it might give us pause to think about our cultural attitudes concerning the elderly. While there is a relative lack of discussion about impact, there are a couple of ways in which the impact of abuse on the elderly is addressed in the professional literature. For one, there are numerous case studies that tell individual stories, and such stories tend to be emotionally moving. Some of the impacts of abuse can be inferred from the indicators, as reviewed above, since we can think of these as the consequences of maltreatment (see Quinn & Tomita, 1986; Administration on Aging, 1996a).

In terms of examining the impact of maltreatment on the elderly, we might start by summarizing the factors believed to be associated with the impact of maltreatment generally. In children, we feel certain that age and developmental level are important considerations. If this also holds for older people, we might ask "What developmental considerations are important when considering the impact of maltreatment?" A closely related consideration would be the level of functioning, including both strengths and limitations, of the older person. Type of abuse, or abuses, is also an important consideration. Many forms of maltreatment have specific physical impacts, yet many assert that it is the psychological aspect of virtually every form of abuse that seems to mediate the impact of abuse (see Chapter 3). Severity of abuse would be another consideration we might look for, assuming the more severe the maltreatment the more traumatic its effects. A final consideration might be the extent and type of the relationship between the older person and the mistreating care provider.

Most social scientists seem to agree that we are constantly learning, adapting, and developing. It is a process that does not necessarily stop just because a person has become elderly; in fact, social psychologist Erik Erikson indicates that social development continues throughout the life cycle. He believes that the last stage of social development occurs in old age and says that this stage is marked by a developmental crisis between "integrity" and "despair." The integrity refers to whether or not all the aspects of a person's life add up to mean something or not. If the older person is unable to envision life as having overall meaning, Erikson suggests, he or she may fall into despair.

How can this relate to the impact of elder abuse? The answer may lie in the kind of meaning that elderly people assign to their abuse, and we should remember that individuals vary greatly on such matters. Many in the field have commented that when the abusive caregiver is an adult child, elderly persons may often blame themselves and feel guilty. The logic behind this seems to be that they are ashamed of raising children who would behave this way. While we don't have good evidence to either confirm or disconfirm the next possibility, we might also speculate on whether or not at least some elderly people see their old age as one last chance to make an impact. To do this, they might be willing to be patient and tolerant with their abusive adult child in the hope that by perservering they might both keep some semblance of a relationship in place. They might feel that they can improve their adult child's behavior.

The elderly person's level of functioning would also seem likely to mediate the effects of abuse in some ways. A fairly healthy individual with a relatively intact psychological constitution might be better equipped to weather maltreatment. A less well functioning individual, perhaps one who has had more adjustment problems in life, might have fewer personal and psychological resources to draw upon. As has been commented on by a number of experts in the field, it could also be noted that elders who have physical limitations may be less well equipped to defend themselves, get away, or even call for assistance. In a similar vein, a person with severe dementia may be less able to understand and explain to others just what has happened to them.

As with virtually every category of family maltreatment (child abuse, domestic violence, or elder abuse), the form of maltreatment (that is, physical, sexual, psychological, and so on) seems important. While some now think that the psychological elements may be the salient feature of all forms of maltreatment (see Chapter 3), the traumatic effects of severe physical abuse cannot be denied, and we would expect traumatic adaptations regardless of the advanced age of the victim. In fact, because of the relative ease with which older people can be seriously injured, they may be even more traumatized. Sometimes physical maltreatment includes the use of restraints to keep the person immobile while the caregiver goes out. The effect of such activity also involves isolating the elderly person. Since social contact and stimulation seems necessary to human functioning and development, we can only expect this isolation to add to the impact of whatever other maltreatment the person might be experiencing.

Finally, the relationship with the care provider may be an important mediating variable on the impact of the maltreatment. If the maltreatment is perpetrated by a person with whom the elderly person has a close personal relationship, we might reasonably presume that the elderly person would experience greater emotional turmoil, disappointment, and perhaps even a sense of betrayal.

While we have anecdotal accounts, and speculation about the effects of elder maltreatment, there has been very little written in the professional literature. In contrast, there has been a great deal of professional concern about the impact of abuse on children. We can ponder the reasons, but what seems clear is that we need more information about this subject. It seems rich ground for thoughtful research.

EXPLANATIONS
AND RISK FACTORS

While there seems to be less research in the literature on elder abuse than on other forms of family maltreatment, generally, the literature on research that tries to answer the question "Why?" is fairly consistent with what we've found with other forms of maltreatment. For one, there appears to be no single explanation that adequately deals with its many aspects. In trying to understand the problem, the literature has identified four primary factors associated with elder maltreatment: (1) individual characteristics of the perpetrator, (2) intergenerational transmission, (3) dependency of the abused, and (4) external stress (O'Malley, et al., 1983, as cited in Quinn & Tomita, 1986; Pillemer, 1986; Pillemer & Suitor, 1988; Tatara, 1996; Wolf, 1986). Social isolation is also sometimes included as a risk factor (Lachs et al., 1994; Lachs & Pillemer, 1995; Pillemer, 1986; Pillemer & Suitor, 1988; Wolf, 1986).

In an effort to unify the information we do have, we'll be reviewing the array of proposed explanations and risk factors of elder abuse as well as taking a look at some additional possible explanations. In keeping with the format adopted throughout this text, we'll be organizing our review into the three-level systems or ecological model we adopted in Chapter 1. This means that we will be discussing three broad levels of explanation: macro, meso, and micro.

The Macro Level—
Broad Cultural and Social Factors

In comparison to other family maltreatment specializations, elder maltreatment has come to public attention late in the game. For whatever reasons, elder abuse didn't get noticed until after the public became concerned about child battering, domestic violence, and then child sexual abuse. Being at the end of the line may say something about our society's values, and these values, as a reflection of our culture, are probably important to understanding elder maltreatment.

Groups and cultures tend to have collective notions about appropriate behavior (Rathbone-McCuan, 1996). Take a moment to think about what's considered important in our society. Independence, appearance, strength, youthfulness, physical fitness, athletic prowess, sex appeal, and financial and personal power usually come to mind. If these are indeed the things we value in our society, what does it say about their opposites: becoming dependent, declining in physical strength, graying, the loss of intellectual powers, and a less involved social role? None of these traits are thought of as desirable, and each is associated with old age.

Whereas the term *patriarchy* is used to describe the cultural pattern in which men are dominant, **ageism** is the term that has been coined to denote the form of bigotry that devalues and stereotypes elderly people (Butler, 1969, as cited in Johnson, 1991). Quinn & Tomita (1986) suggest that stereotypes about the old and the aging process are widespread and seem to contribute to widespread prejudicial attitudes about the elderly. Tanya Johnson (1991), a sociologist with an interest in the field, tells us that as a consequence of this prejudice, elderly people are at greater risk for maltreatment. Johnson identifies three primary types of ageism that cause difficulty for older people: (1) **societal ageism,** (2) **community ageism,** and (3) **professional ageism.**

Societal ageism can be thought of as an overarching societal attitude about the elderly, which is often reflected in official policies about older people. These could include policies, for example, that require people to retire at a certain age, that limit access to health care, or that discriminate against the old simply because they are old (Johnson, 1991). Health care policies that deny payment for services at home, though less costly, but pay for institutional care, thereby making the elderly person dependent is another possible example. *Community ageism,* in Johnson's framework (1991), occurs when local communities disproportionately emphasize services for younger populations instead of for the old. *Professional ageism* is a kind of paternalistic attitude expressed by those professionals who infantilize the elderly. Rather than being treated with dignity and respect, they are spoken down to and almost treated as children. According to Johnson (1991), professional ageism is often expressed in the form of ignoring the needs of the elderly, exploitive billing practices, careless diagnosis, and inappropriate medication (overmedicating for behavior management reasons or undermedication for real physical problems).

In addition to biases about aging and stereotypes of elderly people, there may be other cultural values that might indirectly contribute to elder maltreatment. Individualism, self-determination, and independence are all valued (Motenko & Greenberg, 1995) in this society. However, many elderly people need to be dependent on others due to physical and mental debilities, yet won't do so because of social attitudes about independence and self-determination. They are also highly reluctant to go to nursing homes. While there has been a move in recent years to try to provide supportive services and home health care so they can remain at home, these programs may not be as available as are needed.

While cultural attitudes seem to be very important, there isn't much question that these attitudes don't in and of themselves directly cause elder abuse. They probably do, however, contribute to it indirectly. For example, most of the current literature indicates that isolation is a significant risk factor. Stereotypical views and attitudes about the elderly seem likely to contribute to the isolation and neglect, since people who hold these views may avoid the elderly person. Public policies that don't take care of their needs and circumstances can also sometimes contribute to the problem. With limited financial opportunities, fixed incomes, and a rising cost of living, many elderly, especially those who do not own their own homes, probably have limited options and feel they have to "scrimp." Taken as a whole, these can all contribute to a climate in which elderly people feel overlooked, cast off, and afraid.

While biases about age exist in our society, we should also remember that many elderly people feel well treated. Many tell us that they are very satisfied with their lives and how others treat them. While the Pillemer and Finkelhor (1988) study found that 32 per 1000 elderly people experienced maltreatment, they also found that 968 per 1000 didn't. So, rather than saying society is uniformly biased about the elderly, perhaps we should say we are ambivalent. On one hand, we have ageist views. On the other hand, society as a whole seems willing to be considerate. This is reflected in the discounts for restaurants, public transportation, and entertainment events that are commonly given to elderly people.

External stress is another broad social factor that has sometimes been implicated in elder abuse. By this we are referring to such factors as economic conditions, unemployment, and environmental conditions, including generalized crime, overcrowding, and community and neighborhood conditions. While there is no direct cause-and-effect relationship between social stress and elder maltreatment, researchers have found positive correlations between social stress and other forms of maltreatment (Gil, 1970; Straus et al., 1980). Anecdotal reports, which have not found their way into the literature, tell us that elderly people in some communities are victimized by gang members, who will sometimes start by helping the person out in the yard and ultimately begin to exploit and terrorize the elderly person.

Although there is very little in the literature about the role of culture per se, this doesn't mean it isn't important. It is almost an invisible factor that is often hard to identify and study. On a practical level, workers in the field tell us that there seem to be real differences between the degree to which communities are willing to support their elderly members. Mark Lachs and associates Berkman, Fulmer, and Horwitz (1994), in the first-known prospective study on elder maltreatment, report that being a member of a racial minority may be a risk factor. They also comment that this may be more a result of an increased willingness of members of certain minority communities to help elderly people in their own homes, thereby increasing the likelihood of an adult protective service referral.

In contrast to reports of an increased risk associated with minority status, there is some professional opinion that some ethnic communities actually do a better job of caring for their elder citizens. Some believe, for example, that there are disproportionately fewer referrals in Asian communities because of the important role seniors play in many Asian cultures. There is also the perception that there may be more willingness in African American communities to help their older citizens, especially among churchgoers. Members of Native American communities often describe reverence for the elders of the tribe as being an essential part of their culture. Since we believe that culture is integral to human social behavior, and since there has been so little work done to explore its influence on elder maltreatment, it seems reasonable to say that much more emphasis in this area is needed if we are to better understand why people behave as they do toward the elderly.

The Meso Level— Family and Relationship Factors

At an intuitive level, one of the first relationship factors that comes to mind when thinking about elder maltreatment is that of a **cycle of violence**. While the term first became popular in the domestic violence literature (Walker, 1979), it has been imported into the literature about elder abuse. In the context of elder maltreatment, the term is usually used in reference to the idea that violence repeats itself in families. There's a popular expression that goes something like, "What goes around comes around." The idea is that children who are treated abusively when they are growing up are more likely to be abusive caretakers of their elderly parents should the time come that they are called upon to provide such care. This use of the term is very different from the way Walker (1979) used it in her classic work about woman battering. Another term often used for this idea about abused children becoming abusive toward their aging parents is **intergenerational transmission** (Fulmer & O'Malley, 1987). Again, the idea we're talking about here is different from the way it is used in the child abuse literature. As first introduced in the child abuse field (see Chapter 2), it refers to an increased likelihood that persons who have been abused will grow up to abuse their own children. Intergenerational transmission is an explanation based upon social learning theory, wherein abusive behavior is learned by observing it. When applied to elder abuse, the term **role inversion** is used to describe a twist to this explanation. Role inversion as a concept is used to suggest that adult victims of abuse have learned to be abusive to dependent people by having been abused themselves when in a dependent role (Johnson, 1991).

As discussed in the context of child abuse and domestic violence (see Chapters 2 and 7), there is good evidence to suggest that people who have been exposed to violence in childhood are at increased risk of becoming violent themselves as adults (Gelles & Cornell, 1990; Hotaling & Sugarman, 1986; Straus, et al., 1980). What this means, however, is simply that it happens significantly more often than we would expect. This evidence cannot be responsibly construed to imply there is a clear cause-and-effect relationship (Kaufman & Zigler, 1987, 1989; Widom, 1989). As discussed elsewhere in this text (especially in Chapter 2), there is good evidence to suggest that while witnessing or experiencing abuse might increase the risk of abuse, it doesn't cause it. Any explanation that proposes intergenerational transmission must also account for this. Writers in the field of elder abuse draw on the child abuse and domestic violence literature when discussing intergenerational transmission, which has been identified as one way to explain why adult children become abusive toward their elderly parents (Fulmer, 1988; Johnson, 1991; Pillemer & Suitor, 1988; Quinn & Tomita, 1986). What is lacking in the elder abuse literature, however, is clear empirical evidence validating that it is a factor in *elder* maltreatment. To date there are no studies that can clearly demonstrate that even the 30% rate of intergenerational transmission that can be estimated in the child abuse field (Kaufman & Zigler, 1987, 1989; Widom, 1989) also applies in the field of elder abuse. Before such claims can be responsibly made, more research needs to be done into this question. This is where the elder abuse field might profit from the work that has gone on in the child abuse area. *If* intergenerational transmission can be established as a significant factor, we will want to know when and under what conditions it is most likely to occur. New research would probably also have to do a better job explaining how it is transmitted, since social learning theory, as currently applied, seems to be limited in its ability to explain how this could occur between adult children and their elderly parents.

Another possible relationship-based explanation for elder maltreatment is the relationship history between the maltreated older person and the perpetrator. It is an intuitively derived explanation, which suggests that unresolved conflict between adult children and their parents can get "acted out" in certain circumstances. According to this view, when there are unresolved conflicts between the adult child and the elderly parent,and the adult child becomes the aging parent's caregiver, the conflict is likely to surface. From this frame of reference, frustrations associated with the demands of the caretaking role are likely to agitate the dormant angry feelings of the caretaker, making maltreatment more likely, especially if violence has been used in the family as a way to settle disputes. While not discussed much in the literature, relationship history can sometimes include the elderly person's own history of alcohol or drug use. In other words, if the person had a substance abuse problem while raising children, the children might be more likely to abuse both substances and their elderly parents.

While it has not been discussed much in the literature, relationships between siblings may also play a role in reports of maltreatment. This issue centers around the type of relationship that the siblings themselves have. At an informal level, most of us understand that relationships formed in childhood tend to carry over into adulthood. The question, then, is what happens when one child gains access to an elderly person's assets. What kind of sibling rivalries ensue, and to what degree is financial exploitation the result, or the cause, of these conflicts? This is an interesting area that could benefit from some original research.

Family stress is another possible relationship issue that could be associated with elder maltreatment, even in relatively well functioning families. Suzanne Steinmetz (1988) has written a book that deals with the issue of family stress. Suggesting that stress may be associated with the inability of adult children to care for their aging parents, she notes that elderly parents often need special care at the same time their adult children are facing other stresses, such as sending their own children to college. The term *sandwich generation* is sometimes used to refer to being caught in the middle between the needs of an aging parent and those of one's own nuclear family. While at an intuitive level, the family stress theory seems a plausible way to explain some family maltreatment, other evidence we will review shortly points to single dependent caregivers as likely perpetrators rather than blended nuclear and extended families.

There are a number of other factors associated with the quality of the relationship between elderly people and those close to them. Karl Pillemer and Jill Suitor (1988), working at the Family Research Laboratory at the

University of New Hampshire, reviewed suspected relationship issues with the idea that they might help us understand how the quality of relationships influences maltreatment. The factors they reviewed, which seem to be associated with the quality of the elder and adult child relationship, include:

- The status of the elderly person's health
- The degree to which the elderly person is dependent upon the adult child
- How satisfied each is with the way the other carries out his or her family role
- Similarity in status (for example, both are mothers, and so on)

While we often think in terms of adult children who abuse their parents, as you will recall, Pillemer and Finkelhor (1988) identified spouses as perpetrators of much of the elderly abuse. Pillemer and Suitor (1988) also identified a number of spousal relationship factors that seem to be associated with whether or not maltreatment occurrs. These include:

- Overall psychological well-being
- How transitions from one status to another occur (for example, was retirement planned or sudden and involuntary)
- Level of satisfaction with how each performs family roles
- Similarity in values
- Equity and equality
- Religiosity

The factors identified above should be thought of as suspected risk factors in an area of research that is still developing, and this assumes we are thinking of the problem in terms of elder maltreatment. There is also another question that we should probably consider when looking at elder abuse perpetrated by spouses: Is this maltreatment part of a cycle of domestic violence that has persisted throughout the marriage, or is it precipitated by factors associated with one or both partners reaching seniority? The answer to this question is currently unknown, suggesting yet another area where more research is needed.

The Micro Level—
Individual and Personality Factors

There are two basic types of individual factors that are usually examined when trying to explain why elder maltreatment occurs: those associated with the maltreated elderly themselves and those associated with those who maltreat them.

One theory focuses on the level of disability of the elderly people. According to this theoretical way of looking at the problem, some elderly people suffer from severe mental and/or physical disabilities. Their caretakers may want to do the right thing by their elderly charges, and in trying to accomplish this end, may underestimate just how much will be required in order to provide adequate care. Debilitation could be caused by a number of physical and mental health problems, including **Alzheimer's disease**, a disorder of the brain that causes severe problems with memory and, often, changes in personality and behavior. For some individuals these changes can include aggressiveness and a tendency to violent acting out. Other debilitating conditions affecting elderly people include problems with hygiene, and toileting, and difficulty getting around.

One way of explaining the causes of elder maltreatment which occurs under such conditions is to resort to a theoretical framework called **exchange theory**. According to exchange theory, most of us operate in keeping with certain unwritten principles, which suggest that human relationships should be governed by a give-and-take in relationships. The unstated expectation is that there will be a balance between what one gives and what one gets back (Phillips, 1986). To take it a step further, Phillips (1986) points out that when things are not equal in some relationships, a power imbalance occurs, and the person with the power to control outcomes has little to lose by being unfair or unjust. It is easy to see how one could couple this unequal power balance with such problems as resentment about care demands, personality conflicts, or unresolved family problems and perhaps have increased risk of maltreatment. This certainly might happen in some cases; the question is, does the evidence support the idea that there is increased risk when an elderly person has severe debility? We turn to this next.

In a recent discussion of the topic, Lachs and Pillemer (1995) comment that recent studies show no evidence to support the idea that there is a cause-and-effect relationship between level of frailty, functional impairment, or excessive dependence on the caregiver and an increased risk for maltreatment. They further note that even the early work of Phillips herself, as a proponent of this theory, does not establish significant differences in maltreatment based on the level of impairment. While clear evidence is currently lacking, Lachs and Pillemer (1995) concede that the elderly person's level of functioning plays at least some role in maltreatment. They suggest that, rather than causing maltreatment, frailty probably limits the ability of elderly people to get out of the situation or to protect themselves. The final answer is not in on this issue, and Lachs and Pillemer tell us that a comprehensive longitudinal study is probably needed in order to settle it.

The only known prospective study of risk factors was recently completed (Lachs et al., 1994); in an interesting twist on the issue, it turns out that dependency may be a risk but not the way we had thought of it. It seems that it's not the dependency of the elderly person on the caregiver that is the problem, but the dependency of the supposed caregiver on the elderly person. There are now numerous studies that suggest that dysfunction and dependency on the part of the abusive caregiver is a risk factor.

Consistent with the conclusions we can draw in the domestic violence field, elder maltreatment seems to be a perpetrator-driven phenomenon. Wolf, Strugnell, and Godkin (1982) found that two-thirds of the abusers in their study were financially dependent upon the maltreated elderly person. Pillemer (1985a) compared a group of maltreated elders to a control group, and found that the abused elderly were no more ill than their non-abused counterparts. Pillemer (1985a) also found that abusive caregivers were more likely to be financially dependent upon their elderly parents than those in the non-abusive comparison group. Similar results were found in another controlled study (Hwalek, et al., 1984, as cited in Pillemer & Suitor, 1988).

To generalize a bit, a "typical" nonspouse maltreating caretaker seems to be a middle-aged individual, without stable income, who may have an alcohol or drug abuse problem. Such individuals often seem to be heavily dependent, sometimes with disabilities, and often have a hard time separating from their parents and establishing their own lives (Lachs & Pillemer, 1995; Pillemer & Suitor, 1988; Wolf, 1986). Rosalie Wolf (1986) reviews an interesting discussion (Pillemer, 1985b), which suggests that, when dependent adult children abuse their elderly parents, they may be doing so, at least in part, out of a sense of powerlessness. Pillemer (1985b, as cited in Wolf, 1986) observes that being dependent on one's parent in middle age runs contrary to society's expectations. According to this discussion, acting out violently against the elderly parent may be a way of overcoming feelings of inadequacy.

We don't want to be guilty of stereotyping or overgeneralizing about those who mistreat elderly people, yet there are a number of characteristics that seem to pop up fairly often. In addition to dependency on the elderly person, Lachs and Pillemer (1995) identify three characteristics of caregivers that are often associated with elder maltreatment:

- Mental health problems
- Substance abuse
- Violent behavior in other contexts

Pillemer (1986) comments that a disproportionately high number of abusive caregivers have histories of having been institutionalized themselves for mental health reasons. There is a substantial amount of discussion in the literature suggesting that many seem to have significant mental health issues, personality disturbances, or substance abuse problems (Fulmer & O'Malley, 1987; Pillemer & Suitor, 1988; Quinn & Tomita, 1986; Wolf, 1986; Wolf, Strugnell, & Godkin, 1982).

The last factor to be discussed is that of isolation. While I've decided to include it as an individual factor, it could also be considered a relationship issue, depending on how you look at it. As with so many factors, while we might be able to look at it individually, it is potentially interconnected with other risk factors. From a broad social level, one could argue that, because the society is ageist, the elderly tend to get left out. On the other end of the explanatory spectrum—the individual level—one could argue that severe mental or physical disability might contribute to a lack of mobility and to isolation from others. Based upon our understanding of domestic violence, we can speculate that elders who are victims of abuse at the hands of their spouses might also be isolated by them, an identified risk factor associated with domestic violence (see Chapter 7).

In the elder abuse literature, isolation is frequently cited as an important risk factor (Johnson, 1991; Lachs et al., 1994; Pillemer, 1986; Pillemer & Suitor, 1988; Wolf, 1996). Wolf (1996) indicates that it is strongly associated with both financial exploitation and neglect. We can think of social isolation as a factor that might predispose some elderly people to bring into their homes people they might not otherwise want there. We can also think of it as a consequence of the controlling behavior of abusive caregivers. Abusive individuals may drive other family and friends away from the elderly person, on purpose or indirectly. When the elderly person has a good social network, we can also think of this as a protective factor since abusers may be less likely to behave abusively if they know others will find out. When abuse has occurred, both the victim and the perpetrator may be invested in keeping it a secret. The victim may be too embarrassed to have others know they raised a child who would behave this way. Fear of being placed in a nursing home is motivation for others. And the perpetrators can be expected to want to keep it secret in order to avoid detection.

Concluding Words on Explanations and Risk Factors

We have reviewed some of the major theoretical explanations about elder abuse. There are several, but not many, such proposed theoretical explanations. Some are based on anecdotal reports and observations, some on clinical experience. There is at least one large sample survey, modeled after the National Family Violence Surveys (Pillemer & Finkelhor, 1988), which has provided some good descriptive information about the incidence of elder maltreatment as well as the characteristics of its victims and perpetrators. A number of correlational studies, some of which use comparison groups, have done a good job in exploring possible relationships between the various factors. This has made it possible to identify the factors associated with maltreatment. The kinds of studies that can tell us more about causal relationships—long term longitudinal studies and controlled prospective research—are not yet common in the literature.

While the body of research in the field of elder maltreatment is not as well developed as in other speciality areas, the field does seem to be developing some fairly good tentative ideas about causes and risk factors, though a number of questions remain unanswered. The only prospective study I'm aware of at this writing was done recently by Dr. Mark Lachs and his colleagues (Lachs et al., 1994). Based on a sample of approximately 2,800 elderly people, they were able to do a prospective, forward-looking study to evaluate a group of suspected risk factors. This study had the advantage of a large cohort, making it possible to compare cases involving maltreatment with a comparison group. It identifies four factors as being positively associated with domestic elder maltreatment: (1) functional disability, (2) being a member of a minority racial group, (3) older age, and (4) poor social networks. This and other studies that attempt to test ideas about causes and risk factors seem to be the kind of efforts on which to build a greater understanding of this issue, yet they also need to be replicated.

It's probably safe to say that we have some ideas about how elder maltreatment operates, including a fair idea about a number of tentative risk factors. We don't yet understand all the ins and outs of how these risk factors operate, however. If functional impairment is a risk factor, for example, we don't know what kind of abuse is likely to result. Why does abuse occur in such cases? Is isolation merely a "marker" that follows maltreatment or is there something about isolation that puts the elderly person at risk? If intergenerational transmission operates in elder abuse (which still is not clear), how does it work? Under what circumstances? How do we explain it when one or more risk factors are present but there is no maltreatment? As in child abuse and domestic violence, does an aggregation of risk factors result in an increased likelihood of maltreatment? If so, how many and which ones? These and other similar questions remain, and they can probably best be answered by further, well-designed longitudinal studies, controlled research, and prospective studies that build on, and even challenge, the work that has already been completed. As seems to be the case in the areas of child maltreatment and domestic violence, we may well find an interconnected web of factors, each of which plays some part in the overall phenomenon.

EFFORTS TO DEAL WITH ELDER MALTREATMENT

While it is important to understand whatever problem we are trying to deal with, doing something about the problem usually can't wait until all the research is in. In an attempt to tackle elder maltreatment, a number of efforts have already been initiated. In this section, we'll look at some of those endeavors.

Federal Initiatives

Until federal legislation was enacted in the 1970s that made child abuse a priority (see Chapter 2), state efforts were inconsistent and unfocused. A similar phenomenon has probably occurred in the area of elder abuse. There have been two significant federal programs that have played a role: Title XX of the Social Security Act and Title VII of the Older Americans Act. Title XX of the Social Security Act, enacted by Congress in 1975, was designed to strengthen state social service programs, including those for the elderly. A stipulation to the states receiving these funds included compliance with a requirement that they provide protective services to children, the elderly, and disabled adults (Mixson, 1996). While no funding was provided under Title XX to implement these new initiatives, the states began to develop legislation on elder abuse intervention, including mandatory reporting laws, in anticipation of regulation (Mixson, 1996). Prior to 1980, only 16 states had such legislation (Landes et al., 1993), yet by 1992, 42 states had mandatory reporting laws (Tatara & Blumerman, 1996c).

The Older Americans Act was initially passed in 1965 and has been reauthorized several times since. It established the Administration on Aging, now housed in the U. S. Department of Health and Human Services. It also established State Units on Aging, at the state level, as well as what are called Area Agencies on Aging. There are 57 state units (territories and District of Columbia are included) and approximately 660 area agencies (Administration on Aging, 1996c). The state units are often designated existing state human service agencies. Area agencies on aging vary; sometimes they are part of local governmental bodies and at other times they are independent bodies with their own boards and organizational structures. They try to coordinate services in their area, sometimes actually providing services.

In addition to coordinating with the state and area agencies, the Administration on Aging provides advocacy and serves as a federal point of contact. Some of the work of this office also involves research and education. One of the most visible results of this activity is creation of the National Center on Elder Abuse (NCEA) through the awarding of a grant to the American Public Welfare Association (APWA) (Tatara, 1996). The NCEA is operated by a consortium of the APWA—the National Association of State Units on Aging, the University of Delaware, and the National Committee for the Prevention of Elder Abuse (Tatara, 1996). NCEA operates the Clearinghouse on the Abuse and Neglect of the Elderly, develops and disseminates reports, and participates in a variety of professional activities, such as national conferences, training efforts, and workshops (Tatara, 1996). One of its most important current activities is the completion of a full-fledged national incidence study on elder maltreatment.

It's one thing to enact legislation, and it's another to provide the money in order to implement it. Federal support did not come until 1987, when Congress authorized $5 million for the program (Mixson, 1996). It was not actually funded, however, until 1991, when $2.9 million was allocated (Mixson, 1996). In 1992, Title VII, Chapter 3, which deals with elder maltreatment prevention, was added to the Older Americans Act. From 1992 to the time of this writing, about $4.5 million has been allocated to the states each year for elder abuse prevention (Administration on Aging, 1996b). Approximately the same amount is allocated to support the Long-Term Care Ombudsman Program (Administration on Aging, 1996b). Just to give you an idea about how small this amount really is, if the combined elder abuse prevention and ombudsman dollars are divided evenly among each of the State Units on Aging (and if territories and other jurisdictions are excluded), it works out to slightly less than $160,000 per year. Even as small as this amount appears to be, at this writing the 104th Congress was discussing the elimination of Title VII. Should this occur, the future of federal participation in prevention efforts would be uncertain (Mixson, 1996).

State and Local Efforts

While the federal funding of programs for elder maltreatment prevention and intervention is limited, two distinct prevention and intervention activities have sprung from these federal efforts. The first of these is often referred to as **adult protective services.** The other is the **Long-Term Care Ombudsman Program,** under which each state has a long-term care ombudsman who is in charge of both paid and volunteer ombudsmen at the county and local levels. A chief distinction between the jurisdiction of adult protective services (APS) and the ombudsman program is defined by whether the maltreatment occurs at home or in an institution. Allegations of abuse or neglect that occur in the home (domestic maltreatment) are usually investigated by adult protective services, while alleged maltreatment that occurs in a facility or professional adult care home (institutional maltreatment) is generally the responsibility of the long-term care ombudsman.

Intervention with Domestic Maltreatment

There are no specific federal standards and no real consistency among states in terms of how they run their adult protective services programs (Mixson, 1996). Most states investigate all referrals of elder maltreatment and will generally investigate cases of self-neglect. While self-neglect is not usually what most people think of when we talk about elder maltreatment, a study by the National Association of Adult Protective Services Administrators (Duke, 1996) and anecdotal reports of APS workers suggest that it makes up the vast majority of reported cases.

Once APS receives a case, most agencies will send a social worker out to investigate the allegations and determine the degree of intervention needed to protect the older person. Adult protective services is a completely voluntary program in most jurisdictions. This means that a competent elderly person cannot be compelled to cooperate with the investigation or to agree to the recommendations of the investigating social worker. There are a number of reasons why an elderly person might not cooperate with the investigation. First of all, as discussed earlier, elderly persons may be afraid that if the true extent of the problem were known, they might be placed in a nursing home and thereby lose their independence. Another possible reason is cultural in nature. As one professional in the field related to me, "Many members of the current generation of elderly people are of a generation that doesn't like to admit to "weakness" or the need for outside help." When the maltreatment does involve a family member or other caregiver, the elderly person may also be afraid of retribution of various kinds. According to one APS worker, some perpetrators are very blatant in telling the victim what they will do if the elderly person complains. In addition, some elderly people may genuinely think they are responsible for the problem and may not want to get the care provider in trouble.

Once a case is identified, assessment usually takes place. There can be a great deal of variability in how an assessment is done unless standardized *protocols,* or sets of procedure, are used. While assessments are often quite variable, there are some standardized guidelines that can assist human service workers with this task (Johnson, 1991; Quinn & Tomita, 1986; Epstein, et al., 1996). One such protocol is available on-line through the Internet. Adapted for use in a major medical center, this protocol was developed at a major school of social work (Epstein et al., 1996). It outlines some specific steps, which include doing a complete review of the patient's chart, consulting with medical staff, interviewing the patient, and taking a history. In addition to a review of basic interviewing strategies (including contacting other family, friends, and neighbors, with consent), the protocol identifies some specific signs and symptoms of maltreatment (see the discussion of indicators earlier in this chapter), outlines how to do a functional assessment, lists suggested interview topics and questions, and provides a format for developing a social work intervention plan and outcome goals.

Once an assessment has been completed and maltreatment is identified, intervention is the next logical step. Intervention, even when maltreatment can be substantiated, varies according to a number of factors. Each case is different and individual. Adult Protective Services workers have less authority to intervene than do Child Protective Services workers. Without evidence to the contrary, APS workers have to assume they are dealing with adults who are able to reason and make decisions for themselves. In addition, the APS worker has fewer tools with which to intervene. A CPS worker can peremptorily remove a child from a home if he or she believes the child to be in danger, pending a court hearing. Adult Protective Services workers have no such authority. There is no separate court system set up to handle allegations of elder maltreatment as there is in the child abuse field. If an elderly person refuses to cooperate with the APS worker, the worker has little recourse but to allow the person to make this choice.

Intervention in cases of financial exploitation can often be difficult. Such exploitation can occur without the knowledge of the elderly person, who is often very trusting of the exploiter. Sometimes this person is a family member, but it can also be an outsider who has gained the elderly person's trust. These are often difficult cases to detect, since a person's finances are generally a private matter. Interestingly, bank tellers are becoming increasingly savvy about the financial exploitation of the elderly, and often initiate action. An observant teller can contact both police, in the case of non–family member exploitation, and adult protective services. There is one aspect of this form of maltreatment that makes it very difficult and discouraging. As one worker put it, "By the time you identify what's happening the money's all gone, and there's rarely anything you can do about it." Rather than doing the work on the back end, we might be able to prevent this sort of problem by earlier identification. Another approach that is now appearing on the scene is to provide bill-paying services and financial management programs for the elderly at reputable community agencies.

Local Adult Protective Services help at-risk elderly people stay in their own homes whenever possible.

The emphasis now in adult protective services seems to be on assisting the elderly person to be as independent as possible. This includes doing whatever is necessary to help the person remain in his or her own home. This approach of providing services in the **least restrictive** way possible is also being used because adult protective services has limited authority to intervene against the will of the older person. While they don't have lots of authority, however, they often have a number of resources they can use to help. In many jurisdictions, chief among these are home assistance services. These services can include assistance with cooking, cleaning, eating, getting to the store, and any number of other tasks that can help the elderly person in their efforts to remain independent. Sometimes adult protective services can also access home health services for elderly people who are medically fragile. Adult day care programs, which provide a range of support and structured activities, are another example of a service that might be available. Such programs can often provide a break for stressed caregivers. Residential respite care may make it possible for caregivers to take a break from time to time (for example, go on vacation), so that they can continue to provide long-term care. Another popular service that APS workers can sometimes access is meals delivered directly to the elderly person's home, often called "meals-on-wheels."

While adult protective services attempts to broker whatever services are needed to keep elderly persons in their own homes, these services, depending upon the state or jurisdiction, will usually not be paid for if the elderly person has the financial resources to pay for them. Often persons are not eligible to have these services funded if they have more than a few thousand dollars in savings. One way to meet this requirement, depending on the jurisdiction, is for the elderly person to transfer cash resources to a spouse. (Transfers made to nonspouses sometimes make the person automatically ineligible for funding.) Unfortunately, this makes the elderly person vulnerable to yet another form of exploitation. Once this has been done, the person no longer has control over these funds, and there is nothing that can legally prevent the spouse from taking the money and leaving the dependent elderly person.

At the present time intervention is primarily aimed at assisting and supporting the elderly person, but workers can sometimes function as brokers or intermediaries to help get services for the suspected abusive person as well. These could include referral to a substance abuse treatment program, employment services, transportation, counseling, or educational services to help the abusive caregiver better understand the abilities and limitations of the older person. However, funding is often difficult to get for intervention with the suspected perpetrator of maltreatment, since it isn't direct assistance for the elderly person.

One model intervention program for assisting elderly persons at risk, called the Gatekeeper Program, not only does early identification but follow-up treatment as well (Raschko, 1990; R. Raschko, personal communication, July 19, 1996). It has gotten a fair amount of both national and local attention (see Box 8-2 for a brief description). Programs like Gatekeeper are aimed more toward clients who have become debilitated and who neglect themselves, and as we've already discussed, this seems to be the most common type of case that adult protective services deals with.

When Maltreatment Is
Defined as Domestic Violence

As you recall, some of the earliest research done with large representative samples has been able to determine that a great deal of elder maltreatment is perpetrated by a spouse (Pillemer & Finkelhor, 1988, 1989). This puts the abused person in a difficult situation. Domestic violence programs for victims, especially shelters, seem intended for younger women and don't seem equipped to handle the needs of the elderly. Adult protective services is a completely voluntary program, and, especially if the abuse is of a long-standing nature, APS workers may have a great deal of difficulty doing anything about the abusive spouse. This just goes to show how difficult it can become when dealing with those cases that don't fit clearly into either the elder maltreatment or the domestic violence category. Regardless of whether the alleged primary aggressor is a spouse or an adult child, however, when violence is involved, the case can often be treated as any other case of domestic violence.

Many states are enacting legislation that defines domestic violence as any physical abuse that occurs by *any* person related by blood or role to the maltreated person. When such is the case, laws designed to intervene with domestic violence perpetrators can be used with perpetrators of elder maltreatment, especially in cases of physical abuse. As discussed in Chapter 7, this can include long-term programs that put perpetrators in the position of

BOX 8-2   The Gatekeeper Program:
Outreach and Support for At-Risk Elderly

The Gatekeeper Program represents a new way to reach out to elderly people who are at risk for serious problems. Its goal is to do whatever it can to make it possible for the elderly person to remain independent. It had its beginnings in Spokane, Washington, as the brainchild of clinical social worker Ray Raschko, who is the current director of elder services for Spokane Community Mental Health Center. Since then, the program has been adopted in a number of places around the country. It uses people who come in contact with elderly people as part of their daily activities (bank tellers, people who work in telephone company credit departments, meter readers, property tax appraisers, apartment managers, pharmacists, and law enforcement officers) to look out for warning signs that might mean an elderly person is in trouble. Once they identify an at-risk elderly person, they call in a referral to the program. Sometimes an elderly person gets the attention of one of the volunteers when the person hasn't picked up mail, or when a good customer stops paying the utility bill, or maybe hasn't bought heating fuel for the winter.

The program is usually able to quickly send out a team to determine if the elderly person is okay. There are examples of the team finding the elderly person helpless after falling and breaking a hip. At other times, elderly persons wave the team away, saying they don't want help. The team will make another call later to try to earn the trust of the elderly person.

Clients often suffer from dementia (a disorder associated with brain degeneration), Alzheimer's disease, depression, substance abuse problems, and a range of other mental health concerns. The program in Spokane has teams of professionals who are multidisciplinary. They often include a case manager, nurse, psychiatrist, and primary care physician. Many on the teams are qualified to provide substance abuse counseling.

The program goal is to provide enough support so that elderly persons can remain in their own homes, but be reasonably safe. In order to do this, individual needs require careful attention. Some clients can have significant impairment yet may be unwilling to accept placement in a residential facility. The program tries to help the person with those things that will make it possible to remain at home. Coordination, or case management, typically includes nutrition, medication, self-care, assistance with paying bills, transportation, contact with family and friends, and any number of other things.

having to look at and stop their abusive behavior. In severe domestic violence cases, some jurisdictions, such as San Diego County, will prosecute with or without the willing cooperation of the victim of abuse. In addition to mandatory treatment and jail time, judges often have fairly wide discretion to impose conditions of probation, including staying away from the maltreated person. Another legal option available to elderly people in many jurisdictions is the order of protection, sometimes called a restraining order. This can be served on perpetrators, requiring them to stay away from the victim (though compliance is often problematic).

Involuntary Services—Conservatorship and Involuntary Commitment

If APS workers believe that certain elderly persons are unable to make reasoned decisions for themselves, they can use civil legal proceedings to pursue a guardianship or conservatorship to oversee the elderly person's affairs. The term used varies from state to state. If elderly persons are found to be incompetent to handle their own affairs, their civil rights, including the right to manage their own affairs, can be taken away from them. A disinterested third person, sometimes called a **guardian ad litem**, is often appointed to watch out for the best interests of the person and to make a report to the court. Once the person is found to be incompetent, a guardian or conservator is generally appointed by the court, and this person will be entrusted with the authority to manage the older person's affairs. The decisions the guardian or conservator could make include evicting an abusive caregiver or placing the elderly person in an out-of-home placement.

States also have procedures for the involuntary commitment of persons believed to be mentally ill *and* a danger to self or others; often this can include being gravely disabled, which might be consistent with definitions of self-neglect. Dementia, or brain impairment, caused by old age is generally not in itself considered a mental illness for this purpose, but standards vary from state to state. A number of other serious debilitating mental health conditions, such as severe depression, often afflict elderly people, and can sometimes justify mental health treatment, including placing an elderly person in an inpatient psychiatric facility. When this occurs, the legal proceedings are governed by strict judicial standards. In such proceedings it is necessary to establish both that a mental disorder exists and that there is a danger to self or others. Legal representation for the person is required, and due process procedures must be followed to ensure that the person's rights are protected.

Intervention with Institutional Maltreatment

In addition to raising fears and concerns of elderly people, the subject of abuse and neglect in nursing homes has also received considerable attention from the general public and the media (Pillemer & Bachman-Prehn, 1991). The public perception is that nursing home abuse is a problem. In an article about finding good nursing homes, one review reports on a series of articles about nursing homes that appeared in *Consumer Reports*, noting that many facilities may be providing a poor quality of care (Administration on Aging, 1996d). To a certain degree, these observations are borne out by the professional literature (see Pillemer & Bachman-Prehn, 1991). In their research on the subject, Karl Pillemer and Ronet Bachman-Prehn (1991) found that 10% of nursing home staff admitted to having committed one or more physically aggressive acts on their elderly clients, the most common form being excessive restraint. In the same study, 40% of the staff who responded indicated having committed at least one act that could be construed as psychological maltreatment during the previous year. The most commonly reported form of psychologically aggressive behavior was yelling at a patient.

Based on this recent work, we can be fairly certain that aggressive behavior by staff in nursing homes is often a problem. Before we can talk about specific strategies for dealing with nursing home maltreatment, however, we probably need to talk briefly about why it happens. The dynamics may be somewhat different from those we've already discussed for domestic abuse. Based on their review of the literature, Pillemer and Bachman-Prehn (1991) have identified three kinds of predictors for nursing home maltreatment: (1) facility characteristics, (2) staff characteristics, and (3) situational characteristics. The facility characteristics that Pillemer and Bachman-Prehn chose to look at included the size of the facility (that is, number of beds), whether it was operated as a profit-making business or as a nonprofit, and the rates charged (higher rates being associated with better funding and better care). The staff characteristics they looked at included educational level, age, occupational position (that is, nursing aide versus professional nurse), and amount of experience working with the aged. The situational characteristics Pillemer and Bachman-Prehn explored included levels of job stress and burnout, amount of conflict between patients and caregivers, and patient aggressiveness. The results of their study (1991) suggest that maltreatment in nursing homes is more likely to happen when staff members are burned out and are experiencing aggression from patients. They further suggest that low pay, low prestige, and the physically taxing nature of the work all contribute to the problem.

Long-term care ombudsmen who investigate institutional abuse are limited in their ability to intervene. While their position was created as a result of federal legislation, and while the states receive some funding to support their programs, the ombudsmen have virtually no legal authority to compel residential facilities to do anything. One of the things they can do is work with the elderly person and the facility to try to resolve problems. A recent report on the effectiveness of the Long-Term Care Ombudsman Program notes the limitations imposed on the program but also points out the significant contributions it has made to the prevention of institutional elder maltreatment (National Academy of Science, Institute of Medicine, 1995).

In addition to mediating complaints, perhaps one of the best services ombudsmen provide is to attend to complaints and make appropriate referrals to other individuals or agencies that might have the legal authority to take more decisive steps with residential facilities. Depending upon the location, this can be the state, county, or local licensing authority, health agency, or social service agency. Criminal behavior by a staff member can be referred to law enforcement for prosecution.

A referral to law enforcement or the licensing agency is always an option when the health and well-being of elderly patients is at stake, especially when the violations are blatant. Many violations are probably not sufficiently blatant to result in legal sanctions, however. As you can see from the discussion about risk factors, the likelihood of maltreatment is greater when the staff is overworked, underpaid, and unappreciated, and when the population is difficult. While, as a society, we seem to react when conditions get out of control, a more proactive approach to addressing the problem might prove more successful. Proactive strategies might include an increased emphasis on professional development by providing more staff training opportunities. One of the goals of such training would be to improve the quality of care and reduce maltreatment. This might be done by providing the staff with more information about the causes of behavior problems of elderly patients, positive approaches to managing behavior, strategies for self-care, and team-building efforts. While training staff members to take better care of themselves and their patients is one approach to improving care, we should probably also recognize that we may need to reassess the wages we pay caregivers and the amount of respect we pay them for doing a difficult job.

CHAPTER SUMMARY

In this chapter we surveyed the issue of elder maltreatment—an issue that has arrived late on the scene in terms of public awareness and concern. While conservative estimates suggest that between 500,000 and 1 million elderly people are maltreated each year, nearly as many as children, the issue simply has not attracted as much public attention as other family abuse issues. In trying to get a sense of the issue, we began with a discussion of the historical context, noting that, while we may imagine that in times past families cared for themselves, the reality seems to be that neglect, abandonment, and abuse of the elderly is not a new thing. When changes in economic conditions have resulted in social upheaval, the elderly have been vulnerable. Our own welfare system can trace its roots to efforts to curb this tide. Institutions such as poorhouses, almshouses, and workhouses developed in England and became part of our own social welfare system. Nursing homes may be the modern-day successor in this tradition—places elderly people almost always want to avoid.

We noted that elder maltreatment is a complex phenomenon and that it has many forms. We reviewed three basic categories—domestic maltreatment, institutional maltreatment, and self-neglect. We also reviewed a number of specific types such as physical abuse, sexual abuse, psychological maltreatment, neglect, financial exploitation, abandonment, and violation of basic human rights. In the area of neglect, we noted that it is often classified as either intentional or unintentional. We briefly discussed the kind of data we have about maltreatment and reviewed what we know about incidence and prevalence rates. As a result of this, we noted that there may be some fuzzy boundaries, since the only large sample survey indicates a great deal of abuse by spouses. Whether to call this form of abuse elder maltreatment or domestic violence is a question. We discussed some general indicators of maltreatment but cautioned about interpreting these indicators too quickly.

We noted that there isn't much written in the literature about the impact of maltreatment, and we discussed this topic in general and speculated on some possibilities.

When we got to the subject of explaining why maltreatment occurs, we reviewed the five dominant theories in the field. We framed our discussion within the macro-meso-micro framework we have adopted throughout the text; noting the relative poverty of theory compared to other areas, we included additional possibilities. Within this context, we first explored broad social and cultural factors (macro level), including ageism. Although we lack good information about cultural issues, we noted a paradox: recent research tells us that being a member of a minority racial group increases the risk of elder maltreatment, yet anecdotal reports from the field tell us that racial minority communities may do a better job of caring for their seniors. We explored ways to understand and resolve these disparate reports. In terms of relationships—the meso level—we discussed intergenerational transmission theory as applied to elder abuse, as well as other suspected family dynamics. At the individual, micro, level we looked at factors associated with both the elderly person and others.

In the final section of the chapter, we reviewed intervention efforts. Included here was a discussion of federal initiatives, including Title XX of the Social Security Act, and the Older Americans Act. We briefly discussed the role of the Administration on Aging and the creation of the National Center on Elder Abuse (NCEA). We noted that the NCEA operates a clearinghouse on information and helps coordinate a number of federal and state activities, including data collection on reports of domestic elder maltreatment. As part of the Older Americans Act, we also reviewed the role and functions of the Long-Term Care Ombudsman Program in preventing and investigating institutional maltreatment. We distinguished between the activities of adult protective services and the long-term care ombudsman. We reviewed current philosophies of intervention, including an emphasis on helping elderly people remain as independent as possible. We highlighted one innovative program, the Gatekeeper Program, which uses community volunteers to identify seniors who are at risk. In addition to reviewing these efforts, we also discussed intervention that is possible when elder maltreatment is thought of as domestic violence. We also surveyed the use of guardianship or conservatorship proceedings in cases when elderly persons can no longer make reasoned decisions about their own care.

LEGAL AND ETHICAL CONCERNS: CRITICAL THINKING QUESTIONS

1. As we now know from the best available research, many perpetrators of violence against the elderly are themselves elderly, most often the spouse. Should these cases be handled as elder abuse or domestic violence? Please support your position.

2. When the elderly are restricted from doing the things they want, this is sometimes thought of as a violation of their basic rights. When is it

appropriate to prevent an elderly person from engaging in some activity and when is it a violation of their basic human rights?

3. While we might become aware of indicators of abuse, the elderly person may deny them or refuse to cooperate in an investigation of maltreatment. Should we try to compel the elderly person to cooperate? Why or why not? How can this be justified?

4. Because of public concern about child abuse and domestic violence, many more dollars and resources seem to be put into these issues than into elder maltreatment. Is this justified? Do the citizens of the United States have a moral obligation to do a better job of funding research and programs to help prevent abuse? Why or why not?

5. Some elderly people live with a caregiver who maltreats them, yet they refuse to ask the person to leave. Should we ever be allowed to compel this person to leave?

6. Some severely debilitated elderly people continue to live on their own and neglect themselves. If the elderly person refuses to consider a nursing home placement, when, if ever, should we take steps to do it anyway?

7. When an elderly person is no longer competent to make reasoned choices, guardianship or conservatorship proceedings can be started so a guardian can be appointed. One of the reasons we might want to appoint a guardian is to prevent financial exploitation, yet there are no clear-cut standards about the behavior of guardians. What, if anything, should be done about this?

8. Both domestic and institutional elder maltreatment exist. When we move elderly persons from their own homes because of neglect, when is it justified, if ever, to place them in a nursing home where they may also be at risk?

9. Staff members in nursing homes are underpaid, undervalued, and stressed. Do we share some of the responsibility when they become aggressive with elderly patients? Why or why not?

SUGGESTED ACTIVITIES

1. Contact your local or county long-term care ombudsman. Find out about some of the nursing homes in your area. Are there any that are considered particularly good? Get as much information from the ombudsman as possible. If you can't find the number, try stopping by a nursing home and look for a poster with the phone number.

2. Contact adult protective services in your area and find out what kind of cases they are getting, what they are able to offer clients, and how they intervene. What do they do when they encounter persons who neglect themselves and don't seem able to make reasoned decisions? What do they do if the person seems mentally ill?

3. Contact elder services at your community mental health center and find out if they have any programs like the Gatekeeper Program. If they do,

get whatever information they have and interview someone with the program. Prepare a presentation and deliver it to your class. Would being a Gatekeeper volunteer be something you'd want to do?

4.   Contact a local nursing home and find out what volunteer opportunities they have. Ask if you can spend a day observing. Keep a log of your observations and prepare a short paper about your experiences.

REVIEW GUIDE

1.   Be fully familiar with the historical context of elder maltreatment, as outlined in this chapter:

- Medical and income security
- Conditions during the depression
- Shifts from rural to urban living
- Feudal society and its breakdown
- Poor Law of 1601 and Settlement Act of 1668
- Creation of institutions such as poorhouses

2.   Be familiar with all definitions of elder maltreatment:

- Domestic elder abuse
- Institutional elder abuse
- Self-neglect
- Physical abuse
- Sexual abuse
- Emotional or psychological maltreatment
- Intentional neglect (active neglect)
- Unintentional neglect (passive neglect)

3.   Be familiar with the statistics related to both domestic and institutional abuse. Be familiar with the Pillemer and Finkelhor (1988) study as well as the two counterpart studies in Great Britain and Canada. What are the differences between official reports and survey data? What kind of abuse, and how much, is reflected in each kind of data? How can we explain or reconcile differences in the data?

4.   Be familiar with indicators for each type of maltreatment.

5.   Be conversant with the discussion about the impact of elder maltreatment.

- What is the difference in professional interest between elder maltreatment and other forms of abuse?
- What are some possible explanations for this, as discussed in the text?
- What factors are associated with maltreatment generally?
- What stage does Erikson propose that elderly people are in?
- What factors do we think mediate the effects of abuse? Be able to discuss each.

6.   Be familiar with the macro, meso, and micro explanations and risk factors.

- Be fully familiar with the five main theories that have been used to explain elder maltreatment.
- Be especially able to discuss ageism and its impact.
- Be able to discuss the role of culture in elder maltreatment.
- Be fully familiar with how intergenerational transmission applies, or doesn't apply, to elder maltreatment. In this context be able to discuss role inversion. Be familiar with the results of Widom's work (1989). Be able to distinguish between increased risk and the actual proportion of abused people who become abusive.
- Be familiar with the risk factors identified by Pillemer and Suitor (1988). Be sure to know both those associated with elder spousal violence and those perpetrated by adult children.
- Be familiar with exchange theory explanations of elder maltreatment.
- Be familiar with the results of the one long-range prospective study that was completed by Lachs and Pillemer (1995). Be sure to know the three characteristics of caregivers that they associate with elder maltreatment.
- Be able to discuss isolation as a risk factor.

7. Be fully familiar with federal initiatives to deal with elder maltreatment:

- Title XX of the Social Security Act
- Title VII of the Older Americans Act
- Long-Term Care Ombudsman Program
- Administration on Aging
- Creation of the National Center on Elder Abuse (NCEA)
- State and Area Agencies on Aging

8. Be fully familiar with the following:

- Adult protective services (APS)
- Local long-term care ombudsmen
- Components of the outlined assessment protocol
- Ability, and limitations, of APS to act
- Least restrictive policy
- The Gatekeeper Program
- Steps that can sometimes be taken when elder maltreatment is defined as domestic violence
- Guardianship or conservatorship
- Involuntary mental health institutionalization
- Steps that can be taken with nursing homes and other residential placements.
- Risk factors associated with institutional maltreatment
- Powers of ombudsmen compared to licensing authority

SUGGESTED READING

Administration on Aging. (1996). *Aging*, Number 367. Washington, DC: Administration on Aging, Department of Health and Human Services. Available from the U.S. Government Printing Office.

This special, and final, issue of Aging is devoted to the issue of elder abuse. This is a well-done magazine, written in a popular style. It is a wonderful resource for anyone wanting to know more about elder abuse. Due to government cutbacks, the magazine will no longer be published. Free copies are no longer available but a limited number of copies are still available from the Government Printing Office for $2.50 each.

Epstein, M., Estacio-Decker, J., Krajewski, J., & Schellie, K. (1996). Social work department standard of practice. School of Social Work, University of Washington. [On-line]. Available: http://weber.u.washington.edu/-uwmcsw/eldsop.htm.

If you have a computer and access to the Internet, this is a very nice assessment protocol. Originally developed for use by social workers at a major teaching hospital, it is easily adapted to other settings. It includes both basic considerations as well as sophisticated points that should be explored when trying to determine if an elderly person is being maltreated or the degree to which an elderly person may be at risk. It can be easily downloaded or printed.

Quinn, M. J., & Tomita, S. K. (1986). *Elder abuse and neglect: Causes, diagnosis, and intervention strategies.* New York: Springer Publishing.

This book is a bright spot in an emerging field that has many technical books and journal articles, but no real textbooks. It is designed to familiarize and help individuals interested in joining the ranks of those who want to do something about elder maltreatment. It is a real resource for those who need to learn how to assess and treat the problem. It also contains a nice section about how to do this kind of work without burning out.

A RESOURCE

Those interested in replicating the Gatekeeper Program in their own communities may contact: Ray Raschko, M.S.W., Elder Services, Spokane Community Mental Health Center, 5125 N. Market, Spokane, WA 99207. Phone: (509) 458-7450. Videos and training manuals are available to a limited number of eligible agencies.

CHAPTER GLOSSARY

Active neglect	See intentional neglect.
Adult protective services	A local or state agency charged with the responsibility of investigating and intervening when the elderly or disabled have been abused or neglected or are at risk.
Ageism	Societal negative attitudes and prejudices about the elderly.
Alzheimer's disease	A disorder more common with advancing age, in which the person experiences mental deterioration, especially loss of memory. Progressive in nature. The person can become so debilitated that it can be very difficult to care for the person at home.

Community ageism	A form of ageism characterized by discriminatory practices of communities, whereby services and programs are disproportionately provided for younger populations.
Domestic elder abuse	A form of abuse of the elderly that usually takes place either in the person's own home or the home of a volunteer caregiver.
Emotional or psychological abuse	A form of elder maltreatment that can cause emotional or psychological anguish or the risk of it.
Exchange theory	A theory that, when used to explain elder maltreatment, proposes that maltreatment is more likely to result when caregivers begin to feel resentment about the lack of reciprocity in their relationship with the elderly person.
Financial or material exploitation	Using a relationship of trust or trickery in order to deprive an elderly person of their resources. Some propose that the elderly are especially vulnerable because of loneliness and isolation.
Guardian ad litem	In cases involving the elderly, a person appointed by the court, often an attorney, to look after the best interests of an elderly person who is the subject of a guardianship or conservatorship proceeding.
Institutional elder abuse	A form of abuse of the elderly that takes place in a nursing home or other out-of-home placement by professional or volunteer staff.
Intentional neglect	Willful withholding of things needed by the elderly person in order to control or punish the person.
Intergenerational transmission	A theory that attempts to explain maltreatment as behavior that is learned because of one's own experience of seeing it or being subject to it. Originally developed in the child abuse field, it proposes that children who have been victimized will be more likely to victimize their own children. In elder abuse the concept of role inversion is necessary in order for the explanation to be consistent.
Least restrictive	A philosophy that asserts that services should be provided in the most natural surroundings possible; in the case of the elderly, in their own homes if feasible.
Long-term Care Ombudsman Program	An office established as part of an amendment to the Older Americans Act. Each state has an ombudsman who is responsible for investigating complaints about poor care in nursing homes and other residential facilities. County and local ombudsmen are also often appointed.
National Center on Elder Abuse	An agency established with a grant from the Administration on Aging and coordinated by a consortium of other entities: the American Public Welfare Association, the National Association of State Units on Aging, the University of Delaware, and the National Committee for the Prevention of Elder Abuse. Performs various coordination functions and operates a clearinghouse of information on elder maltreatment. Involved in a national incidence study of elder maltreatment.
Neglect	Failure to provide for the necessities of life by a person who has the responsibility to so provide.
Passive neglect	See unintentional neglect.
Physical abuse	In the case of elder maltreatment, the intentional infliction of physical pain or injury, or the risk of same, in order to coerce or control.
Professional ageism	A paternalistic set of attitudes about the elderly, held by professionals, in which the desires of the professional often supplant the wants and needs of the elderly person.

Self-neglect
A term used to describe neglect of one's own needs and putting oneself at risk when responsible for one's own care.

Sexual abuse
Any kind of sexual contact with an elderly person when the person cannot or does not consent.

Societal ageism
A set of negative or stereotypical attitudes about the elderly that permeates the society. Often reflected in official policies that either ignore their needs or restrict their full participation in the society.

Unintentional neglect
The nondeliberate, nonplanned disregard of an elderly person's needs by a person who has a responsibility to ensure they are met.

Violation of basic human rights
In the context of elder maltreatment, the disregard for the person's free exercise of his or her rights, by virtue of status as an elderly person or resident of a given facility.

REFERENCES

Administration on Aging. (1996a). *Aging,* Number 367. Washington, DC: Administration on Aging, Department of Health and Human Services.

Administration on Aging. (1996b). Title VII—vulnerable elder rights protection activities. [On-line]. http://www.aoa.dhhs.gov/aoa/pages/titlevii.html.

Administration on Aging. (1996c). The administration on aging and Older Americans Act. [On-line]. http://www.aoa.dhhs.gov/aoa/pages/aoafact.html.

Administration on Aging. (1996d). Are good nursing homes hard to find? *Aging,* Number 367. Washington, DC: Administration on Aging, Department of Health and Human Services.

Allen, D. M., & Tarnowski, K. J. (1989). Depressive characteristics of physically abused children. Journal of Abnormal Child Psychology, 17, 1–11.

Altemeier, W., O'Connor, S., Vietze, P., Sandler, H., and Sherrod, K. (1984). Prediction of child abuse: A prospective study of feasibility. *Child Abuse & Neglect,* 8, 393–400.

American Humane Association. (1989). *Highlights of official aggregate child neglect and abuse reporting.* Denver, CO: American Humane Association.

American Professional Society on the Abuse of Children. (1990). *Guidelines for psychosocial evaluation of suspected sexual abuse in young children.* Chicago: Author.

American Professional Society on the Abuse of Children. (1995a). *Practice guidelines: Use of anatomical dolls in child sexual abuse assessments.* Chicago: Author.

American Professional Society on the Abuse of Children. (1995b). *The APSAC Advisor, 8* (4).

American Psychiatric Association. (1994). *Diagnostic & statistical manual of mental disorders, 4th Edition.* Washington, DC: Author.

American Psychological Association. (1996). *PsychLit database on CD-ROM,* a derivative of PsychInfo.

Anton, J., & Fortune, M. M. (Exec. Producers), and Garguilo, M. (Writer-Director). (1994). *Broken vows: Religious perspectives on domestic violence.* [Videotape]. (Available from Center for the Prevention of Sexual and Domestic Violence, 1914 North 34th Street, Suite 105, Seattle, WA 98103-9058. Phone: (206) 634-1903.)

Araji, S., & Finkelhor, D. (1986). Abusers: a review of the research. In D. Finkelhor, S. Araji, L. Baron, A. Browne, S. D. Peters, & G. E. Wyatt (Eds.), *A sourcebook on child sexual abuse.* Newbury Park, CA: Sage Publications.

Asher, R. (1951). Munchausen Syndrome. *Lancet, 1,* 339–341.

Asher, S. J. (1988). The effects of childhood sexual abuse and of issues and evidence. In L. Walker (Ed.),

Handbook on sexual abuse of children, assessment and treatment issues. New York: Springer Publishing.

Associated Press, 1997. *Houston Cronicle,* June 24.

Bandura, A. (1973). *Aggression: A social learning perspective.* Englewood Cliffs, NJ: Prentice Hall.

Bandura, A., & Walters, R. H. (1963). *Social learning and personality development.* New York: Holt, Rinehart and Winston.

Barbaree, H. E., Hudson, S. M., & Seto, M. C. (1993). Sexual assault in society: The role of the juvenile offender. In H. E. Barbaree, W. L. Marshall, & S. M. Hudson (Eds.), *The juvenile sex offender.* New York: Guilford Press.

Barbaree, H. E., Marshall, W. L., and Hudson, S. M. (1993). *The juvenile sex offender.* New York: Guilford Press.

Barnett, G., Manly, J. T., and Cicchetti, D. (1991). Continuing toward an operational definition of psychological maltreatment. *Development and Psychopathology, 3,* 19–29.

Barnett, O. W., Miller-Perrin, C. L., & Perrin, R. D. (1997). *Family violence across the lifespan: An introduction.* Thousand Oaks, CA: Sage Publications.

Barry, R. C., & Weber, T. R. (1994). Thoracoabdominal injuries associated with child abuse. In J. A. Monteleone & A. E. Brodeur (Eds.), *Child maltreatment: A clinical guide and reference.* St. Louis, MO: G. W. Medical Publishing.

Becker, J. V., Kaplan, M. S., Kavoussi, R. (1988). Measuring the effectiveness of treatment for the aggressive adolescent sexual offender. *Annals of the New York Academy of Sciences, 528,* 215–222.

Beitchman, J. H., Zucker, K. J., Hood, J. E., DaCosta, G. A., et al. (1991). A review of short term effects of child sexual abuse. *Child Abuse & Neglect, 15* (4), 537–556.

Beitchman, J. H., Zucker, K. J., Hood, J. E., DaCosta, G. A., et al. (1992). A review of long-term effects of child sexual abuse. *Child Abuse & Neglect, 16* (1), 101–118.

Belsky, J. (1980). Child maltreatment: An ecological integration. *American Psychologist, 35,* 320–335.

Belsky, J. (1984). The determinants of parenting: A process model. *Child Development, 55,* 83–96.

Belsky, J. (1991). Psychological maltreatment: Definitional limitations and unstated assumptions. *Development and Psychopathology, 3,* 31–36.

Bensley, L., & Meengs, M. (1996). *Prevention of child abuse and neglect: A review of the literature.* Olympia, WA: Washington State Department of Health. (Available from Washington State Department of Health, Non-Infectious Conditions Epidemiology, P. O. Box 47812, Olympia, WA 98504-7812.)

Berk, R. A. (1993). What the scientific evidence shows: On the average, we can do no better than arrest. In R. J. Gelles & D. R. Loseke (Eds.), *Current controversies on family violence.* Newbury Park, CA: Sage Publications.

Berliner, L. (1991). The effects of sexual abuse on children. *Violence Update, 1* (10), 1, 8, 10–11.

Berliner, L. (1993). Is family preservation in the best interests of children? *Journal of Interpersonal Violence, 8* (4), 556–557.

Berliner, L. (1994). The problem with neglect. *Journal of Interpersonal Violence, 9* (4), 556.

Berliner, L., Schram, D., Miller, L. L., & Milloy, C. D. (1995). A sentencing alternative for sex offenders: A study of decision making and recidivism. *Journal of Interpersonal Violence, 10* (4), 487–502.

Berliner, L., Stephenson, C., & Stern, P. (1992). Commentary—should investigative interviews of children be videotaped. *Journal of Interpersonal Violence, 7* (2), 277–288.

Black, C. (1981). *It will never happen to me.* Denver, CO: M.A.C., Printing and Publications Division.

Black, R. & Mayer, J. (1980). Parents with special problems: Alcoholism and opiate addiction. *Child Abuse & Neglect, 4,* 45–54.

Blau, G. M., Dall, M. B., & Anderson, L. M. (1993). Assessment and treatment of violent families. In Hampton, R. L., Gullotta, T. P., Adams, G. R., Potter, E. H., & Weissberg, R. P. (Eds.), *Family Violence.* Newbury Park, CA: Sage Publications.

Blythe, B. J., Salley, M. P., & Jayaratne, S. (1994). A review of intensive family preservation services research. *Social Work Research, 18,* 213–224.

Borduin, C. M., Hengeler, S. W., Blaske, D. M., & Stein, R. J. (1990). Multisystemic treatment of adolescent sexual offenders. *International Journal of Offender Therapy and Comparative Criminology, 34* (2), 105–113.

Boudreau, F. A. (1993). Elder abuse. In R. L. Hampton, T. P. Gullotta, G. R. Adams, E. H. Potter, & R. P. Weissberg (Eds.), *Family Violence.* Newbury Park, CA: Sage Publications.

Bowlby, J. (1980). *Attachment and loss: Volume 3, Loss.* New York: Basic Books.

Bowlby, J. (1984). Violence in the family as a disorder of the attachment and caregiving systems. *American Journal of Psychoanalysis, 44* (1), 9–27.

Bradford, J., & McCleon, D. (1984). Sexual offenders, violence and testosterone: A clinical study. *Canadian Journal of Psychiatry, 29,* 335–343.

Bradford, J. M., & Pawlak, A. (1993a). Double-blind placebo crossover study of cyproterone acetate in the treatment of the paraphilias. *Archives of Sexual Behavior, 22* (5), 383–402.

Bradford, J. M., & Pawlak, A. (1993b). Effects of cyproterone acetate on sexual arousal patterns of pedophiles. *Archives of Sexual Behavior, 22* (6), 629–641.

Bradshaw, J. (1988). *Bradshaw on the family.* Deerfield Beach, FL: Health Communications.

Brassard, M. R., Germain, R., and Hart, S. N. (Eds.). (1987). *Psychological maltreatment of children and youth.* New York: Pergamon Press.

Brieland, D., & Lemmon, J. (1977). *Social work and the law.* St. Paul, MN: West Publishing.

Briere, J. (1992). *Child Abuse Trauma.* Newbury Park, CA: Sage Publications.

Briere, J. (1996). A self-trauma model for treating adult survivors of severe child abuse. In J. Briere, L. Berliner, J. A. Bulkley, C. Jenny, & T. Reid (Eds.), *The APSAC Handbook on Child Maltreatment.* Thousand Oaks, CA: Sage Publications and the American Professional Society on the Abuse of Children.

Briere, J., Berliner, L., Bulkley, J. A., Jenny, C., & Reid, T. (Eds.). (1996). *The APSAC Handbook on Child Maltreatment.* Thousand Oaks, CA: Sage Publications and the American Professional Society on the Abuse of Children.

Briere, J., & Runtz, M. (1990). Differential adult symptomatology associated with three types of child abuse histories. *Child Abuse and Neglect, 14* (3), 357–364.

Briere, J., & Runtz, M. (1993). Childhood sexual abuse: Long-term sequelae and implication for psychological assessment. *Journal of Interpersonal Violence, 8,* (3), 312–330.

Bronfenbrenner, U. (1977a). Toward an experimental ecology of human development. *American Psychologist, 32,* 513–531.

Bronfenbrenner, U. (1977b). *The ecology of human development.* Cambridge, MA: Harvard University Press.

Browne, A. (1987). *When battered women kill.* New York: Free Press.

Browne, A., & Finkelhor, D. (1985). The traumatic impact of child sexual abuse: A conceptualization. *American Journal of Orthopsychiatry, 55,* 530–541.

Browne, A., & Finkelhor, D. (1986). Impact of child sexual abuse: A review of the research. *Psychological Bulletin, 99,* 66–77.

Browne, A., & Williams, K. R. (1989). Exploring the effect of resource availability and the likelihood of female-perpetrated homicides. *Law & Society Review, 23,* 75–94.

Brunk, M., Henegeler, S. W., & Whelan, J. P. (1987). Comparison of multisystems therapy and parent training in the brief treatment of child abuse and neglect. *Journal of Consulting and Clinical Psychology, 55,* 171–178.

Bryant, D., Kessler, J., & Shirar, L. (1992). *The family inside.* New York: Norton.

Bulkley, J. A., Feller, J. N., Stern, P., & Roe, R. (1996). Child abuse and neglect laws and legal proceedings. In J. Briere, L. Berliner, J. A. Bulkley, C. Jenny, & T. Reid (Eds.), *The APSAC Handbook on Child Maltreatment.* Thousand Oaks, CA: Sage Publications and the American Professional Society on the Abuse of Children.

Burgess, A., & Holmstrom, L. (1974). Rape trauma syndrome. *American Journal of Psychiatry, 131,* 981–986.

Burgess, R. L., & Garbarino, J. (1983). Doing what comes naturally? An evolutionary perspective on child abuse. In D. Finkelhor, R. J. Gelles, G. T. Hotaling, & M. A. Straus (Eds.), *The dark side of families: Current family violence research.* Newbury Park, CA: Sage Publications.

Butler, R. N. (1969). Ageism: Another form of bigotry. *The Gerontologist, 9,* 243–246.

Calhoun, C., & Ritzer, G. (1992). *Introduction to social problems.* New York: McGraw-Hill.

Caliso, J. A., & Milner, J. S. (1994). Childhood physical abuse, childhood social support, and adult child abuse potential. *Journal of Interpersonal Violence, 9,* (1), 27–44.

Cantwell, H. B. (1980). Child neglect. In C. H. Kempe & R. E. Helfer (Eds.), *The battered child.* Chicago: University of Chicago Press.

Carden, A. (1994). Wife abuse and wife abuser: review and recommendations. *The Counseling Psychologist, 22* (4), 539–582.

Caribou Tribal Council (1991). Impact of the residential school. Williams Lake, B. C., Canada: Caribou Tribal Council.

Carnes, P. (1983). *Out of the Shadows.* Center City, MN: Hazelden Educational Materials.

Carnes, P. (1989). *Contrary to love.* Center City, MN: Hazelden Educational Materials.

Case, M. E. S. (1994). Head injury in child abuse. In J. A. Monteleone & A. E. Brodeur (Eds.), *Child maltreatment: A clinical guide and reference*. St. Louis, MO: G. W. Medical Publishing.

Chaffin, M., Bonner, B. L., Worley, K. B., & Lawson, L. (1996). Treating abused adolescents. In J. Briere, L. Berliner, J. A. Bulkley, C. Jenny, & T. Reid (Eds.), *The APSAC Handbook on Child Maltreatment*. Thousand Oaks, CA: Sage Publications and the American Professional Society on the Abuse of Children.

Christophoulus, C., Cohn, D. A., Shaw, D. S., Joyce, S., Sullivan-Hanon, J., Kraft, S. P., & Emery, R. (1987). Children of abused women: Adjustment at time of shelter residence. *Journal of Marriage and the Family, 49,* 611–619.

Cicchetti, D., & Aber, L. A. (1980). Abused children—abusive parents: An overstated case? *Harvard Educational Review, 50,* 244–255.

Cicchetti, D., & Carlson, V. (1989). *Child maltreatment: Theory and research on the causes and consequences of child abuse and neglect*. New York: Cambridge University Press.

Cicchinelli, L. F. (1995). Risk assessment: Expectations and realities. *The APSAC Advisor, 8* (4), 3–8.

Claussen, A. H., & Crittenden, P. M. (1991). Physical and psychological maltreatment: Relations among types of maltreatment. *Child Abuse & Neglect, 15,* 5–18.

Coleman, V. E. (1994). Lesbian battering: The relationship between personality and the perpetuation of violence. *Violence and Victims, 9* (2), 139–152.

Conte, J. R. (1991). Child sexual abuse: Looking backward and forward. In M. Q. Patton (Ed.), *Family sexual abuse*. Newbury Park, CA: Sage Publications.

Conte, J. R. (1993). Sexual abuse of children. In R. L. Hampton, T. P. Gullotta, G. R. Adams, E. H. Potter, & R. P. Weissberg (Eds.), *Family violence*. Newbury Park, CA: Sage Publications.

Cooper, A. J. (1995). Review of the role of two antilibidinal drugs in the treatment of sex offenders with mental retardation. *Mental Retardation, 33* (1), 42–48.

Corson, J., and Davidson, H. (1987). Emotional abuse and the law. In M. R. Brassard, R. Germain, and S. N. Hart (Eds.), *Psychological maltreatment of children and youth*. New York: Pergamon Press.

Cowan, G., and Curtis, S. R. (1994). Predictors of rape occurrence and victim blame in the William Kennedy Smith case. *Journal of Applied Social Psychology, 24* (1), 12–20.

Cox, S. M. & Conrad, J. J. (1991). *Juvenile justice: A guide to practice and theory*. Dubuque, IA: William C. Brown Publishers.

Crittenden, P. M. (1996). Research on maltreating families. In J. Briere, L. Berliner, J. A. Bulkley, C. Jenny, & T. Reid (Eds.), *The APSAC handbook on child maltreatment*. Thousand Oaks, CA: Sage Publications and the American Professional Society on the Abuse of Children.

Cruz, O. A., & Giangiacomo, J. (1994). Ophthalmic manifestations of child abuse. In J. A. Monteleone & A. E. Brodeur (Eds.), *Child maltreatment: A clinical guide and reference*. St. Louis, MO: G. W. Medical Publishing.

Curan, T. F. (1995). Legal issues in the use of CPS risk assessment instruments. *APSAC Advisor, 8* (4), 15–20.

Curtis, G. C. (1963). Violence breeds violence—perhaps? *American Journal of Psychiatry, 120,* 386–387.

Davidson, H. A., & Loken, G. A. (1987). *Child pornography and prostitution: Background and legal analysis*. Washington, DC: National Center for Missing and Exploited Children and the U.S. Department of Justice.

Davies, D., Cole, J., Albertella, G., McCulloch, L., Allen, K., & Kekevian, H. (1996). A model for conducting forensic interviews with child victims of abuse. *Child Maltreatment, 1* (3), 189–199.

Davis, D. (Producer-Director). (1987). *The unquiet death of Eli Creekmore*. [Videocassette]. Seattle, WA: KCTS Channel 9. (Available from Filmakers Library, 124 East 40th St., New York, NY 10016. Phone: (212) 808-4980.)

Davis, L. V., & Hagen, J. L. (1994). The problem of wife abuse: The interrelationships of social policy and social work practice. *Social Work, 37,* 15–20.

Davis, L. V., Hagen, J. L., & Early, T. J. (1994). Social services for battered women: Are they adequate, accessible, and appropriate? *Social Work, 39* (6), 695–704.

Davis, R. C., & Smith, B. (1995). Domestic violence reforms: Empty promises or fulfilled expectations? *Crime & Delinquency, 41* (4), 541–552.

Davis, T. C., Peck, G. Q., and Storment, J. M. (1993). Acquaintance rape and the high school student. *Journal of Adolescent Health, 14* (3), 220–224.

Dean, D. (1979). Emotional abuse of children. *Children Today, 8* (4), 18–20.

de Koster, K., & Swisher, K. L. (1994). *Child abuse: Opposing viewpoints.* San Diego, CA: Greenhaven Press.

Denson-Gerber, J. (1979). Sexual and commercial exploitation of children: Legislative responses and treatment challenges. *Child Abuse and Neglect, 3,* 61–66.

DePanfilis, D. (1996). Social isolation of neglectful families: A review of social support assessment and intervention models. *Child Maltreatment, 1* (1), 38–52.

Dickstein, L. (1988). Spouse abuse and other domestic violence. *Psychiatric clinics of North America, 2,* 611–625.

Dietz, P. E. (1993). Sex offenses: Behavioral aspects. In S. H. Kadish, A. F. Morrison, & M. T. Morrison (Eds.), *Encyclopedia of Crime and Justice.* New York: Free Press.

Dobash, R. E., & Dobash, R. B. (1979). *Violence against wives.* New York: Free Press.

Douglas, L. (1988). *Domestic mistreatment of the elderly: Towards prevention.* Washington, DC: American Association of Retired Persons.

Dubowitz, H. (1994). Neglecting the neglect of neglect. *Journal of Interpersonal Violence, 9* (4), 556–560.

Dubowitz, H., Black, M., Starr, R. H., Jr., & Zuravin, S. (1993). A conceptual definition of child neglect. *Criminal Justice and Behavior, 20* (1), 8–26.

Dubowitz, H., & Newberger, E. (1989). Pediatrics and child abuse. In D. Cicchetti and V. Carlson (Eds.), *Child maltreatment.* New York: Cambridge University Press.

Duke, J. (1996). Study found 79% of adult protective service cases were self-neglect. *Aging,* Number 367. Washington, DC: Administration on Aging, Department of Health and Human Services.

Dutton, D. G. (1988). Profiling of wife assaulters: Preliminary evidence for a trimodal analysis. *Violence and Victims, 3,* 5–30.

Edleson, J. L., Eisikovits, Z. C., Guttman, E., & Sela-Amit, M. (1991). Cognitive and interpersonal factors in woman abuse. *Journal of Family Violence, 6* (2), 167–182.

Edleson, J. L., & Tolman, R. M. (1992). *Intervention for men who batter: An ecological approach.* Newbury Park, CA: Sage Publications.

Egeland, B. (1988). In National Center on Child Abuse and Neglect (Ed.), *Child neglect monograph: Proceedings from a symposium.* Washington, DC: National Clearinghouse on Child Abuse and Neglect Information.

Egeland, B., & Erickson, M. F. (1987). Psychologically unavailable caregiving. In M. R. Brassard, R. Germain, and S. N. Hart (Eds.), *Psychological maltreatment of children and youth.* New York: Pergamon Press.

Egeland, B., & Jacobvitz, D. (1984). *Intergenerational continuity of parental abuse: Causes and consequences.* Paper presented at the Conference on Biosocial Perspectives in Abuse and Neglect, York, Maine.

Egeland, B., & Sroufe, A. (1981). Developmental sequelae of maltreatment in infancy. In R. Rizley & D. Cicchetti (Eds.), *New directions in child development: Developmental perspectives in child maltreatment.* San Francisco: Jossey-Bass.

Eisikovits, Z. C., & Edleson, J. L. (1989). Intervening with men who batter: A critical review of the literature. *Social Science Review, 37,* 385–414.

Ellenberger, H. (1970). *The discovery of the unconscious.* New York: Basic Books.

Else, L., Wonderlich, S. A., Beatty, W. W., Christie, D. W., & Staton, R. D. (1993). Personality characteristics of men who physically abuse women. *Hospital and Community Psychiatry, 44* (1), 54–58.

Elwell, M. E., & Ephros, P. H. (1987). Initial reactions of sexually abused children. *Social Casework, 68,* 109–116.

Emory, L. E., Cole, C. M., & Meyer, W. J. (1992). The Texas experience with DepoProvera: 1980–1990. *Journal of Offender Rehabilitation, 18* (3–4), 125–139.

Epstein, M., Estacio-Decker, J., Krajewski, J., & Schellie, K. (1996). Social work department standard of practice. School of Social Work, University of Washington. [On-line]. http://weber.u.washington.edu/-uwmcsw/eldsop.htm.

Erikson, E. (1968). *Identity, youth and crisis.* New York: Norton.

Everson, M. D., & Boat, B. W. (1994). Putting the anatomical dolls in sexual abuse controversy in perspective: an examination of the major uses and criticisms of the dolls in child sexual abuse evaluations. *Child Abuse and Neglect, 18,* 113–130.

Faller, K. C. (1996). Interviewing children who may have been abused: A historical perspective and overview of controversies. *Child Maltreatment, 1* (2), 83–95.

Family Policy Council. (1995). *Youth and family services reform in Washington State*. Olympia, WA: Author. (Available from Family Policy Council, 14th & Jefferson, P. O. Box 45015, Olympia, WA 98504-5015.)

Fantuzzo, J. W., & Lindquist, C. U. (1989). The effects of observing conjugal violence on children: A review and analysis of research methodology. *Journal of Family Violence, 4,* 77–90.

Federal Bureau of Investigation. (1985). *Crime in the United States*. Washington, DC: Department of Justice.

Federal Bureau of Investigation. (1992). *Crime in the United States*. Washington, DC: Department of Justice.

Fein, L. G. (1979). Can child fatalities, end product of child abuse, be prevented? *Children and Youth Services Review, 1,* 75–89.

Figley, C. R. (1985). From victim to survivor: Social responsibility in the wake of catastrophe. In C. R. Figley (Ed.), *Trauma and its wake: The study and treatment of post-traumatic stress disorder*. New York: Brunner/Mazel.

Finkelhor, D. (1979). *Sexually victimized children*. New York: Free Press.

Finkelhor, D. (1984a). How widespread is child sexual abuse? *Children Today, 13,* (4), 18–20.

Finkelhor, D. (1984b). *Child sexual abuse: New theory and research*. New York: Free Press.

Finkelhor, D. (1985, October). An overview of current knowledge about child sexual abuse. A paper prepared for the Surgeon General's Conference on Violence, Leesburg, VA.

Finkelhor, D. (Ed.). (1986a). *A sourcebook on child sexual abuse*. Newbury Park, CA: Sage Publications.

Finkelhor, D. (1986b). Abusers: Special topics. In D. Finkelhor (Ed.), *A sourcebook on child sexual abuse.* Newbury Park, CA: Sage Publications.

Finkelhor, D. (1992). Preface in Briere, J., *Child abuse trauma*. Newbury Park, CA: Sage Publications.

Finkelhor, D. (1994). The international epidemiology of child sexual abuse. *Child Abuse & Neglect, 18* (4), 409–417.

Finkelhor, D., & Araji, S. (1986). Explanations of pedophilia: A four factor model. *Journal of Sex Research, 22,* (2), 145–161.

Finkelhor, D., & Browne, A. (1985). The traumatic impact of child sexual abuse: A conceptualization. *American Journal of Orthopsychiatry, 55,* 530–541.

Finkelhor, D. & Browne, A.. (1986), Initial and long-term effects: A review of the research. In D. Finkelhor, et al., (Eds.), *A sourcebook on child sexual abuse*. Newbury Park, CA: Sage Publications.

Finkelhor, D., Hotaling, G., Lewis, I. A., & Smith, C. (1990). Sexual abuse in a national survey of adult men and women: Prevalence, characteristics, and risk factors. *Child Abuse & Neglect, 14 ,* 19–28.

Finkelhor, D., Hotaling, G., & Sedlak, A. J. (1992). The abduction of children by strangers and nonfamily members: Estimating the incidence using multiple methods. *Journal of Interpersonal Violence, 7* (2), 226–243.

Finkelhor, D., & Yllo, K. (1982). Forced sex in marriage: a preliminary research report. *Crime and Delinquency, 28,* 459–478.

Finkelson, L, and Oswalt, R. (1995). College date rape: Incidence and reporting. *Psychological Reports, 77,* 526.

Fortin, A., & Chamberland, C. (1995). Preventing the psychological maltreatment of children. *Journal of Interpersonal Violence, 10* (3), 275–295.

Freud, S. (1896). The aetiology of hysteria. In Strachy, J. (Ed. & Trans.), *The standard edition of the complete psychological works of Sigmund Freud.* Vol. 3. New York: Norton.

Freund, K., & Blanchard, R. (1989). Phallometric diagnosis of pedophilia. Journal of Consulting and Clinical Psychology, 57 (1), 100–105.

Friedrich, W. N. (1996). An integrated model of psychotherapy for abused children. In J. Briere, L. Berliner, J. A. Bulkley, C. Jenny, & T. Reid (Eds.), *The APSAC handbook on child maltreatment.* Thousand Oaks, CA: Sage Publications and the American Professional Society on the Abuse of Children.

Friedrich, W. N., Enbender, A. J., & Luecke, W. J. (1983). Cognitive and behavioral characteristics of physically abused children. *Journal of Consulting and Clinical Psychology, 51,* 313–314.

Fromuth, M. E. (1986). The relationship of childhood sexual abuse with later psychological and sexual adjustment in a sample of college women. *Child Abuse and Neglect, 10,* 5–15.

Fromuth, M. E., & Burkhart, B. R. (1989). Long-term psychological correlates of childhood sexual abuse in two samples of college men. *Child Abuse and Neglect, 13,* 533–542.

Fulmer, T. (1988). Elder abuse. In Straus, M. B. (Ed.), *Abuse and victimization across the life span.* Baltimore, MD: Johns Hopkins University Press.

Fulmer, T. T., & O'Malley, T. A. (1987). *Inadequate care of the elderly: A health care perspective on abuse and neglect.* New York: Springer Publishing.

Furby, L., Weinrott, M. R., & Blackshaw, L. (1989). Sex offender recidivism: A review. *Psychological Bulletin, 105* (1), 3–30.

Furniss, E. M. (1992). *Victims of benevolence: Discipline and death at the Williams Lake Indian Residential School, 1891—1920.* Williams Lake, B. C., Canada: Caribou Tribal Council.

Gaines, R., Sandgrund, A., Green, A., and Power, E. (1978). Etiological factors in child maltreatment: A multivariate study of abusing, neglecting, and normal mothers. *Journal of Abnormal Psychology, 87,* 531–540.

Garbarino, J. (1989). Troubled youth, troubled families: Dynamics of adolescent maltreatment. In D. Cicchetti and V. Carlson (Eds.), *Child maltreatment: Theory and research on the causes and consequences of child abuse and neglect.* New York: Cambridge University Press.

Garbarino, J., & Crouter, A. (1978). Defining the community context for parent-child relations: The correlates of child maltreatment. *Child Development, 49,* 604–616.

Garbarino, J., & Gilliam, G. (1980). Understanding abusive families. Lexington, MA: Lexington Books.

Garbarino, J., Guttmann, E., & Seeley, J. W. (1986). *The psychologically battered child.* San Francisco, CA: Jossey-Bass.

Garbarino, J., & Kostelny, K. (1992). Child maltreatment as a community problem. *Child Abuse & Neglect, 16,* 455–464.

Garbarino, J., & Sherman, D. (1980). High-risk neighborhoods and high-risk families: The human ecology of child maltreatment. *Child Development, 51,* 188–198.

Gardner, L. I. (1972). Deprivation dwarfism. *Scientific American, 227* (4), 76–82.

Garmezy, N. (1976). Vulnerable and invulnerable children: Theory, research, and practice. *Master lectures in developmental psychology.* Washington, DC: American Psychological Association.

Garmezy, N., Masten, A., Nordstrom, L., & Ferrarese, M. (1979). The nature of competence in normal and deviant children. In M. W. Kent and J. E. Rolf (Eds.), *Primary Prevention and Psychopathology, Vol. 3.* Hanover, NH: University Press of New England.

Gaudin, J. M., & Polansky, N. A. (1986). Social distancing of the neglectful family: Sex, race, and social class influences. *Children and Youth Services Review, 8,* 1–12.

Gelles, R. (1980). Violence in the family: A review of research in the seventies. *Journal of Marriage and the Family, 42,* 873–885.

Gelles, R. (1992). Family violence. In C. Calhoun & G. Ritzer (Eds.), *Introduction to social problems.* New York: McGraw-Hill.

Gelles, R. (1993a). Family violence. In R. L. Hampton, T. P. Gullotta, G. R. Adams, E. H. Potter, & R. P. Weissberg (Eds.), *Family violence.* Newbury Park, CA: Sage Publications.

Gelles, R. (1993b). Family reunification/family preservation: Are children really being protected. *Journal of Interpersonal Violence, 8* (4), 557–562.

Gelles, R. (1995). *Violence toward men: Fact or fiction?* (Report prepared for the American Medical Association, Council on Scientific Affairs). Kingston, RI: Family Violence Research Program, University of Rhode Island.

Gelles, R., & Conte, J. R. (1990). Domestic violence and sexual abuse of children: A review of research in the eighties. *Journal of Marriage and the Family, 52,* 1045–1058.

Gelles, R., & Cornell, C. P. (1990). *Intimate violence in families* (2nd ed.). Newbury Park, CA: Sage Publications.

Gelles, R., & Harrop, J. W. (1989). Violence, battering, and psychological distress among women. *Journal of Interpersonal Violence, 4,* 400–420.

Gelles, R., & Straus, M. (1988). *Intimate violence.* New York: Simon & Schuster.

Gelles, R., & Straus, M. (1990). *Physical violence in American families: Risk factors and adaptations to violence in 8,145 families.* New Brunswick, NJ: Transaction Publishers.

Gelles, R. J., & Loseke, D. R. (Eds.). (1993). *Current controversies on family violence.* Newbury Park, CA: Sage Publications.

Gil, D. (1970). *Violence against children: Physical child abuse in the United States.* Cambridge, MA: Harvard University Press.

Gil, E., & Johnson, T. C. (1993). *Sexualized children: Assessment and treatment of sexualized children and children who molest.* Rockville, MD: Launch Press.

Giovannoni, J. (1989). Definitional issues in child maltreatment. In D. Cicchetti and V. Carlson (Eds.), *Child maltreatment: Theory and research on the causes and consequences of child abuse and neglect.* New York: Cambridge University Press.

Giovannoni, J. (1991). Social policy considerations in defining psychological maltreatment. *Development and Psychopathology, 3,* 51–59.

Goetting, A. (1989). Patterns of marital homicide: A comparison of husbands and wives. Annual Meeting of the American Sociological Association (1988, Atlanta, Georgia). *Journal of Comparative Family Studies, 20* (3), 341–354.

Gondolf, E. W. (1985). *Men who batter.* Holmes Beach, FL: Learning Publications.

Gondolf, E. W. (1988). Who are these guys? Toward a behavioral typology of batterers. *Violence and Victims, 3,* 3.

Gondolf, E. W. (1993). Male Batterers. In R. L. Hampton, T. P. Gullotta, G. R. Adams, E. H. Potter, & R. P. Weissberg (Eds.), *Family violence.* Newbury Park, CA: Sage Publications.

Gondolf, E. W. (1996). Characteristics of batterer in a multi-site evaluation of batterer intervention systems. [On-line]. http://www.umn.edu/mvncava/papers/gondolf/batchar.htm.

Gondolf, E. W. (In press). Batterer programs: What we know and need to know. *Journal of Interpersonal Violence.*

Gondolf, E. W., Fisher, E. E., & McFerron, R. (1991). Racial differences among shelter residents: A comparison of Anglo, Black, and Hispanic battered women. In R. Hampton (Ed.), *Black family violence: Current research and theory.* Newbury Park, CA: Sage Publications.

Gondolf, E. W. & Russell, D. (1986). The case against anger control treatment programs for batterers. *Response to the Victimization of Women and Children, 9,* 3.

Goodman, G. S., & Bottoms, B. L. (1993). *Child victims, child witness.* New York: Guilford Press.

Gordon, A., Holden, R., & Leis, T. (1991). Managing and treating sex offenders: Matching risk and needs with programming. *Forum of Corrections Research, 3* (4), 2–22. [On-line]. http//198.103.98.138/crd/forum/e03/e034.htm.

Gottman, J. M., Jacobson, N. S., Rushe, R. H., Shortt, J. W., Babcock, J., La Taillade, J. J., & Waltz, J. (1995). The relationship between heart rate reactivity, emotionally aggressive behavior, and general violence in batterers. *Journal of Family Psychology, 9,* 227–248.

Gould, C., and Cozolino, L. (1992). Ritual abuse, multiplicity, and mind-control. *Journal of Psychology and Theology, 20* (3), 194–196.

Graziano, A. M., & Diament, D. M. (1992). Parent behavioral training: An examination of the paradigm. *Behavior Modification, 16,* 3–28.

Groth, A. N., Hobson, W. F. & Gary, T. S. (1982). The child molester: Clinical observations. In J. R. Conte, & D. A. Shore (Eds.), *Social work and child sexual abusers.* New York: Haworth Press.

Haden, D. C. (Ed.). (1986). *Out of harm's way: Readings on child sexual abuse, its prevention and treatment.* Phoenix, AZ: Oryx Press.

Hagan, M. P., King, R. P., & Patros, R. L. (1994). Recidivism among adolescent perpetrators of sexual assault against children. *Journal of Offender Rehabilitation, 21* (1–2), 127–137.

Hamberger, L. K. (1994). Domestic partner abuse: Expanding paradigms for understanding and intervention. *Violence and Victims, 9* (2), 91–94.

Hamberger, L. K., & Hastings, J. E. (1986). Personality correlates of men who abuse their partners: A cross-validation study. *Journal of Family Violence, 1,* 323–341.

Hamberger, L. K., & Hastings, J. E. (1988). Characteristics of male spouse abusers: Consistent with personality disorders. *Hospital and Community Psychiatry, 39* (7), 763–770.

Hamberger, L. K., & Hastings, J. E. (1991). Personality correlates of men who batter and nonviolent men: Some continuities and discontinuities. *Journal of Family Violence, 6* (2), 131–147.

Hamberger, L. K., & Hastings, J. E. (1993). Court-mandated treatment of men who assault their partner: Issues, controversies, and outcomes. In Z. Hilton (Ed.), *Legal responses to wife assault.* Newbury Park, CA: Sage Publications.

Hampton, R. L. (1987a). *Violence in black families.* Lexington, MA: Lexington Books.

Hampton, R. L. (1987b). Race, ethnicity and child maltreatment: An analysis of cases recognized and reported by hospitals. In R. E. Staples (Ed.), *The black family essays and studies* (4th ed.). Belmont, CA: Wadsworth.

Hampton, R. L. (1991). *Black family violence.* Lexington, MA: Lexington Books.

Hampton, R. L., & Coner-Edwards, A. F. W. (1993). Physical and sexual violence in marriage. In R. L. Hampton, T. P. Gullotta, G. R. Adams, E. H. Potter, & R. P. Weissberg (Eds.), *Family violence.* Newbury Park, CA: Sage Publications.

Hampton, R. L., Gullotta, T. P., Adams, G. R., Potter, E. H., & Weissberg, R. P. (Eds.), (1993). *Family violence.* Newbury Park, CA: Sage Publications.

Hampton, R. L., & Newberger, E. H. (1985). Child abuse incidence and reporting by hospitals: The significance of severity, class, and race. *American Journal of Public Health, 75* (1), 56–60.

Harlow, H. F. & Harlow, M. K. (1966). Learning to love. *American Scientist, 54* (3), 244–272.

Harlow, H. F. & Zimmerman, R. R. (1959). Affectional responses in the infant monkey. *Science, 130,* 421–431.

Hart, S. N., & Brassard, M. R. (1991). Psychological maltreatment: Progress achieved. *Development and Psychopathology, 3,* 19–29.

Hart, S. N., Brassard, M. R., & Karlson, H. C. (1996). Psychological maltreatment. In J. Briere, L. Berliner, J. A. Bulkley, C. Jenny, & T. Reid (Eds.), *The APSAC handbook on child maltreatment.* Thousand Oaks, CA: Sage Publications and the American Professional Society on the Abuse of Children.

Hart, S. N., Germain, R. B., and Brassard, M. R. (1987). The challenge: To better understand and combat psychological maltreatment of children and youth. In M. R. Brassard, R. Germain, and S. N. Hart (Eds.), *Psychological maltreatment of children and youth.* New York: Pergamon Press.

Harway, M., & Hansen, M. (1994). *Spouse abuse: Assessing & treating battered women, batterers, & their children.* Sarasota, FL: Professional Resource Press.

Haugaard, J. J. (1987). The consequences of child sexual abuse: A college survey. Unpublished manuscript, Department of Psychology, University of Virginia, Charlottesville. (As cited in Haugaard & Repucci, 1988).

Haugaard, J. J., & Repucci, N. D. (1988). *The sexual abuse of children.* San Francisco: Jossey-Bass.

Hay, T., & Jones, L. (1994). Societal interventions to prevent child abuse and neglect. *Child Welfare, 73* (5), 379–403.

Hayes, H. E., & Emshoff, J. G. (1993). Substance abuse and family violence. In R. L. Hampton, T. P. Gullotta, G. R. Adams, E. H. Potter, & R. P. Weissberg (Eds.), *Family violence.* Newbury Park, CA: Sage Publications.

Hegar, R. L., Zuravin, S. J., & Orme, J. G. (1994). Factors predicting severity of physical child abuse injury: A review of the literature. *Journal of Interpersonal Violence, 9,* (2), 170–183.

Herrenkohl, E. C., Herrenkohl, R. C., & Toedter, L. J. (1983). Perspectives on the intergenerational transmission of abuse. In D. Finkelhor, R. J. Gelles, G. T. Hotaling, & M. A. Straus (Eds.), *The dark side of families.* Newbury Park, CA: Sage Publications.

Herzberger, S. D. (1983). Social cognition and the transmission of abuse. In D. Finkelhor, R. J. Gelles, G. T. Hotaling, & M. A. Straus (Eds.), *The dark side of families.* Newbury Park, CA: Sage Publications.

Hickox, A. & Furnell, J. R. G. (1989). Psychological and background factors in the emotional abuse of children. *Child: Care, Health, and Development, 15,* 227–240.

Hilberman, E. (1980). Overview: The wife beater's wife reconsidered. *American Journal of Psychiatry, 137,* 1336–1346.

Hilberman, E., & Munson, K. (1977). Sixty battered women. *Victimology, 2,* 460–470.

Hoglund, C. L., & Nicholas, K. B. (1995). Blame, guilt, and anger in college students exposed to abusive family environments. *Journal of Family Violence, 10* (2), 141–157.

Hotaling, G. T. & Sugarman, D. B. (1986). An analysis of risk markers in husband to wife violence: The current state of knowledge. *Violence and Victims, 1* (2), 101–124.

Hunter, R., and Kiltrom, N. (1979). Breaking the cycle of abusive families. *American Journal of Psychology, 136,* 1320–1322.

Hwalek, M., Sengstock, M. J., & Lawrence, R. (1984, November). *Assessing the probability of abuse of the elderly.* Paper presented at the Annual Meeting of the Gerontological Society of America, San Antonio, TX.

Ivey, A. (1994). *Intentional interviewing and counseling: Facilitating client development in a multicultural society.* Pacific Grove, CA: Brooks/Cole.

Jacobson, N. (1993). Keynote address to the 1993 Annual Conference of the American Association for Marriage and Family Therapy, Santa Ana, CA.

Jacobson, N. S., Gottman, J. M., & Shortt, J. W. (1995). The distinction between Type 1 and Type 2 Batterers—further considerations: Reply to Ornduff et al. (1995), Margolin et al. (1995), and Walker (1995). *Journal of Family Psychology, 9* (3), 272–279.

James, B. (1994). *Handbook for treatment of attachment-trauma problems in children.* New York: Lexington Books.

Jason, J., & Andereck, N. D. (1983). Fatal child abuse in Georgia: The epidemiology of severe physical child abuse. *Child Abuse and Neglect, 7,* 1–9.

Jayaratne, S. (1977). Child abusers as parents and children: A review. *Social Work, 22,* 5–9.

Jewett, C. L. (1978). *Adopting the older child.* Harvard, MA: The Harvard Common Press.

Johnson, C. F. (1996). Physical abuse: Accidental versus intentional trauma in children. In J. Briere, L. Berliner, J. A. Bulkley, C. Jenny, & T. Reid (Eds.), *The APSAC handbook on child maltreatment.* Thousand Oaks, CA: Sage Publications and the American Professional Society on the Abuse of Children.

Johnson, T. C., & Feldmeth, J. R. (1993). Sexual behaviors: A continuum. In E. Gil and T. C. Johnson (Eds.), *Sexualized children: Assessment and treatment of sexualized children and children who molest.* Rockville, MD: Launch Press.

Johnson, T. F. (1991). *Elder maltreatment: Deciding who is at risk.* New York: Greenwood Press.

Jones, R. L., & Jones, J. M. (1987). Racism as psychological maltreatment. In M. R. Brassard, R. Germain, and S. N. Hart (Eds.), *Psychological maltreatment of children and youth.* New York: Pergamon Press.

Kadushin, A. (1974). *Child welfare services.* New York: Macmillan.

Kalmus, D., & Straus, M. (1983). Feminist, political, and economic determinants of wife abuse services. In D. Finkelhor and M. S. Straus (Eds.), *The dark side of families: Current family violence research.* Newbury Park, CA: Sage Publications.

Kaplan, H. I., & Sadock, B. J. (Eds.). (1989). *Comprehensive textbook of psychiatry/V.* Baltimore: Williams & Wilkins.

Karlin, N. J. (1995). Munchausen syndrome by proxy. [On-line]. http://www.bratretreat.org.brpr/v4n1.html.

Kaufman, J., & Zigler, E. (1987). Do abused children become abusive parents? *American Journal of Orthopsychiatry, 57* (2), 186–192.

Kaufman, J., & Zigler, E. (1989). The intergenerational transmission of child abuse. In D. Cicchetti and V. Carlson (Eds.), *Child maltreatment: Theory and research on the causes and consequences of child abuse and neglect.* New York: Cambridge University Press.

Kavanagh, K. A., Youngblade, L., Reid, J. B., & Fagot, B. I. (1988). Interactions between children and abusive versus control parents. *Journal of Clinical Child Psychology, 17,* 137–142.

Kazdin, A. E., Moser, J., Colbus, D., & Bell, R. (1985). Depressive symptoms among physically abused and psychiatrically disturbed children. *Journal of Abnormal Psychology, 94,* 298–307.

Kempe, C. H., & Helfer, R. E. (Eds.). (1980). *The battered child.* Chicago: University of Chicago Press.

Kempe, C. H., Silverman, F. N., Steele, B. F., Droegmuller, W., & Silver, H. K. (1962), The battered child syndrome. *Journal of the American Medical Association, 181* (1), 17–24.

Kempe, R., Cutler, C., & Dean, J. (1980). The infant with failure-to-thrive. In C. H. Kempe, & R. E. Helfer (Eds.), *The battered child.* Chicago: University of Chicago Press.

Kiersch, T. A. (1990). Treatment of sex offenders with Depo-Provera. *Bulletin of the American Academy of Psychiatry and the Law, 18* (2), 179–187.

Kinard, E. M. (1982). Emotional development in physically abused children. *American Journal of Orthopsychiatry, 50,* 686–696.

Kinard, E. M. (1996). Social support, self-worth, and depression in offending and nonoffending mothers of maltreated children. *Child Maltreatment, 1* (3), 272–283.

Kinney, J., Haapala, D. A., Booth, C., & Leavitt, S. (1991). The HOMEBUILDERS model. In E. M. Tracy, D. A. Haapala, J. Kinney, & P. Pecora (Eds.), *Intensive family preservation services: An instructional source book.* Cleveland, OH: Mandel School of Applied Social Sciences.

Kinsey, A. C., Pomeroy, W. B., Martin, C. E., & Gebbhard, P. H. (1953). *Sexual behavior in the human female.* Philadelphia: W. B. Saunders.

Knockwood, E. (1992). *Out of the depths: The experiences of Mi'kmaw children at the Indian Residential School at Shubenacadie, Nova Scotia.* Lakeport, Nova Scotia: Roseway Publishing.

Kolko, D. J. (1992). Characteristics of child victims of physical violence. *Journal of Interpersonal Violence, 7,* (2), 244–276.

Kolko, D. J., Kazdin, A. E., Thomas, A. M, & Day, B. (1993). Heightened child physical abuse potential: Child, parent, and family dysfunction. *Journal of Interpersonal Violence, 8,* (2), 169–192.

Kolko, J. R., Blakely, E. H., & Engleman, D. (1996). Children who witness domestic violence: A review of empirical literature. *Journal of Interpersonal Violence, 11* (2), 281–293.

Korbin, J. (Ed.). (1981). *Child abuse and neglect: Cross-cultural perspectives.* Berkeley: University of California Press.

Korbin, J., Coulton, C. J., & Furin, J. J. (1995). A neighborhood based approach to risk assessment. *The APSAC Advisor, 8* (4), 3–8.

Koss, M. P. (1992). Defending date rape. *Journal of Interpersonal Violence, 7,* 122–126.

Kurz, D. (1993). Physical assaults by husbands: A major social problem. In R. J. Gelles & D. R. Loseke (Eds.), *Current controversies on family violence.* Newbury Park, CA: Sage Publications.

Lachs, M. S., Berkman, L., Fulmer, T., & Horwitz, R. I. (1994). A prospective community-based pilot study of risk factors for the investigation of elder maltreatment. *Journal of the American Geriatrics Society, 42* (2), 169–173.

Lachs, M. S., & Pillemer, K. (1995). Abuse and neglect of elderly persons. *New England Journal of Medicine, 332* (7), 437–443.

Landes, A., Foster, C. D., & Siegel, M. A. (1991). *Domestic violence: No longer behind the curtains.* Wylie, TX: Information Plus.

Landes, A., Siegel, M. A., & Foster, C. D. (1993). *Domestic violence: No longer behind the curtains.* Wylie, TX: Information Plus.

Lanning, K. V. (1987). *Child molesters: A behavioral analysis for law-enforcement officers investigating cases of child sexual exploitation.* Washington, DC: National Center for Missing and Exploited Children.

Lanning, K. V. (1991). Ritual abuse: A law enforcement view or perspective. *Child Abuse and Neglect, 15,* 171–173.

Lanning, K. V. (1996). Criminal investigation of sexual victimization of children. In J. Briere, L. Berliner, J. A. Bulkley, C. Jenny, & T. Reid (Eds.), *The APSAC handbook on child maltreatment.* Thousand Oaks, CA: Sage Publications and the American Professional Society on the Abuse of Children.

Launius, G. D., Silberstein, M. J., Luisiri, A., & Graviss, E. R. (1994). Radiology of child abuse. In J. A. Monteleone & A. E. Brodeur (Eds.), *Child maltreatment: A clinical guide and reference.* St. Louis, MO: G. W. Medical Publishing.

Laws, D. R. (Ed.). (1989). *Relapse prevention with sex offenders.* New York: Guilford Press.

Leonard, K. E., & Jacob, T. (1988). Alcohol, alcoholism, and family violence. In V. B. van Hasselt, R. L. Morrison, A. S. Bellack, & M. Hersen (Eds.), *Handbook of family violence.* New York: Plenum.

Letellier, P. (1994). Gay and bisexual domestic violence victimization: Challenges to feminist theory and response to violence. *Violence and Victims, 9* (2), 95–106.

Levinson, D. (1981). Physical punishment of children and wifebeating in cross-cultural perspective. *Child Abuse and Neglect, 5* (4), 193–196.

Lockhart, L. L., White, B. W., Causby, V., & Isaac, A. (1994). Letting out the secret: Violence in lesbian relationships. *Journal of Interpersonal Violence, 9* (4), 469–492.

Lynch, M. A., & Cicchetti, D. (1991). Patterns of relatedness in maltreated and nonmaltreated children: Connections among multiple representational models. *Development and Psychopathology, 3,* 207–226.

Mack, R. N. (1989). Spouse abuse—a dyadic approach. In G. R. Weeks (Ed.), *Treating couples: The intersystem model of the Marriage Council of Philadelphia.* New York: Brunner/Mazel.

Madanes, C. (1990). *Sex, love, and violence.* New York: Norton.

Maletzky, B. M. (1991). The use of medroxyprogesterone acetate to assist in the treatment of sexual offenders. *Annals of Sex Research, 4* (2), 117–129.

Maletzky, B. M. (1993). Factors associated with success and failure in the behavioral and cognitive treatment of sexual offenders. *Annals of Sex Research, 6* (4), 241–258.

Marshall, W. L., & Barbaree, H. E. (1988). The long-term evaluation of a behavioral treatment program for child molesters. *Behavior Research and Therapy, 26,* 499–511.

Marshall, W. L., & Eccles, A. (1991). Issues in practice with sex offenders. *Journal of Interpersonal Violence, 6* (1), 68–93.

Marshall, W. L., Laws, D. R., & Barbaree, H. E. (Eds.), (1990). *Handbook of sexual assault: Issues, theories, and treatment of the offender.* New York: Plenum Press.

Maslow, A. (1954). *Motivation and personality* (2nd ed.). New York: Harper & Row.

Maslow, A. (1968a). *Toward a psychology of being.* New York: Van Nostrand Reinhold.

Maslow, A. (1968b). *Toward a theory of human motivation.* New York: Harper & Row.

Masson, J. M. (1984). *Assault on truth: Freud's suppression of the seduction theory.* New York: Addison-Wesley.

McClear, S. V., & Anwar, R. A. (1989). A study of battered women presenting in an emergency department. *American Journal of Public Health, 79,* 595–599.

McGee, R. A., & Wolfe, D. A. (1991). Psychological maltreatment: Toward an operational definition. *Development and Psychopathology, 3,* 3–18.

McNulty, F. (1980). *The burning bed.* New York: Harcourt Brace Jovanovich.

Meadow, R. (1977). Munchausen syndrome by proxy: The hinterland of child abuse. *Lancet, 2,* 343–345.

Melton, G. B. (1990). Child protection: Making a bad situation worse? *Contemporary Psychology, 35,* 213–214.

Melton, G. B., & Barry, F. D. (Eds.). (1994). *Protecting children from abuse and neglect.* New York: Guilford Press.

Miller, A. (1990). *For your own good.* New York: Noonday Press.

Millon, T. (1983). *Millon clinical multiaxial inventory manual.* Minneapolis, MN: Interpretive Scoring Systems.

Milner, J. S., & Chilamkurti, C. (1991). Physical child abuse perpetrator characteristics. *Journal of Interpersonal Violence, 6,* (3), 345–366.

Milner, J. S., & Crouch, J. L. (1993). Physical child abuse. In R. L. Hampton, T. P. Gullotta, G. R. Adams, E. H. Potter, and R. P. Weissberg (Eds.), *Family violence.* Newbury Park, CA: Sage Publications.

Milner, J. S., & Robertson, K. R. (1990). Comparison of physical child abusers, intrafamilial sexual child abusers, and child neglecters. *Journal of Interpersonal Violence, 5,* (1), 37–48.

Mixson, P. M. (1996). How adult protective services evolved, and obstacles to ethical casework. *Aging,* Number 367. Washington, DC: Administation on Aging, Department of Health and Human Services.

Monteleone, J. A. (1994). Munchausen syndrome by proxy. In J. A. Monteleone, & A. E. Brodeur, (Eds.), *Child maltreatment: A clinical guide and reference.* St. Louis, MO: G. W. Medical Publishing.

Monteleone, J. A., Brewer, J. R., & Fete, T. J. (1994). Physical examination in sexual abuse. In J. A. Monteleone, & A. E. Brodeur (Eds.), *Child maltreatment: A clinical guide and reference.* St. Louis, MO: G. W. Medical Publishing.

Monteleone, J. A., & Brodeur, A. E. (Eds.). (1994a). *Child maltreatment: A clinical guide and reference.* St. Louis, MO: G. W. Medical Publishing.

Monteleone, J. A., & Brodeur, A. E. (1994b). Identifying, interpreting, and reporting injuries. In J. A. Monteleone & A. E. Brodeur (Eds.), *Child maltreatment: A clinical guide and reference.* St. Louis, MO: G. W. Medical Publishing.

Monteleone, J. A., Glaze, S., & Bly, K. M. (1994). Sexual abuse: An overview. In J. A. Monteleone & A. E. Brodeur (Eds.), *Child maltreatment: A clinical guide and reference.* St. Louis, MO: G. W. Medical Publishing.

Motenko, A. K., & Greenberg, S. (1995). Reframing dependence in old age: A positive transition for families. *Social Work, 40* (3), 382–390.

Mulhern, S. (1994). Satanism, ritual abuse, and multiple personality disorder: A sociohistorical perspective. *International Journal of Clinical and Experimental Hypnosis, 42* (4), 265–288.

Munkel, W. I. (1994). Neglect and abandonment. In J. A. Monteleone & A. E. Brodeur (Eds.), *Child maltreatment: A clinical guide and reference.* St. Louis, MO: G. W. Medical Publishing.

Murphy, W. D., & Smith, T. A. (1996). Sex offenders against children: Empirical and clinical issues. In J. Briere, L. Berliner, J. A. Bulkley, C. Jenny, & T. Reid (Eds.), *The APSAC handbook on child maltreatment.* Thousand Oaks, CA: Sage Publications and the American Professional Society on the Abuse of Children.

Myers, J. E. B. (1992). *Legal issues in child abuse and neglect.* Newbury Park, CA: Sage Publications.

Myers, J. E. B. (1996). Taint hearings to attack investigative interviews: A further assault on children's credibility. *Child Maltreatment, 1* (3), 213–222.

Nagayama Hall, G. C. (1995). Sexual offender recidivism revisited: A meta-analysis of recent treatment studies. *Journal of Consulting and Clinical Psychology, 63* (5), 802–809.

National Academy of Science, Institute of Medicine. (1995). Real people real problems: An evaluation of the Long-Term Care Ombudsman Program of the Older Americans Act (summary). [On-line]. http://www.nap.edu/nap/online/rprp/summary.html.

Navarre, E. L. (1987). Psychological maltreatment: The core component of child abuse. In M. R. Brassard, R. Germain, and S. N. Hart (Eds.), *Psychological maltreatment of children and youth.* New York: Pergamon Press.

NCCAN (National Center on Child Abuse and Neglect), (1981). *Study findings: National incidence and prevalence of child abuse and neglect.* Washington, DC: Department of Health, Education, and Welfare.

NCCAN (National Center on Child Abuse and Neglect), (1988). *Study findings: National incidence and prevalence of child abuse and neglect-1988.*

Washington, DC: Department of Health and Human Services.

NCCAN (National Center on Child Abuse and Neglect). (1994). *Child maltreatment 1992: Reports from the states to the National Center on Child Abuse and Neglect.* Washington, DC: U.S. Government Printing Office.

NCCAN (National Center on Child Abuse and Neglect). (1995a). *Child abuse and neglect fact sheet, 1993.* Washington, DC: U.S. Government Printing Office.

NCCAN (National Center on Child Abuse and Neglect). (1995b). *Child maltreatment 1993: Reports from the states to the National Center on Child Abuse and Neglect.* Washington, DC: U.S. Government Printing Office.

NCCAN (National Center on Child Abuse and Neglect). (1996). *Child abuse and neglect fact sheet, 1994.* Washington, DC: U.S. Government Printing Office.

NCPCA (National Committee for the Prevention of Child Abuse). (1992). *Current trends in child abuse reporting and fatalities: The results of the 1991 annual fifty state survey.* Chicago: National Committee for the Prevention of Child Abuse.

Neidig, P. H., & Friedman, D. H. (1984). *Spouse abuse: A treatment program for couples.* Champaign, IL: Research Press.

Ney, P. G. (1987). Does verbal abuse leave deeper scars: a study of children and parents. *Canadian Journal of Psychiatry, 34 ,* 371–378.

Oates, R. K., Forrest, D., & Peacock, A. (1985). Self-esteem and abused children. *Child Abuse & Neglect, 9,* 159–163.

Oates, R. K., Peacock, A., & Forrest, D. (1984). Development in children following abuse and nonorganic failure to thrive. *American Journal of Diseases in Children, 138,* 764–767.

Ogg, J., & Bennett, G. (1992). Elder abuse in Britain. *British Medical Journal, 305,* 988–989.

Oldershaw, L, Walters, G. C., & Hall, D. K. (1986). Control strategies and noncompliance in abusive mother-child dyads: An observational study. *Child Development, 57,* 722–732.

O'Malley, T. A., Everett, E. D., O'Malley, H. C., & Campion, E. W. (1983). Identifying and preventing family mediated abuse and neglect of elderly persons. *Annals of Internal Medicine, 90* (6), 998–1005.

Pagelow, M. (1981). *Women-battering: Victims and their experiences.* Newbury Park, CA: Sage Publications.

Patten, S. B., Gatz, Y. K., Jones, B., & Thomas, D. L. (1989). Posttraumatic stress disorder and the treatment of sexual abuse. *Social Work, 34* (3), 197–203.

Patterson, G. R., Chamberlain, P., & Reid, J. B. (1982). A comparative evaluation of a parent-training program. *Behavior Therapy, 13,* 638–650.

Patterson, G. R., & Fleischman, M. J. (1979). Maintenance of treatment effects: Some considerations concerning family systems and follow-up data. *Behavior Therapy, 10,* 168–185.

Pecora, P. J., Whittaker, J. K., and Maluccio, A. N. (1992). *The child welfare challenge.* New York: Aldine de Gruyter.

Peled, E., & Edleson, J. L. (1992). Multiple perspectives on groupwork with children of battered women. *Violence and Victims, 7* (4), 327–346.

Pence, E., & Paymar, M. (1993). *Education groups for men who batter: The Duluth Model.* New York: Springer Publishing.

Perry, J. C., & Vaillant, G. E. (1989). Personality disorders. In H. I. Kaplan, & B. J. Sadock (Eds.), *Comprehensive textbook of psychiatry/V.* Baltimore: Williams & Wilkins.

Peters, S. D., Wyatt, G. E., & Finkelhor, D. (1986). Prevalence. In D. Finkelhor (Ed.), *A sourcebook on child sexual abuse.* Newbury Park, CA: Sage Publications.

Phillips, L. R. (1986). Theoretical explanations of elder abuse: Competing hypotheses and unresolved issues. In K. A. Pillemer & R. S. Wolf (Eds.), *Elder abuse: Conflict in the family.* Dover, MA: Auburn House.

Phillips, M., & Frederick, C. (1995). *Healing the divided self.* New York: Norton.

Pillari, V. (1991). *Scapegoating in families.* New York: Brunner/Mazel.

Pillemer, K. A. (1985a). The dangers of dependency: New findings on domestic violence against the elderly. *Social Problems, 33,* 146–158.

Pillemer, K. A. (1985b, October). *Domestic violence against the elderly: A discussion paper.* Paper presented at the Surgeon General's Workshop on Violence and Public Health, Leesburg, VA.

Pillemer, K. A. (1986). Risk factors in elder abuse: Results from a case control study. In K. A. Pillemer and R. S. Wolf (Eds.), *Elder abuse: Conflict in the family.* Dover, MA: Auburn House.

Pillemer, K., & Bachman-Prehn, R. (1991). Helping and hurting: Predictors of maltreatment of patients in nursing homes. *Research on Aging, 13* (1), 74–95.

Pillemer, K., & Finkelhor, D. (1988). Prevalence of elder abuse: A random sample survey. *Gerontologist, 28,* 51–57.

Pillemer, K., & Finkelhor, D. (1989). Causes of elder abuse: Caregiver stress versus problem relatives. *American Journal of Orthopsychiatry, 59* (2), 179–187.

Pillemer, K., & Suitor, J. J. (1988). Elder abuse. In V. B. van Hasselt, R. L. Morrison, A. S. Bellack, & M. Hersen (Eds.), *Handbook of family violence.* New York: Plenum Press.

Pillemer, K., & Wolf, R. S. (Eds.). (1986). Elder abuse: Conflict in the family. Dover, MA: Auburn House.

Pithers, W. D. (1990). Relapse prevention with sexual aggressors: A method for maintaining therapeutic gain and enhancing external supervision. In W. L. Marshall, D. R. Laws, & H. E. Barbaree (Eds.), *Handbook of sexual assault: Issues, theories, and treatment of the offender.* New York: Plenum Press.

Pithers, W. D. (1991). Relapse prevention with sexual aggressors. *Forum of Corrections Research, 3* (4), 36–48. [On-line]. http//198.103.98.138/crd/ forum/e03/e034.htm.

Pithers, W. D., & Cumming, G. F. (1989). Can relapse be prevented?: initial outcome data from the Vermont treatment Program for Sexual Aggressors. In D. R. Laws (Ed.), *Relapse prevention with sex offenders.* New York: Guilford Press.

Pithers, W. D., Kashima, K. M., Cumming, G. F., Beal, L. S., et al. (1988). Relapse prevention of sexual aggression: *Current perspectives. Annals of the New York Academy of Sciences, 528,* 244–260.

Podkieks, E. National survey on abuse of the elderly in Canada (1992). *Journal of Elder Abuse and Neglect, 4,* 5–58.

Polansky, N. A., Chalmers, M. A., Buttenwieser, E., & Williams, D. P. (1981). *Damaged parents: An anatomy of child neglect.* Chicago: University of Chicago Press.

Polansky, N. A., & Gaudin, J. M. (1983). Social distancing of the neglectful family. *Social Service Review, 57* (2), 196–208.

Poole, D. A., Lindsay, D. S., Memon, A., & Bull, R. (1995). Psychotherapy and the recovery of memories of childhood sexual abuse: U.S. and British practioners' opinions, practices, and experiences. *Journal of Consulting and Clinical Psychology, 63* (3), 426–437.

Putnam, F. W. (1989). *Diagnosis and treatment of multiple personality disorder.* New York: Guillford Press.

Putnam, F. W. (1991). The Satanic ritual abuse controversy. *Child Abuse and Neglect, 15,* 175–179.

Quinn, M. J., & Tomita, S. K. (1986). *Elder abuse and neglect: Causes, diagnosis, and intervention strategies.* New York: Springer Publishing.

Quinton, D., Rutter, M., and Liddle, C. (1984). Institutional rearing, parental difficulties and marital support. *Psychological Medicine, 14,* 107–124.

Raschko, R. (1990). Gatekeepers do the casefinding in Spokane. *Aging,* Number 361. Washington, DC: Administration on Aging, Department of Health and Human Services.

Rathbone-McCuan, E. (1996). Self-neglect in the elderly: Knowing when and how to intervene. *Aging,* Number 367. Washington, D.C: Administration on Aging, Department of Health and Human Services.

Reed, L. D. (1996). Findings from research on children's suggestibility and implications for conducting child interviews. *Child Maltreatment, 1* (2), 105–120.

Renzetti, C. M. (1995). Building a second closet: Third party responses to victims of lesbian partner abuse. In S. M. Stith and M. A. Straus (Eds.), *Understanding partner violence.* Minneapolis, MN: National Council on Family Relations.

Reschly, D., and Graham-Clay, S. (1987). Psychological abuse from prejudice and cultural bias. In M. R. Brassard, R. Germain, and S. N. Hart (Eds.), *Psychological maltreatment of children and youth.* New York: Pergamon Press.

Research and Statistics Branch, Correctional Service of Canada. (1991). Everything you always wanted to know about Canadian federal sex offenders and more. *Forum of Corrections Research, 3* (4), 2–22. [On-line]. http//198.103.98.138/crd/ forum/e03/e034.htm.

Rohner, R. P., & Rohner, E. C. (1980). Antecedents and consequences of parental rejection: a theory of emotional abuse. *Child Abuse and Neglect, 4,* 189–198.

Rosenbaum A., & O'Leary, K. D. (1981). Marital violence: Characteristics of abusive couples. *Journal of Consulting and Clinical Psychology, 49,* 63–71.

Rosenfeld, B. D. (1992). Court-ordered treatment of spouse abuse. *Clinical Psychology Review, 12,* 205–226.

Rosenthal, J. A. (1988). Patterns of reported child abuse and neglect. *Child Abuse & Neglect, 12,* 263–271.

Rush, F. (1977). The Freudian cover-up. *Chrysalis, 1,* 31–45.

Russell, D. E. H. (1983). The incidence and prevalence of intrafamilial and extrafamilial sexual abuse of female children. *Child Abuse and Neglect, 7,* 133–146.

Russell, D. E. H. (1984). *Sexual exploitation, rape, child sexual abuse, and work place harassment.* Newbury Park, CA: Sage Publications.

Rutter, M. (1979). Protective factors in children's responses to stress and disadvantage. In M. W. Kent and J. E. Rolf (Eds.), *Primary prevention of psychopathology.* Hanover, NH: University Press of New England.

Ryan, K. M. (1995). Do courtship-violent men have characteristics associated with a "battering personality." *Journal of Family Violence, 10* (1), 99–120.

Sagatun, I. J., & Edwards, L. P. (1995). *Child abuse and the legal system.* Chicago: Nelson-Hall Publishers.

Salter, A. C. (1992). Response to the "Abuse of the child sexual abuse accommodation syndrome." *Journal of Child Sexual Abuse, 1* (4), 173–177.

Salzinger, S., Kaplan, S., Pelcovitzz, D., Samit, C, & Krieger, R. (1984). Parent and teacher asessment of children's behavior in child maltreating families. *Journal of the American Academy of Child Psychiatry, 23,* 458–464.

Sarason, S. B. (1981). *Psychology misdirected.* New York: Free Press.

Satir, V. (1988). *The new peoplemaking.* Mountain View, CA: Science and Behavior Books.

Saunders, D., & Azar, S. (1989). Treatment programs for family violence. In L. Ohlin & M. Tonry (Eds.), *Family violence* (*Crime & justice, volume 2*). Chicago: University of Chicago Press.

Saunders, D. G. (1992). A typology of men who batter: Three types derived from cluster analysis. *American Journal of Orthopsychiatry, 62* (2), 264–275.

Scalzo, A. J. (1994). Burns and child maltreatment. In J. A. Monteleone & A. E. Brodeur (Eds.), *Child maltreatment: A clinical guide and reference.* St. Louis, MO: G. W. Medical Publishing.

Schecter, S. (1983). *Women and male violence.* Boston: South End Press.

Schecter, S., & Ganley, A. (1995). Understanding domestic violence. In *Domestic violence: A national curriculum for family preservation practitioners.* San Francisco: Family Violence Prevention Fund.

Sgroi, S. (1982). *Handbook of clinical intervention in child sexual abuse.* Lexington, MA: Lexington Books.

Shaffer, R. E., and Cozolino, L. J. (1992). Adults who report childhood ritualistic abuse. *Journal of Psychology and Theology, 20* (3), 188–193.

Sheets, D. A. (1996). Caseworkers, computers, and risk assessment: A promising partnership. *The APSAC Advisor, 9* (1), 7–11.

Sheldrick, C. (1991). Adult sequelae of child sexual abuse. *British Journal of Psychiatry, 158* (Suppl. 10), 55–62.

Shepard, M. (1992). Predicting batterer recidivism five years after community intervention. *Journal of Family Violence, 7* (3), 167–178.

Sherman, L. W. (1992). *Policing domestic violence.* New York: Free Press.

Sherman, L. W., & Berk, R. (1984). The specific deterrent effects of arrest for domestic assault. *American Sociological Review, 49,* 261–272.

Simon, L. M. J., Sales, B., Kaszniak, A., & Kahn, M. (1992). Characteristics of child molesters: Implications for the fixated-regressed dichotomy. *Journal of Interpersonal Violence, 7* (2), 211–225.

Small, M. A., & Tetreault, P. A. (1990). Social psychology, "marital rape exceptions," and privacy. *Behavioral Sciences and the Law, 8,* 141–149.

Smith, R. (1995, September). What to do with sexual abusers? *NASW News, 40* (8), 3.

Smith, S. (1975). *The battered child syndrome.* London: Butterworths.

Smith, S. M., & Hanson, R. (1975). Interpersonal relationships and childrearing practices in 214 parents of battered children. *British Journal of Psychiatry, 127,* 513–525.

Spanos, N. P. (1994). Multiple identity enactments and multiple personality disorder: A sociocultural analysis. *Psychological Bulletin, 116,* 143–165.

Spinetta, J. (1978). Parental personality factors in child abuse. *Journal of Consulting and Clinical Psychology, 46,* 1409–1414.

Spitz, R. (1945). Hospitalism: An inquiry into the genesis of psychiatric conditions in early childhood. *Psychoanalytic Study of the Child, 1,* 53–74.

Spitz, R. (1946). Anaclitic depression. *Psychoanalytic Study of the Child, 2,* 313–342.

Sprenkle, D. H. (1994). Wife abuse through the lens of "systems theory." *The Counseling Psychologist, 22* (4), 598–602.

Stark, E. (1985). Women battering, child abuse, and social heredity: What is the relationship? *Marital Violence: Sociological Review Monographs, 31,* 147–171.

State vs. Michaels 642 A. 2d 1372 (N.J. 1994).

Steele, B. J., & Pollock, C. B. (1968). A psychiatric study of parents who abuse infants and small children. In C. H. Kempe & R. E. Helfer (Eds.), *The battered child.* Chicago: University of Chicago Press.

Steinberg, M., & Westhoff, M. (1988). Behavioral characteristics and physical findings: A medical perspective. In K. C. Faller (Ed.), *Child sexual abuse: An interdisciplinary manual for diagnosis, case management, and treatment.* New York: Columbia University Press.

Steinman, M. (1990). Lowering recidivism among men who batter women. *Journal of Police Science and Administration, 17,* 124–132.

Steinmetz, S. (1988). *Duty bound: Elder abuse and family care.* Newbury Park, CA: Sage Publications.

Stewart, W. F., & Young, R. (1992). The rehabilitation of the child sexual abuse accommodation syndrome in trial courts in Kentucky. *Journal of Child Sexual Abuse, 1* (4), 133–141.

Stoolmiller, M., Duncan, T., Bank, L., & Patterson, G. R. (1993). Some problems and solutions in the study of change: Significant patterns in client resistance. *Journal of Consulting and Clinical Psychology, 61,* 920–928.

Straus, M. (1974). Foreword. In R. E. Gelles (Ed.), *The violent home: A study of physical aggression between husbands and wives.* Newbury Park, CA: Sage Publications.

Straus, M. (1978). *Family patterns and child abuse in a nationally representative American sample.* Paper presented at the Second International Congress on Child Abuse and Neglect, London.

Straus, M. (1979). Measuring intrafamily conflict and violence: The conflict tactics (CT) scales. *Journal of Marriage and the Family, 41,* 75–88.

Straus, M. (1993). Physical assaults by wives: A major social problem. In R. J. Gelles and D. R. Loseke (Eds.), *Current controversies on family violence.* Newbury Park, CA: Sage Publications.

Straus, M. (1994). *Beating the devil out of them: Corporal punishment in American families.* New York: Lexington Books.

Straus, M. B. (Ed.). (1988). *Abuse and victimization across the life span.* Baltmore, MD: Johns Hopkins University Press.

Straus, M., & Gelles, R. J. (1986). Societal change and family violence from 1975 to 1985 as revealed by two national surveys. *Journal of Marriage & the Family, 48,* 465–479.

Straus, M., & Gelles, R. J. (Eds.) (1990). *Physical violence in American families: Risk factors and adaptations to violence in 8,145 families.* New Brunswick, NJ: Transaction Publishers.

Straus, M., Gelles, R. J., & Steinmetz, K. L. (1980). *Behind closed doors: Violence in the American family.* Garden City, NY: Anchor.

Straus, M., & Smith, C. (1990). Family patterns and child abuse. In R. Gelles, & M. Straus (Eds.), *Physical violence in American families: Risk factors and adaptations to violence in 8,145 families.* New Brunswick, NJ: Transaction Publishers.

Sugarman, D., & Hotaling, G. (1989). Dating violence: Prevalence, context, and risk markers. In M. A. Pirog-Good & J. E. Stets (Eds.), *Violence in dating relationships: Emerging issues.* New York: Praeger.

Summit, R. C. (1983). The child sexual abuse accommodation syndrome. *Child Abuse & Neglect, 7,* 177–193.

Summit, R. C. (1992a). Abuse of the child sexual abuse accommodation syndrome. *Journal of Child Sexual Abuse, 1* (4), 153–163.

Summit, R. C. (1992b). The rehabilitation of the child sexual abuse accommodation syndrome in trial courts in Kentucky: Commentary. *Journal of Child Sexual Abuse, 1* (4), 147–151.

Syers, M., & Edleson, J. L. (1992). The combined effects of coordinated criminal justice intervention in woman abuse. *Journal of Interpersonal Violence, 7* (4), 490–502.

Tarter, R. E., Hegedus, A. M., Winsten, N. E., & Alterman, A. I. (1984). Neuropsychological, personality, and familial characteristics of physically abused delinquents. *Journal of the American Academy of Child and Adolescent Psychiatry, 23,* 668–674.

Tatara, T. (1996). *Elder abuse: Questions and answers—an information guide for professionals and concerned citizens.* Washington, DC: National Center on Elder Abuse.

Tatara, T., & Blumerman, L. (1996a). Elder abuse information series #1: Elder abuse in domestic settings. Washington, DC: National Center on Elder Abuse.

Tatara, T., & Blumerman, L. (1996b). Elder abuse information series #2: Elder abuse in domestic settings. Washington, DC: National Center on Elder Abuse.

Tatara, T., & Blumerman, L. (1996c). Elder abuse information series #3: Elder abuse in domestic settings. Washington, DC: National Center on Elder Abuse.

Tolman, R. M., & Bennett, L. W. (1990). A review of quantitative research on men who batter. *Journal of Interpersonal Violence, 5* (1), 87–118.

Tolman, R. M., & Edleson, J. L. (1995). Intervention for men who batter: A review of research. In S. R. Stith & M. A. Straus (Eds.), *Partner violence: Prevalence, causes and solutions.* Minneapolis, MN: National Council on Family Relations.

Tooker, E. (1978). The league of the Iroquois: Its history, politics, and ritual. *Handbook of North American Indians, 15,* 418–441. Washington, DC: Smithsonian Institution.

U.S. Department of Justice. (1992). Criminal victimization in the U.S., 1990: *Survey Report NCJ 134126.* Washington, DC: U.S. Department of Justice.

U.S. Department of Justice. (1994, March). Elderly Crime Victims: National Crime Victimization Survey. Washington, DC: Bureau of Justice Statistics, Office of Justice Programs, U.S. Department of Justice.

U.S. Department of Justice. (1995). *Helping to prevent child abuse—and future criminal consequences: Hawaii Healthy Start.* Washington, DC: National Institute of Justice.

Van Hasselt, V. B., Morrison, R. L., Bellack, A. S., & Hersen, M. (Eds.) (1988). *Handbook of family violence.* New York: Plenum Press.

Vicary, J. R., Klingaman, L. R., and Harkness, W. L. (1995). Risk factors associated with date rape and sexual assaults of adolescent girls. *Journal of Adolescence, 18,* 289–306.

Victor, J. S. (1992). Ritual abuse and the moral crusade against Satanism. *Journal of Psychology and Theology, 20* (3), 248–253.

Vida, S. (1994). An update on elder abuse and neglect. *Canadian Journal of Psychiatry, 39,* Supplement 1, S34–S40.

von Bertalanffy, L. (1934). *Modern theories of development: An introduction to theoretical biology.* London: Oxford University Press.

von Bertalanffy, L. (1968). *General systems theory.* New York: Braziller.

Walker, L. (1979). *The battered woman.* New York: Harper Perennial.

Walker, L. (1995). Current perspectives on men who batter women—implications for intervention and treatment to stop violence against women: Comment on Gottman et al. (1995). *Journal of Family Psychology, 9* (3), 264–271.

Walsh, B. (1996). Criminal investigation of physical abuse and neglect. In J. Briere, L. Berliner, J. A. Bulkley, C. Jenny, & T. Reid (Eds.), *The APSAC handbook on child maltreatment.* Thousand Oaks, CA: Sage Publications and the American Professional Society on the Abuse of Children.

Warren, A. R., Woodall, C. E., Hunt, J. S., & Perry, N. W. (1996). It sounds good in theory, but . . . do investigative interviewers follow guidelines based on memory research? *Child Maltreatment, 1* (3), 231–245.

Wauchope, B., & Straus, M. (1990). Age, gender and class differences in physical punishment and physical abuse of American children. In M. Straus & R. J. Gelles (Eds.), *Physical violence in American families: Risk factors and adaptations to violence in 8,145 families.* New Brunswick, NJ: Transaction Publishers.

Wegscheider, S. (1981). *Another chance.* Palo Alto, CA: Science and Behavior Books.

Wekerle, C., & Wolfe, D. A. (1993). Prevention of child physical abuse and neglect: Promising new directions. *Clinical Psychology Review, 13,* 501–540.

Werner, E. E. (1989a). Children of the garden island. *Scientific American,* April, 106–111.

Werner, E. E. (1989b). High risk children in young adulthood: A longitudinal study from birth to 32 years. *American Journal of Orthopsychiatry, 59* (2), 72–81.

Werner, E. E. (1992). The children of Kauai: Resiliency and recovery in adolescence and adulthood. *Journal of Adolescent Health, 13* (4), 262–268.

Werner, E. E. (1993). Risk, resilience, and recovery: Perspectives from the Kauai Longitudinal Study. Special issue: Milestones in the development of resilience. *Development and Psychopathology, 5* (4), 503–515.

Werner, E. E. (1995). Resilience in development. *Current Directions in Psychological Science, 4* (3), 81–85.

Whatley, M. A. (1993). For better or worse: The case of marital rape. *Violence and Victims, 8* (1), 29–39.

White J. W., and Koss, M. P. (1991). Courtship violence: Incidence in a national sample of higher education students. *Violence and Victims, 6* (4), 247–256.

Widom, C. (1989). Does violence beget violence? *Psychological Bulletin, 106* (1), 3–28.

Wiese, D., & Daro, D. (1995). *Current trends in child abuse reporting fatalities: The results of the 1994 annual fifty-state survey.* Chicago: National Committee to Prevent Child Abuse.

Williams, L. M. (1994). Recovered memories of abuse in women with documented child sexual victimization histories. *Consciousness and Cognition* (special issue), January.

Wilson, M. I., & Daly, M. (1992). Who kills whom in spouse killings? On the exceptional sex ratio of spousal homicide in the United States. *Criminology, 30,* 189–215.

Wolf, R. S. (1986). Major findings from three model projects on elder abuse. In K. A. Pillemer & R. S. Wolf (Eds.), *Elder abuse: Conflict in the family.* Dover, MA: Auburn House.

Wolf, R. S. (1996). Understanding elder abuse and neglect. *Aging,* Number 367. Washington, DC: Administration on Aging, Department of Health and Human Services.

Wolf, R. S., Strugnell, C., & Godkin, M. (1982). *Elder abuse and neglect: Findings from three model projects.* Worcester, MA: University of Massachusetts Medical Center, University Center on Aging.

Wolfe, D. A. (1985). Child abusive parents: An empirical review and analysis. *Psychological Bulletin, 97,* 462–482.

Wolfe, D. A. (1987). *Child abuse: Implications for child development and psychopathology.* Newbury Park, CA: Sage Publications.

Wolfe, D. A. (1991). *Preventing physical and emotional abuse of children.* New York: Guilford Press.

Wolfe, D. A. (1994). The role of intervention and treatment services in the prevention of child abuse and neglect. In G. B. Melton & F. D. Barry (Eds.), *Protecting children from abuse and neglect.* New York: Guilford Press.

Wolfe, D. A., Edwards, B., Manion, I., & Koverola, C. (1988). Early intervention for parents at risk of child abuse and neglect: A preliminary investigation. *Journal of Clinical and Consulting Psychology, 56,* 40–47.

Wolfe, D. A., & Jaffe, P. (1990). The psychosocial needs of children in care. In L. C. Johnson & D. Barnhorst (Eds.), *Children, families, and public policy in the 1990's.* Toronto: Thompson Educational Publishing.

Wolfe, D. A., & Mosk, M. D. (1983). Behavioral comparisons of children from abusive and distressed families. *Journal of Consulting and Clinical Psychology, 51,* 702–708.

Wolock, I., & Horowitz, B. (1984). Child maltreatment as a social problem: The neglect of neglect. *American Journal of Orthopsychiatry, 54* (4), 530–543.

Wong, N. (1989). Classical psychoanalysis. In H. I. Kaplan, & B. J. Sadock (Eds.), *Comprehensive textbook of psychiatry/V.* Baltimore: Williams & Wilkins.

Zigler, E., & Hall, N. W. (1989). Physical abuse of children in America: Past, present, and future. In D. Cicchetti and V. Carlson (Eds.), *Child maltreatment: Theory and research on the causes and consequences of child abuse and neglect.* New York: Cambridge University Press.

Zimbardo, P. G. (1979). *Psychology and life, 10th edition.* Palo Alto, CA: Scott, Foresman.

Ziveny, O. A., Nash, M. R., & Hulsey, T. L. (1988). Sexual abuse in early versus late childhood: Differing patterns of pathology as revealed on the Rorschach. *Psycholotherapy, 25,* 99–106.

Zuravin, S. J. (1989). *Suggestions for operationally defining child physical abuse and physical neglect.* Paper prepared for Meeting on Issues in the Longitudinal Study of Child Maltreatment, Toronto. (Cited in Pecora, Whittaker, & Maluccio [1992].)

Zuravin, S. J., & DiBlasio, F. A. (1992). Child-neglecting adolescent mothers: How do they differ from their nonmaltreating counterparts? *Journal of Interpersonal Violence, 7* (4), 471–489.

INDEX

Items printed in bold appear in the end-of-chapter glossaries.

Abandonment, 274
Abrasions, elder maltreatment, 278
Abuse related accommodation, 163, 239–240, **267**
Activity level, as a resiliency to abuse, 177
Active neglect, 274, **305**
Acute phase, cycles in domestic violence, 240, 241
Acute stress disorder, 126
Adaptations to abuse, 163
Addiction theory, 27, **35**
Addiction cycle, 198–199, **216**
Addiction model of sexual abuse, 198–199
Addictive system, 198, **216**
Adler, Alfred, 22
Administration on Aging, 292, 305
Adolescent abuse, 59, 60
Adolescent sex offenders, 165, 189, 193, 199–202
Adult protective services, 293, **305**
Adult psychological maltreatment, 227
Ageism, 282–283
Aid to Families with Dependent Children (AFDC), 172, **184**
Air Force Office of Special Investigations (AFOSI), 158
Alcohol abuse (see Substance abuse)
Alcoholics Anonymous, 155, 1157, 198
Almshouses, 272–273
Alzheimer's Disease, 288, 297, **305**
American Humane Association, 114
American Psychiatric Association, 128
American Professional Society on the Abuse of Children (APSAC), 146, 150, 151, 162, 184
American Association for Marriage and Family Therapy, 251
American Medical Association, 233
American Public Welfare Association, 292
Anatomically detailed dolls, 149–150
  in criminal proceedings, 162
  objections to their use, 149
Anger turned inward hypothesis, 99, **106**
Antiandrogens, 201, **216**
Antisocial personality disorder, 192, **216**
  and domestic violence, 248
Antisocial batterers, 248–249, **267**
Anxiety, and acute stress disorder, 126
  and child sexual abuse, 123
  and domestic violence, 237, 239
  and elder maltreatment, 277

child physical abuse, 51
Anxious attachment, 247
Apathy-futility syndrome, 99, **106**
APSAC, **184**
The APSAC handbook on child maltreatment, 183
Area Agencies on Aging, 292
Army Criminal Investigative Service (CID), 158
Arraignment, 159, **184**
Assault, 5–6, **35**
Attachment problems related to child abuse, 50
Attention deficit hyperactivity disorder, 51
Avoidance, 126, **139**
  and domestic violence impact, 239
  in child physical abuse, 50
  in posttraumatic stress disorder, 239

Basic human needs, 6–8
  and child psychological maltreatment, 77–78, 89
Bateson, Gregory, 26, **35**,
Battered child syndrome, 3–4, 42–43, **68**, 145, 162, 224
Battered women's shelters, 224–225, 253
Battered woman syndrome, 236
Batterers (see domestic violence perpetrators)
Battering, 225, 234, **267**
Behavior problems, 50, 57, 77, 157, 238, 246
Behaviorally oriented programs, 175, **184**
Belief system, 198, **216**
Betrayal, 130, 131, **139**
Beyond a reasonable doubt, 160, **184**
Bipolar I disorder, 128, **139**
Bipolar II disorder, 128, **139**
Blockage, **139**, 197, **217**,
Borderline personality disorder, 129, **139**
  child sexual abuse, 128–129
  signs and symptoms of, 129
  child physical abuse, 50
  domestic violence, 248
Borderline personality, category of domestic violence perpetrator, 249
Bureau of Alcohol, Tobacco and Firearms, 204
Bureau of the Census, 14, 232
Burns, and child physical abuse, 48
  and elder maltreatment, 278
  stocking and mitten, 48, **69**
  types of, 48

Carnes, Patrick, 27, 198–199, 216
CASA (Court Appointed Special Advocate), 194
Case studies in domestic violence, 231
Causation, 11–12, 35
Child abuse (see also Child physical abuse, Child
  psychological maltreatment, Child sexual abuse,
  and Child neglect)
  and Dependency proceedings, 153
  and domestic violence, 30–31, 173, 247
  fatalities, 20, 171
  forms of, 43
  reporting, 144–145
  and substance abuse, 31, 174
Child abuse hearsay exception, 161, 185
**Child Abuse Prevention and Treatment Act of
  1974, 44–45, 68, 144**
Child neglect, basic components of, 95
  categories of, 95–96
  consequences of, 93
  legal proceedings in, 153, 157–165
  definition of, 95
  and depression, 99
  description of, 92
  extent of, 93
  family risk factors, 98
  family characteristics, 173
  fatalities, 93
  forms of, 95–96
  government policy on, 94
  individual risk factors for, 98–100
  intergenerational transmission, 95
  intervention with, 168–178
  investigation of, 145
  media attention to, 92
  neglect of, 93
  perpetrators of, 40–41
  physical indicators of, 145
  and poverty, 94
  professional attention to, 4–5, 70, 92–93
  public attention to, 92
  resiliency and protective factors, 100–101
  and sexual abuse, 99
  social cost of, 94–95
  social and economic contributors, 23
  and social development, 95
  social services for, 156–157
  socio-cultural risk factors, 98
  sources of data on, 14
  statistics on, 20, 92–93, 114–115
  and substance abuse, 31, 99–100
Child physical abuse, 39–69
  continuum of, 46
  criteria for identifying and diagnosing, 42
  cultural influences, 57–58
  definition of, 43–46

developmental factors associated with, 51
and domestic violence, 238
family risk factors, 59
fatality statistics, 41
history of, 41–43
impacts of, 50–51
intergenerational transmission of, 52–56
investigation of, 145–46
major types of injuries, 47–49
Munchausen Syndrome by Proxy, 63, 64
and oppression, 61–62
perpetrators of, 29, 40–41, 55–57, 59
physical indicators of, 145
professional attention to, 3–4, 42
psychological impact of, 49–52
public attention to, 41–43
resiliency and protective factors, 62
social and economic contributors to, 23
statistics on, 20, 40–41, 60, 92–93
substance abuse, 31, 59–60
Child pornography, 158, 159
  and the Internet, 159
  pedophiles, 204
  sex offenders, 190
  sex offenders, 203–204
Child protection, 170, 171, 185
**Child Protective Services (CPS), 21, 45, 46, 92, 94,
  95, 120, 144–145, 151–153, 158–159, 171, 185**
Child prostitution and sex offenders, 190
Child psychological maltreatment,
  and behavior disorders, 77
  and basic human needs, 77–78, 89
  categories of, 74–75
  character disorders associated with, 77
  characteristics of, 90
  and child protective factors, 91
  and critical/sensitive periods, 81
  definitions of, 73–77
  and development, 79, 89
  effects of, 79–81
  family structure, 88
  culture, 86–88
  intergenerational transmission of, 88
  and other forms of abuse, 70, 72, 76, 85
  parental characteristics, 89
  parental protective factors, 91
  prosecution of, 77
  professional attention to, 70
  and self-esteem, 78
  and substance abuse, 90
Child sexual abuse, 6
  and acute stress disorder, 126
  between children, 119
  child sexual abuse accommodation syndrome, 163
  civil court proceedings, 165–166

credibility assessments, 150
definitions of, 116, 118–119
dissociative disorders, 127, 133–135
signs and symptoms of, 121–123
extent of, 113–118, 121,
four-factor traumagenic model, 29, 130
Freudian theory about, 111–112
history, 2–5, 111–112, 135
impact of, 111, 121–124, 135–136
indicators of, 122–123
media attention to, 109, 113
perpetrators of, 41, 109–110, 188–220
professional attention to, 3–5, 109–113
psychiatric diagnosis, 129–130
public attitude toward, 163
public attention to, 5, 109–112
self-efficacy, 131
signs and symptoms of, 121–123
statistics on, 114–115
substance abuse, 121
validating complaints of, 150
Child sexual abuse accommodation syndrome, 163,
162–164
Child sexualization, a continuum of, 201–202
Civil rights movement and domestic violence,
224
Clearinghouse on the Abuse and Neglect of the
Elderly, 298
Client matching, 252, **267**
Clinical sample, 13, **35**, 130, **139**
Clinton, William J., 173, 204
Clitorectomies, 44
Cognitive development, 79–81, **106**
Cognitive-behavioral programs, 175, **185**
Cognitive-behavioral school, 258, **267**
Cognitively oriented programs, 175, **185**
Common law, 223, **267**
Community ageism, 283, **306**
Community intervention projects, 255, **267**
Comorbidity, 31, **35**
Compensatory factors, 56
Competency, 160, **185**
Compulsive and dependent personality types, 249
Computed tomography, 48, **68**
Conduct disorders and child physical abuse, 51
Conflict Tactics Scale, 231, 233, 250, 251, **267**
Conjugal violence, 225
Consensus-based models, 152, **191**
Consent, 118, **139**
Conservatorship, 298
Continuums of abuse, 5, 8–10, 12, **35**, 46, 119,
201–202
Controlled studies, 12
Conversion disorders, 111, **139** (see also
Dissociative disorders)

Cooperating, 118, **139**
Corporal punishment, 59, 162
Correlational data, 12, **36**
Correlational studies, 12
Corrupting, 75, **106**
Couples counseling and domestic violence interven-
tion, 256, 259
Courtship violence, 228, 230, **267**
Credibility assessments, 150, **185**
Crime Control and Safe Streets Act of 1968, 204
**Crimes Against Children and Sexually Violent
Offender Registration Act**, 204, **217**
Criminal proceedings, 157–165
child sexual abuse cases, 157–165
interviewer testimony in, 161–162
perpetrator profiles, limitations on use of, 164, 196
sentencing in, 165
tainted victim testimony in, 160
victim competency to testify in, 160
Critical periods, 81, **106** (see also Sensitive periods)
Culture of helping, 125, **139**
Culture, and child abuse,41–43, 56–58, 86, 100, 172
cross cultural data in family abuse, 22, 244–245
and defining abuse, 44–45
and elder maltreatment, 280, 282–284
and individuality, 28
Iroquois, 22
oppression and abuse 61–62
patriarchy, 23, 244
and family abuse, 22–23
and sexual abuse, 23
western European influence, 22–23, 58, 244
Cunnilingus, 119, **139**
Cybernetics, 17
Cycle of violence, 240–242, 285
Cyclothymic disorder, 128, **139**
Cyproterone acetate, 217 **223**

Date rape, 230
Decubitous ulcers, 279
Defensive independence, 84, **106**
Degrade, 75, **106**
Delayed discovery rule, 166, **185**
Dementia, 281, 297–298
Denial, 50, 111–112, **140**, 209
Denying essential stimulation, as a form of child
psychological abuse, 75, **106**
Dependency proceedings, 153–156, **185**
Dependency petition, 154, **185**
Depersonalization disorder, 127, **140**
Depo Provera, 211, **217**
Depression, 127, **140**
and acute stress disorder, 126
and child abuse, 174
and child neglect, 99

Depression *(continued)*
  and child physical abuse, 51
  and child sexual abuse, 123
  and domestic violence 237, 239, 242
  and elder maltreatment, 277, 297–298
  learned helplessness, 242
  and major depressive episodes, 127–128
  and mood disorders, 127–128
  symptoms of, 128
Descriptive statistics, 13, **36**
Despair, 199, **217**
Developmental blockage, 197, **217**
Diagnostic and Statistical Manual, 126, 133, 191, 192, 193, 237
Disclosure in child sexual abuse cases, 163
Discovery rule, 166, **185**
Discovery, 159, **185**
Disinhibition, 197, 198, **217**
Disorder, 125, **140**
Disposition hearings, 155, 165, **185**
Dissociation, 133, **140** (see also Dissociative disorders)
  child sexual abuse, 123, 132
  child physical abuse, 50
  domestic violence impact, 239
  memory, 166
  victims of domestic violence, 241
Dissociative disorders, 127, **140**
  and child sexual abuse, 127
  conversion disorder, 127
  depersonalization disorder, 127
  dissociative amnesia, 127, **140**
  dissociative identity disorder, 127, **140**
  dissociative fugue, 127, **140**
  hysterical neurosis, 127
  multiple personality disorder (see Dissociative identity disorder)
  and child sexual abuse, 133–135
Dissociative symptoms, 127, **140**
Domestic elder abuse, 273, **306**
Domestic violence, 6, **36**, 225, 234, **268**
  abuse related accommodation, applied to, 239
  battered women's shelters, 224–225
  child abuse, 30–31, 173, 238
  continuums of abuse, 9
  couples counseling, 259–262
  courtship violence, 228, 230
  cross-cultural comparisons of, 245
  cultural influences, 22–23
  cycle of violence, 240–242
  date rape, 230
  definition of, 225–229
  Duluth Model 256
  Equality Wheel, 258
  elderly, 276, 287, 293, 296

expressive violence, 259
fatalities, 20, 232, 234
feminist theory applied to, 229, 233, 244
financial dependency, 243
frequency of, 228, 231–232
gay and lesbian relationships, 228, 229, 244
homicides, 234
impact of, 235–238
instrumental violence, 259
intergenerational transmission of, 25
interpersonal perspective, 259
intervention, 252–262
learned helplessness, 5, 242
O. J. Simpson, 4, 221, 222
pathologizng victims, 238–239
patriarchy, 23, 58, 223
perpetrators, 248–252
posttraumatic stress disorder, 239
Power and Control Wheel, 257
presumptive arrests, 255
profeminist position, 244, 256–257, **268**
programs for battered women, 224–225
psychological assault, 226–227
psychological dependency, 243
public and professional attention to, 4, 221–222, 254
risk factors, 245–246
rule of thumb, 223
social and economic factors, influence of, 23
social learning theory, 238, 246
statistics on, 20,25, 233
status incompatibility, 246
substance abuse, 31
women's movement, 224
women's advocacy, 254
Domestic violence perpetrators, 248–252
  assessment of, 262
  demographic variables associated with, 245
  Gondolf's topology, 248–249
  Hamberger–Hastings typology, 249
  Jacobson's topology, 250–252
  recidivism, 260–261
  risk markers, 247
  psychiatric diagnosis, 248
  physiological differences in vagal reactors, 250
  Saunders' typology, 249
  statistics on, 232, 247
  treatment programs, 224–225, 256–262
  philosophies and controversies, 16, 261–262
Drug Enforcement Administration, 204
Dry intercourse, 119
Due process requirements, 211
Duluth Model, 256–257, 260, 261, **268**
Duluth Abuse Intervention Project, 258, 261
Dysthymic disorder, 128, **140**

Ecological model, understanding child psychological maltreatment, 85
Ecological model, 15, **36**, 15–29
    Belsky's four levels, 18
Economic status and family maltreatment, 56, 62, 284
Education and family maltreatment, 1, 172, 245, 247, 292
Ego dystonic, 129, **140**
Ego syntonic, 129, **140**
Elder maltreatment, **active neglect**, 274, **305**
    Adult Protective Services, 293
    ageism, 282, 283
    behavioral indicators of, 278–279
    categories of, 273
    cultural values, 283
    cycle of violence in, 285
    caregiver dependency, 288– 289
    dementia, 281
    domestic elder abuse, 273, **306**
    domestic violence, 276, 287, 293, 296
    emotional abuse, 274, **306**, 299
    exchange theory, 2288
    federal initiatives on, 291
    financial exploitation, 274, **306**
    forms of, 274–276
    Gatekeeper Program, 297
    history of, 271–273
    human development, 280
    impact of, 277, 280
    indicators of, 278–279
    institutional elder abuse, 273, 276, 298–300, **306**
    intentional neglect, **306**
    intergenerational transmission of, 285, 291
    involuntary services in cases of, 298
    isolation , 281, 289–290
    mandatory reporting laws for, 275
    material exploitation, 274, **306**
    neglect, 274, **306**
    nursing homes, 283, 299
    passive neglect, 274, **306**
    perpetrators of, 289
    physical abuse, 274, **306**
    psychological abuse, 280, **312**, 305
    public policies, 283
    public and professional attention to, 5, 270, 280, 298
    relationship factors in, 281, 286–287
    research on, 274–277, 282
    restraint, as a form of, 281, 299
    risk factors for, 282, 288, 291
    self-neglect, 273, **307**
    state and local initiatives on, 293
    statistics on, 20, 276, 284
    substance abuse, 286

unintentional neglect, 274, **307**
Electra complex, 111, **140**
Emergency Assistance for Families, 253
Emergent characteristics, 17, **36**
Emotional abuse, 6, 20, **36**, 72, 76, 83, **106**, 274, 306 (see also Psychological maltreatment)
Emotional assault, 76, **107**
Emotional maltreatment, 6
Emotional neglect, 72, 76, **107**
Empirically based models, 152 **186**
Environmental context, 85–86, **107**
Equality Wheel, 258, **268**
Erikson, Erik, 51, 79–81, 83, 84, 85, 280
Exchange theory, 288, **306**
Excited utterance exception, 161, **186**
Exhibitionism, 119, 192, 199
Exosystem level, 18
Experiential school, 26, **36**
Experimental studies, 12
Exploiters, 190, **217**
Exploiting, 75, **107**
Explosion phase, in cycle of violence, 240, **268**
Expressive violence, in domestic violence, 259
Extraneous variables, 11, **36**

Fact finding hearing, in dependency proceedings, 155, **186**
Failure to thrive syndrome, 93, 96, 97, **107**, 145
False memory/repressed memory debate, 13, 165–166
False Memory Foundation, 166
Family Adaptability and Cohesion Evaluation Scales (FACES II), 27
Family advocacy programs, 158
Family context, 85, **107**
Family Maltreatment Matrix, 7
Family therapy, 173, 174, 210, 245
Family preservation, 176, **192**
Family preservation/child protection, 175–178, 180
Family Research Laboratory, 293
Family systems model, 25–26, 205
Family Therapy Institute of Washington D.C., 216
Family Violence Prevention and Services Act, 259
Family Violence Research Program, 57
Federal Bureau of Investigation, 210, 238
    FBI Official Crime Statistics, 14, **274**
Feedback, 18
Fellatio, 119, **140**, **223**
Feminist theory, 235, 239, 250 (see also profeminist)
Fetal alcohol syndrome, 100, **107**
Fetal alcohol effect, 100, **107**
Fifteenth Amendment to the United States Constitution, 229
Financial exploitation, 280, , 285, **312**
Finding of fact, 161, **192**
Fixated molester, 199, **223**

Fixated-regressed sex offender profile model, 199–202
Flight of ideas, 128
Fondling, 119, **140**, **217**
Foster care, 169, 175
Fosterparentscope, 169
Four-factor sex offender model, 196–198
Four-factor traumagenic model, 130, 131, 140
Fractures and elder maltreatment, 278
Freud, Sigmund, 2, 3, 111–112, 113, 125, 127, 135, 136, 195
Freudian theory, 111–112, 194
Friction burns and elder maltreatment, 278
Frotteurism, 192, **217**
Functional, 132, **140**

Gatekeeper Program, 296, 297 305
Guardian ad litem, 154, **186**, 298, **306**
Guardianship, and the elderly, 298
Gender issues and abuse, 57–58, 232–235
General systems theory, 16–18
Generalizations, 12, **36**
Grandiosity, 128, **140**
Grooming, 10, 130, **141**

Hamberger–Hastings typology, 249
Hazards in physical environment, 96
Head injuries, child physical abuse, 47
Head Start Program, 94, 173, **186**
Healthy Start Program, 177, **186**
Hearsay evidence, 161, **186**
Hearsay exclusion, 161, **186**
Hitler, Adolf, 61
History, child physical abuse, 41–43
    child sexual abuse, 2–5, 111–113, 135
    battered women's shelters, 224–225
    domestic violence, 222–225
    elder maltreatment, 271–273
    family maltreatment, 2–5
Homebuilders family preservation model, 171
Homeostasis, 17, **36**
Honeymoon phase, in cycle of violence, 240, **268**
Hormone therapy and sex offender treatment, 208, 210, 211
Human development, 96
    child sexual abuse, 129
    child psychological maltreatment, 78–81, 83, 89
    child physical abuse, 50, 51
    children and domestic violence, 238
    critical periods, 81
    elder maltreatment, 280
    failure to thrive, 96
    hierarchy of needs, 7
    pedophilia, 197
    psychosexual, 197

    sensitive periods, 81
    sex offenders, 194
    traumatic sexualization, 130–131
Hyperarousal, 126, **141**
Hypothesis testing, 11, **36**
Hypothesis, 11, **36**
Hysterical neurosis, 3, 111, 127, **141**

Impaired thinking, 198–199, **217**
Inadequate molester, 195, **217**
Incest, 6
    avoidance failure, 198
    and sex offender treatment, 208
    and sex offenders, 197
Incest taboo, 6
Incidence, 19, *114*
Indicated abuse, 114, 115, **141**
Inferential statistics, 13, **36**
Initial reaction, 240
Institutional elder abuse, 273, 293, **306**
Instrumental violence, 259
Intentional neglect, 274, **306**
Intercourse, 119, **141**
Interfemural intercourse, 119, **141**
Intergenerational transmission, 24, 285, **306**
Intergenerational transmission theory, 36, 52, 61, 68
    child neglect, 95
    child psychological maltreatment, 88
    domestic violence, 25, 238
    elder maltreatment, 282, 291
    family abuse, 24, 25
    oppression, 61–62
    statistics, 53–55
Internalize, 25
Interpersonal perspective, 259, **268**
Intervention, with sex offenders, 203–212
    child abuse and neglect, 168–178
    domestic violence, 252–262
    elder maltreatment, 291–300
Intervening variables, 11, **36**
Interview techniques, 146–148, 160, 162
    protocol, 151
Introverted molester, 195, **217**
Intrusive reexperiencing, 126, **141**
Involuntary commitment, and the elderly, 298
Isolation, 75, **107**, 277, 281, 283, 289

Juvenile courts, 153–156, **186**
Juvenile sex offenders, 200–202,
    contributing factors, 200
    levels of sexualization, 201–202
    mens rea, 200
    statistics on, 200
    treatment of, 201

Kauai Longitudinal Study, 177, **186**
Kelley–Frye hearing, 164, **186**
Kent State University, 207
Kentucky Supreme Court,
    ruling on child sexual abuse accommodation syndrome, 163–164
Kinsey, A. C., 116

Learned helplessness, 5, 242, **268**
Least restrictive, 295, **306**
Lesbian and gay relationships,
    domestic violence in, 228, 229, 244
Levels of addiction, 199
Locus of control, 57, 59
Long-Term Care Ombudsman Program, 275, 276, 292, 293, 299, **306**

Macro level, 18, 19, **36**
Magnetic resonance imaging, 48, **69**
Major depressive episode, 127–128, **141**
Major depressive disorder, 128
Mandatory reporting law, 44, **69**, 115, 144–145, 275, 292
Manic episode, 128, **141**
Marital violence, 225
Marital rape, 226
Markers, 12, **36**
Maslow, Abraham, 7, 78
Maslow's hierarchy, **36**, 78, 98
Material exploitation, 274, **306**
McMartin day care case, 4, 5
Mediating variables, 56
Medicaid, 168, 173
Medical model and child sexual abuse, 125
Medicare, 271
Medroxyprogesterone acetate, 211, **217**
Megan's Law, 204, **217**
Mens rea, 200, **218**
Mental disorders, 126, **141**, **218**
Meso level, 19, **37**
Micro level, 18, 19, **37**
Miller, Alice, 61,87, 68
Millon Clinical Multiaxial Inventory, 249
Minneapolis Police Experiment, 255, **268**
Minnesota Mother Child Interaction Project, 84
Missing and Exploited Children's Task Force, 204, **218**
Molesters, 190, 195, **218**
Mood disorders, 127–128, 237
Moral development, 79, **107**
Morally indiscriminate molester, 195, **218**
Mother-child relationships, intervention with, 174
Multiple personality disorder, 123, **127**, 133, 136, **141**
Munchausen Syndrome by Proxy, 63, 64, **69**

Narcotics Anonymous, 157
National Association of Adult Protective Service
    Administrators, 293
National Association of State Units on Aging, 292
National Center on Child Abuse and Neglect, 20, 40, 43, 60, 114, 92
National Center on Elder Abuse, 276, 277, 292, **306**
National Child Abuse and Neglect Data System, 114
National Coalition Against Domestic Violence, 225, **268**
National Committee for the Prevention of Elder
    Abuse, 292
National Council of Governors, Planning Advisors, 177
National Crime Victim Survey, 14, 20, **37**, 232, 243, **268**, 276, 279
National Family Violence Surveys, 14, 30, **37**, 231–234, 244, 246–247, **268**, 275–276, 290
National Incidence Studies, 115
National Institute of Justice, 255
National Organization of Women (NOW), 4, 224, 253, **268**
Naval Investigative Services (NIS), 158
Neglect, 5–8, **37**, 274, 276, 283, **306**
Neglect of neglect, 92
New Jersey Supreme Court, taint hearings, 161
Nineteenth amendment to the United States
    Constitution, 223
Nonorganic failure to thrive (FTT), **107**
Nursing homes, 273, 283

Occupational status and domestic violence, 245, 247
Oedipus complex, 111, **141**
Office of Juvenile Justice and Delinquency
    Prevention, 119
Official crime statistics, **37**
Older Americans Act, 291, 292
Operational definition, **107**
Operationalize, 11, **37**
Oppression, 61–62, **69**
Orphanage system, 273

Palo Alto Group, 26, **37**
Parental and child characteristics and behaviors, 85
Parental expectations, in child physical abuse cases, 57
Parents Anonymous, 157
Parsimony, **37**, 19
Passive neglect, **306**
Pathologizing, 132, **141**
Pathology, 125, **141**, **218**
Patria potestas, 41, **69**
Patriarchy, 23, **37**, 58, 223, 244, **268**
Pedophiles, 6, 29, 158, 193, 204, 208

Pedophilia, 192, 197, **218**
Penile plethysmograph, 209, **218**
Permanency planning, 155, **186**
Perpetrator groups,
    and domestic violence intervention, 256
Personality disorders, 128–129, **141**, 209, **218**
Phenomenological, 132, **141**
Physical abuse, 5–6, **37**, 39–64, 2874, **306**
    child, 39–64
    domestic violence, 226–227, 235–238, 240–242
    elder maltreatment, 276, 278, **306**
Piaget, Jean, 79–81, 83
Plea bargaining, 159, **186**
Poisonous pedagogy, 61, 69
Polygraph examinations, 209, **218**
Poor houses, 272–273
Poor Law of 1601, 272
Population samples, 13, **37**
Pornography, 158–59
    and the Internet, 159
    and pedophiles, 204
    and sex offender treatment, 211
    and sex offenders, 190, 203–204
Post sexual abuse syndrome, 129
Posttraumatic stress disorder (PTSD), 123, 126,
    141, 237, 239
Poverty, 56, 94, 98, 172
Power and Control Wheel, 257, **268**
Powerlessness 130, 131, **141**
Pragmatic, 132, **142**, **218**
Predictors, 12, **37**
Preferential molesters, 195, **218**
Preliminary hearing, 159, **186**
Preoccupation, and sexual addiction cycle, 199, **218**
Preponderance of the evidence, 154, **186**
Pressured speech, 128, **142**
Presumptive arrests, 255, **268**
Pretrial motions, 159, **187**
Prevalence estimates, 19, 115, **142**
Profeminist position, 244, 256–257, **268**
    limitations of, 244
    and Duluth Model, 256–257
Professional ageism 273, **306**
Progression, 199, **218**, 254
Protective and **resiliency** factors, 62, 90–92,
    100–101, **108**, 176–178
Protocols, 254, 294
Provera, 201, **218**
Psychiatric diagnosis, and child abusers, 175
    and child physical abuse, 50
    and child sexual abuse, 129–130
    and domestic violence, 248
    and sex offenders, 191–192
Psychological abuse, 6, 36, 72, 74, **107**, 274, **306**
    (see also Psychological maltreatment)

and interaction with other forms of abuse, 8
public and professional attention to, 5
Psychological maltreatment, 6, 71, 72 ,74, **107** (see
    also Psychological abuse)
Psychological neglect, 74, **108**,
Psychomotor agitation, 128, **142**

Rape, 163, 199
Rapists, 190, **218**
Red flags, 211
Regression, **142**, 194, **219**
Regressed situational molester, **219**
Regressed molester, 195, **219**
Regressed, 193, 194–195
Regressive behaviors in child sexual abuse cases, 122
Reify, 125, **142**
Reinforcement, 246, **268**
Rejection, 75, **108**
Relapse prevention model, 208, **219**
Reliability, **37**
Repressed memory/false memory debate, 13,
    165–166
Repression and child physical abuse, 50
Research, 11–15, 81–84, 113, 115–116, 130, 193, 243,
    274–277, 282, 292, 285–286
Residential respite care, 295
Residential schools, 273
Residual exception, 161, **187**
Resiliency and protective factors, 62, 90–92,
    100–101, **108**, 176–178
Respite phase, in cycle of violence, 240–241
Retinal hemorrhaging, 48–49, **69**
    in shaken infant syndrome, 49
    in elder maltreatment, 278
Retraction, in child sexual abuse cases, 163
Retrospective analysis, 91, **108**
Retrospective studies, 13, **37**, 115–116
Review hearings, 155, **187**
Risk factors, 30, 56–60, 85–90, 97–100, 243–248,
    282–291
Risk assessment,
    in child abuse intervention, 151–152
    instruments (RAI), 151–152 **187**
Ritualistic abuse, 119, 120, **142**, **219**
Ritualistic abusers, 190
Ritualization, 123, **219**
Role inversion, 285
Roles, 25, **37**
Rule of thumb, 223, **269**

Sadistic abuse, 119, **142**, **219**
Sadistic molester, 190, 195, **219**
Satanic ritual abuse controversy, 120
Satir, Virginia, 25–26, 35, **37**, 88, 89
Saunders' typology, 249

Scientific method, 11
Secrecy in child sexual abuse, 163
Seduction theory, 111, **142**
Seductive molester, 195, **219**
Selectively permeable boundaries, 18, **37**
Self-efficacy, 131, **142**, 253
Self-esteem, in child abuse, 174
   and child psychological maltreatment, 78
   and child physical abuse, 50–51, 57, 59
   and domestic violence, 236, 247
   and hierarchy of needs, 7
   and major depressive disorder, 128
   and child psychological maltreatment, 83, 91
   and juvenile sex offenders, 200
   and sex offenders, 197
   and sex offender treatment, 210
Self-neglect, 273, **307**
Sensitive periods, 81, **108**
Sensitivity, 53, **69**, **108**
Sentencing, 159, 165, **187**
Severe physical abuse, 46, **69**, 154, **187**
Sex offender intervention and treatment, 203–212
   assessment, 208–209
   behavioral approaches, 208
   case management, 211
   cognitive-behavioral approaches, 208, 210
   community based approaches, 206
   comprehensive approaches, 208–212
   family therapy, 210
   group treatment, 210
   hormonal approaches, 208, 210
   outpatient programs, 207, 212
   post release models, 212
   programs in correctional institutions , 206
   recidivism, 206–208, 211
   relapse prevention model, 208, 211
Sex offenders, 188–213
   addiction model, 198
   adolescent, 189, 193, 199
   categories of, 190, 192
   developmental blockage, 197, **217**
   fixated molester, 193–194 **217**
   fixated-regressed profile model, 193–196
   four-factor sex offender model, 196–198
   intervention and treatment,189, 201, 203–212
   juvenile sex offenders, 200–202
   pedophilia, 193, 197, **218**
   preferential molester, 195, **218**
   profile models, 193–196
   progression in, 199
   psychiatric diagnosis of, 191, 192
   psychosexual development, 194, 197
   public concern about, 203
   public image, 190

   recidivism, 203, 206–208, 211
regressed molester, 194, **219**
   research and treatment, 193
   sexual psychopath laws, 205
   situational blockage, 197, **220**
   situational molesters, 195, **220**
   situational-preferential profile model, 196–196
   statistics on, 121, 188, 196, 203
Sex ring abusers, 190, **219**
Sex roles, in domestic violence, 247
Sexual abuse, 37, **307** (see also Child sexual abuse,
   Domestic violence, and Elder maltreatment)
Sexual assault, domestic violence, 226
Sexual addiction model, 198
Sexual arousal, in sex offenders, 197, **219**
Sexual compulsivity, 199, **219**
Sexual exploitation, 119, 219
Sexual predators, 190, **219**
Sexual predator laws, 205
Sexual sadism, 192, **220**
Sexually indiscriminate molester, 195, **219**
Sexually reactive children, 201–202, **220**
Sexually violent predators, 204, **220**
Shaken infant syndrome, 47, **69**, 162
   retinal hemorrhaging in, 49
   signs and symptoms, 47
Shelter care hearing, 153, **187**
Sibling abuse, 59, 60
Simpson, O. J., 2, 4, 221, 222
Single parenthood, in child physical abuse cases, 56
Situational blockage, 197, **220**
Situational molesters, 195, **220**
Situational-preferential sex offender profile model,
   195–196
Sleep disturbance, in child sexual abuse cases, 123,
   136
   in domestic violence, 237
   as indicator of depression, 128
   elder maltreatment, 277
Sociability, resiliencies to abuse, 177
Social development, 51, 79, **108**
   in child neglect, 95
Social isolation, in child abuse and neglect, 57, 59,
   98, 172,173
   domestic violence, 246
   juvenile sex offenders, 200
Social learning theory, 24, **37**, 52, **69**, 238, 246,
   269, 285–286
Social Services Block Grants, 253
Social Security, 271, 291
Societal ageism, 283, **307**
Society for the Prevention of Cruelty to Animals,
   41–42
Society for the Prevention of Cruelty to Children,
   42

Sociopathic batterers, 248, **269**
Specificity, 53, **69**
Spousal abuse, 225
Standard of evidence, 154, 156, 160, **187**
State legislation, violent predator laws, 204
State funded care, 168–169
State Units on Aging, 292
Statements made to professionals providing diagnosis and treatment, 161, **187**
Statistics on, adolescent abuse, 60
  child abuse, 20, 25, 40, 114–115
  child abuse and neglect, risk assessment, accuracy of, 152
  child abuse and domestic violence, 173
  child abuse fatalities, 20, 41, 47, 171
  on child abuse intervention, 177
  emotional abuse, 20
  intergenerational transmission theory, 53–55
  child physical abuse, 20, 40–41, 92, 93
  child physical abuse, burns, 48
  child physical abuse, perpetrators of, 55
  child physical abuse and substance abuse, 31
  child neglect, 20, 92, 93, 114–115
  child neglect and substance abuse, 31
  child sexual abuse, 20, 93
  child sexual abuse, frequency, 121
  child sexual abuse, incidence of, 114–115
  child sexual abuse, force, use in, 119
  child sexual abuse, perpetrators of, 41
  child sexual abuse, prevalence of, 115–118
  child sexual abuse, types of, 119
  courtship violence, 230
  date rape, 230
  domestic violence, 20, 25, 231
  domestic violence and child abuse, 30–31, 238
  domestic violence fatalities, 20, 232
  domestic violence and gender, 233, 234
  domestic violence intervention, 254
  domestic violence perpetrators, 232, 247–249, 250, 261
  domestic violence treatment, 260
  domestic violence and substance abuse, 31
  in elder maltreatment, 20, 276, 284
  juvenile sex offenders, 200
  sex offender treatment and recidivism, 206, 207, 211
  sex offenders, 121, 188, 196, 203
Status incompatibility, 246 **269**
Statute of limitation, 166, **187**
  discovery rule, 166, **185**
  delayed discovery rule, 166, **185**
Stigmatization, 130, 131, **142**
Stocking and mitten burns, **69**
Strategic family therapy, 26, **38**
Strengths-based perspective, 81, **108**

Stress, associated with maltreatment, 57, 59, 174, 194, 237, 282
Structural family therapy, 26, **38**
Subdural hematomas, 42
  in elder maltreatment, 278
Subdural hemorrhaging, 47
Substance abuse, and child maltreatment, 31, 50, 57, 59–60, 90, 99–100, 121, 123, 132, 174
  and domestic violence, 31, 239, 247, 248
  and sex offenders, 194, 198, 211
  and the elderly, 286, 297
  and elder maltreatment, 289
  and sex offender treatment, 211
Substantiated abuse, 114–115, 115, **142**
Subsystems, 18, **38**
Suicide, and borderline personality disorder, 129
  and child physical abuse, 50
  and child sexual abuse, 123
  and depression 128
  and domestic violence, 239
Sunken eyes, in elder maltreatment, 279
Support groups, child abuse intervention, 175
  in domestic violence, 253
Survivors, 132, **142** (see also Victims)
  of child sexual abuse 118
  labeling of, 130
  mood disorders in, 128
  victimology, 125
Sybil, 133
Syndrome 125, **142**
Systemic approach in child psychological maltreatment, 85–91
Systems approaches, 15, 16–29, **38**

Taint hearings, 161, **187**
Temporary care, 153, **187**
Tension–building phase, in cycles of domestic violence, 240, 241, **269**
Termination proceedings, 156, **187**
  standard of evidence for, 156
Terrorizing, 75, **108**
Therapeutic foster care, 175
Thoracoabdominal trauma, 47, **69**
Thurman v. City of Torrington, 255
Title XX of the Social Service Block Grant, 253
Title XX of the Social Security Act, 291
Title XX of the Social Security Act, mandatory reporting laws, 292
Title VII of the Older Americans Act, 291, 292
Trauma bonds, 247–248
Traumagenic event, 126, **142**
Traumatic reexperiencing **142**
Traumatic sexualization, 130–131, **142**
Trial, 160, **187**
Twelve-step programs, 198, **220**

Type I batterers, 250–252, **269**
Type II batterers, 250–252, **269**
Type 1 batterers, 249, **269**
Type 2 batterers, 249, **269**
Type 3 batterers, 249, **269**
Typical batterer, 249, **269**
Typologies, 190, **220**, 248

U.S. Attorney General's Task Force on Domestic
    Violence, 255
U. S. Marshall's Service, 204
U.S. Children's Bureau, 43
U. S. Customs, 158, 203–204
U.S. Department of Health and Human Services, 292
U. S. Postal Inspector, 158, 203–204
U. S. Supreme Court rulings,
    indefinite commitment of sexually violent preda-
        tors, 205
    videotaped interviews, 148
    wife battering, 223
Unintentional neglect, 274, **307**
Unmanageability, 199, **220**

Vagal reactors, 250, **269**
    history of violence in childhood, 251
    criminal populations, 251
Validating complaints, 150, **187**
Validity, **38**
Variance, **38**
Vegetative symptoms, 128, **142**

Vicarious punishment, 52, **69**, 246, **269**
Vicarious reinforcement, 52, **69**, 246, **269**
Victim blaming, 5, 27, **38**
Victims, (see also Survivors)
    of child sexual abuse, 132
    competency, 160
    credibility of, 150, 158
    labeling, 130
    public attitude toward, 163
    testimony in criminal cases, 160
Victims of Crime Act, 253
Videotaping interviews, 148–149
Violation of basic human rights, as a form of elder
    maltreatment, 274, **307**
Visceral injuries, 47, **69**
Voyeurism, 192, 199, **220**

Wee Care Nursery School, 161
Withdrawal, in child physical abuse, 50
    in child psychological maltreatment, 83
    in child sexual abuse, 122, 136
    in elder maltreatment, 277
Women and domestic violence, 233
Women's movement, and child sexual abuse issues,
    112–113
    and domestic violence issues, 224
    historic role in family maltreatment awareness, 4
Work houses, 272

Zeitgeist, 112–113, **142**